Christianity and Private Law

This volume examines the relationship between Christian legal theory and the fields of private law.

Recent years have seen a resurgence of interest in private law theory, and this book contributes to that discussion by drawing on the historical, theological, and philosophical resources of the Christian tradition. The book begins with an introduction from the editors that lays out the understanding of "private law" and what distinguishes private law topics from other fields of law. This section includes two survey chapters on natural law and biblical sources. The remaining sections of the book move sequentially through the fields of property, contracts, and torts. Several chapters focus on historical sources and show the ways in which the evolution of legal doctrine in areas of private law has been heavily influenced by Christian thinkers. Other chapters draw out more contemporary and public policy-related implications for private law.

While this book is focused on the relationship of Christianity to private law, it will be of broad interest to those who might not share that faith perspective. In particular, legal historians and philosophers of law will find much of interest in the original scholarship in this volume. The book will be attractive to teachers of law, political science, and theology. It will be of special interest to the many law faculty in property, contracts, and torts, as it provides a set of often overlooked historical and theoretical perspectives on these fields.

Robert F. Cochran, Jr. is Louis D. Brandeis Professor of Law, Pepperdine University Caruso School of Law and Senior Fellow, Institute for Advanced Studies in Culture, University of Virginia, USA.

Michael P. Moreland is University Professor of Law and Religion and Director of the Eleanor H. McCullen Center for Law, Religion and Public Policy, Villanova University Charles Widger School of Law, USA.

Law and Religion

The practice of religion by individuals and groups, the rise of religious diversity, and the fear of religious extremism, raise profound questions for the interaction between law and religion in society. The regulatory systems involved, the religion laws of secular government (national and international) and the religious laws of faith communities, are valuable tools for our understanding of the dynamics of mutual accommodation and the analysis and resolution of issues in such areas as: religious freedom; discrimination; the autonomy of religious organisations; doctrine, worship and religious symbols; the property and finances of religion; religion, education and public institutions; and religion, marriage and children. In this series, scholars at the forefront of law and religion contribute to the debates in this area. The books in the series are analytical with a key target audience of scholars and practitioners, including lawyers, religious leaders, and others with an interest in this rapidly developing discipline.

Titles in this series include:

Law and the Christian Tradition in Italy
The Legacy of the Great Jurists
Edited by Rafael Domingo and Orazio Condorelli

Church Laws and Ecumenism
A New Path for Christian Unity
Edited by Norman Doe

Christianity and Private Law
Edited by Robert F. Cochran, Jr. and Michael P. Moreland

For more information about this series, please visit: www.routledge.com/Law-and-Religion/book-series/LAWRELIG

Christianity and Private Law

Edited by
Robert F. Cochran, Jr.
and Michael P. Moreland

Routledge
Taylor & Francis Group
LONDON AND NEW YORK

Produced by the Center for the Study of Law and Religion, Emory University

First published 2021
by Routledge
2 Park Square, Milton Park, Abingdon, Oxon OX14 4RN

and by Routledge
605 Third Avenue, New York, NY 10017

First issued in paperback 2022

Routledge is an imprint of the Taylor & Francis Group, an informa business

British Library Cataloguing-in-Publication Data
A catalogue record for this book is available from the British Library

Library of Congress Cataloging-in-Publication Data
Names: Cochran, Robert F., 1951– editor. | Moreland, Michael P., editor.
Title: Christianity and private law / edited by Robert F. Cochran, Jr. and Michael P. Moreland.
Description: Milton Park, Abingdon, Oxon ; New York, NY : Routledge, 2021. | Includes bibliographical references and index.
Identifiers: LCCN 2020026074 (print) | LCCN 2020026075 (ebook) | ISBN 9780367893460 (hardback) | ISBN 9781003018704 (ebook)
Subjects: LCSH: Christianity and law—History. | Religion and law. | Christianity—Philosophy. | Civil law.
Classification: LCC K3280 .C47 2021 (print) | LCC K3280 (ebook) | DDC 346/.001—dc23
LC record available at https://lccn.loc.gov/2020026074
LC ebook record available at https://lccn.loc.gov/2020026075

ISBN 13: 978-0-367-62777-5 (pbk)
ISBN 13: 978-0-367-89346-0 (hbk)
ISBN 13: 978-1-003-01870-4 (ebk)

DOI: 10.4324/9781003018704

Typeset in Galliard
by codeMantra

Contents

Foreword

A quarter century ago, Robert F. Cochran, Jr. teamed up with fellow legal heavyweights Michael McConnell and Angela Carmela to assemble a pathbreaking study titled *Christian Perspectives on Legal Thought.* That welcome and courageous volume explored the interaction of various Christian traditions with prominent schools of legal thought at the time: political liberalism, legal realism, critical legal studies, feminist legal theory, critical race theory, and law and economics. It also explored the past, present, and potential contributions of Christianity to substantive legal topics in environmental law, criminal law, family law, contracts, torts, and legal ethics. Two dozen law professors contributed original chapters to that volume, which the editors adroitly arranged as the first dots on a very large canvas depicting various modes of interaction between law and Christianity.

Today, a good bit more of this canvas has been filled in, owing to the work of some 1,500 scholars worldwide who are now part of a rapidly growing guild of law and religion study. Some 50 centers, institutes, and programs in law and religion have popped up on campuses around the globe—more than half in the United States, but with growing numbers in Europe, the Mediterranean basin, sub-Saharan Africa, Latin America, Australia, New Zealand, Southeast Asia, and the Pacific Rim. These groups are being further integrated by international and regional consortia of law and religion study and by dozens of periodicals and blogs on law and religion newly available. Several leading presses—Ashgate, Brill, Cambridge, Eerdmans, Mohr Siebeck, Orbis, Oxford, Routledge, Schöningh, Vandenhoeck & Ruprecht—have each established new book series or collections on law and religion, and the body of law and religion scholarship in multiple world languages is growing briskly.

The interaction of law and Christianity continues to be a central theme of this burgeoning global law and religion literature, yielding a much more nuanced picture of Christian contributions to various areas of law historically and today. This volume on *Christianity and Private Law* is a welcome and novel contribution to this literature. It again features the editorial leadership of Professor Cochran and his Nootbaar Institute of Law, Religion, and Ethics at Pepperdine. Joining him on the masthead is distinguished Catholic legal scholar, Michael P. Moreland, new director of the Eleanor H. McCullen Center for Law, Religion and Public Policy at Villanova. Included are 16 fresh chapters by several senior legal heavyweights like Dick Helmholz and James Gordley and a sturdy company of other legal stars, including Angela Carmella and David Caudill, who were part of the earlier overview volume on *Christian Perspectives on Legal Thought*.

"Private law" is a common phrase for Europeans who readily divide the legal world into public, private, penal, and procedural law categories, building in part on ancient Roman law, medieval canon law, and modern civil law. "Private law" is a less common term for Anglo-American common lawyers. They are more familiar with several discrete legal subjects that Europeans gather under the canopy of private law—contracts, property, and torts at the center of the canopy, associational law, family law, testamentary law, civil procedure, remedies, and other topics nearer the periphery. In both civil law and common law lands, private law focuses on the voluntary and involuntary legal relationships between private parties, whether individuals or private groups. The laws of the state—sometimes the laws of other non-state associations, too—facilitate and support those private relationships, articulate and vindicate interests and expectations that emerge from them, and offer remedies for harms that result from misfeasance, non-feasance, or breach of duty by another. The editors and several chapter authors do a fine job defining and defending "private law" as a category, and drawing interesting relationships between contracts, torts, and property which are the main subjects treated in these pages.

"Christianity" comprises all manner of Christian ideas and institutions, norms and habits that are shaped by the familiar quadrilateral of Scripture, tradition, reason, and experience. Distinct Catholic, Calvinist, Lutheran, Anglican, Anabaptist, and Evangelical voices, both historical and contemporary, come through in these pages, as does the powerful new Jewish voice of Michael Helfand. The authors variously trace, describe, interpret, and critique the discrete contracts, property, and torts topics assigned to them. Opening chapters in each of the four sections are devoted to biblical and traditional Christian teachings. They underscore the depth, nuance, and complexity of Christian engagement with these fundamental private legal relationships. Constructive and critical chapters later in each section highlight and illustrate the enduring value of these traditional Christian teachings for addressing discrete modern private law questions. At the heart of many of these Christian reflections on torts, property, and contracts is the fundamental biblical question about how to love all of our neighbors—even our enemies and others who hurt us. Do we "turn the other check" to the tortfeasor? Do we give aid and comfort to the stranger in imitation of the Good Samaritan? Do we give our "second coat" to the thief who has stolen our first? How do we responsibly acquire and use, have and hold, share and steward our property? How do we balance freedom and fairness in contract? Is it just price or just market price that sets the bargain? Do we sue, arbitrate, or mediate our private conflicts, given the biblical injunction to "Go tell it to the church"? And how do we judge and reason through the private law conflicts in a way that balances justice and mercy, rule and equity, principle and prudence? These and many other questions have inspired centuries of deep thought by Christian jurists and judges who have variously drawn on biblical, theological, jurisprudential, historical, and natural law arguments to work out their legal systems. That rich world of Christian perspectives on private law is nicely illustrated in these authoritative but accessible chapters that will edify novices and experts alike.

This volume is one of several new introductions to Christianity and law commissioned by the Center for the Study of Law and Religion at Emory University. Each volume is an anthology of some two dozen chapters written by leading scholars. Each volume has historical, doctrinal, and comparative materials designed to uncover Christian sources and dimensions of familiar legal topics. Each volume is authoritative but accessible, calibrated to reach students, scholars, and instructors in law, divinity, graduate, and advanced college courses as well as educated readers from various fields interested in what Christianity has, can, and perhaps should offer to the world of law. Earlier titles in this series of introductions include *Christianity and Law* (2008), *Christianity and Human Rights* (2011), *Christianity and Family Law* (2017), and *Christianity and Natural Law* (2017). New titles just out are on *Christianity and Global Law* (2020), *Christianity and Criminal Law* (2020), and *Christianity and Juridical Ecumenism* (2020). Other introductions are forthcoming on Christianity and "Conscience," "Constitutionalism," "Economic Law," "International Law," and "Migration Law." We aim, over time, to commission other such volumes on Christianity and bankruptcy law, education law, elder law, environmental law, health law, labor law, procedural law, remedies, and other familiar legal topics.

This volume on *Christianity and Private Law*—together with the two volumes on *Christianity and Global Law* and *Christianity and Criminal Law*—was made possible by a generous grant from Fieldstead and Company, a private California foundation. We give thanks to the Fieldstead board and directors for their generous support, and to the program officers, Dr. Steven Ferguson and Dr. Joe Gorra, for their wise counsel as we planned these volumes. We also express our warm thanks to our Emory colleagues, Ms. Anita Mann and Ms. Amy Wheeler, for their skillful administration of this and other scholarly projects.

It was a joy to work with such a range of leading scholars from North America and Europe who contributed fresh chapters to this volume. Our collective efforts were greatly enhanced by the two roundtable conferences held at Pepperdine Law School in 2017 and 2018. Those intense discussions helped us identify the major themes for this study of Christianity and private law, a topic which has not been much explored in recent scholarship. The editors and I express our warm thanks to Dean Paul Caron, Associate Dean of Faculty Research and Development Babette Boliek, Nootbaar Institute Program Director Jenna DeWalt, and Research Assistant Analise Nuxol for organizing these two meetings and providing such generous hospitality in the glorious setting of Malibu. Thanks also to Villanova law students and research assistants Jillian Brennan and Christopher Molony for their assistance in preparing the final version of the manuscript.

We are delighted to publish this volume and several others in the distinguished "Law and Religion" series edited by one of the world's preeminent scholars of law and religion, Professor Norman Doe. Professor Doe and his many colleagues in the Cardiff Centre for Law and Religion have been vital trans-Atlantic allies with our Emory Center for the Study of Law and Religion. We give thanks for their leadership in this expanding global field of interdisciplinary legal study, and for their partnership with us in publishing this and parallel volumes on law and Christianity.

Finally, the editors and I express our warm thanks to Alison Kirk and her colleagues at Routledge in taking on this volume and applying their usual standards of excellence in their editing, production, and marketing.

John Witte, Jr.
Director, Center for the Study of Law and Religion
Emory University

Contributing authors

William S. Brewbaker III, William Alfred Rose Professor of Law, University of Alabama School of Law

Angela C. Carmella, Professor of Law, Seton Hall University School of Law

Robert F. Cochran, Jr., Louis D. Brandeis Professor of Law, Pepperdine University Caruso School of Law and Senior Fellow, Center for Advanced Studies in Culture, University of Virginia

David S. Caudill, Professor of Law and Arthur M. Goldberg Family Chair, Villanova University Charles Widger School of Law

Wim Decock, Research Professor of Law, University of Leuven

Paula A. Franzese, Peter W. Rodino Professor of Law, Seton Hall University School of Law

James Gordley, W.R. Irby Chair in Law, Tulane University Law School

Michael A. Helfand, Associate Dean for Faculty and Research and Professor of Law, Pepperdine University Caruso School of Law

R. H. Helmholz, Ruth Wyatt Rosenson Distinguished Service Professor of Law, University of Chicago Law School

Adam J. MacLeod, Professor of Law, Faulkner University Thomas Goode Jones School of Law

Michael P. Moreland, University Professor of Law and Religion, Director of the Eleanor H. McCullen Center for Law, Religion and Public Policy, Villanova University Charles Widger School of Law

Nathan B. Oman, Rollins Professor of Law and Co-Director, Center for the Study of Law and Markets, Marshall-Wythe School of Law, The College of William & Mary

David W. Opderbeck, Professor of Law and Co-Director of the Gibbons Institute of Law, Science & Technology, Seton Hall University School of Law

David F. Partlett, Asa Griggs Candler Professor of Law, Emory University School of Law

Jeffrey A. Pojanowski, Professor of Law, Notre Dame Law School

C. Scott Pryor, Professor of Law, Campbell University Norman Adrian Wiggins School of Law

Val D. Ricks, Professor of Law, South Texas College of Law Houston

Brent A. Strawn, Professor of Old Testament and Professor of Law, Duke University

John Witte, Jr., Robert W. Woodruff Professor of Law, McDonald Distinguished Professor of Religion, and Director of the Center for the Study of Law and Religion, Emory University

Part I
Introduction

1 Introduction

Robert F. Cochran, Jr. and Michael P. Moreland

What is private law? And what does it have to do with Christianity? These are the animating questions of this book. This volume is part of a series on "Christianity and Law" sponsored by the Center for Law and Religion at Emory University. Some books in the series are on particular topics in law such as immigration or religious freedom, but there are also books in the series on Christianity and general fields of law—Christianity and family law, Christianity and natural law, and Christianity and criminal law, for example. But that leaves a large opening for the vast range of topics covered by "private law." The volumes in the series are intended to be introductions, written for law students, lawyers, and non-specialists in areas of law to help orient them to how Christianity relates to those fields.

What is private law?

A word of clarification at the outset about this term "private law," which may be unfamiliar to some readers. Law students discover early in their legal education that their basic courses can be divided into "public" and "private" law. There is a longstanding historical and conceptual tradition that denotes some topics as "private law"—namely property, contracts, business associations, and torts. Several of the chapters in this book address how those fields developed. A separate volume in this series addresses business associations, another topic often designated as private law.

One way of approaching what constitutes private law and how it is distinct from public law is found at the outset of an influential account of the sociology of law, Max Weber's *Economy and Society.* Weber writes that "[o]ne of the most important distinctions in modern legal theory and practice is that between 'public' and 'private' law," though the distinction is sometimes difficult to draw. Broadly speaking, public law directly involves the state—as Weber puts it, "the total body of those norms which regulate state-oriented action, that is, those activities which serve the maintenance, development, and the direct pursuit of the objectives, of the state."[1] In the usual American law school curriculum,

1 Max Weber, *Economy and Society: An Outline of Interpretive Sociology*, vol. 2, ed. Gunther Roth and Claus Wittich (Berkeley: University of California Press, 1978), 641.

criminal law and constitutional law, then, are "public law" courses, as are such areas as tax law and administrative law. By contrast, private law is, as Weber puts it, "the totality of those norms which, while issuing from the state, regulate conduct other than state-oriented conduct"; private law regulates the interests of individual parties.

Another difference between public law and much of private law is that whereas public law is created by the state—constitutional law, legislative enactments, and administrative regulation—much of private law is created by individuals. Individuals draft contracts, buy and sell property, and create and operate businesses. As to all of these areas of private law, the state creates the framework, but individuals organize and create many of the specific obligations under which individuals will govern themselves.

A third way of approaching the distinction between public and private law is the way private parties confront each other (in, say, a property or torts dispute) as opposed to the government initiating a legal action against private person (as Weber terms it, the difference between the law of coordination and the law of subordination). On this view, private law is "concerned with those legal affairs in which several parties are confronting each other so that the law treats them as being coordinated and that their legal spheres are to be 'properly' defined against each other...." In public law (a criminal prosecution, for example), "a holder of preeminent power, having authoritative power of command, is confronting those persons who are his subjects by virtue of the legal meaning of the norms."[2]

An important insight shared by many of the contributors to this volume is that private law is not public law by another name—there is an integrity to private law that is not reducible to merely functional or instrumental concerns. As summarized by Ernest Weinrib in his *The Idea of Private Law* (a work that played a significant role in rejuvenating interest in private law theory), functionalist accounts of law assume "that no distinction exists between private and public law." On this view, because private law is always in the pursuit of public objectives, "private law is public law in disguise."[3] A widely influential such functionalist view would be law and economics, or at least some forms of economic analysis of law. For law and economics, legal rules (as a descriptive or normative matter) are shaped by economic efficiency or some other policy objective or function—thus Weinrib's charge of functionalism. A recurring question raised by the chapters in this volume is whether Christianity is committed to non-instrumentalist and more formalist (in Weinrib's sense) views of private law, and, if so, how such non-instrumentalist views might be vindicated. But there is also a recurring theme in this volume that private law is not simply empty formalism. As pointed out by Brian Leiter, "vulgar formalism" holds that "judicial decision-making

2 Ibid., 642.

3 Ernest Weinrib, *The Idea of Private Law*, revised edition (Oxford: Oxford University Press, 2012), 7.

involves nothing more than mechanical deduction on the model of the syllogism."[4] Still, there is an inner logic to the law, and we might think that private law partakes of what Weinrib terms "immanent moral rationality"—there is a "normative force" to private law.[5]

Christianity and private law

In this collection, the content of that moral rationality in private law is spelled out in terms of the historical and conceptual ways in which the Christian tradition has informed the development and articulation of private law. A tentative hypothesis advanced in this collection is that a consideration of the Christian tradition helps us answer the question of what might be the special or distinctive aspects of private law. To that question there are conceptual answers tied to justice in particular forms and also historical answers (as private law emerged as a field), both of which are presented in these chapters. A besetting question for scholarship about law and religion is a concern that work at the intersection of Christianity and law ends up with crude "legal moralism." That is rejected by the contributions to this volume.

Instead, we might look to what Stephen A. Smith writes in his book *Contract Theory*, where he lays out four types of views that one can take toward any area of law: historical, prescriptive, descriptive, and interpretive. In historical accounts, we "seek to explain how and why the law has developed the way it has; they reveal the law's causal history." This volume has many such contributions, mining the resources of the Christian tradition for clues to how central concepts in private law came to be as they are. In a prescriptive account, we seek to say "what the law should be" or the "ideal law." Here, too, we have several chapters that critique the current state of fields of private law, pushing against (for example) aspects of individualism in property law or the demise of the doctrine of unconscionability in contract law. A descriptive account "aim[s] to describe the law as it is now or as it was at a certain time." The reader will encounter much in this book that tries to summarize the state of current legal doctrine in private law or shows how, for example, property law in medieval England was understood. Finally, an interpretive account "aim[s] to enhance understanding of the law by highlighting its significance or meaning." In that regard, each chapter in this volume is in some sense interpretive because each tries to "reveal an intelligible order in the law—it helps to 'make sense' of the law—and thereby helps us better understand it."[6] The bold claim advanced throughout this book is that the Christian tradition provides such an interpretive account of private law—not exhaustive, to be sure, but a valuable and neglected perspective on the fields of property, contracts, and torts.

4 Brian Leiter, "Legal Formalism and Legal Realism: What Is the Difference?" *Legal Theory*, 16 (2010): 111.

5 Weinrib, *The Idea of Private Law*, 23–24.

6 Stephen A. Smith, *Contract Theory* (Oxford: Oxford University Press, 2004), 4–5.

One way of examining this interpretive view is to consider the typology regarding the relationship of Christianity and forms of culture (we would include here legal culture) famously developed by H. Richard Niebuhr in his book *Christ and Culture*. Some of our authors address private law from one of these perspectives. Others describe the thought of Christian thinkers who have addressed an aspect of private law from one of them.

Under Niebuhr's synthesist perspective ("Christ above culture"), culture is good, but Christian faith has insights to add to it. Thomas Aquinas is the classic example of this view. According to Niebuhr, "In his system of thought he combined without confusing philosophy and theology, state and church, civic and Christian virtues, natural and divine laws, Christ and culture."[7] As to law, synthesists believe that Christian teaching can be reconciled with natural law and ultimately yield the best of positive law. Much of the history of private law can be understood this way, as canon and common lawyers took Roman law and developed it in light of Christian morality. Several of our authors[8] trace this history through the development of both canon and common law.

The next three motifs, in contrast to that of the synthesist, see culture as radically sinful. They suggest that the mere addition of Christian insight to culture is insufficient to redeem culture. Conversionists[9] ("Christ transforming culture") seek to convert a fallen culture in light of the insights of Christian teaching. A classic statement of this perspective is from Dutch Calvinist, Abraham Kuyper: "There is not one square inch on the earth as to which Christ does not scream 'mine'."[10]

The chapters of several authors in this volume are characterized by a conversionist stamp.[11] One area where many conversionist Christians have sought to reform law has been in its treatment of the poor and disenfranchised. See the chapter herein by David Opderbeck, and the chapter by Paula Franzese and Angela Carmella. Conversionists do not necessarily suggest that law should be the dominant means of transforming culture. As the chapters by David Caudill (on contracts) and Robert Cochran (on torts) indicate, Kuyper himself advocated sphere sovereignty—the division of authority within the institutions of society, of which government is only one. One thing to note is that conversionist Christians often wind up on opposite sides of legal issues. An example in this collection is the contrasting positions in the chapters of Val Ricks and Scott Pryor on the degree to which the state should regulate contracts.

7 H. Richard Niebuhr, *Christ and Culture* (New York: Harper & Row, 1951), 130.

8 See the essays by James Gordley, Adam MacLeod, Wim Decock, Michael Moreland and Jeffrey Pojanowski, and David Partlett.

9 John Calvin is often seen as the classic conversionist in arguing that "all the world is a theater for the glory of God."

10 *Abraham Kuyper: A Centennial Reader*, ed. James D. Bratt (Grand Rapids, MI: Eerdmans, 1998), 488.

11 See the essays by David Opderbeck, R.H. Helmholz, Paula Franzese and Angela Carmella, David Caudill, Val Ricks, and Scott Pryor.

Niebuhr's dualist category (Christ and Culture in Paradox) consists of those who see a necessary incompatibility between Christ and culture, but who see a role for the Christian in each. Martin Luther, for example, held Christ and culture uncomfortably in tension. For example, he said specifically that a Christian judge should not look to Christ for answers to legal problems. "You do not have to ask Christ about your duty. Ask the imperial or the territorial law."[12] Dualists see value in secular law as a necessary restrainer of evil in this fallen world, but view law as ultimately unredeemable. Though there are elements of all of Niebuhr's motifs in Augustine, as William Brewbaker's chapter herein illustrates, Augustine's view of property is best characterized as dualist. Property law in this world protects the possession of people who will use it for evil, but to not protect it would be worse. Christian practices, however, with respect to their property should be quite different than that permitted by the civil law. Christians do what they can in the City of Man, but we should never pretend that it can be ruled in the same way as the City of God.

In response to the evil of the world, separatists ("Christ against culture") come apart from it.[13] "[T]he political task of Christians is to be the church rather than to transform the world."[14] Separatists build their own institutions, rather than conform or compromise with the dominant culture. Separatists reject the use of the coercion that is an inherent part of law. They reject the (mere) cultural demands of justice and law and replace them with love within the Christian community.

In some respects, however, separatists may transform the world (and even law). Their alternate culture at times attracts the outside world. An example of such transformation within legal scholarship and the legal profession has been their influence on the alternative dispute resolution (ADR) movement. Separatists have long made use of non-adversarial methods of dispute resolution, and they were at the forefront of the ADR movement.[15] Two chapters within this collection reflect separatist approaches to private law. Nathan Oman's chapter in Part IV discusses John Calvin's approach to litigation. Though Calvin to many is the preeminent conversionist, he condemns Christian use of the courts. Michael Helfand's chapter in Part III addresses the practice of many Jews of agreeing to resolve disputes before Jewish arbitrators, rather than turn to secular courts. Such contract provisions can be a means of private law controlling both the substance and the procedure of public law.

12 Martin Luther, "Sermon on 'The Sermon on the Mount,'" in *From Irenaeus to Grotius: A Sourcebook in Christian Political Thought*, eds. Joan Lockwood O'Donovan and Oliver O'Donovan (Grand Rapids, MI: Eerdmans, 1999), 599.

13 In Niebuhr's typology, Anabaptist churches are the "separatist branch" of the Protestant Reformation.

14 Stanley Hauerwas and William H. Willimon, *Resident Aliens: Life in the Christian Colony* (Nashville, TN: Abingdon Press, 1989), 38.

15 See, for example, Andrew W. McThenia and Thomas L. Shaffer, "For Reconciliation," *Yale Law Journal*, 94 (1985): 1660–68.

Those in Niebuhr's final category, Culturalists ("The Christ of culture") draw no distinction between Christ and culture. Their Christian faith merely reflects the culture around them. "They feel no great tension between church and world, the social laws and the Gospel."[16] They merely provide another vocabulary or set of concepts for what the culture already instantiates. The danger is that one who takes this perspective (whether consciously or not) will fail to see the ways Christ should transform culture or law. There is an especially strong temptation for those who benefit from the laws of a culture to give it the blessings of religious faith. This can be an issue in all areas of private law, as those who make law, either creating private law's public framework or drafting contracts and buying and selling property within that framework, use law for their own benefit at the expense of those with no power. Moreover, interpretations of Christianity have often been used to protect those interests.

Cutting across Niebuhr's categories, the chapters fall into one (sometimes more than one) of four other categories. First, some chapters consider the biblical sources and how they have shaped the emergence of private law. A second approach taken in several chapters is historical—showing how figures working within the Christian tradition in various historical periods have contributed to our understanding of property, contracts, and torts. These accounts are often "genealogical" in their concerns, gathering sources and showing how a concept in private law (obligation in the law of contracts for example) emerged. A third and related approach looks to Christian philosophical sources, particularly natural law. Finally, some chapters take a prophetic or critical perspective.

The chapters in this collection

The volume begins with two overview chapters that examine the biblical and philosophical sources of private law. Brent Strawn notes that the Old Testament contains several discussions of contract, property, and tort law (or at least a nascent understanding of these topics). Through an exegesis of particular illustrations of private law in the Old Testament, Strawn draws out consistent themes from the biblical sources: concern for the vulnerable, God's pervasive involvement with law-making, and his abiding interests in covenant, ownership, and familial lineage as forces shaping the emergence of private law.

James Gordley, working from within the Thomistic and Catholic tradition, points out that what we term "private law" has its sources in Roman law, and he explores the ways in which medieval jurists and canonists adapted those Roman sources in Christianity. Gordley argues that principles of justice (compared to charity) were at work in the emergence of private law in Christianity, worked out in such areas as fault (in tort law) and a just price (in contracts). Gordley also unpacks the complicated relationship between canon law and civil law in the medieval period, as ecclesiastical and civil rulers looked to multiple sources of law for resolving conflicts in areas that we now denote as private law.

16 Niebuhr, *Christ and Culture*, 83.

Following these two general orientations to the topic, the volume takes up particular areas of private law—property, contracts, and torts. The section on property law sets forth a range of historical, critical, and philosophical approaches from a Christian perspective. David Opderbeck's chapter "Christian Thought and Property Law" opens the section by exploring how certain themes from the early modern period—particularly aspects of Protestantism and individualism—sit uneasily with earlier aspects of Christian thought that emphasize the communal nature of property and a radical critique of private property rights. Adam MacLeod's "The Boundaries of Dominion" provides a natural law perspective on property law, drawing upon the so-called New Natural Law theory's account of basic goods and practical reasonableness. MacLeod attempts to provide a conceptual account of dominion as the core of property law, over and against rival accounts of property law that are focused on property as "a bundle of rights," a right to exclude, or a norm of social obligation.

In "Augustinian Property," William Brewbaker considers property law's relation to Augustine's account of political authority and the punitive function of civil law. On such a view, property is less a right of use than an entitlement rooted in providence, a view that once again challenges certain modern individualistic and narrowly rights-focused ways of understanding property. R. H. Helmholz carries the discussion forward chronologically in a chapter on religion and English property law in the period from 1500 to 1700, the Tudor and Stuart periods and the time of the English Reformation. Mining original source material, Helmholz shows that discussions of property law in that period were marked by a ready invocation of scriptural arguments, the importation of canon law into common law decision making, and a generally permeable boundary between theological and legal argumentation. Helmholz's contribution suggests that the emergence of property in the English common law is more theologically inflected and less crudely "secular" than modern views might suggest.

The section of the volume on property law concludes with a chapter by Paula Franzese and Angela Carmella applying Catholic social teaching to modern public housing policy. As Franzese and Carmella note, Catholic social teaching holds that "property has a specific social function, subordinated to the right to common use," and that housing is not simply a "market commodity," but instead various agencies must coexist in order to ensure that there is "just distribution of housing." They use these insights to assess aspects of zoning and access to affordable housing in New Jersey, underscoring the contemporary policy implications of some of the insights about property law developed in the other chapters.

Turning next to contracts, this section of the volume begins with a historical exploration by Wim Decock of "The Theological Roots of Contractual Obligation." Decock's historical research—like Helmholz's in the property context—shows how theologians (most especially in his chapter, Spanish scholastic theologians working in the Thomistic natural law tradition) contributed to the formation of the law of contracts at the outset of the modern period. The language of these moral theologians was also profoundly legal, and scholasticism shaped such important contract law doctrines as liberty among contracting parties, private autonomy in making contracts, and commutative justice in contractual relations.

Working in the different theological and philosophical idiom of the influential Dutch jurist Herman Dooyeweerd and the Reformed (Calvinist) Christian tradition, David Caudill explores the system upon which Dooyeweerd based his jurisprudence. Dooyeweerd, according to Caudill, developed a profound taxonomy of private and public life, with a central importance placed on law within those spheres. Dooyeweerd's account also underscores the importance of a limited state and corresponding limitations on interference with freedom of contract.

Turning to another important doctrine in contract law, Val Ricks offers "A Christian Critique of Consideration." Ricks rejects the view of Oliver Wendell Holmes that the doctrine of consideration is a mere empty formality, and he draws on philosophical sources to provide a reconstruction of consideration as a doctrine enabling human freedom. C. Scott Pryor then argues for rehabilitating the doctrine of unconscionability. Pryor looks to such biblical themes as righteousness and fairness in dealing to argue for a view of contracts centered on right ordering and commutative justice. Because a Christian perspective on contract law will emphasize righteousness and sociability, Pryor argues for a more robust doctrine of unconscionability to constrain unfair or unscrupulous dealing with others in contractual relationships. As noted earlier, there is a tension in the underlying justifications of these two chapters. Though they both present a Christian critique of an aspect of contract law, Ricks argues for greater freedom of contract, Pryor for greater legal oversight of contracts.

In the final chapter of the contracts section, Michael Helfand draws on contemporary discussions of legal pluralism to explore "Privatization and Pluralism: Promoting Religious Values Through Contract." In a sense, Helfand's chapter is inversely related to the other chapters exploring contract law—while others explore religious (particularly historical) influences on the civil law of contracts, Helfand argues for the importance of religious forms of dispute resolution (such as religious arbitration) within a private law framework. Whereas generally there has been a tendency for public law to expand through greater regulation of private law, Helfand explores the possibility that substantive and arbitration provisions in contracts might wrest control of some aspects of law back from the state into the private arena.

The final section of the volume takes up tort law. Jeffrey Pojanowski and Michael Moreland engage issues raised by contemporary tort theory and its division into externalist and internalist accounts, somewhat along the lines of the functionalist and formalist division noted earlier in discussing Ernest Weinrib's view. The challenge for efforts at a comprehensive account of tort law is that many aspects of tort doctrine seem contingent, such that current theoretical approaches—be they law and economics, corrective justice, or civil recourse views—fail to account for particular features of tort law. In order to address this debate between comprehensive and contingent theories of tort law, they turn to insights from Thomas Aquinas's discussion of the relation of natural law and positive (human) law to sort out essential aspects of tort law as providing a means for redressing harms through justice and contingent aspects of tort law that are not fully arbitrary but could be otherwise.

In a similar effort to clear up some ambiguities in contemporary tort doctrine, David Partlett focuses on the element of duty in tort law and posits views rooted in Christianity against certain modern limitations on tort liability. Partlett emphasizes the pillars of community, individual autonomy, and protection of the vulnerable. These expansive themes, on Partlett's view, run contrary to modern developments such as federal statutory preemption of state tort liability and First Amendment free speech limitations on defamation and intentional infliction of emotional distress.

In "Christian Perspectives on Torts and Intermediate Communities," Robert Cochran argues against prevailing views of tort law as enshrining individualism and autonomy and shows how important dimensions of tort law are also solicitous of communities. Drawing on the principles of subsidiarity in Catholic social thought and sphere sovereignty in Dutch Reformed theology, Cochran illustrates how these principles can provide both descriptive and normative accounts of this overlooked communitarian dimension of tort law.

Finally, in a chapter that begins describing a contemporary development in tort law (the civil recourse account of John Goldberg and Benjamin Zipursky) but moves out to considerations of civil litigation more generally, Nathan Oman outlines "Christianity's Quarrel with Civil Recourse Theory." Oman points out that for at least one representative tradition in Christian legal theory (Calvinism), litigation in civil courts was suspect and only legitimate when done in a public spirit. Oman notes concerns from this Christian perspective about the elevation in civil recourse theory of litigation as an appropriate forum for achieving a just legal order.

It is the hope of the editors that, taken together, these chapters will show that there is a range of intelligible answers to the questions with which this introduction began. The fields of private law have a historical and conceptual core that is deeply indebted to Christianity. Through a set of biblical, historical, philosophical, and critical perspectives on property, contracts, and torts, the reader will see numerous connections between Christianity and private law.

2 Christian origins of private law

James Gordley

Repentance and private law

Would God forgive a thief who refused to return what he stole? Answering that question led the Christian teachers of the Middle Ages to investigate what the Roman jurists had called problems of "private law." Public law deals with the relations between the state and its citizens or other states. Private law deals with the relations between citizens. They own property. They make contracts. If one person harms another, the victim may be owed compensation. If one Christian takes another's property, or breaks a contract, or hurts him, has he committed a sin, and, if so, must he compensate the other person if he wishes to be forgiven? The medieval Canon lawyers answered these questions with the help of Roman legal texts.

St. Augustine had said,

> If the thing of another person, for which a sin was committed, is not returned when it can be returned, there is not penance but rather pretense. If indeed it is truly done, the sin is not forgiven unless restitution is made of the thing that was taken away.[1]

The Roman Empire fell, barbarians conquered Western Europe, urban life disintegrated, and, in the twelfth century, as cities again began to flourish and intellectual life resumed, this passage was included in the *Decretum*, a collection of sources that Christians regarded as authoritative and which became the basis for the study of Canon law. We know little about its origins, except that it is said to have been compiled by a man named Gratian. Its compilation was part of what Kenneth Pennington called "the big bang,"[2] an explosion of legal thought centering in Bologna, which became one of the first Western universities.

1 C. 14 q. 6 c. 1.

2 Kenneth Pennington, "The 'Big Bang': Roman Law in the Early Twelfth-Century," *Rivista internazionale di diritto comune*, 18 (2007): 70.

It coincided with the renewed study of Roman law based on a compilation of legal texts that became known as the *Corpus iuris civilis*, made in the sixth century under the Emperor Justinian.

The Canon lawyers read the passage from St. Augustine to mean that one who had committed a sin by harming another person could not be forgiven without *restitutio*, that is, without compensating the victim for the harm he suffered. In Roman law, *restituere* meant to restore something, such as a damaged building or road, to its former condition. *Restitutio in integrum* was an extraordinary remedy which allowed a person to set aside a transaction and be placed in his former position when he had suffered an inequitable loss. The Canonists broadened the meaning of the term. It meant making compensation for any kind of loss one person had wrongfully caused another.

The Canonists were familiar with Roman law. Many of them had a degree in Roman as well as Canon law – the so-called "double doctorate." In determining when a loss had been caused wrongfully, and *restitutio* must be made, they consulted Roman sources.

The Roman law had rules about private law but they were not organized systematically into doctrines or explained by principles. It recognized the rights of property owners but had no general theory of property. As has often been said, the Romans had no general law of torts – which is the law that governs when a person who has been harmed can seek compensation. There were particular actions that could be brought by an injured party. Two of the most important were an action under the *lex Aquilia* and an action for *iniuria*. The former held a person liable who intentionally or negligently harmed another's property, or, according to two Roman texts, his person. The medieval Roman lawyers generalized those two texts to allow the action whenever his person had been harmed. The action for *iniuria* imposed liability for various offences to another's reputation or honor. Still other actions imposed liability on a person who was not at fault, for example, the *actio de pauperie*, for harm done by animals. Similarly, Roman contract law was a law of particular contracts. Some, such as gratuitous loans and deposits for safekeeping, were binding when the object in question was delivered. Others, such as sale, lease, and partnership, were binding on consent. Some, such as sale, lease, and partnership, were contracts of good faith (*bonae fidei*). A party was bound, not only by what he said, to all the obligations that good faith required. In contrast, the formal contact *stipulatio* (in the Middle Ages, a notarized contract) could be used to make any promise binding. But it was not a contract of good faith, and a party was bound only to what he said.

The Canon lawyers borrowed selectively from these rules. One example is liability for fault. A person needed to make *restitutio* when he caused another harm intentionally or negligently but not when he did so without fault. A person who could not have acted otherwise could not have sinned.

That principle was not obvious, at least to Gratian. In a text included in the *Decretum*, the Eighth Council of Toledo had said that "if an inescapable danger compels one to perpetrate one of two evils, we must choose the one that makes us less guilty."[3] In another text, Pope Gregory I had said:

> when the mind is torn between greater and lesser sins, if absolutely no path of escape lies open without sin, lesser evils are always to be chosen. A man swears to keep a secret that another man is about to confide to him. The secret turns out to be a plan to murder the husband of a woman with whom he is committing adultery. A man promises obedience to a spiritual director who then forbids him to do what is good and commands him to do what is evil.[4]

Gratian concluded that a "dispensation… from natural law" could be permitted "when one is compelled to choose between two evils."[5]

This conclusion was quickly rejected by the Canonists. According to an authoritative compilation of notes to the *Decretum* that became known as the *Glossa ordinaria* or Standard Gloss, "the Master (Gratian)" spoke "badly."

> For it would then follow that necessity could make one do something evil. But the canons say that God will never punish anyone unless he has done wrong voluntarily. [citing *Decretum* C. 23 q. 4 c. 23.] Furthermore, if necessity really required us to do something evil, that the law that prohibited this would be impossible to obey. But every law must be possible. [citing *Decretum* D. 4 c. 2.][6]

The man who swore to keep the secret does not sin by revealing it "for an oath was not invented to be a chain of iniquity."[7] The man who promised to obey his spiritual director does not sin by disobeying since his promise "is to be understood only of whatever is lawful and honest."[8]

Although Gratian thought a sin could be committed without fault, nevertheless, he also said that an act could not be punished when it was done "*contra animum*," against one's will.[9] The Canonists adopted the principle of the *lex Aquilia* that a person was responsible if he acted intentionally or negligently.

3 D. 13 c. 1.
4 D. 13 c. 2.
5 *D. G. ante* D. 13 c. 1.
6 *Gl. ord.* to *Decretum* to *d.G. ante* D. 13 c. 1 to *Item adversus.*
7 *Gl. ord.* to D. 13 c. 2 to *transgressionis contagione.*
8 *Gl. ord.* to *formidat.* For similar solutions, see *Summa 'Elegantius in iure divino' seu Coloniensis*, ed. Gerard Fransen and Stephan Kuttner (New York: Fordham University Press, 1969), pars 1, cap. 79; *The Summa Parisiensis on the Decretum Gratiani*, ed. Terence P. McLaughlin (Toronto: Pontifical Institute of Medieval Studies, 1952), to D. 13 cc. 1–2; *Summa 'Omnis qui iuste iudicat sive Lipsiensis,'* eds. Rudolf Weigand, Peter Landau and Waltraud Kozur (Vatican City: Biblioteca Apostolica Vaticana, 2007), 1: to D. 13 c.2; Huguccio, *Summa*, Admont Stiftsbibliothek M.S 7, to D. 13 pr.
9 *D.G. ante* D. 50 c. 46.

In their view, the Roman texts that imposed legal liability without fault did not concern moral obligations, whatever pragmatic purposes they may have served.

There were three texts in the *Decretum* to support their position. One suspects that Gratian, or someone else familiar with Roman law, had looked rather hard to find them. All three were from the ninth century – Pope Nicolas I, the Council of Worms, and the Council of Tribourg – and all of them dealt with someone who cut down a tree that fell on another. He is not to be blamed if the harm was not due to his "will" or "fault (*culpa*) or neglect";[10] if it was not caused "intentionally or by negligence (*negligentia*)" and he was doing a "necessary work";[11] or if he had called "look out."[12] Whatever the authors of the ninth-century texts had in mind, the Standard Gloss identified this rule with that of the *lex Aquilia*, citing a Roman text which resembled those in the *Decretum*. It said that one who prunes a tree is not liable if a branch falls on someone if he does so in a private place and calls out.[13]

Thus the Canonists reached the conclusion suggested by Roman law: one must make compensation if he had caused harm intentionally or by negligence. This conclusion was confirmed by text in the *Decretals*. The *Decretals* was a compilation made under Pope Gregory IX of excerpts from papal letters that resolved disputed points of Canon law. It and the *Decretum* were called the *Corpus iuris canonici*, in contrast to the compilation of Justinian, which was called the *Corpus iuris civilis*. A text in the *Decretals* exonerated a priest who dropped a beam and killed a man who was helping him to build a church provided that "he was taking care to be diligent" and "called out in a loud voice" because one is not responsible for "chance events." The Standard Gloss explained that "chance events are not imputed to one unless fault intervenes," citing, again, the Roman text about the man who prunes a tree. According to a text from Gregory IX, "If harm is done through your fault or injury inflicted… or it occurs by your lack of skill or negligence, by law you must make satisfaction for it…."[14] The principle of civil law, that one was liable for harm done intentionally or negligently, had become a principle of moral and religious law governing when a person had sinned and must make compensation.

The Standard Gloss to the *Decretals* then placed this interpretation on four texts taken from the book of Exodus in which fault was not mentioned. A man must make compensation when he leaves a pit uncovered and an ox or donkey falls into it (Ex. 21:33–34);[15] when his ox harms another's ox (Ex. 21:35)[16]; when he lets his animals to graze in a field or vineyard and they graze in another's

10 D. 50 c. 49 (Pope Nicolas I).
11 D. 50 c. 50 (Council of Worms).
12 D. 50 c. 51 (Council of Triburg).
13 *Gl. ord.* to D. 50 c. 49 to *inculpabiles*; to D. 50 c. 51 to *Si duo*, citing Dig. 9.2.31.
14 X 5.36.9.
15 X 5.36.2.
16 X 5.36.3.

field (Ex. 22:5);[17] and when his fire spreads and destroys grain (Ex. 22:6).[18] In Jewish law, the *Mishna* refers to these cases as "the four generative causes of damages." "What they have in common is that they customarily do damage, and taking care of them is your responsibility."[19] "In the case of anything of which I am liable to take care, I am deemed to render possible whatever damage it might do."[20] In contrast, the Standard Gloss to the *Decretals* explained all four cases by citing the *lex Aquilia*.[21] In the case of the pit, it said that the one is not responsible if the pit is in a private rather than a public place.[22] In the case of the ox and the fire, it said that the man is responsible on account of fault (*culpa* or *negligentia*).[23]

As described earlier, in Roman law, a person was liable under the *lex Aquilia* for inflicting physical harm. He was liable for *iniuria* for injuring another person's dignity or reputation. The Canonists accepted the principle that one was liable for injuring another person's dignity, but they extended the remedy. In Roman law, one was required to pay damages. Raymond of Penafort[24] said that in addition, in order to make restitution, he should publicly announce that he had been in error or at least apologize.[25] To reach this conclusion, they again read their texts broadly. Raymond cited two texts from the *Decretum*. According to one, a person must give back another's thing that he acquired by sin.[26] According to the other, a person who had posted an accusation at night in a public place will not be suspended from communion or anathematized if he confesses.[27] He also cited Matthew 5:23 which said that you should go and be reconciled with your brother before presenting your offering at the altar. Hostiensis cited a text from the *Decretales*[28] which said that a person implicated in heresy should denounce the heresy in question at various public places. Here again, the remedy was adopted by civil law. By the sixteenth century, secular courts were allowing the plaintiff an action for *recantatio*, *revocatio* or *palinodia* to force the defendant to confess his error or apologize.[29]

17 X 5.36.4.
18 C. 5.36.5.
19 *The Mishnah*, trans. Jacob Neusner (New Haven, CT: Yale University Press, 1988), Babba Qamma 1:1, at 503.
20 *Mishnah* 1:2, at 503.
21 *Gl. ord.* to X 5.36.2 *to reddat pretium*; to X 5.36.3 to *reddet bovem*; to X 5.36.4 to *aestimationem restituit*; X 5.36.5 to *reddet damnum*.
22 *Gl. ord.* to X 5.36.2 to *reddet pretium*.
23 *Gl. ord.* to X 5.36.to *reddet damnum*.
24 Raimundus de Penafort, *Summa de poenitentia*, eds. Xaverio Ochoa and Alosio Díez (Rome: Commentarium pro religiosis, 1976), II.5.42.
25 *See* Karl Weinzierl, *Die Restituionslehre der Frühscholastik* (Munich: M Hueber, 1936), 132–46.
26 C. 14, c. 6, c. 1.
27 C. 5, q. 1, c. 2.
28 X 5.34.10 (vers. *precipias*).
29 Udo Wolter, *Das Prinzip der Naturalrestitution in § 249 BGB Herkunft, historische Entwicklung und Bedeutung* (Berlin: Duncker & Humblot, 1985), 72. *See generally* Reinhard Zimmermann, *The Law of Obligations Roman Foundations of the Civilian Tradition* (Cape Town:

The medieval Roman lawyers thus borrowed rules from the Canonists, as the Canonists did from the Roman lawyers. For the Canonists, however, the rules they borrowed had a different significance. The medieval Roman lawyers, like the ancient Roman jurists, were concerned with when one party could successfully sue another. The Canonists were concerned with moral responsibility for harming another person. They recognized that certain Roman rules instantiated general moral principles. They distinguished these rules from others which, in their judgment, did not. The rules of the *lex Aquilia* that held a person liable for harm caused by fault, intentionally or negligently, did concern moral responsibility. Rules that held a person liable for harm caused without fault did not, such as those of the *actio de pauperie*. What mattered was moral principle, not the distinctions among Roman actions.

In a similar way, in discussing contract law, the Canonists borrowed only those rules of Roman law that, in their view, concerned moral obligation. Most Canonists rejected the Roman rule that only certain contracts were binding on consent. In principle, all promises were morally binding. The *Decretum* contained two texts in which promises were said to be binding which, the Canonists observed, would not be enforceable in Roman law.[30] According to one, if remuneration is promised for doing something for the Church, the promise must be kept. According to the other, when an Archbishop promised goods to a monastery before he died, his successor should keep the promise.[31] A text in the *Decretals* contained the general statement, "agreements are to be served, agreements are to be kept (*pacta servetur, pacta custodiantur*)."[32] The statement had been made by a Church council in Africa to explain why a bishop should be disciplined who had promised another bishop not to attract away members of his congregation and then had broken his promise. The Canonists read these texts broadly. They concluded that agreements were enforceable in Canon law without regard to the Roman distinctions between contract that are enforceable on consent and those that are not.[33] The reason, according to the standard gloss to the *Decretals*, is that "God does not distinguish between simple speech and an oath."[34]

Some modern scholars have concluded that Canon law gave birth to the idea that, in principle, all contracts are binding in principle.[35] The medieval Roman lawyers, however, had concluded that all contracts are binding in principle

---

Juta, 1990), 1072; C. von Wallenrodt, "Die Injurienklagen auf Abbitte, Widerruf und Ehrenerklärung in ihrer Entstehung, Fortbildung und ihrem Verfall," *Zeitschrift für Rechtsgeschichte*, 3 (1864): 238.

30 C. 1, q. 2 c. 66.

31 C. 12 q. 5 c. 3.

32 X 1.35.1 (*pacta servetur, pacta custodiantur*).

33 *Gl. ord.* to C. 12 q. 2 c. 66 to *promiserint*; *Gl. ord.* to X 1.35.1 to *pacta custodiantur.*

34 *Gl. ord.* to X 1.35.1 to *pacta custodiantur.*

35 Jules Roussier, *Le Fondement de l'obligation contractuelle dans le droit de l'église* (Paris: Domat-Montchrestien,1933), 20–94, 177–216; F. Schupfer, *Il diritto delle obligationi in Italia: nell'età dell'Risorigimento* (Turin: Bocca, 1920), 1:51.

or by nature even though not all are legally enforceable.[36] The difference, as Guido Astuti pointed out, is that the Canonists were concerned with a different question: not when a contract is enforceable, but when breaking a promise is a sin.[37]

The Canonists limited the principle with a doctrine taken from the medieval Roman law. To be binding, the promise must have a *causa*. The *causa* could be liberality or the receipt of something in return. This doctrine was unknown to the Roman jurists. Nevertheless, the medieval lawyers read it into the Roman texts.[38] Baldus degli Ubaldi, one of the greatest medieval jurists, then read it into the Canon law.[39]

The Canonists were more hesitant to reject the Roman distinction between contracts of good faith and contracts of strict law. They repeated the Roman rule that in contracts of good faith, unlike those of strict law, the parties are bound to the unexpressed obligations that good faith requires.[40] They often described the difference in the same way as the civilians without any hint that the distinction does not matter in Canon law.[41] Baldus claimed that in Canon law all contracts were contracts of good faith.[42] He noted, however, that he was merely giving his own opinion. Perhaps the hesitancy was due to the technical meaning of "good faith" in Roman contract law. It meant that associated with types of contracts such as sale and lease were packages of terms to which a party is obligated without his express consent. In modern law they are called the "implied terms" of a contract, and, as in Roman law, they depend on the type of contract a party entered into. In a sale, he is bound by those of the law of sales, in a lease, by those of the law of leases, and so forth

In this way, the Canonists created what one might call a distinct body of private law. Like Roman law, it was a set of rules and principles setting out the duties people owe to each other. Unlike Roman law, it purported to be a moral law binding in conscience. The Roman law was applied in courts by professionally trained judges in those parts of Europe in which it had been adopted. The Canon law counseled every Christian as to when he might need forgiveness. Its rules, developed by scholars in universities, had to be put into a form which could be understood by priests who might have no legal education who could advise lay people who might have no education at all. One of the greatest

36 James Gordley, *Philosophical Origins of Modern Contract Doctrine* (Oxford: Oxford University Press, 1991), 41–45.

37 Guido Astuti, "I principii fondamentale dei contratti nella storia del diritto italiano," *Annali di storia del diritto*, 1 (1957): 34–37.

38 Gordley, *Philosophical Origins*, 49–57; James Gordley, *The Jurists: A Critical History* (Oxford: Oxford University Press, 2013), 48–49.

39 Baldus de Ubaldis, *Commentaria Corpus iuris civilis* (Venice, 1577) to C. 3.36.15 no. 3; *see* Baldus de Ubaldis, *In Decretalium volumen commentaria* (Venice, 1595), to X. 1.35.1.

40 *Gl. ord.* to X 3.17.6 to *restituerent*; to X 2.25.6 to *bonae fidei.*

41 *Gl. ord.* to X 3.17.3 to *deceptione*; Sinibaldus Fliscus (Innocent IV), *Commentaria, apparatus in V libros Decretalium* (Frankfurt: Minerva, 1968), to X 3.17.3.

42 Baldus de Ubaldis, *In quinque volumen Decretalium commentaria* (Venice, 1595), to X 2.11.1 no. 12 (ego puto quod in aequitate canonica omnes contractus mundi sit bonae fidei).

Canonists, St. Raymond of Penafort, included this discussion of the culpability of a person who kills another in a manual for confessors:

> Homicide may occur by chance, as when someone throws a stone at a bird and someone else unexpectedly passing by is struck and dies, or when someone cuts down a tree which, by chance, crushes someone, and so forth.... If ... the work was done lawfully, the killing is not imputed to him if he uses the diligence that he should, namely, in looking about and calling out, not too late or too softly but at an appropriate time, and loudly, so that if someone were there he could escape and look out for himself, or if a teacher does not go beyond due measure in beating a student. It is otherwise if, engaged in a lawful work, he does not use due diligence. As has been said, then the killing is imputed to him. This distinction is proved from D. 50 c. 50; c. 51; X 5.12.25. Finally, some homicide is voluntary. It may be said without distinction that voluntary homicide is a mortal sin and a very great one. D. 50 c. 44.[43]

If a man confessed to a priest that he had killed someone, the priest could ask him questions about his intentions and his degree of diligence. He might, in the end, tell the man that he not committed a sin at all. Similarly, if a man had broken a promise a priest might tell him that he must keep it, whether the promise was enforceable in secular law or not. Guided by manuals such as these, the priest could do so without himself knowing the many sources, Roman and Christian, on which it was based.

There had been earlier manuals for confessors.[44] They lacked the legal content that Canon lawyers now provided. Later confessional manuals integrated this legal content with the theology of St. Thomas Aquinas. An early example was the *Summa confessorum* of Johannes von Freiburg (d. 1314).[45] A notable one was that of St. Antoninus (1389–1459), the Archbishop of Florence and confessor of Cosimo di Medici.[46] An influential one that was more of a digest than a traditional handbook for confessors was the *Summa Sylvestrina* of Sylvester da Prierio (1456?–1527?).[47]

Christian influence?

To what extent this distinct body of law rested on specifically Christian principles is not clear. James Whitman believes that there were serious tensions between Roman law, which was, after all, the work of pagan authors, and the values of

43 Raimundus de Penafort, *Summa de poenitentia*, II.1.

44 Lugger Körntgen, *Studien zu den Quellen der frühmittelalterlichen Bussbücher* (Sigmaringen: J. Thorbecke, 1993).

45 Johannes von Freiburg, *Summa confessorum* (Augsburg, 1476).

46 Antoninus, *Summula confessionalis utilissima* (Venice, 1538).

47 Silvestro da Prierio (Mazzolini), *Summae Syluestrinae, quae Summa summarum, merito nuncupatur* (Venice, 1591).

medieval Christians. One of his examples is how the medieval jurists dealt with a classical Roman text that said that by nature it is permitted for each contracting party to circumvent the other by proposing a price more favorable to himself.[48] A post-classical Roman text gave a remedy to a person who sold land for less than half its "true price."[49] Early on, the medieval Roman jurists generalized this text to provide a remedy for goods as well as land, for buyers as well as sellers, and for parties in kindred transactions such as a lease.[50] Did they do so under the influence of a Christian aversion to hard bargains? It is hard to say. In any event, they allowed a remedy only for those disparities of more than half the just price – for what became called *laesio enormis* – and, by a papal decretal, that rule became accepted in Canon law.[51]

In other instances, the Canonists took the lead in tempering the strictness of Roman law. One instance concerned the rights of an owner. The Canonists said that these rights were qualified, relying on excerpt from St. Ambrose denouncing the sin of greed which had been included in the *Decretum*. A greedy person "always sees gold, always silver" and "asks gold even in his prayer and supplication to God."

> But, you say, what is the injustice if I diligently care for my own without seizing what is another's? Oh, imprudent saying! Your own you say? What things? From what horde did you bring them into this world? When you came into the light, when you left your mother's womb, stuffed with what possessions and goods, I ask, did you come?... Let no one call his own what is common.[52]

The Canonists concluded that an owner of property could not disregard the needs of others. If he had more than enough for himself, he should give the rest away. Moreover, in a case of urgent necessity, property became literally common. Raymond of Penafort put the case of a person who, when fleeing his enemies, met a priest riding a horse. When the priest refused to give the horse, the man took it by force, fled, and when he was safe, gave the horse back to the priest. Raymond said that "I believe that if there was no other way to escape, he is not bound in any way" citing the text from St. Ambrose along with others.[53]

The Romans had not formulated a general doctrine that one could use another's property in time of necessity. In support of their doctrine, however, the Canonists cited Roman rules on jettisoning cargo at sea to save a ship in

48 James Q. Whitman, "Long Live the Hatred of Roman Law!" *Rechtsgeschichte*, 2 (2003): 48–49.

49 C. 4.44.2.

50 See *Brachylogus*, ed. Eduard Böcking (Berlin: F. Dümmler, 1829), iii.xiii.8; Accursiis, *Glossa ordinaria* to C 4.44.2 to *auctoritate iudicis.*

51 X 3.17.3.

52 D. 47 c.8.

53 Raymundus de Penyafort, *Summa iuris*, ed. Joseph Rius y Serra (Barcelona: Barchinonae, 1945).

a storm.[54] There were several other Roman texts allowing one person to use another's property in discrete situations. The Standard Gloss to the *Decretum* listed some of them:

> There are cases in which one is allowed to pass through another's field: if there is a servitude, C. 3.34.11, or if one wants to dig up one's own treasure, D. 10.4.19 (at the end), if my fruit fell into your field, Dig. 43.27.1, when I am looking for a fugitive, Dig. 11.4.4 ... and when a public road is destroyed, Dig. 8.6.14.1.[55]

The Canonists had to work to reconcile this rule with some of their own texts. One, which was included in the *Decretals*, came from an early manual for priests used to prescribe the penance to be done by those who had confessed their sins. It said that "if a person stole food, clothing or money because of necessity, being hungry or naked, he should do three weeks penance, and if he returned what he stole, he should not be compelled to fast."[56] The Canonists' difficulty was why he should have to do penance at all, even a light penance, since by their doctrine he could not have committed a sin. According to the Standard Gloss: "From the facts that penance is imposed, it may be gathered that the necessity was moderate. Penance would not have been imposed if it had been great… for in necessity all things are common."[57] They thus formulated what came to be called the "doctrine of necessity."

Another instance in which the Canonists tempered the strictness of Roman law concerning the circumstances in which a person was not bound by a contract. As we have seen, the Canonists had concluded that promises were binding, whether they were enforceable in Roman law or not: "*pacta servetur, pacta custodiantur*."[58] In asking whether a person always must keep a promise, they relied on a text from St. Augustine included in the *Decretum* in which he considered a question put by Cicero. Suppose one person deposited his sword with another, who promised to return it when asked to do so. If the owner of the sword asked for it after he had become insane or wished to use it to hurt himself or another, should the promise be kept? Augustine, like Cicero, answered that it should not.[59] According to the Standard Gloss, "[t]herefore, this condition is always understood: if matters remain in the same state."[60] It cited a Roman text in support.[61] According to the text, if a person had promised by *stipulatio* that something be given to himself or to Titius, it was better to give it to Titius "if

54 *Gl. ord.* to D. 47 c. 8 to *commune*.
55 *Gl. ord. to D.* 1 c. 2.
56 X 5.18.3.
57 *Gl. ord.* to X 5.18.3. to *poenitentia*.
58 X 1.35.1 (*pacta servetur, pacta custodiantur*).
59 C. 22 q. 2 c. 14.
60 *Gl. ord.* to C. 22 q. 2 c. 14 to *furens*.
61 *Gl. ord.* to C. 22 q. 2 c. 14 to *furens*.

he remain in the same position as he was when the *stipulatio* was made." But the payment should not be made to Titius if he had been adopted, or exiled, or become a slave "for there appears to be in the *stipulatio* the tacit agreement 'if he remain in the same legal position'."[62] As in the case of necessity, the Canonists used a general doctrine to explain a particular case in a Roman text. As in the case of necessity, they did so by finding a legal standard in the moral reflections of one of the Church fathers. Baldus then read the doctrine that a promise need not be kept in changed circumstances into the Roman law.[63]

The doctrines of necessity and changed circumstances were unknown to the ancient Roman jurists, although the Canonists found particular cases in Roman law that these doctrines could explain. Neither did the ancient Romans recognize a generalized remedy for relief for an unjust price, although the medieval Roman lawyers based it on a Roman text. Were these instances in which a Roman concern for justice was modified by a Christian concern for charity?

The medieval jurists would have rejected that view. They thought these doctrines concerned a person's obligations as a matter of justice. The medieval Roman lawyers followed by Canonists such as Hostiensis[64] described the remedy for an unjust price as a remedy for a type of fraud: *dolus ex re ipsa*, or fraud that appears from the thing itself. Intentional fraud or *dolus ex propositio* might also result in an unjust price, but because of a misrepresentation.[65]

The Canonists distinguished between obligations of justice and obligations of charity. As a matter of charity, a rich man might be under a duty to forgive a poor debtor, but as a matter of justice he was not. One who violated a duty of charity would be forgiven if he were genuinely sorry, but one who violated a duty of justice must also compensate the person he had wronged. As a matter of justice, in time of necessity, a person was entitled to use another's property without his consent. If circumstances had changed, he was not obligated to keep a promise.

It may be, however, that these doctrines address problems that were more likely to trouble Christians concerned about sin than to ancient Roman jurists concerned about litigation. If Whitman is correct, the medieval Roman lawyers generalized the relief given for an unjust price because, as Christians, they were offended by the classical Roman text that said that the parties are allowed to circumvent each other. The Canonists based the doctrine of necessity on St. Ambrose's denunciation of greed. In developing the doctrine of changed circumstances, they were concerned about what a person should do if he promised to do act which turned out to be sinful. It was a problem put by St. Augustine,

62 Dig. 46.3.38.pr.

63 Baldus de Ubaldis, *Commentaria Corpus iuris civilis* to Dig. 12.4.8.

64 Hostiensis, *Summa aurea* (Venice 1574), iii. 17, par. 7.

65 Azo Portius, *Summa Codicis* (Lyon, 1557), to C. 2.20, no. 9; *Summa trecensis*, ed. H. Fittting (Berlin: J. Guttentag, 1894) (published under the title *Summa Codicis des Irnerius*) lib. 4, tit. 41; Vacarius, *Liber pauperum*, ed. F. Zulueta (London: Quaritch, 1927) 51 to Dig. 19.2.23.3.

and also, as we have seen, one raised by the cases of a person promised to keep the secret of a friend who then confided his intention to commit murder, or to obey a spiritual director who then instructed him to do evil. The extent to which a party was bound by the words of his promise may have been particularly important for those Canonists who agreed with Baldus that a formal promise made by *stipulatio* was also a contract of good faith.

Be that as it may, these doctrines were later explained by considerations of justice in the moral theology of Thomas Aquinas, and then in the synthesis of the Roman and Canon law and Thomistic moral theology achieved in the sixteenth and early seventeenth centuries by a group of theologian-jurists centered in Spain and known to historians as the late scholastics. Among the leaders were Francisco de Vitoria (1492–1546), Domingo de Soto (1494–1560), Luis de Molina (1535–1600), Leonard Lessius (1554–1623), and Francisco Suárez (1548–1617).

For Aquinas and the late scholastics, the doctrine of necessity did not compromise the protection of private property. They explained the doctrine by drawing on Aristotle's account of the purposes of private property. His teacher Plato had said that property should be held in common. Aristotle pointed out the disadvantages: under common ownership, people would quarrel and those who worked hard would receive no more than those who did not.[66] Aquinas and the late scholastics gave a similar explanation.[67] They concluded that the protection of private property should extend no further than the purposes for which it was instituted. One could take another's property when it was necessary to preserve one's own life. [68]

Followed by the late scholastics, Aquinas explained relief for *laesio enormis* as a consequence of Aristotle's teachings on commutative justice. Commutative justice required that neither party become richer or poorer at the other's expense.[69] Consequently, in contracts such as sale or lease, the parties must exchange resources of equal value. The law required a discrepancy of more than half because for pragmatic reasons, the law could not correct every evil.[70]

As we have seen, the Roman jurists had said that the parties to certain contracts are bound to the obligations required by "good faith." Canonists such as Baldus had said that all contracts are contracts of good faith. The late scholastics explained that these terms were consequences of the principle of equality in exchange. Aquinas had said that the seller must warrant his goods on account of

66 *Politics* II. v.

67 Aquinas, *Summa theologiae* II-II Q. 66, a. 2; Domenicus Soto, *De iustitia et iure libri decem* (Salamanca, 1553), lib. 4, q. 3, a. 1; Luis de Molina, *De iustitia et iure tractatus* (Venice, 1614), disp. 20; Leonard Lessius, *De iustitia et iure ceterisque virtutibus cardinalis* (Paris, 1628), lib. 2, cap. 5, dubs. 1–2.

68 *Summa theologiae* II-II, Q. 66 a.7; Lessius, *De iustitia et iure* lib. 2, cap. 12, dub. 12; Soto, *De iustitia et iure* lib. 5, q. 3, a. 4; Molina, *De iustitia et iure tractatus* disp. 20.

69 Aristotle, *Nicomachean Ethics* V.ii 1130^{b}–1131^{a}.

70 *Summa theologiae* II-II, Q. 77, a.1, ad 1.

that principle.[71] The late scholastics agreed.[72] Molina explained that he could waive the warranty but only if he preserved equality by lowering his price.[73]

Aquinas and the late scholastics explained the doctrine of changed circumstances by applying Aristotle's teachings on *epikeia* which concerned how laws should be applied. A law should not be followed when circumstances arose which the lawmaker did not consider and in which he would never have intended the law to be binding.[74] They said that the same exception applied to contracts, since they were a sort of law that the parties gave to themselves.[75]

Moral duties and personal rights

The late scholastics were also the first to speak generally of an injustice as a violation of a person's "rights" (*iura*). Aquinas had rarely used the term "right" (*ius*) in this sense. In discussing harms done to another he had not asked whether a "right" was violated but whether the conduct in question was allowed (*licet*). For example, in discussing property, Aquinas asked whether one person is allowed to possess a thing as his own.[76] In discussing murder, he asked whether one person is allowed to kill another.[77] He used the term "thing" (*res*) when he described commutative justice: in buying and selling, someone "voluntarily transfers his thing (*rem*) to another."[78] He also used the word "thing" when he described *restitutio*. "*Restitutio* appears to be nothing else than to reinstate someone in the possession or ownership of his own thing (*res*)."[79] He was using the language of Gratian, who had used that of St. Augustine. St. Augustine had said that "the sin is not forgiven unless restitution is made of the thing (*res*) that was taken away."[80] Gratian explained, "Penance is not done if another's thing (*res*) is not restored."[81]

When Aquinas and the Canonists spoke of a "thing," they meant not just a physical thing but honor, reputation and whatever else belonged to a person. When Vitoria discussed *restitutio* in his commentary on Aquinas, he proposed using the term "right." A right (*ius*) ... is nothing other than what one is allowed to do or what the law (*lex*) allows. ... We say, indeed, "I do not have the right of doing this," that is, "it is not allowed for me to do it," and again, "I am using

71 *See Summa theologiae* II-II Q. 77, aa. 2–3.

72 Soto, *De iustitia et iure* lib. 2., cap. 21, dub. 11; lib. 6, q. 3, a. 2; Molina, *De iustitia et iure* disp. 353; Lessius, *De iustitia et iure* lib. 2, cap. 21, dub. 11.

73 Molina, *De iustitia et iure* disp. 353.

74 Aristotle, *Nicomachean Ethics* V.x.

75 Aquinas, *Summa theologiae* II–II, q, 88, a. 10; q. 89, a. 9; Lessius, *De iustitia et iure* lib. 2, cap. 17, dub. 10; cap. 18, dub. 10.

76 *Summa theologiae* II–II, Q. 66, a. 2.

77 *Summa theologiae* II–II, Q. 64, aa. 2–7.

78 *Summa theologiae* II–II, Q. 61, a. 3.

79 *Summa theologiae* II–II, Q. 62 a. 1.

80 C. 14 q. 6 c. 1.

81 *D. G. ante* C. 14 q. 6 c. 1 (Poenitentia non agitur, si res aliena non restituatur.)

my right," that is, "it is allowed'."[82] Lessius defined right, in this sense, as a "legitimate power ... the violation of which constitutes an injury." [83] According to Molina, a right is a "faculty or power to something a man has ... or to use something by his own right."

> Nor do I see it possible to define this meaning of *ius* more appropriately than if we say, it is a faculty to do something, to obtain something, or to claim it or in another way to have it, such that, if it is contravened, without a legitimate ground (*sine legitima causa*), one suffers an injury (*iniuria*).[84]

In Latin, the word *ius* can mean a body of law or principles: for example, civil law (*ius civile*) or Canon law (*ius canonici*). Aquinas used the word in a similar sense when he defined *ius* as the object of the virtue of justice (*iustitia*). In Roman law, *ius* can also mean the right of a person to have something or do something. For example, one could have a variety of rights in the land of another: the right to walk across it (*ius ambulandi*),[85] to drive animals across it (*ius agenda*),[86] to have water flow across it (*ius aquaeductus*),[87] to burn limestone on it (*ius calcis coquendae*)[88] and to take sand from a sandpit (*ius harenae foedienae*).[89] A person with a usufruct had the right to use and take produce from the land (*ius utendi fruendi*).[90] A debt was a *ius debiti.*[91] A creditor had a *ius crediti.*[92] The Romans spoke of particular rights such as these. The late scholastics used the word as a general term for whatever a person was entitled to have or to do.

As Brian Tierney noted, some modern scholars interpreted the new terminology of the late scholastics as a shift from medieval to a modern conception of rights. Some Catholic authors have argued that they betrayed a medieval idea that one could not speak of a person's rights apart from the principles of justice they reflected. Some secular authors congratulated the late scholastics for founding a modern conception of individual rights.

Brian Tierney has shown that neither of these views is correct. Vitoria was not launching a new concept of law but using the terms "rights" to state the doctrine of *restitutio* more clearly. "Vitoria's problem was that he could not discuss

82 Francisco de Vitoria, *Commentarios a la Secunda Secundae de Santo Tomas*, ed. Vicente Beltrán de Heredia (Salamanca: Apartado 17, 1932), to II-II Q. 61, a. 1.

83 Lessius, *De iustitia et iure* lib. 1, cap. 2, dub. 1, no. 3.

84 Molina, *De iustitia et iure* II, disp. I, no. 2.

85 J. 2.3.pr.

86 Ibid.

87 Ibid.

88 J. 2.3.2.

89 Ibid.

90 D. 7.1.1.

91 D. 4.2.13.

92 Ibid.

restitution adequately without considering the concept of *ius* as a subjective right. The definition he had earlier accepted from Aquinas did not include any such concept."[93]

Nor did the innovation concern the assertion of rights against oppression. When Vitoria defended the inhabitants of the new world against pillage by their Spanish conquerors, he defended their rights without using that term. He said that "[b]ecause they were in peaceful possession of things both public and private, therefore in all respects ... they are to be recognized as owners, nor is their possession to be disturbed."[94] Like "Moslems or Jews or other infidels" "it is not permitted to seize from [them] the things that they possess on the ground that they are infidels, but it is theft and robbery no less than if they were Christians."[95] According to Molina, "if the king fell into tyranny or attempted to do that which in no way benefitted the republic, "it would be the same as if the throne fell vacant.

> [T]he entire right and power of the republic would devolve on the republic itself that it previously had to constitute [a government]... It could constitute a new king, who it wished, or laws that it wished to limit, extend or diminish his power, or to choose whatever other kind of regime it wished.[96]

He said all that without using the term "rights."

Nevertheless, there is a difference as to the meaning of individual rights to many modern philosophers and jurists and to the late scholastics. For Immanuel Kant, the right to property meant the right of an owner to do as he chooses with what belongs to his property and to exclude others from using it.[97] A promise is the expression of will of one party to a contract; a contract is the expression of will of both.[98] In the nineteenth century, both civil and common law jurists defined property and contract in the same way, although not, I have argued elsewhere, because of the influence of Kant.[99] Property was defined in terms of the will of the owner.[100] Contract was defined in terms of

93 Brian Tierney, *The Idea of Natural Rights Studies on Natural Rights, Natural Law, and Church Law 1150–1625* (Grand Rapids, MI: William B. Eerdman, 1997), 259.

94 Francesco de Vitoria, *De Indis*, in *Relecciones del Maestro Fray Francisco de Vitorira*, ed. Alonso Getinao (Madrid, 1933), no. 4.

95 Vitoria, *De Indis* no. 7.

96 Molina, *De iustitia et iure* V, disp. 3 no. 2.

97 *Die Metaphysik der Stitten Erster Theil. Metaphysische Angangsgründe der Rechtslehre* in *Kant's gesammelte Schriften*, ed. Königlich Preussischen Akademie der Wissenschaft (Berlin: Deutsche Akademie der Wissenschaften zu Berlin, 1914), 6: 203 at 245.

98 *Metaphysische Angangsgründe der Rechtslehre*, 272.

99 Gordley, *Philosophical Origins*.

100 *E.g.*, Christopher Columbus Langdell, "Classification of Rights and Wrongs" (pt. 1), *Harvard Law Review*, 13 (1900): 537, 537–38; Frederick Pollock, *A First Book of Jurisprudence for Students of the Common Law* (London: Macmillan & Co., 1896), 160; Charles Aubry and Charles Rau, *Cours de droit civil français*, 4th ed. (Paris: Marchal et Billard, 1869–71), 2: § 190; François Laurent, *Principes de droit civil français* (Paris: Auguste Durand et Pedone

the will of the parties.[101] There were no limits, in principle, on the right of the owner to use his property as he chose or the right of the parties to contract on whatever terms they agreed. Legal scholars remember the nineteenth century as an age of "will theories."

Jurists in the twentieth and early twenty-first centuries have been trying to escape from this unqualified idea of private rights.[102] Among its other difficulties, it fails to explain the doctrines we have just considered, which have passed into modern law.

Some modern legal systems recognized the doctrine of necessity, which is hard to square with an unqualified right of an owner to exclude others from using his property.[103]

Many modern legal systems have adopted the doctrine of changed circumstances.[104] The nineteenth-century jurists had trouble explaining the doctrine. If the parties are bound by what they willed, what they might have done under circumstances they never contemplated should not matter.

Many modern legal systems give relief when the terms of exchange are unfair.[105] If contracts are the will of the parties, it is hard to understand why sometimes they are not bound by terms which they did will. Conversely, it is hard to understand why often they are bound by terms that they did not contemplate, yet in all modern legal systems, they are bound by "implied terms" which they may not have considered. The Roman jurists read such terms into certain contracts on account of good faith. Baldus said that in Canon law, all contracts were contracts of good faith. The late scholastics tried to show that these terms followed from the principle of equality in exchange. The nineteenth-century jurists had difficulty explaining them at all.

The "will theories" are now discredited but no generally accepted theory of property or contract has taken their place.[106] We cannot live with the modern conception of rights accepted by Kant and by nineteenth-century jurists, but we are at a loss trying to do without it.

Lauriel, 1869–78), 6: § 101; Charles Demolombe, *Cours de Code Napoléon* (Paris: Auguste Durand, 1854–82), 9: § 543; Bernhard Windscheid, *Lehrbuch des Pandektenrechts*, 7th ed. (Düsseldorf: J. Buddeus, 1891), 1: § 167.

101 *E.g.*, Christopher C. Langdell, *A Summary of the Law of Contracts*, 2nd ed. (Boston, MA: Little, Brown, 1880), 1–21; Stephen Leake, *Elements of the Law of Contracts* (London: Stevens & Sons, 1867), 7–8; Frederick Pollock, *Principles of Contract* (London: Stevens & Sons, 1885), 1–9; Demolombe, *Cours de Code Napoléon,* 24: § 12; Léon Larombière, *Théorie et pratique des obligations* (Paris: Auguste Durand, 1857), 1: § 41; Laurent, *Principes de droit civil français*, 15: §§ 424–27; Georg Friedrich Puchta, *Pandekten* (Leipzig: Johann Ambrosius Barth, 1844), §§ 49, 54; Friedrich Carl von Savigny, *System des heutigen Römischen Rechts* (Berlin: Veit und Comp., 1840–8), 3: § 134; Windscheid, *Lehrbuch*, 1: § 69. See generally Gordley, *Philosophical Origins*, 161–213.

102 Gordley, *Jurists*, 222–75.

103 James Gordley, *Foundations of Private Law* (Oxford: Oxford University Press, 2009), 130–40.

104 Gordley, *Foundations*, 336–51.

105 Ibid., 361–76.

106 Gordley, *Jurists*, 222–81.

The late scholastics may have been the first to use the term "rights" to refer to everything to which a person is entitled, but they did not accept this modern conception of rights. For them, the right to exclusive use of one's property and to hold another person to his promise was qualified, and in ways that were described by Aquinas and the medieval Canonists, although they did not use the term "rights." For all of them, the reason was not that justice must sometimes give way to claims based on charity or on the social welfare. The reason was that, as a matter of justice, respect for rights was conditioned on the reasons that both limit their exercise and explain why they should be respected. Perhaps the Canonists, Aquinas, and the late scholastics found that idea easier to grasp because they were Christian teachers. They were speaking, however, about what is just for everyone, not just for Christians.

3 Biblical understandings of private law

Brent A. Strawn

The roots of much contemporary law can be traced back to the Bible due to its importance in (Western) thought, generally, and in jurisprudence, more specifically, given certain developments in late antiquity and the Middle Ages.[1] To label this relationship between contemporary law and the Bible one of "trace," rather than something more bold, is necessary because, on the one hand, the connection between the Bible (ancient as it is) and (much) later law is rarely simple, and, on the other hand, because the Bible's legal material is only one instance of a much larger ancient legal world[2]—a good bit of which antecedes biblical law and at least some of which was influential on if not generative of the law now located in Scripture.[3] Apart from Greco-Roman sources, which loom large for the New Testament and Early Christianity, ancient Near Eastern legal material is of even more fundamental significance for the Old Testament. To be sure, cultural influence from ancient Mesopotamia and Egypt may be found in many parts of the Hebrew Bible, but the legal materials are often the clearest instances of the Bible's "belonging" to its wider cultural context.[4] In any event, the shared heritage between the Bible and its ancient Near Eastern congeners indicates that the latter, too, are significant traces with regard to the Bible's influence on later law—even if these earlier lights are only known dimly, "through a glass darkly," as it were.

Although the Bible's legal legacy is vast, this chapter attends to "private law," which is typically understood as pertaining to those matters wherein legal

1 See, e.g., *OEBL*, *passim*, esp. the editorial preface (1:xiii–xviii).

2 See *HANEL*, *passim*, esp. the introduction by Raymond Westbrook, "The Character of Ancient Near Eastern Law" (1:1–90); see also idem, *Law from the Tigris to the Tiber: The Writings of Raymond Westbrook*, eds. Bruce Wells and F. Rachel Magdalene, 2 vols. (Winona Lake, IN: Eisenbrauns, 2009).

3 For example, David P. Wright, *Inventing God's Law: How the Covenant Code of the Bible Used and Revised the Laws of Hammurabi* (Oxford: Oxford University Press, 2009) has argued that Exod 20:23–23:19 is directly dependent on the Laws of Hammurabi.

4 See Kenton L. Sparks, *Ancient Texts for the Study of the Hebrew Bible: A Guide to the Background Literature* (Peabody, MA: Hendrickson, 2005), esp. 417–34; and John H. Walton, *Ancient Near Eastern Thought and the Old Testament: Introducing the Conceptual World of the Hebrew Bible*, 2nd ed. (Grand Rapids, MI: Baker Academic, 2018), esp. 269–91.

resolution is largely left to private parties. Private law may thus be contrasted with "public law," which requires the involvement of official entities like government agents.[5] Private law includes, therefore, inter alia: torts, contract, and property law. A sampling of how each of these three areas are treated in biblical law comprises the bulk of the present chapter with a particular focus on the Old Testament since it is the primary repository of legal material in Holy Scripture.[6] Treatment of Scripture is essential, in turn, to any investigation of a Christian understanding of any particular subject given the centrality of the Bible to Christian faith and practice. Since the topic at hand is large, but space limited, what follows is necessarily introductory and selective. In what follows, therefore, I have selected three examples from different corpora of biblical law as touchstones to highlight some of the main issues and, hopefully, to serve as entrées into the larger discussion.[7]

Three preliminaries: on "understandings," "privacy," and "(practiced) law"

Before proceeding, three important preliminary matters must be considered. *First*, what one finds in the Bible on matters like the one at hand are various understandings (plural), not one singular understanding. This is an obvious point, especially to those familiar with the Bible and biblical scholarship, but should be repeated, in any event, especially for those less familiar with either (or both). So, for example—and painting with a broad brush—scholars have identified no less than four major blocks of legal material in the first five books of the Bible known as the Torah or Pentateuch. These are, in chronological order, the Book of the Covenant or Covenant Code (Exod 20:22–23:19), the Deuteronomic Law (Deuteronomy 12–26), the Priestly Law (Leviticus 1–15 + Numbers 1–9), and the Holiness Code (Leviticus 17–26).[8] This chronological ordering would be debated by some scholars, as would the precise delineation of the texts (verses)

5 Modern definitions for these various categories can be conveniently found in *BLD*, 1390 ("private law") and 1425 ("public law"); cf. also 1016 ("law: special law").

6 But note the brief coda on the New Testament below; see also other chapters in this collection.

7 For a more extensive presentation of the full range and content of biblical law, see Tikva Frymer-Kensky, "Israel," in *HANEL*, 2:975–1046.

8 See Eckart Otto, "Book of the Covenant," in *OEBL*, 1:69–77; Daniel I. Block, "Deuteronomic Law," in *OEBL*, 1:182–95; Jeffrey Stackert, "Holiness Code and Writings," in *OEBL*, 1:389–96; and William K. Gilders, "Priestly Law," in *OEBL*, 1:166–75; as well as standard introductory treatments such as that found in Dale Patrick, *Old Testament Law* (Atlanta, GA: John Knox, 1985); and, more recently, Frymer-Kensky, "Israel," 2:975–81; and William S. Morrow, *An Introduction to Biblical Law* (Grand Rapids, MI: Eerdmans, 2017). The listing above does not yet include legal sub-collections such as the Ten Commandments or different sources of biblical law like narratives that involve law or legal customs, various mentions of law or legal topics outside the Pentateuch, or two important ostraca recovered from Israel that address legal matters (see Frymer-Kensky, "Israel," 2:975–76, 979–81; Edward L. Greenstein, "Decalogue," in *OEBL*, 1:164–72; Christopher A. Rollston, "Epigraphic Texts," in *OEBL*, 1:266–71).

that belong to these "codes"—even the language of "legal code" (as opposed to "collection") is not uncontroversial.[9] The main point to be made, regardless, is that these legal collections do not always agree, and in some instances are plainly, explicitly, even extensively at odds.[10] In fact, one of the more recent developments in the study of biblical law is to investigate how one legal collection seems to have made use of another, with some scholars going so far as to suggest that those responsible for later collections sought to displace and entirely replace earlier ones.[11] The plural form when it comes to "biblical *understandings* of private law" is thus quite apropos and must constantly be kept in mind. For a number of reasons, biblical law—and this holds true for much ancient Near Eastern legal material as well—is not as regular (nor as regulated!) as modern law. Of course modern law, too, has its fair share of discrepancies that are constantly subjected to review and revision.

The *second* important preliminary is to wonder, if not challenge, the category of private law when it comes to the Bible. While it has long been clear to scholars that the laws in the Pentateuch date from different periods—in part because they belong to distinct collections—the present form of the Pentateuch places all of these laws, chronology and content aside, in the time between Israel's departure from Egypt and its arrival in Canaan.[12] The oddness of this is quite palpable: laws pertaining to agriculture, for example (see, e.g., Lev 19:9–10, 19), just don't make sense in the time of Israel's wandering in the desert; such laws reflect later concerns and practices—as would a host of other laws pertaining to, say, officials (e.g., Deut 17:8–13), to architecture (Deut 22:8), and so forth. Not only does the Pentateuch place all of its legislation in the period of Sinai and the wilderness journey thereafter, it also ascribes that regulation almost entirely to God, even if God's law is extensively mediated via Moses.

9 For the niceties, see the works cited in the previous note. For a challenge to the chronological priority of the Book of the Covenant, see John Van Seters, *A Law Book for the Diaspora: Revision in the Study of the Covenant Code* (Oxford: Oxford University Press, 2003).

10 See, famously, the differences between Lev 17:1–8 and Deut 12:13–16, 20–22 on the question of profane slaughter; or Exod 21:2–6, Deut 15:12–18, and Lev 25:39–43 on slave manumission.

11 See, e.g., Bernard M. Levinson, *Deuteronomy and the Hermeneutics of Legal Innovation* (Oxford: Oxford University Press, 1997); idem, *Legal Revision and Religious Renewal in Ancient Israel* (Cambridge: Cambridge University Press, 2008); Jeffrey Stackert, *Rewriting the Torah: Literary Revision in Deuteronomy and the Holiness Legislation* (Tübingen: Mohr Siebeck, 2007). Of course, not all scholars agree. See, recently, Joshua A. Berman, *Inconsistency in the Torah: Ancient Literary Convention and the Limits of Source Criticism* (Oxford: Oxford University Press, 2017). Cf. also Christine Hayes, *What's Divine about Divine Law? Early Perspectives* (Princeton, NJ: Princeton University Press, 2015).

12 David P. Wright has called this the "pseudoarchaeographic context" of the Pentateuchal law collections, deeming it a "narrative fiction" that would have affected "to some degree whatever customs they may have picked up from practice or from sources used to fit" it (review of *Everyday Law in Biblical Israel: An Introduction* by Raymond Westbrook and Bruce Wells, *JHS*, 11 [2011]: 1–4 [2], http://dx.doi.org/10.5508/jhs.2011.v11.r35).

The effects of the geographical location and divine placement of biblical law are several,[13] but one primary one is to problematize any notion of law, or bit of law, in the Bible as entirely devoid of larger, more public or official agents—that is, as private. In the Bible, that is, the location and placement of Pentateuchal law means that *the Deity is always somehow involved in biblical law*. Any "privacy" that is present or at work in biblical law, therefore, will likely be of a different sort than what is often understood by such terminology today.[14]

The *third* preliminary matter concerns the nature of the law we have in the Bible and questions surrounding its implementation, functionality, and practice. Put simply, was this law ever used in actual jurisprudence: was it a functioning law "code" or not? This question pertains equally to ancient Near Eastern legal material.[15] In general, the scholarly judgment on the question of real-life implementation has been negative, or at least agnostic. Speaking specifically of ancient Israel, Raymond Westbrook and Bruce Wells state:

> We cannot be sure of the extent to which the laws set out in the Bible were actually put into practice during the Iron Age—the time of ancient Israel and Judah. As we shall see, some of them may have been purely utopian; some were rules of practice transfigured by ideology; and others, although pragmatic in content, were most probably the product of academic circles, that is, of groups of scribes engaged in a theoretical endeavor. Nonetheless, the laws in the Bible represent in many instances what people at the time considered the law to be, and even if not always put into practice, they reveal the underlying processes of juridical thought that were prevalent in the society.[16]

13 See, e.g., Terence E. Fretheim, "Law in the Service of Life: A Dynamic Understanding of Law in Deuteronomy," in *A God So Near: Essays on Old Testament Theology in Honor of Patrick D. Miller*, eds. Brent A. Strawn and Nancy R. Bowen (Winona Lake, IN: Eisenbrauns, 2003), 183–200.

14 And for more than one reason, one of which would be different understandings of the self and personal status back then vs. now. See, e.g., Westbrook, "Character," 1:35–44; Frymer-Kensky, "Israel," 2:999–1007; and more generally Susan Niditch, *The Responsive Self: Personal Religion in Biblical Literature of the Neo-Babylonian and Persian Periods* (New Haven, CT: Yale University Press, 2015) as well as Charles Taylor, *Sources of the Self: The Making of the Modern Identity* (Cambridge, MA: Harvard University Press, 1989).

15 For a convenient collection of the pertinent text, see Martha T. Roth, *Law Collections from Mesopotamia and Asia Minor*, 2nd ed. (Atlanta, GA: Scholars Press, 1997). Secondary treatments may be found in *OEBL* and *HANEL*.

16 Raymond Westbrook and Bruce Wells, *Everyday Law in Biblical Israel: An Introduction* (Louisville, KY: Westminster John Knox, 2009), 3. Cf. Bruce Wells, "Law and Practice," in *A Companion to the Ancient Near East*, ed. Daniel C. Snell (Oxford: Blackwell, 2005), 199–211 (202), on ancient Near Eastern law more generally: "Ultimately it seems that the law collections represent the practiced law of their societies accurately to some degree and inaccurately to some degree. But in either case, we do not know to what degree." Note also Westbrook, "Character," 1:71:

> Since the intellectual method of the codes was to set out principles by the use of often extreme examples, and they were based, if at some remove, on the activity of the courts, it is probable that they inform us what the courts could do and in perfect justice should

The question of whether biblical and ancient Near Eastern law was actually practiced, therefore, must remain somewhat open ended, especially as the earlier points about the pluriform nature of biblical law and its apparently intentional editorial placement bear directly on the question of "everyday law" and legal practice in the biblical world.

Torts: "If other damage ensues..." (Exod 21:23)

With these important matters out of the way, the way is clear to turn to tort law, but not without encountering yet one more important issue that must be addressed. Writing about law in ancient Egypt, Russ VerSteeg states:

> There is no compelling evidence to indicate that the ancient Egyptians formally recognized or even abstractly appreciated a general theory of legal recovery remotely similar to modern tort law. Rather, for them it appears that criminal laws fulfilled some of the functions that modern tort law serves. As is true in many ancient legal systems, the Egyptians did not distinguish between tort and crime in the same fashion that modern societies do.[17]

The biblical "system," if it may be monolithized for the moment, is one such "ancient legal system" similar to Egyptian law at this point. The same is also true of cuneiform law collections according to Bruce Wells, who writes that in contrast "to most modern systems, the legal systems of the Ancient Near East do not appear to have had a distinction between civil law and criminal law."[18] Hence, as per VerSteeg: "today it is, as a practical matter, virtually impossible for us to distinguish ancient Egyptian tort law from criminal law in any meaningful way."[19] As per Wells, the same judgment holds for Mesopotamian sources.

The situation is further complicated, in the case of the Bible, due to our limited knowledge regarding the nature and extent of juridical officials and procedures.[20] We know these existed in ancient Israel, at least to some degree, but we don't know nearly as much about them as we would like, especially not enough to allow for an altogether clear distinction between private and public

---

do, whereas the courts themselves, in dealing with less tidy situations, were more flexible in their judgments. Accordingly, we can reconstruct a picture of how the ancients thought about crime [among other legal topics]—what they regarded as wrongs and what means they devised for redressing them—even if we cannot always be sure how they applied their ideas on a day-to-day basis.

17 Russ VerSteeg, *Law in Ancient Egypt* (Durham, NC: Carolina Academic Press, 2002), 151.

18 Wells, "Law and Practice," 209.

19 VerSteeg, *Law in Ancient Egypt*, 152.

20 For a collation of the available evidence, see Frymer-Kensky, "Israel," 2:981–99. See also Michael LeFebvre, "Legal Institutions," in *OEBL*, 1:536–43; Trevor W. Thompson, "Punishment and Restitution," in *OEBL*, 2:183–93; and Shalom E. Holtz, "Trial Procedure," in *OEBL*, 2:414–20.

law. Consider, for example, the fact that laws concerning homicide in the Bible vary on whether or not the crime is taken up formally with official entities. Exodus 21:12–14 differentiates between intentional and unintentional homicide and mentions a place of asylum but is otherwise brief and tight-lipped about other legal apparatus. Deuteronomy 19:12 mentions "city elders" (*ziqnê ʿîr*) who expel an intentional homicide from an asylum city to which the killer has fled because in this case asylum is not permitted. Numbers 35:24 speaks not of elders but of a "congregation" (*ʿēdāh*) that "judges" (*špṭ*) between the killer and the one seeking vengeance on the basis of "these ordinances" (*hammišpāṭîm hāʾēlleh*; cf. 35:22–23). But even if the congregation somehow finds in favor of the killer—namely, that it was a case of unintentional manslaughter—the murderer is still confined to an asylum city for an unspecified period of time. Otherwise, the avenger of blood can retaliate with no negative repercussions (35:25–28). Whatever the case, the blood avenger in question is almost certainly a close family member (Lev 25:48–49), not a formal agent of the state.[21]

Given this overlap, "[o]ne theoretical means of distinguishing tort from crime is to categorize laws and legal situations based on types of punishments (*i.e.*, the legal consequences)."[22] Generally speaking, therefore, compensation made to a victim may be associated with torts while bodily punishment (especially as enacted or required by legal authorities) would be reserved for crime.[23] This distinction would mean that the biblical laws of homicide discussed above are crime, not tort, despite the fact that, at least in some cases, judgment for a murder would have been something that private parties saw to themselves.

Raymond Westbrook thinks this type of "modern classification is unhelpful," however, because ancient law "had a different theoretical basis, albeit never expressed in the native sources."[24] So, while a modern bipartite distinction based on punishments may be convenient, Westbrook believes that, "[f]rom the pattern of treatment and remedies," there are actually three major categories of wrongdoing that can be identified: "wrongs against a hierarchical superior; serious wrongs against the person, honor, or property of an individual; and minor harm to an individual's person or property."[25] In this schema, homicide belongs to the second category. Yet another emic way of proceeding would be to draw a

21 See Assnat Bartor, "Bloodguilt and Blood Feud," in *OEBL*, 1:64–68, esp. 66–67.

22 VerSteeg, *Law in Ancient Egypt*, 152.

23 Ibid., 152; cf. Westbrook, "Character," 1:75.

24 Westbrook, "Character," 1:75. Cf. Russ VerSteeg, *Early Mesopotamian Law* (Durham, NC: Carolina Academic Press, 2000), 129–31, who also notes how it is difficult to distinguish, with precision, certain modern categories of torts (whether, for example, intentional, negligent, or strictly liable) in the ancient sources.

25 Westbrook, "Character," 1:75. Note that, in some cases, the correspondence between crime and punishment was more poetic than jurisprudential. See, e.g., Patrick D. Miller, *Sin and Judgment in the Prophets: A Stylistic and Theological Analysis* (Chico, CA: Scholars Press, 1982). Cf. Martha C. Nussbaum, *Poetic Justice: The Literary Imagination and Public Life* (Boston, MA: Beacon, 1995).

distinction, as Douglas Knight has for ancient Israel, between law in the villages, law in the cities and states, and law in the cult.[26]

There is obviously some overlap between the classificatory systems offered by VerSteeg, Westbrook, and Knight—not least given the fact that so much of ancient Israelite life was rural, which would mean that much of its law was, by our definitions at least, private, if only because there would not have been any state-sanctioned authorities around to enforce it. In any event, with these important considerations duly entered, a concrete example from the Book of the Covenant concerning injury may serve as a useful entrée into biblical tort law:

> When men fight, and one of them pushes a pregnant woman and a miscarriage results (*wĕyaṣĕʾû yĕlādêhā*), but no other damage (*ʾāsōn*) ensues, the one responsible shall be fined according as the woman's husband may exact from him, the payment to be based on reckoning (*wĕnātan biplīlîm*).[27] But if other damage (*ʾāsōn*) ensues, the penalty shall be life for life, eye for eye, tooth for tooth, hand for hand, foot for foot, burn for burn, wound for wound, bruise for bruise. (Exod 21:22–25; NJPSV)

This short unit raises a host of questions. It is clear enough that the situation is one of unintentional injury caused by brawling, which unchecked ends up causing harm to a pregnant woman (*aberratio ictus*). It is not clear in the Hebrew text—despite the English translation above—if the woman miscarries or simply gives birth prematurely. In any event, if there is no further "damage" or "harm" (*ʾāsōn*), the one responsible for the initial blow will pay the fine the

26 See Douglas A. Knight, *Law, Power, and Justice in Ancient Israel* (Louisville, KY: Westminster John Knox, 2011); and, earlier, idem, "Village Law and the Book of the Covenant," in *"A Wise and Discerning Mind": Essays in Honor of Burke O. Long*, eds. Saul M. Olyan and Robert C. Culley (Providence, RI: Brown Judaic Studies, 2000), 163–79. Cf. similarly Morrow, *An Introduction to Biblical Law*.

27 This meaning of this final clause is uncertain. Cf. the NRSV translation: "paying as much as the judges determine." The Hebrew word *pĕlīlîm* is not the usual term for judges, however, though perhaps it could be taken as "assessors" or the like. But the fact that the fee is apparently set arbitrarily by the husband seems to suggest that *pĕlīlîm* is an abstract noun of some sort, which is how the Septuagint understood the phrase "with a valuation" (*meta axiōmatos*; cf. NETS: "with judicial assessment"), and is also how the NJPSV translates it (see above); cf. also Frymer-Kensky, "Israel," 1:1033: "and will render account." Contrast, however, the considered opinion of Bernard S. Jackson, *Wisdom-Laws: A Study of the Misphatim of Exodus 21:1–22:16* (Oxford: Oxford University Press, 2006), 209–39, esp. 225–27, who argues that third-party adjudicators (here designated *pĕlīlîm*) are certainly involved. For additional discussion, see E. A. Speiser, "The Stem PLL in Hebrew," *JBL*, 82 (1963): 301–306; Samuel E. Loewenstamm, *Comparative Studies in Biblical and Ancient Oriental Literatures* (Kevelaer: Butzon and Bercker and Neukirchen-Vluyn: Neukirchener, 1980), 517–25; and Raymond Westbrook, "*Lex Talionis* and Exodus 21.22–25," *RB*, 93 (1986): 52–69. My own sense is that the third-party option, while possible, is less likely given the formulation, which is exceedingly spare, and that it may require too much of the Hebrew preposition *bĕ-* ("in, with").

woman's husband demands. But if other damage does come about, the law becomes talionic—and (in)famously so: eye for eye, tooth for tooth, and so forth.

But what is this "damage"? It is not clear if the harm in question refers to the baby or to the mother. As in the translation presented above, many interpreters think the brawlers caused a miscarriage; otherwise, one wonders why "the early birth of a perfect baby would be considered a punishable injury."[28] In this light, the "harm" in question must refer to the woman and refer to further injuries *beyond* the loss of her child, perhaps even *because* of that loss.[29] But another option is that the damage in question refers to the baby, which somehow survived its premature birth.

While these matters cannot be decided here, this example from Exodus 21 suffices to show how an act, depending on its result(s), could be considered a tort, remediated by compensation, or a crime, punishable by corporeal means up to and including death. The wrong is, therefore—at least potentially—at once *both* civil *and* criminal, public *and* private. It is also clear that the wrong that has been done in this instance was not intentional, at least in the strongest sense of that term: with criminal or felonious intent. Even so, the brawlers had general intent to fight even if they didn't foresee or desire all of the possible consequences of their brawl. They were reckless, that is: consciously disregarding a high probability of loss since a reasonable person would worry that damage might come from violent physical altercation near a pregnant woman.[30] Some scholars have argued that the case is less severe, merely one of negligence.[31] Depending on how all of this is determined, there may even be an element of strict liability involved since a wrong was committed, with or without *mens rea*, and must now be rectified.

To be sure, the case of the injured pregnant woman in Exod 21:22–25 is somewhat odd if not extreme; at the very least it is complicated, in part due to its peculiar and not altogether transparent formulation which has led scholars to posit a wide range of interpretations. There are other passages from the Book of the Covenant, or from the other legal corpora in the Old Testament, that might be used to discuss biblical tort law more straightforwardly. Even so, this passage is instructive in highlighting the overlap between crime and tort in biblical law in a case of what appears to be mostly a matter of private law. It is, after all, the husband of the injured woman who sets the fee in the case of no further harm. Even if that fee is ultimately assessed by some third party (which remains unclear), the latter do not play a major role—at least not explicitly. And

28 Frymer-Kensky, "Israel," 1:1033.

29 See additional options in ibid., 1:1033; Jackson, *Wisdom-Laws*, 214–20.

30 Cf. *BLD*, 930, on "constructive intent." Transferred intent is another possible category: the brawlers intended one wrongful act which can now be shifted to apply to the wrongful act that they ended up actually doing (ibid., 931). For intention and negligence in biblical law, see Brent A. Strawn, "Intention," in *OEBL*, 1:433–46.

31 See Jackson, *Wisdom-Laws*, 234–35 and n. 135–140 for examples of scholars who have argued for intentional, accidental/negligent, and indirect action in Exod 21:22–25.

if further damage does ensue, no adjudicatory body is mentioned at all. Instead the text addresses the judgment to "you" (singular): "you shall give (*wĕnātattāh*) life for life..." (NRSV). The particular verbal form used here is not formally an imperative but may function, syntactically, as a command. Perhaps the singular subject of the verb is complex in some way, representative of the corporate body. Regardless, the general sense of this case puts it more on the private side of the public-private law spectrum. And yet, if one goes back to the beginning of the Book of the Covenant, one finds that all of what is contained herein is prefaced with "[t]he LORD said to Moses" (Exod 20:22), which is followed, with God still speaking, by "[t]hese are the ordinances that you [Moses] shall set before them" (21:1). If, all things considered, Exod 21:22–25 is an example of private law, it is nevertheless a law mandated by the highest and most official of authorities: *God*—who evidently cares even about inadvertent harm done to a woman and her child during a fisticuffs.

Three additional comments are in order:

1 This peculiar law in Exod 21:22–25 shows that private law in the Bible, no less than other types, especially modern ones, is *flexible and dynamic.* "If no further harm follows, then *x*, but if further damages ensue, then *y*." Among other things, such dynamism allows the law to be appropriately responsive: in terms of punishment scenarios, for example, which are flexed according to the extent of the wrong done and the damage incurred.

2 Exodus 21:22–25 demonstrates that biblical private law is attentive to highly atypical situations, *especially at the point of the most vulnerable.*[32] The Book of the Covenant has, after all, a more general law pertaining to injury to combatants during a fight earlier in the same chapter (Exod 21:18–19). What the case of the injured pregnant woman adds, therefore, is *compassionate range*: even in the most unusual of circumstances, the law must account for—and protect!—those who are most at risk, even from accidental harm. Still further, the presence of this sort of concern in legal form indicates that those under the law, too, should behave similarly and generally.[33]

3 In this way, biblical law anticipates and encapsulates claims that David Partlett has made about tort law more generally: "while the law of torts is not necessarily coextensive with Christian ethics, its core values are focused on human dignity and regard for the welfare of others"; and, further, "tort law deeply influences social norms by infusing those norms with ideas of right

32 Cf. Michael Welker, "The Power of Mercy in Biblical Law," *JLR*, 29 (2014): 225–35.

33 See Westbrook, "Character," 1:71 (cited in n. 16 above) for his theory of extreme instances serving as useful examples for less-extreme situations. Cf. also Elaine Scarry, *On Beauty and Being Just* (Princeton, NJ: Princeton University Press, 1999), who argues that there is an intrinsic relationship between beautiful things and justice because beauty calls forth care. Many modern readers might find *lex talionis* in Exod 21:23–25 unlovely, but the carefully crafted legal attention to pregnant mothers and their in utero children on display in this passage certainly summons correlate carefulness.

action even where no legal sanction prevails."[34] Partlett argues that "biblical law and tort law share a root"—namely:

> *community*. In many ways, this common root is the strength of both types of law. In the case of tort law, legal rulings grow organically from the affairs of the community and not from abstractions of generalized codes with theoretical glosses. Judges must reflect the norms of the community and the urgent needs of the citizens in rendering justice.[35]

Seen in this light, much of biblical law, insofar as it is private and not criminal, could be considered tort law, in which case there are not two types of law—tort and criminal—but just one, with the earlier considerations discussed above dutifully recalled. Even more to the point with regard to the Book of the Covenant, it is worth noting that Bernard S. Jackson, in his learned analysis of Exod 21:1–22:16, has argued that most of the ordinances found here are what he calls "wisdom-laws": meaning "that they manifest wisdom values, namely (a) the desireability of the *avoidance* of judicial settlement of disputes, in favour of 'self-executing rules' and (b) the law as 'wisdom' (teaching)."[36] Jackson's first point suggests a biblical preference for private law (at least in this specific legal corpus), with his second point suggesting that law both emerges from traditional community-based norms (so, similarly, Partlett) and that it functions as a repository for successful living.[37] It is small wonder, then, to find that the Hebrew word *tôrāh* can also be used of prophetic words "and even includes the words of instruction from a father or mother to their child" (see, e.g., Prov 1:8; 3:1; 4:2; 6:20, 23; 7:2).[38]

The calculus of the preceding, especially Partlett's remarks in conjunction with Jackson's, puts us not far from Lord Atkin's remarks on tort law, especially after the important *Donoghue v. Stevenson* case of 1932 (A.C. 562)—namely, that "I doubt whether the whole law of tort could not be comprised in the golden maxim to do unto your neighbor as you would that he should do unto you."[39] If Jackson is right about at least some of the legislation in the Book of the Covenant, the compassion that is at work in the Good Samaritan story is equally present—even legislated—long before Luke 10:25–37. Of course, what the lawyer (*nb*!) in Luke learns is not an answer to the question "And who is my neighbor?" (10:29) but rather an answer to the question "Which of these three, do you think, was a neighbor to the man who fell into the hands of the robbers?"

34 David Partlett, "Torts," in *OEBL*, 2:407–414 (408).

35 Ibid., 2:409 (emphasis added).

36 Jackson, *Wisdom-Laws*, vii (his emphasis).

37 See ibid., *passim*, esp. 23–39, 40–74. For wisdom in ancient Israel more generally, see William P. Brown, *Wisdom's Wonder: Character, Creation, and Crisis in the Bible's Wisdom Literature* (Grand Rapids, MI: Eerdmans, 2014).

38 Pete Enns, "Law of God," *NIDOTTE*, 4:893–900 (893), esp. 895–96.

39 See Partlett's discussion in "Torts," 2:410–11.

(10:36; NRSV). The "wisdom" of Exod 21:22–25 would be comparable: the unusual case of a pregnant woman injured inadvertently in a brawl should give the community great pause whenever its members are tempted to physical violence even as this case suggests that the community go to great lengths to ensure the greatest of care be taken even in far less extreme—or less litigated—scenarios.[40] "An analogous principle," that is, "holds good in every case of *aberration ictus*."[41] But not only there. One can see this compassionate range at work in all sorts of nooks and crannies of the law—for example, the duty to return a wandering animal to its owner, even if the owner is your enemy (Exod 23:4); or the requirement to help an overloaded beast of burden, even if you are inclined not to help (Exod 23:5)![42]

Contract: "You may not charge interest..." (Deut 23:19)

Contractual elements are found at many points in the Bible, but perhaps above all in the notion of "covenant" (*bĕrît*), which is a notion largely at home in international relations where the idea signified agreements made between equal (parity) and unequal (suzerain-vassal) parties. In the Old Testament this notion has been theologized and applied to the relationship between God and the people of Israel. Covenantal agreements obligated constituent parties to the agreement in various ways: to not rebel against an overlord, for example, or to pay appropriate tribute, in the case of ancient Near Eastern treaties;[43] or, in the case of the Bible, for Israel to be God's people and for God to be Israel's God (Exod 6:7; Lev 26:12; Deut 26:17; 29:13; cf. Gen 17:1–14).[44] Though the dating of covenantal ideas in ancient Israel is heavily debated, it can be seen, conceptually at least, as the facilitating environment of all biblical law. This is one effect, after all, of placing the entirety of the Pentateuch's legislation in the mouth of God and locating it during the covenant-making at Mt. Sinai and in the wilderness journey thereafter up to and including the covenant-document par excellence, Deuteronomy.[45] The fifth and final book of the Torah is perhaps the clearest instance of

40 Cf. Partlett, "Torts," 2:413: "what the best common law courts do is to establish a conversation about the application of proper conduct and values that should pervade human relationships beyond liability rules." See Westbrook's various works for his opinion that the biblical laws are exemplary and not comprehensive: they are representative and do not purport to account for every possible scenario.

41 Loewenstamm, *Comparative Studies*, 522.

42 In both instances the Hebrew verbal construction is emphatic. See also the parallel law in Deut 22:1–4, which extends it to a neighbor's garment or anything else that a neighbor loses: "You may not withhold your help" (v. 3b; NRSV).

43 See Simo Parpola and Kazuko Watanabe, *Neo-Assyrian Treaties and Loyalty Oaths*, repr. ed. (Winona Lake, IN: Eisenbrauns, 2014); and Kenneth A. Lawrence and Paul J. N. Lawrence, *Treaty, Law and Covenant in the Ancient Near East*, 3 vols. (Wiesbaden: Harrassowitz, 2012).

44 For a classic treatment, see Rolf Rendtorff, *The Covenant Formula: An Exegetical and Theological Investigation*, trans. Margaret Kohl (Edinburgh: T & T Clark, 1998).

45 See the first section above. For more on covenant, see Pauline A. Viviano, "Covenant," in *OEBL*, 1:130–38.

how the covenant requires faithful enactment of God's law, including what Deuteronomy calls the "statutes and ordinances" (*ḥuqqîm umišpāṭîm*). Within the structure of Deuteronomy, these statues and ordinances (12:1–26:19) seem to function as regulations and case laws that are keyed to the Ten Commandments (Deut 5:6–21; cf. Exod 20:1–17).[46] The matters of loan, deposit, and pledge can serve as examples of contract law.

Deuteronomy 23:19, which is found in the section of case law relating to the Seventh Commandment against stealing, states:

> You shall not charge interest on loans to another Israelite, interest on money, interest on provisions, interest on anything that is lent. (NRSV)

The word for interest here is often used of the "bite" of a snake. The imagery is vivid, therefore, and quite apropos. In any event, like Exod 22:25 before it, Deut 23:19 forbids usury when it comes to intra-Israelite business transactions. Deuteronomy 23:20, however, acknowledges things are different if the debtor is not an Israelite, before underscoring the intra-Israelite standard:

> On loans to a foreigner you may charge interest, but on loans to another Israelite you may not charge interest, so that the LORD your God may bless you in all your undertakings in the land that you are about to enter and possess. (NRSV)

The envelope structure of vv. 19–20, coupled with the motivation clause at the end about God's blessing (v. 20b), deemphasizes the allowance for interest with foreigners (v. 20a). This bit is something of an aside, perhaps, somehow less important than the prohibition of usury with one's fellow people which is twice mentioned. Be that as it may, Deuteronomy 15 also distinguishes between interest-free loans to community members and the profit that may be exacted from a foreigner. Perhaps one should see in this insider-outsider distinction less an instance of incipient us vs. them mentality, let alone xenophobia, and something more like the beginnings of international contract law. As Deut 28:12b would have it: "You will lend to many nations, but you will not borrow" (NRSV).

Deuteronomy has additional rules governing intra-Israelite loans, especially in matters of deposit and pledge:

> When you make any type of loan to your neighbor, don't enter their house to receive the collateral. You must wait outside. The person to whom you are lending will bring the collateral to you out there. Moreover, if the person is poor, you are not allowed to sleep in their pawned coat. Instead, be certain to give the pawned coat back by sunset so they can sleep in their own coat.

46 See, e.g., Dennis T. Olson, *Deuteronomy and the Death of Moses: A Theological Reading* (Minneapolis, MN: Fortress, 1994), 62–125, esp. 62–65.

> They will bless you, and you will be considered righteous before the Lord your God. (Deut 24:10–13; CEB)

The not-so-small detail about the creditor waiting outside means the lender cannot seize the pledged item. It must, instead, be surrendered by the debtor. This law protects the debtor even as it limits the creditor: the debtor needn't surrender that which is most prized, the creditor may not take what is most desired. Although the larger unit here in Deuteronomy (24:8–25:4) is apparently keyed to the Eighth Commandment against false witness, perhaps the Tenth Commandment, against coveting, is also operative as it often is elsewhere.[47]

The accent, regardless, is clearly on protection of the weaker, economically vulnerable party—a point underscored by explicit mention of poor persons who will need their pawned coat for adequate warmth at night. This same concern is on display in the following laws as well, which do *not* draw a distinction between Israelite and non-Israelite, but, instead, explicitly include non-Israelites within the legislated activities. So, for example, wages cannot be withheld from poor and needy workers, whether Israelite or immigrant, "because they are poor and their livelihood depends on them." If wages are withheld, "they might cry to the Lord against you, and you would incur guilt" (Deut 24:14–15; NRSV). Or, again

> Don't obstruct the legal rights of an immigrant or orphan. Don't take a widow's coat as pledge for a loan. Remember how you were a slave in Egypt but how the Lord your God saved you from that. That's why I'm commanding you do this thing. (Deut 24:17; CEB).

The references to "crying out" and to Egypt are not incidental. They evoke the language of painful prayer, first, and, second, the saving act of God that delivered Israel from slavery and brought Israel into covenantal relationship with God. So, once again, covenant is the facilitating environment for contract law, no less than other types. God's actions as treaty partner in saving and delivering motivate proper behavior for Israelites even as that action is double-edged: misbehavior would figure Israel as a new Egypt with God motivated to deliver the mistreated poor and oppressed. So it is that contract law, no less than other types, also pays extensive attention to vulnerable members of society—whether native-born or not. Contract law in this light is not at all interested in interest per se, let alone in protecting it; economic gain is ultimately unimportant.[48]

47 See Strawn, "Intention," 1:435 for the reanalysis and reinterpretation that the coveting law, with its accent on interiority, requires "of the entire Decalogue (if not still other laws)."

48 Barbara E. Armacost and Pete Enns, "Crying Out for Justice: Civil Law and the Prophets," in *Law and the Bible: Justice, Mercy and Legal Institutions*, eds. Robert F. Cochran Jr. and David VanDrunen (Downers Grove, IL: IVP Academic, 2013), 121–50, esp. 147–49 have discussed modern-day payday lending in the United States as a troubling counterexample; though their concern is with the biblical prophets, the concern is equally present in the Torah.

What matters instead and by far is *the building of a community (citizen and otherwise) through law.*

Property: "The land shall not be sold in perpetuity, for the land is mine..." (Lev 25:23)

The final category of private law, property, may be considered in the latest of legal collections, the Priestly law and Holiness writings.[49] Ancient Israelite society was, especially in comparison to our own, almost entirely subsistence based. Land, therefore, was the predominant source of wealth in biblical Israel.[50] So, while moveable property existed and laws pertaining to such are known (cf. Lev 19:36; Deut 25:13–15), the most important kind of property was real property. It is not surprising, then, to find a good deal of law—and legal topics—dealing with real property, much of which is theologically fraught. Geoffrey Miller's brief summary is a useful starting point:

> The Bible recognizes that property rights can generally be alienated—transferred to others. The principle of free alienability applies to all forms of property: real estate (e.g., Gen 23:7; 33:18–20); tangible personal property (e.g., Gen 25:34); intangible personal property (e.g., Gen 24:33); and slaves or servants (e.g., Gen 37:28). The right to transfer property was not absolute, however: in certain cases the law imposed restrictions on alienation in order to further important social values such as the interest in maintaining property in family ownership.[51]

Nowhere is the last comment clearer than in terms of familial land, something that the Bible calls *naḥălāh* ("inheritance, possession, property").[52] It may not be going too far to say that the Old Testament is almost obsessed with land.[53] The story of Abraham begins with, and revolves around, the twin promises of land and progeny (see, e.g., Gen 12:1–4; 15:1–16). By the end of Genesis the progeny piece is mostly in place: Israel is a large and fruitful people. The problem is that they now sojourn in the land of Egypt, where they are soon enslaved, precisely because of their size and strength (see Exod 1:1–14).

49 As noted earlier, scholars typically differentiate these two corpora though they have much in common. In any event, some of the material cited in this section comes from Priestly passages of the Pentateuch (including narrative texts) with other material coming from the Holiness writings.

50 Raymond Westbrook, *Property and the Family in Biblical Law* (Sheffield: Sheffield Academic Press, 1991), 11.

51 Geoffrey Parsons Miller, "Property," in *OEBL*, 2:175–82 (175).

52 Another important term, often used in combination with *naḥălāh*, is *ʾăḥuzzāh* ("land holding, property").

53 See, e.g., Walter Brueggemann, *The Land: Place as Gift, Promise, and Challenge in Biblical Faith*, 2nd ed. (Minneapolis, MN: Fortress, 2002); and Norman Habel, *The Land Is Mine: Six Biblical Land Ideologies* (Minneapolis, MN: Fortress, 1995).

The balance of Exodus and the rest of the Pentateuch, extending also into the material in Joshua (even Judges), can be seen as the slow resolution of the second, long-deferred promise of land. Eventually, Israel takes possession of the land promised long ago. Once they do, the land is carefully allotted to various family units (see Joshua 13–19), though concerns for land division are also present within the Pentateuch proper, prior to the settlement (see esp. Num 26:1–65; 32:1–35:34).

The texts concerning land boundaries, tribal allotments, and so forth are not always easy to align; they no doubt reflect different traditions from different periods—the default situation in the case of the multi-layered Pentateuch. Even so, the general point of the land being carefully allotted to different family units within Israel reflects concern with appropriate chain of title and the original root of title. Indeed, one might perhaps see in the divine promise and gift of land to Israel's ancestors the legal justification and/or motivation for the conquest and settlement in Joshua (and Judges).[54] What is certain, regardless, is that the divine promise and gift of land means that Israel's claim on title is, ultimately, only penultimate. By first promising and then gifting the land, God is shown to have ultimate claim on it, to be its original owner. This point is made explicit in several places in the Bible: right at the start of the covenant at Sinai, for example, where God, almost as an aside, reminds Israel, "indeed, the whole earth is mine" (Exod 19:5; cf. Pss 24:1–2; 50:10; etc.). The point is memorably made in a passage from Leviticus 25:

> You shall observe my statutes and faithfully keep my ordinances, so that you may live on the land securely. The land will yield its fruit, and you will eat your fill and live on it securely....The land shall not be sold in perpetuity, for the land is mine; with me you are but aliens and tenants. (Lev 25:18, 23; NRSV)

This passage asserts God's ownership: the land belongs to the LORD. But the passage also indicates that God's root of title has ramifications for the rest of the chain, which in this case means that the land cannot be alienated "in perpetuity" (*liṣmītūt*). Still further, it reveals the legal status of the Israelites: they are not land owners at all, but just "aliens and tenants" (*gērîm wĕtôšābîm*; cf. CEB: "immigrants and foreign guests")—renters, as it were—on what is, and remains, decidedly *God's land*. Such a claim has profound ramifications across the Old Testament, not only because there is a great deal of legal concern for *gērîm* and *tôšābîm*, in the Bible, but also because land *mismanagement* is one of the major reasons given for Israel's *loss* of the land (see, e.g., Lev 26:34–35, 43; 2 Chr 36:21).

The implications of such a perspective—at once both legal and theological—are several; it must suffice to lift up three important points.

54 See Miller, "Property," 2:176–77.

1 Concerns over root and chain of title underlie several of the provisions for transfer of ownership. To be more specific, things could be sold, including real property, but there was often provision—*especially* in the case of real property—for the original seller or other family members to subsequently "redeem" (*gāʾal*; NRSV; cf. CEB: "buy back") what had been sold (see Lev 25:23–55; 27:1–34).[55] Related to such provision, and an ultimate example of it, is the Jubilee legislation which mandates that ownership reverts to the original extended family unit (*mišpāḥāh*) every 50 years (see Lev 25:8–55; cf. Lev 17:17–24; Num 36:4). While most scholars believe that the Jubilee is utopian and would have been almost impossible to practice, it remains a lofty ideal, one grounded, in theory at least, in certain legal precedents known from the ancient Near East.[56] What is novel is the way the Holiness writings took up a tradition of debt release and mandated its regular recurrence every 50 years.[57] Whether utopian or not, practiced or otherwise, such legislation again underscores concrete pragmatic and economic aspects to what some might otherwise misconstrue as solely "spiritual" realities.

2 The notion of divinely given inalienable real property plays a major role in the narrative about Naboth's vineyard in 1 Kings 21. In this story, the acquisitive king Ahab desires Naboth's land, offering to trade him for it or simply buy it outright. He does not receive the answer he wants: "Naboth responded to Ahab, 'Lord forbid that I give you my family inheritance'" (1 Kgs 21:3; NRSV). Not surprisingly, the term Naboth uses here is *naḥălāh*, which explains both his strong refusal and his invocation of God by name.[58] Ahab, spurred on by his queen Jezebel, ends up acquiring the vineyard after all, once Jezebel arranges for two individuals to bring false testimony against Naboth, who is subsequently executed (vv. 4–16). But then, in the very process of taking ownership of the vineyard—no extended kin are mentioned who might have inherited Naboth's land—Ahab is met by the prophet Elijah who roundly condemns him and Jezebel (vv. 17–24). This story stresses that even the most powerful of individuals must not, and indeed *cannot*, trespass the inalienable nature of property law that obtains in the case of the *naḥălāh*. If (and when) they did so, they were subject to a higher law given the ultimate claim of God on land and people.[59]

55 In Westbrook's terms, biblical law developed "special rules…to maintain the link between property and family and to bend ownership of property to the goal of ensuring the family's continuation" (*Property and the Family*, 11). Cf. Miller, "Property," 2:178–79. Note, in this regard, the difference drawn between urban and rural scenarios: homes in cities are allowed to be sold permanently if not redeemed within one year (Lev 25:29–30); not so for pastureland (i.e., property as means of livelihood) outside of cities (cf. Lev 25:34).

56 See Pamela Barmash, "Amnesty and Reform Texts," in *OEBL*, 1:9–13.

57 See Westbrook, *Property and the Family*, 36–57, esp. 50–52; also 16.

58 The Hebrew is quite emphatic, suggesting that any such action by Naboth would be reckoned a desecration (*ḥālîlāh*) by God.

59 Although it does not concern land, the story of David and Bathsheba is not entirely unrelated, especially in terms of an acquisitive king (note the use of the verb "to take" in 2 Sam. 11:4; cf.

3 The final point to be made is that despite the significance—both legal and theological—of biblical laws concerning property, including that of the *naḥălāh*, these laws are not above revision. The story of the daughters of Zelophehad found in Num 27:1–11 is the parade example. Zelophehad died leaving no sons but five daughters: Mahlah, Noah, Hoglah, Milcah, and Tirzah. The daughters come to Moses and, in contrast to the patrilineal system of the time, request that they, too, receive property, just as any male descendant would. Since the situation is unprecedented, the case is brought to God who replies:

> Zelophehad's daughters are right in what they are saying. By all means, give them property as an inheritance [*naḥălāh*] among their father's brothers. Hand over their father's inheritance [*naḥălāh*] to them. (Num 27:7; CEB)

As precedent typically does, what is established here is then further specified, generalized to any others where "a man dies and doesn't have a son," in which case "you must hand his inheritance [*naḥălāh*] over to his daughters" (Num 27:8); still further scenarios are then imagined and delineated. The point to be made here is not solely one about legal revision, but also pertains to the flexibility and dynamism that were noted earlier for biblical law. Of course here, too, the issue is the preservation of the family unit and so, in one way, there has been no real change in the law's ultimate concern when it comes to inalienable family property. In another way, however, the passage is remarkable in showing that the law could be (and was) flexed to accommodate gendered issues in a way that was, at that time, otherwise quite rare.[60] This legal change is prompted, furthermore, by unmarried and now orphaned daughters who were among the more disenfranchised and powerless of society at that time. Still further, their opinion is validated and the legal change requested authorized directly by God.[61]

---

the importance of this verb in the request for kingship [1 Sam. 8:11, 13–14, 16] and in Nathan's parable and its explanation [2 Sam. 12:4, 9–10]) and the fact that at some points in Israelite history wives may have been considered the property of husbands. But note that some scholars, observing the difference in the two versions of the Tenth Commandment in Exodus 20 and Deuteronomy 5, have argued that the latter (from a latter legal collection than the former) reflects a move *away* from considering the neighbor's wife as property in the same way as the other items listed.

60 For discussion, see Jonathan Burnside, *God, Justice, and Society: Aspects of Law and Legality in the Bible* (Oxford: Oxford University Press, 2011), 192–93; and esp. Katharine Doob Sakenfeld, "In the Wilderness, Awaiting the Land: The Daughters of Zelophehad and Feminist Interpretation," *PSB* 9 (1988): 179–96, who shows that the account is not straightforward on the matter of gender.

61 Note also Num 36:1–12 which contains further legal decisions about Zelophehad's daughters—namely, that they are not allowed to marry outside their tribe, lest the *naḥălāh* go to that tribe, rather than stay where it was originally allotted. They can marry anyone they wish, but it must be someone in "a clan [*mišpāḥāh*] of their father's tribe," precisely "so that no inheritance of the Israelites shall be transferred from one tribe to another; for all Israelites shall retain the inheritance of their ancestral tribes" (vv. 6–7; NRSV).

Conclusion: private law, then and now

The present chapter is only a brief introduction to some aspects of biblical private law. Private law, as understood in biblical perspective—or, rather, private law in the multiple and varied texts found in the Bible—seems to challenge, to some degree at least, contemporary notions of the same. The most fundamental challenge is found in the fact that the literary setting of Pentateuchal law makes all legal breach an offense against God and God's covenant—that is a far cry from more individualized modern notions of private law, on the one hand, and from more constrained notions of "religious" or "ceremonial" law, on the others, especially since the latter were typically restricted to offenses like blasphemy, sacrilege, apostasy, and so forth.[62]

Upon closer inspection, however, the invocation (or involvement) of God with *all* law—private law included—may be less different from the contemporary scene than one might think, and in more than one way. According to some scholars, the theological framing of biblical law is little more than "ideology," often in the worst understanding of that term: at best, a thin veneer to justify the power of some, like a royal and/or priestly elite, over all other haven-nots.[63] In such a perspective, the ideological nature of biblical law detracts from its legal force or significance because it is ultimately about something other than (and perhaps far from) real, actual law—especially of a beneficent sort. Biblical law collections, seen in this light, are not "simply" legislative but iconic: they represent or stand for something, though that something is not something very good.

At least two things might be offered in reply. First, *all* law, not just biblical law, is ideological, at least to some degree and according to some interpreters.[64] Biblical law, therefore, need not stand out or stand apart on this point, at least not negatively, especially since there are far less malevolent understandings of the term "ideology" than a gross means for grabbing power. Second, cleansed of negative "ideology," the point about biblical law being iconic in some way can stand with its connections to the divine realm not indicating that biblical law was not also truly legislative, only that it was *divinely legislative*. If parts of biblical law, like the Jubilee, are and remain utopian and unrealizable, well, here, too, one might perhaps say the same thing for at least some parts of contemporary jurisprudence. There seems to be no reason, regardless, why law, biblical or otherwise, cannot or should not be aspirational. Aspiration to wise, successful living—human flourishing, to use a recent phrase—is part of what Jackson believes is at work in the "wisdom-laws" of the Book of the

62 Cf. Westbrook, "Character," 1:76.

63 An extreme example is found in Harold V. Bennett, *Injustice Made Legal: Deuteronomic Law and the Plight of Widows, Strangers, and Orphans in Ancient Israel* (Grand Rapids, MI: Eerdmans, 2002).

64 See, e.g., Roger Cotterrell, *The Politics of Jurisprudence: A Critical Introduction to Legal Philosophy*, 2nd ed. (Oxford: Oxford University Press, 2003).

Covenant and what Partlett (via Lord Atkin) affirms: laws that might end up self-governing and self-regulating even in the absence of liability rules. The aspirational aspects of biblical law extend also to private arenas (e.g., Exod 23:5), as, also, does modern legislation. The presence of aspirational aspects—a legal good, in my judgment—not only in Scripture, but also now, may even suggest that contemporary, secular law also traffics in the ideal, utopian, iconic, perhaps even (dare one say it?) the theological, though often unknowingly and perhaps dangerously.[65] Modern law may be *theological* (sacralized, to use another term) insofar as it arrogates to itself all authority, if not in heaven, then certainly here on earth. Such a move is *dangerous* since, in biblical perspective, no human institution is deemed worthy of or capable of appropriately handling such authority or of sufficiently grounding all that stems from such authority. The Bible and the history of the Christian Church, as well as the history of our own secular age, know of far too many failures in this regard to recount. To come full circle, this may be why—from the very start and also at the end of the day—biblical law is presented as *God's* law. Small wonder, then, that the only thing that the Israelite king is required to do according to Pentateuchal legislation is to write out a copy of the Torah (Deut 17:14–20)!

* * *

Coda: private law in the New Testament

For various reasons, the New Testament does not contain much "law"—not, at least, like that contained in the Old. Some of this is a matter of *literary genre*, though it is clear enough that Jesus is presented as a kind of new Moses in Matthew's Sermon on the Mount and that much of Paul's moral exhortation in his epistles has at least quasi-legal force to it for some communities of faith.[66] Another aspect may be *historical*: the length of time reflected within these respective testaments (and their specific books) and in the compositional histories of the same. Beyond the New Testament canon, later centuries of Christian thought will witness to the development of church law. A closely related, *sociological* factor is that Old Testament law reflects something akin to a polity for a landed people, replete with monarch, government, and the like, whereas the New Testament reflects a community under external imperial

65 Cf. Rémi Brague, *The Law of God: The Philosophical History of an Idea*, trans. Lydia G. Cochrane (Chicago: University of Chicago Press, 2008). Not unrelated discussions include Charles Taylor, *A Secular Age* (Cambridge, MA: Harvard Univeristy Press, 2007); and George Steiner, *Real Presences* (Chicago: University of Chicago Press, 1989). For the gods in ancient law, see also Yochanan Muffs, *The Personhood of God: Biblical Theology, Human Faith and the Divine Image* (Woodstock, VT: Jewish Lights, 2005), 35–44.

66 See, inter alia, Dale C. Allison, *The New Moses: A Matthean Typology* (Minneapolis, MN: Fortress, 1993); Victor Paul Furnish, *Theology and Ethics in Paul* (Louisville, KY: Westminster John Knox, 2009).

hegemony—a community, moreover, that seemed to expect the end of all things to happen rather sooner than later. Once it becomes clear to Christians that the eschaton is delayed, we (again) find the eventual and extensive rise of ecclesiastical law.

These important considerations aside, the New Testament contains much that pertains to private law or at least evidences its presence. Note, for example, texts that attest to private property with free rights of alienability (e.g., Matt 19:21; 25:9; Mark 10:21; Luke 22:36),[67] though in some cases, as in Acts 5:1–11, the community's interest in property was seen to supersede the individual's prerogative (cf. also Acts 2:44–45; 4:37). In several instances, what one finds in the New Testament in terms of private law is entirely in line with the Old, indicating a continuity that extends from earlier stages into the late Second Temple Period. So, for example, Jesus' remarks about usury in Luke 6:34–35 are clearly resonant with Deuteronomy. Of course, the question of continuity—or discontinuity—is a profound one when it comes to Old Testament law and the New Testament, especially in Paul and his use of *nomos*.[68] The literature here is vast but special attention should be paid to the so-called "New Perspective" on Paul which has argued for far greater alignment between Paul and the Judaism of his day than was acknowledged before.[69] Other chapters in this volume take up further aspects of the New Testament in greater detail.

Abbreviations

BLD	Bryan A. Garner, ed., *Black's Law Dictionary* (10th ed.; St. Paul: Thomson Reuters, 2014)
CEB	Common English Bible
HANEL	Raymond Westbrook, ed., *A History of Ancient Near Eastern Law* (2 vols.; Leiden: Brill, 2003)
JBL	*Journal of Biblical Literature*
JHS	*Journal of Hebrew Scriptures*
JRL	*Journal of Law and Religion*
NETS	Albert Pietersma and Benjamin G. Wright, *A New English Translation to the Septuagint* (New York: Oxford University Press, 2007)

67 Miller, "Property," 2:181.

68 See, among many, many others: J. Duncan M. Derrett, *Law in the New Testament* (London: Darton, Longman & Todd, 1970); Frank Thielman, *The Law and the New Testament: The Question of Continuity* (New York: Crossroad, 1999); Enns, "Law of God," 4:898–99; and Cochran and VanDrunen, eds., *Law and the Bible.*

69 See esp. E. P. Sanders, *Paul and Palestinian Judaism: A Comparison of Patterns in Religion* (Philadelphia, PA: Fortress, 1977). But for the most recent rapprochement, see now Stephen J. Chester, *Reading Paul with the Reformers: Reconciling Old and New Perspectives* (Grand Rapids, MI: Eerdmans, 2017).

NIDOTTE	Willem A. VanGemeren, gen. ed., *New International Dictionary of Old Testament Theology and Exegesis* (5 vols.; Grand Rapids: Zondervan, 1997)
NJPSV	New Jewish Publications Society Version
NRSV	New Revised Standard Version
OEBL	Brent A. Strawn, editor in chief, *The Oxford Encyclopedia of the Bible and Law* (2 vols.; Oxford: Oxford University Press, 2015)
PSB	*Princeton Seminary Bulletin*
RB	*Revue Biblique*

Part II
Property

4 Christian thought and property law

David W. Opderbeck

Introduction

Anglo-American property law presents a set of difficult problems for contemporary Christian thought. The dominant concepts of private property in Anglo-American property law trace their roots to sources that include the Westphalian settlement of the wars of religion, the Calvinist work ethic, the English Civil Wars, the Scottish Enlightenment, British Mercantile capitalism, and the entrepreneurial fervor of the American Great Awakenings. These sources supply a heady brew of Christian Protestant religion, patriotism and individualism. Like the old Guinness Stout ads suggested, this brew is not just intoxicating: it does contain some nutrients that have made us bold and strong, particularly against the threats of fascism during World War II and totalitarian communism during the Cold War. But when mixed with even more potent spirits – particularly racism – "property rights" have justified terrible evils, not least the Atlantic Slave Trade. Today elements of the Christian right have aligned themselves with libertarian rhetoric that exalts property rights as the fundamental pillar of society, while other streams of Christianity emphasize a "prosperity gospel" that views wealth as a key sign of God's blessing.[1] At the same time, elements of the Christian left, though exercising a far smaller cultural influence than the religious right, have aligned themselves with movements that at their extreme edges sometimes advocate the forcible redistribution of private property.[2] This chapter seeks to place the concept of "property" within the context of Christian thought, and offers some tentative suggestions for how Christian thinkers should approach property law.

1 Kevin M. Kruse, *One Nation under God: How Corporate America Invented Christian America* (New York: Basic Books, 2015); Chris Lehmann, "How the Prosperity Gospel Explains Trump's Popularity With Christian Voters," *The Washington Post*, July 15, 2016, https://www.washingtonpost.com/posteverything/wp/2016/07/15/how-the-prosperity-gospel-explains-donald-trumps-popularity-with-christian-voters.

2 Jim Wallis, "An Open Letter to the Occupiers from a Veteran Troublemaker," *Sojourners*, October 13, 2011, https://sojo.net/articles/open-letter-occupiers-veteran-troublemaker.

The Biblical witness

All Christian traditions agree that the Bible is a foundational norm for Christian thought, although there is significant disagreement about how to interpret and use it as a source. The Bible has been employed to justify monarchy and serfdom, slavery, strongly libertarian views of personal property, mercantilism, socialism, communism, redistributionism, and every other kind of property regime that could be imagined. One of the difficulties with the Bible as a source of norms concerning property rights is the diversity of its witness on this question. Nevertheless, it is possible to discern some overarching themes that can inform our present discussion.

Creation

The Hebrew scriptures include the Law (*Torah*), the Prophets (*Nevi'im*), and the "Writings" (*Ketuvim*). The first book of the *Torah*, Genesis, includes the Bible's creation narratives.

First, the doctrine of creation establishes that the Earth belongs to God. Most modern mainstream Biblical scholars agree that the Biblical creation narratives are not scientific accounts of how the Earth came into existence, but rather establish the theological truth that God alone is the source and final authority over all creation. In Genesis 2, God places the man and woman in the "Garden," and from that privileged place he gives them dominion over the Earth. From the perspective of the Bible's creation narratives, then, humanity does properly exercise a kind of "right" over the rest of the created order. However, the scope of humanity's authority is entirely derived from and subject to God's ultimate rule.

> The nature of humanity's state in the "Garden" has provoked much theological and philosophical speculation over the millennia that relates directly to our question of property law. Most early and medieval Christian thinkers assumed that the Garden was a perfect state without any need for negative rights or the force of positive law to enforce such rights. Any such need, including the right to exclude from private property and the resulting law of property, arose only because of Adam's Fall, which introduced the depredations of sin into the creation. Private property rights were necessary and important because of the reality of sin, but they were always relative to a higher natural law derived from creation's original perfection, which would be restored in the eschaton. Moreover, in the interregnum between the original creation and the eschaton, private property rights existed within a political framework that subordinated private property rights to the Crown and the Church, which ruled over Christendom on behalf of the New Adam, Christ, until he would return to consummate history.

During the Enlightenment another etiological narrative took shape, given particular force in Thomas Hobbes' *Leviathan*. For Hobbes, the state of nature was one of perpetual conflict and human life without a social contract backed by the rule of law was always "nasty, brutish, and short." In Hobbes' conception, private property rights took on a more "horizontal" aspect as an element of the social contract between individuals. Yet another Enlightenment thinker, John Locke, agreed that raw nature was wild and untamed, but also argued that natural rights in property arise from the improvement of raw nature by rational human effort, first begun by Adam and Eve in the Garden.[3]

Neither Hobbes nor Locke included anything like the Christian doctrine of the Fall in their origin stories, and accordingly their accounts of negative rights in property and of positive law to enforce those rights were more absolute than earlier Christian accounts. Stated another way, private property rights played a more foundational role in Hobbes' and Locke's origin stories than in the Biblical origin stories as interpreted by most Christian thinkers prior to the Enlightenment. This is also reflected in the subtle but significant Enlightenment shift away from referring to "creation" in favor of the term "nature."

Land and covenant

A second major Biblical theme relating to property is that of the relationship between the land and God's covenant with His chosen people, Israel. The *Torah* includes numerous provisions that sound similar to modern concepts of private property law and that are often cited as scriptural sanction for private property regimes. Careful attention to the shape of the narrative and the laws, however, reveals a more complex picture.

The second book of the *Torah*, Exodus, describes the Hebrew people's rescue from Egyptian slavery by God, their sojourn in the desert, and God's giving of the Ten Commandments and other provisions of the law.

Leviticus and Deuteronomy, the third and fifth books of the *Torah* respectively, contain detailed laws that are presented as running from God through Moses on the cusp of the Hebrews' entry into the promised land.[4]

The Levitical and Deuteronomic laws at the heart of the *Torah* include numerous requirements concerning the land. Many scholars suggest that the overall framework reflects a clan-based system of land tenure typical of the ancient near east. Most notably for the purposes of this chapter, the Levitical law rendered title to family land inalienable: "The land, moreover, shall not be sold permanently, for the land is Mine; for you are but aliens and sojourners with Me. Thus

3 For a good discussion of Hobbes' and Locke's genealogies of property, see Jeremy Waldron, "Property and Ownership," § 4*Stanford Encyclopedia of Philosophy*, ed. Edward N. Zalta (Winter 2016 Edition), https://plato.stanford.edu/entries/property/.

4 In fact, the actual historical circumstances of the exodus, the entry into the promised land, and the creation and redaction of these different law codes are certainly far more lengthy and complex than a simple reading of the texts might suggest. *See, e.g.*, John H. Walton, ed., *Zondervan Illustrated Biblical Backgrounds Commentary, Vol. 1* (Grand Rapids, MI: Zondervan, 2009); Margaret Warker, ed., *Ancient Israel in Egypt and the Exodus* (Washington, DC: Biblical Archeology Society, 2012). The ethical, legal, and historical concerns the Biblical conquest narratives present for modern readers are also beyond the scope of this chapter.

for every piece of your property, you are to provide for the redemption of the land" (Leviticus 25:23–24 (NASB)). As Biblical scholar Christopher J.H. Wright has noted, "[t]he combined effect of these regulations was to take the land itself right off the market as a commodity. Speculation in land or amassing huge private estates by permanent land purchase were *technically* impossible in Israel."[5] In addition, a portion of the land – "the edges of the fields" – was to be left for the poor[6] (e.g. Leviticus 23:22). Other portions of the fruits of the land were to be dedicated as offerings, both in thanks to God and to support the Priestly class and the operations of the Temple. Moreover, the land itself was to be given a sabbath rest – a fallow period every seven years (Lev 25:4).

Wealth and wisdom

The Writings (*Ketuvim*) include historical books and poetical and wisdom literature. The poetical and wisdom literature tends to view wealth and property as blessings from God to the faithful, hard-working person. Proverbs 8: 9–10, for example, offers this instruction:

> Honor the Lord from your wealth
> And from the first of all your produce;
> So your barns will be filled with plenty
> And your vats will overflow with new wine.[7]

Proverbs 28:19 is a good example of the wisdom literature's advice about hard work:

> He who tills his land will have plenty of food,
> But he who follows empty pursuits will have poverty in plenty.[8]

At the same time, the wisdom literature stresses that all wealth ultimately belongs to God and that a person who enjoys wealth should share it freely with others. Proverbs 11, for example, states that

> One person gives freely, yet gains even more;
> another withholds unduly, but comes to poverty.
> A generous person will prosper;
> whoever refreshes others will be refreshed.

5 Christopher J.H. Wright, *Old Testament Ethics for the People of God* (Downers Grove, IL: InterVarsity Press, 2004), 163.

6 This concept is picked up by contemporary legal scholar Joseph William Singer in his book *The Edges of the Field* (New York: Beacon Press, 2001).

7 Prov. 8: 9–10 NASB.

8 Prov. 28:19 NASB.

. . . .

> Those who trust in their riches will fall,
> but the righteous will thrive like a green leaf.[9]

Other parts of the wisdom literature, such as the books of Job and Ecclesiastes, stress the fleeting nature of human life and the futility of efforts to acquire wealth. The "preacher" of Ecclesiastes tells us that

> He who loves money will not be satisfied with money, nor he who loves abundance with its income. This too is vanity. When good things increase, those who consume them increase. So what is the advantage to their owners except to look on? The sleep of the working man is pleasant, whether he eats little or much; but the full stomach of the rich man does not allow him to sleep.[10]

These texts highlight the relationship between God's blessing, wealth, property, generosity, and the dangers of greed.

Prophecy and judgment

The Hebrew Scriptures' historical and prophetic books (*Nevi'im*) are in large part commentaries on why Israel and Judah subsequently *lost* the land to the Assyrians and Babylonians. The reason given by the Prophets is that the nation failed to keep the *Torah* or to live according to wisdom, in particular by participating in idol worship and by oppressing the poor. The land belongs to God, who alone is worthy of worship and who requires compassion for the poor. God takes the land away from those who abuse it.

The prophetic literature, however, includes a note of hope. God made a covenant with Israel, which He will keep. Israel will return to the land, and a new era of peace will come. In the books of Ezra and Nehemiah, we see the exiles return to Jerusalem and rebuild the Temple. During this "Second Temple" period, which lasted over 400 years, many Jews expected the fulfillment of their reading of the prophetic literature, that is, a restoration of the land under a king in the line of King David. It proved, however, a tumultuous time of foreign rule by the Ptolemies, Seleucids (prompting the Maccabean Revolt), and Romans. During the Roman period, the Temple was further rebuilt and expanded by Herod the Great. Jewish eschatological movements such as the Essenes continued to draw on the Bible's prophetic literature in constructive vivid accounts of the end of history, and much of Jewish piety centered on the promise of a Messiah who would permanently reestablish David's throne.

9 Prov. 11: 24–25, 28 NASB.
10 Eccles. 5: 10–12 NASB.

Wealth, judgment, and new covenant

From the Christian perspective, the New Testament Gospels pick up the story at this point. Yet the Messiah who comes is not a political king who wrestles the land back from Rome, but rather a suffering servant who dies condemned on a cross and leaves behind loosely organized followers who claim the crucified Messiah has risen again, ascended to heaven, and promised to return. What, then, of the land? To the point of this chapter, what of "property?"

In the Gospels, Jesus is notoriously skeptical of society's religious, political, and economic elites. Many passages in the Gospels seem to suggest that wealth itself is sinful. One classic story here is the encounter between Jesus and the "rich young ruler," narrated in Matthew's and Mark's Gospels (Matthew 19:16–22; Mark 10:17–27). The young man asks Jesus what is necessary for eternal life. Jesus tells the man to "keep the commandments" (Matt 19:17). The man responds, "which ones?" (Matt 19:18 (NASB)). Jesus responds with a list from the Decalogue, and adds "and, You shall love your neighbor as yourself" (Matt 19:18–19, quoting Leviticus 19:18 (NASB)). The young man claims he has kept all these commandments, but asks "what am I still lacking?" Jesus responds: "If you wish to be complete, go and sell your possessions (ὑπάρχοντα) and give to the poor, and you will have treasure in heaven; and come, follow Me" (Matt 19:21 (NASB)). The young man "went away grieving; for he was one who owned much property (κτήματα)" (Matt 19:22 (NASB)).

Another classic story is Jesus' parable of the rich man and Lazarus the beggar in Luke 16. The rich man lives in luxury while the beggar lies at the rich man's gate, hoping to receive even crumbs falling from the rich man's table. The rich man dies and ends up in "Hades," while Lazarus dies and is carried by angels into Abraham's bosom. In Hades, the rich man begs Abraham, "'send Lazarus so that he may dip the tip of his finger in water and cool off my tongue, for I am in agony in this flame'" (Luke 16:24 (NASB)). Abraham replies, "'Child, remember that during your life you received your good things, and likewise Lazarus bad things; but now he is being comforted here, and you are in agony'" (Luke 16:26 (NASB)). It seems that the rich man and Lazarus' reversal of fortunes in the afterlife results directly from the rich man's hoarding of his property in this life.

This parable follows in Luke's Gospel after the parable of the unrighteous steward, who is praised for writing down debts owed by third parties to his master (Luke 16:1–9). Jesus glosses the parable as follows: "And I say to you, make friends for yourselves by means of the wealth of unrighteousness (μαμωνᾶ τῆς ἀδικίας), so that when it fails, they will receive you into the eternal dwellings" – a strange and enigmatic saying! (Luke 16:9 (NASB)). After the parable, Jesus offers another famous teaching: "No servant can serve two masters; for either he will hate the one and love the other, or else he will be devoted to one and despise the other. You cannot serve God and wealth (μαμωνᾷ, KJV "mammon")" (Luke 16:13 (NASB)). The point of the parable of the unrighteous steward seems to be that wealth is a master that enslaves us, so the servant of God should be prepared to give his wealth away for the higher cause of God's Kingdom.

These parables are just a few illustrations of Jesus' teachings about wealth. They reflect an overwhelming emphasis in Jesus' teachings on the dangers of wealth, the sins of the wealthy classes, and the exalted place of the poor in God's economy of justice.

Following on the Gospels, and in fact properly read together with the Gospel of Luke, the book of Acts tells of the story of how the early Christian community became the Church. Famously, Acts 2 says "all those who had believed were together and had all things in common; and they began selling their property (κτήματα) and possessions (ὑπάρξεις) and were sharing them with all, as anyone might have need," and Acts 4 tells us that

> the congregation (πλήθους, multitude) of those who believed were of one heart and soul; and not one *of them* claimed that anything belonging to him (ὑπαρχόντων) was his own, but all things were common property to them. And with great power the apostles were giving testimony to the resurrection of the LORD Jesus, and abundant grace was upon them all. For there was not a needy person among them, for all who were owners of land or houses would sell them and bring the proceeds of the sales and lay them at the apostles' feet, and they would be distributed to each as any had need.
>
> (Acts 2:44–45; 4:32–35 (NASB))

Note that the Greek words translated "property" and "possessions" demonstrate that the community described in Acts 2 and Acts 4 actually satisfied the conditions the rich young ruler could not meet.

The Christian community in the Roman Empire

In addition to the Gospels and Acts, a major portion of the New Testament comprises occasional letters to local churches from the Apostles (or persons writing pseudonymously in an Apostle's name). Unlike the *Torah*, which presumes a religious political community under a temporal authority, these letters are devoid of temporal political legislation. The letters do, however, often touch on how members of the Christian community should handle wealth, and here they uniformly view material wealth as a temptation and charity as a virtue.

Perhaps the most direct statement in the New Testament relating to what we today might call "property law" is found in the Apocalypse of John, better known as the book of Revelation. The text is best understood, in the vein of the Old Testament prophetic literature, as a political commentary on Rome.[11] In effect, Rome is cast in the role of the Assyrians or Babylonians, or (with

11 Michael J. Gorman, *Reading Revelation Responsibly: Uncivil Worship and Witness: Following the Lamb into the New Creation* (Eugene, OR: Wipf & Stock, 2010); Joseph Mangina, *Brazos Theological Commentary on the Bible: Revelation* (Ada, MI: Brazos Press, 2010).

difficulty for later Christian-Jewish relations) in the role of unfaithful Israel, with the Christian faithful cast in the role of the Jewish exiles who will return to rebuild the city. In Revelation 18 an angel (messenger of God) passes judgment on "Babylon the Great" – Rome – shouting that

> all the nations have drunk
> The maddening wine of her adulteries.
> The kings of the earth committed adultery with her,
> And the merchants of the earth grew rich from her excessive luxuries.
>
> (Rev. 18:2–3 (NIV))

Another "voice from heaven" then announces "Babylon's" judgment by "death, mourning and famine" and by "fire": "Give her as much torment and grief," the oracle proclaims, "as the glory and luxury she gave herself" (Rev. 18:6–7 (NIV)). The oracle then offers a poignant and vivid image of what this judgment means for Roman trade:

> The merchants of the earth will weep and mourn over her because no one buys their cargoes anymore— cargoes of gold, silver, precious stones and pearls; fine linen, purple, silk and scarlet cloth; every sort of citron wood, and articles of every kind made of ivory, costly wood, bronze, iron and marble; cargoes of cinnamon and spice, of incense, myrrh and frankincense, of wine and olive oil, of fine flour and wheat; cattle and sheep; horses and carriages; and human beings sold as slaves.
>
> (Rev. 18:11–13 (NIV))

This coming judgment is a disaster for Rome as well as for those whose personal and economic security lies with Rome. But it is offered in the text of Revelation as a word of *hope* for a community at the margins, the Christian community. For Roman rule will be replaced by a new city, the New Jerusalem, come down from heaven, with God at its center. Into this city – with its gold-paved streets and jewel-encrusted walls – all the kings of the earth will bring their treasure.

In short, unlike the Old Testament, the New Testament does not speak directly to property *law*, at least not in terms of positive law. The New Testament literature does, however, continue the Old Testament's theological themes about God's ownership of creation, the dangers of the concentration of power and wealth, and the final vindication of God's purposes by His own acts of judgment. From the New Testament's perspective, the Christian community is outside the mainstream of power and wealth, and should remain outside that mainstream for the sake of its purity and preservation. The Christian community waits patiently for the hope of Christ's return and God's final consummation of history, which is immanent. It seems beyond the historical horizon of the New Testament authors to suggest any positive, redemptive role for anything like property law.

Historical reception

The story of how the New Testament's eschatological vision worked through what became the Church in its first few centuries after the Apostolic age has been told as often as it has been fiercely debated. Christianity originally was seen as, and functioned as, a sect within Judaism.

As the Apocalypse of John suggests, in its first centuries, Christianity held an outsider status.[12] Christians were periodically subject to persecution by Roman authorities, who often viewed Christians as dangerously subversive of the established political-religious order. In the early fourth century CE, however, things changed. Constantine the Great consolidated power in a victory of Maxentius at the Milvian Bridge, spurred on by a vision of the cross. Constantine was active in the Church's life, calling the Council of Nicea to resolve the Arian controversy, at which the assembled Bishops hammered out the Nicene Creed. He also began a project of Christianizing Roman law, for example by issuing the Edict of Milan (313 CE) decriminalizing Christian worship, bringing ecclesiastical leaders in to the civil administration, and by tempering some of the harshness of Roman corporeal punishments.

Constantine's reign marks a continental divide for contemporary political theology, and, accordingly, for any effort to discuss a "Christian perspective" on any aspect of private law, including property law. Perspectives on law and Christianity drawn from the main streams of Roman Catholicism, Eastern Orthodoxy, or the Magisterial Reformation, on the whole, have viewed the "Constantinian shift" as a good thing. Today, dissenting voices that draw on the Radical Reformation, particularly on Anabaptist thought, argue that the Constantinian shift was disastrous. We can identify a third stream of contemporary political theology, which is also highly skeptical of the Constantinian shift, but for somewhat different reasons and with very different results than the Anabaptists: liberation theology. As these categories suggest, careful reflection on private property law from a Christian perspective will implicate broader questions of political theology concerning the Church's relationship to temporal power.

The early church and patristic views

The documents we possess from the first and second centuries suggest that early Christian communities practiced to some degree the kind of voluntary sharing of goods mentioned in Acts 5. Statements about voluntary sharing can be found in the *Didache*, the pseudonymous *Epistle of Barnabas*, the *Epistle to Diognetus*, and the *Shepherd of Hermas*.[13] These documents do not condemn private prop-

12 The Apocalypse may have been written as early as 60 CE, in the time of Nero's reign, but many scholars date it at or within decades after the fall of Jerusalem in 70 CE. *See* Mangina, *supra* note 13.

13 Justo L. Gonzalez, *Faith & Wealth: A History of Early Christian Ideas on the Origin, Significance, and Use of Money* (San Francisco, CA: Harper & Row, 1990).

erty, and in fact assume that some members of the Church will own property, but exhort the wealthy to share with the poor.

In the third century, some important Patristic thinkers evince a more directly negative attitude about wealth and private property. Irenaeus, for example, drawing on the mammon of unrighteousness (μαμωνᾶ τῆς ἀδικίας) in Jesus' parable of the unjust steward, suggested that all wealth, even from otherwise lawful commercial activity, ultimately derives from greed, theft, and other sins. [14] But perhaps the most direct commentary from this period on the dangers of wealth is found in Clement of Alexandria. In his commentary on the parable of the rich young ruler, *Quis dives salvetuer? – Who is the Rich to Be Saved?*"[15] Clement did not claim that it is necessarily wrong to possess things if they were properly used. Indeed, Clement said that

> [r]iches . . . which benefit also our neighbours, are not to be thrown away. For they are possessions, inasmuch as they are possessed, and goods, inasmuch as they are useful and provided by God for the use of men; and they lie to our hand, and are put under our power, as material and instruments which are for good use to those who know the instrument.[16]

However, in his text *The Tutor*, he criticized luxuries such as excessive jewelry and suggested that the original, proper state of human life involved a communal sharing of goods:

> God brought our race into communion by first imparting what was His own, when He gave His own Word, common to all, and made all things for all. All things therefore are common, and not for the rich to appropriate an undue share. That expression, therefore, 'I possess, and possess in abundance: why then should I not enjoy?' is suitable neither to the man, nor to society. . . . . For God has given to us, I know well, the liberty of use, but only so far as necessary; and He has determined that the use should be common. And it is monstrous for one to live in luxury, while many are in want.[17]

These warnings against wealth might reflect the Church's changing demographics, as more members of the higher classes of Roman society became Christians, and the issue of conspicuous wealth became more pressing. For some Romans from wealthy families who had become disaffected with their culture, the Church's criticism of wealth may have in itself been attractive – perhaps as part

14 Ibid., Chapter 6.

15 Clement of Alexandria, "Who Is the Rich that Will be Saved?" trans. William Wilson, *Ante-Nicene Fathers*, vol. 2 (Buffalo, NY: Christian Literature Publishing, 1885), http://www.newadvent.org/fathers/0207.htm.

16 Ibid., XIV.

17 Clement of Alexandria, "The Tutor," trans. Philip Schaff, *The Ante-Nicene Fathers*, vol. 2, http://www.ccel.org/ccel/schaff/anf02.vi.iii.ii.xiii.html.

of the age-old story of a young person coming into adulthood by rejecting his or her parents' culture. Even for those who heeded the call to poverty, the process of divestment may be much more gradual than is often supposed – more like wealthy people today who establish foundations than an immediate fire sale.[18]

The developing "Mainstream" view

As we examine the development of the mainstream of Christian thought about private property, it is useful to compare a transitional figure, Lactantius, with two of the great thinkers in the post-Nicene and Medieval traditions, Augustine and Aquinas. The key text from Lactantius for our purposes is the *Divine Institutes.*[19] Lactantius, a well-trained rhetor later known as the "Christian Cicero," wrote the *Divine Institutes* as an apologetic treatise against the persecution of Christians that had begun under the Emperor Diocletian. He eventually became a key advisor to Constantine I and significantly influenced Constantine's policy favoring Christianity.

Lactantius explained how the Christian concept of "justice" coheres with the Roman tradition. The persecution of Christians under Diocletian was unjust because Rome had lost sight of its original justice. By allowing the Christians to flourish instead, Rome would move back toward its original state of justice. The parallels here with the Christian Biblical narrative of creation-fall-redemption are obvious and intentional.

In the Golden Age as pictured by the famous Greek poet Aratus, Lactantius said,

> It was not even allowed to mark out or to divide the plain with a boundary: men sought all things in common; since God had given the earth in common to all, that they might pass their life in common, not that mad and raging avarice might claim all things for itself, and that that which was produced for all might not be wanting to any… .[20]

This original state of justice, however, was lost through the greed and avarice of men. Lactantius argued that the loss of original justice was particularly evident in the misuse of property:

> [a]nd the source of all these evils was lust; which, indeed, burst forth from the contempt of true majesty. For not only did they who had a superfluity fail to bestow a share upon others, but they even seized the property of

18 Peter Brown, *Through the Eye of a Needle: Wealth, the Fall of Rome, and the Making of Christianity in the West, 350–550 AD* (Princeton, NJ: Princeton University Press, 2013).

19 Lactantius, *Divine Institutes*, trans Alexander Roberts, *The Ante-Nicene Fathers, Vol. 7*, eds. James Donaldson, and A. Cleveland Coxe (Buffalo, NY: Christian Literature Publishing Co., 1886), http://www.newadvent.org/fathers/07015.htm.

20 Lactantuis, *Divine Institutes*, V.5.

> others, drawing everything to their private gain; and the things which formerly even individuals laboured to obtain for the common use of men, were now conveyed to the houses of a few.[21]

Worse, the wealthy and powerful used the law to enforce their greed:

> [t]hey also, under the name of justice, passed most unequal and unjust laws, by which they might defend their plunder and avarice against the force of the multitude. They prevailed, therefore, as much by authority as by strength, or resources, or malice.[22]

With the coming of Christ, Lactantius argued, the true justice of the Golden Age was restored, and is present in the Christian community. This was particularly true concerning wealth and possessions:

> Someone will say, Are there not among you some poor, and others rich; some servants, and others masters? Is there not some difference between individuals? There is none; nor is there any other cause why we mutually bestow upon each other the name of brethren, except that we believe ourselves to be equal. . . . . For men are rich, not because they possess riches, but because they employ them on works of justice; and they who seem to be poor, on this account are rich, because they are not in want, and desire nothing.[23]

Lactantius' negative attitude toward wealth and property was typical in the Patristic era. In addition to the sources we have already mentioned, Clement of Rome, Ambrose of Milan, Tertullian, St. Cyprian, St. Basil the Great, St. Gregory of Nyssa, St. Gregory of Nazianzus, St. John Chrysostom, and St. Jerome all assumed the natural law mandated common ownership and wrote and preached thunderously against the accumulation of private property.[24]

Yet, as Hermann Chroust and Robert Affeldt noted in an excellent article published in 1951, the Church Fathers generally did not advocate the overthrow of extant Roman property laws, but rather focused on the requirement of voluntary sharing.[25] Chroust and Affeldt suggested that this reflected the influence of Stoicism on early Christian thinkers as well as the historical circumstances of these pre- or early-Christendom thinkers. Lactantius' treatment of wealth and property can be seen as a kind of transitional stage between the Apostolic age and Constantinian Christendom. The Christian community, at least as depicted in Lactantius' apologetic, continued to share goods in common like the

21 Lactantius, *Divine Institutes*, V.6.

22 Ibid.

23 Lactantius, *Divine Institutes*, V.16.

24 For an excellent summary, see Hermann Chroust and Robert J. Affeldt, "The Problem of Private Property According to St. Thomas Aquinas," 34 *Marquette Law Review* 151 (1950–51).

25 Ibid., 174–75.

community depicted in Acts 4 and like the people who lived in the Golden Age. The use of the law by greedy people to protect their usurpation of common goods against the poor was for him a prime example of the injustice of the present age, in contrast to the newly restored community present in Christianity. Indeed, even in the *Divine Institutes*, Lactantius qualified his reading of Aratus as "poetical." Private property apparently was not in his mind itself unjust. The question was whether the owner of private property possessed the virtues of justice and charity that would compel him to share his property with those in need, and whether the law would allow the greedy person to hoard necessary resources that should be available to everyone.

A similar transitional dynamic can be observed in St. Augustine's discussions of private property and wealth. One place in which this discussion is somewhat ignominiously apparent is in Augustine's polemics against the Donatists. For example, in an exposition of the Gospel of John's account of the baptism of Jesus (John 1:32–33), Augustine argued against the Donatists that the merits of baptism inhere in the sacrament itself and not in the merits of the officer who performs the sacrament.[26] As part of his battle against the Donatists, Augustine had urged the civil authorities to seize churches and lands held by Donatist sympathizers. The Donatist sympathizers argued that this was unlawful and unjust. In this sermon, Augustine defended the seizures through a crafty distinction between divine and temporal law:

> By what right does every man possess what he possesses? Is it not by human right? For by divine right, *The earth is the LORD's, and the fullness thereof.* The poor and the rich God made of one clay; the same earth supports alike the poor and the rich. By human right, however, one says, This estate is mine, this house is mine, this servant is mine. By human right, therefore, is by right of the emperors. Why so? Because God has distributed to mankind these very human rights through the emperors and kings of this world. Do you wish us to read the laws of the emperors, and to act by the estates according to these laws? If you will have your possession by human right, let us recite the laws of the emperors; let us see whether they would have the heretics possess anything. But what is the emperor to me? You say. It is by right from him that you possess the land. Or take away rights created by emperors, and then who will dare say, That estate is mine, or that slave is mine, or this house is mine?[27]

If property ownership is not a natural right, but only a human, temporal right, the Emperor can define property law however he sees fit. Further, the Emperor is properly charged with the protection of the Church against heresy, and therefore

26 Augustine, *Tractates on the Gospel of John, Tractate 6*, trans. John Gibb, *Nicene and Post-Nicene Fathers, First Series*, Vol. 7, ed. Philip Schaff (Buffalo, NY: Christian Literature Publishing Co., 1888), http://www.newadvent.org/fathers/1701006.htm.

27 Ibid., 6.25.

the Emperor can confiscate the property of heretics. Augustine anticipated the response: why should we care what the Emperor says? We must obey the Emperor, Augustine said, because God ordains the temporal authority and scripture requires us to obey it.[28]

It is interesting to note the shift between Lactantius and Augustine on this point concerning property. Lactantius on the cusp of the Constantinian shift appeals to the Golden Age, not to the authority of an Emperor, to protect the rights of religious dissenters, and in the process marginalizes private property law, although he does not entirely reject the concept of private property. Augustine, shortly after the Constantinian shift, appeals to the authority of the Emperor alone to justify the confiscation of property from religious dissenters. For both Lactantius and Augustine, private property rights do not occupy a central place in a good social order but rather, to the extent private property rights exist, they are decidedly subservient to the demands of charity and to the unity of the Church.[29]

From Aquinas to contemporary Catholic social teaching

Lactantius and Augustine were both products of antiquity. As Christendom moved into the Medieval era, theology began to reflect different intellectual and cultural concerns, and what I have called the "mainstream" of Christian thought about private property thickened. The height of the historic mainstream view is perhaps reflected in Aquinas' discussion in the *Summa Theologiae*. The *locus classicus* for Aquinas' views is in II-II, Question 66 ("Of Theft and Robbery") and Questions 77–78 ("Cheating" and "The Sin of Usury").[30] In his discussion of theft and robbery, Aquinas listed the objections to private property we noted above in the Church Fathers: all things belong to God alone.[31] Aquinas responded by distinguishing the "nature" and "use" of things.[32] In their nature, things belong only to God, but in their use, things are given to the dominion of human beings for their profit. This capacity of dominion consistent with human reason and will is part of the image of God in humanity. Further, Aquinas argued, the exercise of dominion over things is *necessary* to human life because it fosters careful, orderly, industrious action and peaceful relationships

28 Ibid., 6.26. For further discussion of Augustine's views on the limitations of private property, see Richard J. Dougherty, "Catholicism Economy: Augustine and Aquinas on Property Ownership," *Journal of Markets & Morality*, 6, no. 2 (Fall 2003): 479–95. Doughterty helpfully notes that Augustine's views reflect an effort to "navigate between the Manichean attack on private property ownership as immoral and the too-ready embrace of property as an unqualified and essential good." Ibid., 483.

29 See also the chapter by William Brewbaker in this volume.

30 Thomas Aquinas, *Summa Theologiae*, II–II (Question 66, 77–78), trans. Fathers of the English Dominican Province (Cincinnati, OH: Benziger Bros. 1947), http://www.ccel.org/ccel/aquinas/summa.i.html.

31 ST II-II, Q. 66, Art. 1., Obj. 1–2.

32 Ibid., ad.

when each person is contented with his own property.[33] Here, however, Aquinas introduced an important qualification concerning how property should be used: "man ought to possess external things, not as his own, but as common, so that, to wit, he is ready to communicate them to others in their need."[34]

How did Aquinas square his statements about the propriety and need for private property and the requirements of common possession? In typical fashion, he invoked the distinction between positive and natural law: the natural law comprises basic principles built into the creation and is general and universal, while positive law is enacted by temporal authorities and may vary in particular times and places. Positive law, for Aquinas, should be consistent with the natural law, but positive law can never fully embody the natural law because positive law always reflects necessary compromises in this world.

Aquinas believed social "agreement" about the "division of possessions" is a matter for positive law. This sounds much like Augustine's view, but Augustine addressed this aspect of positive law in more occasional texts that were primarily about the respective spheres of authority belonging to Church and State and the role of the State in protecting the Church. Aquinas went further in making a positive case for property rights as part of how the positive law rationally orders society.

Aquinas did not suggest the positive law could properly encode absolute property rights or that the sharing of property with those in need must remain solely voluntary. When addressing the common ethical problem of whether it is lawful to steal "through stress of need," for example, Aquinas argued that

> While it is impossible for all to be succored by means of the same thing, each one is entrusted with the stewardship of his own things, so that out of them he may come to the aid of those who are in need. Nevertheless, if the need be so manifest and urgent, that it is evident that the present need must be remedied by whatever means at hand (for instance when a person is in some imminent danger, and there is no other possible remedy), then it is lawful for a man to succor his own need by means of another's property, by taking it either openly or secretly: nor is this properly speaking theft or robbery.[35]

A full discussion of Questions 77 and 78 of II-II is perhaps best suited to chapters in this book on contract law, since they concern the propriety of obtaining a profit on the exchange of property (acceptable with limitations) and on the charging of interest (unacceptable). However, these sections demonstrate that Aquinas regarded "property" as subsisting only in land and tangible things and that he thought profits on the exchange of property should be limited.

33 Ibid., Art. 2, ad.
34 Ibid.
35 Ibid., ad.

Regarding profit, Aquinas argued that profit generally is not virtuous or necessary because it suggests the goods were sold for more than their intrinsic value. However, he allowed that if a "moderate gain" is directed by a trader to a virtuous purpose, such as "the upkeep of his household or for the assistance of the needy," or as "payment for his labor," profit-taking can be consistent with virtue.[36] This attention to the ends to which a "moderate" profit could be put, rather than only to the inherent character of the act itself, would seem to suggest that the charging of moderate interest also could be consistent with virtue.[37] Here, however, Aquinas echoed the traditional Christian teaching against usury. Money, in Aquinas' view, is not real form of goods, but was created by humans for the pragmatic purpose of facilitating the exchange of goods.[38] When money is exchanged for goods, the money is "consumed," which is its proper function. But when interest is charged on money lent, the money-lender has sold "what does not exist, and this evidently leads to inequality which is contrary to justice."[39]

For Aquinas, then, private property rights in land and tangible things can serve a valuable social purpose and are a proper subject for the positive law. Private property rights, in Aquinas' view, facilitate the cardinal virtue of justice, because in voluntary exchanges of "buying and selling," each person is rendered what is due to him.[40] Both the scope of private property rights and the ability to profit from transactions in property, however, should be limited by the requirements of charity to persons in need.[41]

Contemporary Catholic social teaching is broadly consistent with this Thomistic approach, although in some of its formulations it seems to extend a more basic natural right in private property than suggested by Aquinas.[42] In response to the rise of Marxism, Pope Leo XIII stated in his Encyclical *Rerum Novarum* that "every man has by nature the right to possess property as his own" and that "[t]he fact that God has given the earth for the use and enjoyment of the whole human race can in no way be a bar to the owning of private property."[43] Pope Leo further argued that positive law that guards rights in private property is appropriate:

> With reason, then, the common opinion of mankind, little affected by the few dissentients who have contended for the opposite view, has found in

36 Ibid.

37 Ibid., Q. 78, Art. 1, Obj. 1.

38 Ibid.

39 Ibid.

40 ST II–II, Q. 11, ad. 3.

41 As Dougherty notes, "[t]he principled defense of an absolute or unqualified right to the possession of private property, then, is not found in Aristotle, Augustine, or Aquinas." Dougherty, *supra* note 38, 491.

42 As Ernest Fortin noted, *Rerum Novarum* significantly modified Aquinas' teleological, duty-based view of society with a more modern, non-teleological, rights-based view. Ernest L. Fortin, A.A., "Sacred and Inviolable": *Rerum Novarum* and Natural Rights," *Theological Studies*, 53 (1992): 203–33.

43 Pope Leo XIII, *Rerum Novarum*, May 15, 1891, para. 6, 8.

> the careful study of nature, and in the laws of nature, the foundations of the division of property, and the practice of all ages has consecrated the principle of private ownership, as being pre-eminently in conformity with human nature, and as conducting in the most unmistakable manner to the peace and tranquillity of human existence. The same principle is confirmed and enforced by the civil laws-laws which, so long as they are just, derive from the law of nature their binding force.[44]

At the same time, Pope Leo argued that laborers should be paid a fair wage and supported labor unions.

By the time of the Second Vatican Council, *Rerum Novarum*'s strong affirmation of private property rights was becoming moderated. The Council document *Gaurdium et Spes*, for example, agreed that "[p]rivate property or some ownership of external goods affords each person the scope needed for personal and family autonomy, and should be regarded as an extension of human freedom," but also said that "[o]f its nature private property also has a social function which is based on the law of the common purpose of goods."[45] In his Encyclical *Centesimus Annus*, written in 1991 for the one hundredth anniversary of *Rerum Novarum*, Pope John Paul II affirmed that private property ownership is a natural right, but also noted that "[a]t the same time, the Church teaches that the possession of material goods is not an absolute right, and that its limits are inscribed in its very nature as a human right."[46] Most recently, in his Encyclical on the environment, *Laudato Si*, Pope Francis stated that

> [t]he principle of the subordination of private property to the universal destination of goods, and thus the right of everyone to their use, is a golden rule of social conduct and 'the first principle of the whole ethical and social order'. The Christian tradition has never recognized the right to private property as absolute or inviolable, and has stressed the social purpose of all forms of private property.[47]

Whether this represents a shift or development in modern Catholic social teaching away from *Rerum Novarum*'s strong position on individual property rights remains a subject of intense debate.

The Magisterial Reformers and the "Protestant Work Ethic"

The previous sections discussed the development of the Patristic and Catholic traditions concerning private property. It is often argued that the Protestant

44 Ibid., para. 11.

45 Second Vatican Ecumenical Council, Pastoral Constitution on the Church in the World of Today *Gaudium et Spes*, 69; 71.

46 Pope John Paul II, *Centesimus Annus*, May 1, 1991, para. 30.

47 Pope Francis, *Laudato Si*, May 24, 2015, para. 93.

Reformation unleashed forces of economic individualism that undermined the more holistic Catholic view.[48] The Magisterial Reformers – Luther, Calvin, and their immediate followers – accepted the mainstream view that private property rights are not part of the created order but are necessary for the present stability of society. Indeed, Luther thundered against the Anabaptists (whom we will discuss in the next section) because their views on common ownership were subversive of social order.[49]

Luther and Calvin's views on property, usury, and trade differed, however, because of their social contexts. Luther's view has been called more "provincial" and leaned toward a Medieval view of the agrarian society, while Calvin's views were more suited to the bustling urban environment of Geneva.[50] In his sermon "On Trading and Usury," for example, Luther argued that it is sinful for merchants to sell their goods for the highest possible profit. Here, he said, "occasion is given for avarice, and every window and door to hell is opened."[51] Luther said the ideal civil law would involve a government agency that would set a fair price, but he complained that "we Germans have too many other things to do; we are too busy drinking and dancing to provide for rules and regulations of this sort."[52]

Calvin, in contrast, was more attuned to the economic changes happening in his time. Concerning usury, Calvin said,

> The reasoning of Saint Ambrose and Chrysostom, that money does not beget money, is in my judgment too superficial . . . Certainly if money is shut up in a strong-box, it will be barren – a child can see that. But whoever asks a loan of me does not intend to keep this money idle and gain nothing. The profit is not in the money itself, but in the return that comes from its use. It is necessary then to draw the conclusion that while such subtle distinctions appear on the surface to have some weight, they vanish under closer scrutiny, for they have no substance. I therefore conclude that usury must be judged, not by any particular passage of Scripture, but simply by the rules of equity.[53]

48 Brad S. Gregory, *The Unintended Reformation: How a Religious Revolution Secularized Society* (Cambridge, MA: Belknap Press, 2015).

49 Martin Luther, "Admonition to Peace: A Reply to the Twelve Articles of the Peasants in Swabia," in Hans J. Hillerbrand, ed., *The Annotated Luther, Vol. 5: Christian Life in the World* (Minneapolis, MN: Fortress Press, 2017); "Against the Robbing and Murdering Hordes of Peasants," in *Luther's Works, Vol. 46: The Christian in Society III*, ed. Helmutt T. Lehmann (Minneapolis, MN: Fortress Press, 1967).

50 David H. Eaton, "The Economists of the Reformation: An Overview of Reformation Teaching Concerning Work, Wealth, and Interest," *Sage Open* (July–September 2013): 1–9.

51 Martin Luther, "Trade and Usury," in *Callings: Twenty Centuries of Christian Wisdom on Vocation*, ed. William C. Placher (Grand Rapids, MI: Eerdmans, 2005).

52 Ibid.

53 Cited in David H. Eaton, "The Economists of the Reformation: An Overview of Reformation Teaching Concerning Work, Wealth, and Interest," Sage Open (July–September 2013): 1–9, 6 https://journals.sagepub.com/doi/pdf/10.1177/2158244013494864.

Calvin similarly viewed the ownership and use of private property more as a matter of general equity than of specific Biblical command. Calvin's pragmatism, tied to the Calvinist belief in predestination and election, along with Luther's emphasis on the value of "secular" callings, arguably led to what Max Weber called the "Protestant work ethic" and the rise of global capitalism.[54] The debate over Weber's thesis is vast and beyond the scope of this chapter. At the very least, it seems clear that the mercantile economies that arose after the Westphalian settlement following the post-Reformation wars, intensifying with the ascendancy of the British Empire, early American capitalism, and the Industrial Revolution, reflected a social harmonization of Magisterial Protestant Christianity, capitalism, and private property ownership.[55]

Anabaptist views

The early Anabaptists collectively were often accused by the Magisterial Reformers and their heirs as teaching a community of goods (that is, goods held in common and not as private property) in a way that undermined the stability of society.[56]

The community of goods was part of the views of Thomas Müntzer, who some scholars suggest was the ideological father of modern communism.[57] It was also emphasized by other early radical Anabaptists who held chiliastic views, such as the Melchiorites. This heady brew of social unrest and apocalypticism spilled into the notorious Münster Peasant's Rebellion in 1534–35. As noted in our discussion of Martin Luther, the peasants' actions ultimately provoked Luther's fierce opposition.

The community of goods was also, and remains, a distinctive of the Hutterite branch of Anabaptist Christianity. An excellent historical exposition of the minority Hutterite Anabaptist view on property can be found in Peter Walpot's "Great Article" book, written in 1577.[58] A segment of that text, titled "True Yieldedness and the Christian Community of Goods," lays the foundation for the communal ethos of the Hutterite "Bruderhof" system. Walpot wrote that

54 Max Weber, *The Protestant Ethic and the Spirit of Capitalism* (London: Routledge Classics, 1991).

55 Another important area of study beyond the scope of this chapter is the role of Calvinist theology in justifying African slavery – private property rights in persons, or at least in the labor of persons – in America. *See* Mark A. Noll, *The Civil War as a Theological Crisis* (Chapel Hill, NC: The University of North Carolina Press, 2015).

56 James M. Strayer, *The German Peasant's Revolt and Anabaptist Community of Goods* (Montreal: MQUP, 1991), Chapter 4.

57 Strayer, *The German Peasant's Revolt*, Chapter 5.

58 "Peter Walpot," in Daniel Liechty, ed. and trans., *Early Anabaptist Spirituality: Selected Writings* (New York: Paulist Press, 1994), 137.

> Private property does not belong in the Christian Church. Private property is a thing of the world, of the heathen, of those without divine love, of those who will have their own way. For there would be no property if it were not for selfish will. But the true community of goods belongs among believers. For by divine law all things should be held in common and nobody should take for himself what is God's any more than the air, rain, snow or water, the sun or other elements. Just as these cannot be divided up, so it is with temporal goods, which God has given in the same portion and measure for the common good. These should not be made private, and surely this cannot be done according to divine or Christian law. For owning private property is contrary to the nature and conditions of his creation. Whoever encloses and holds privately that which is and should be free, sins and goes against the One who created it free and made it free.[59]

For most Anabaptist traditions, in contrast to the more radical Hutterites, the "ideal of realizing the prescriptions of Acts 2 and 4 eventually took the form of Christian mutual aid instead of Christian community of goods."[60] The Swiss Brethren statement at the Frankenthal Disputation of 1571, for example, said that

> A Christian may have personal property and buy and sell. However, he must follow the teaching of Paul that he serve the poor with his property, and have it as though he had it not. That the People in Moravia [the Hutterites] practise community of goods, we wish neither to praise nor to defend.[61]

In his outstanding contemporary Anabaptist systematic theology, Thomas Finger notes the affinity between Anabaptist perspectives on wealth and property with liberation theology, the subject of this chapter's next section.[62] However, Finger notes that Anabaptists' stress on personal conversion, regardless of class, differs in some respects from liberation theology's preferential option for the poor, which seems to place the poor in a special soteriological category in virtue of being poor. Consistent with the mainstream of Anabaptist thought, Finger does not suggest private property should be abolished, but rather that voluntary "economic sharing" in the form of mutual aid across economic and class divides should characterize the Church's life.[63]

Liberation theology

Liberation theology began as a Catholic movement in Latin America in the 1950s. The liberationist view is that individualistic concepts of property rights

59 Ibid., 191, § 145.
60 Ibid., 160.
61 Quoted in ibid., 161
62 Finger, *A Contemporary Anabaptist Theology*, 243–48.
63 Ibid.

have led to forms of global capitalism through which the poor have systematically been oppressed. Drawing on Marxist thought, many liberation theologians argue that the "Christian view of property" requires a political order that restricts property rights over capital goods. Some liberationists even argue that violence is justified to overthrow the existing legal-political order, not least in redistributing capital to the poor.[64]

The relationship between liberation theology and Marxism is a significant point of tension that bears directly on our consideration of Christian thought and property law. Marx, of course, rejected the concept of private property. The Communist Manifesto tells us that "the theory of Communists may be summed up in the single sentence: Abolition of private property."[65] Scholars dispute precisely what Marx's opposition to "private property" meant – many argue that Marxism seeks common ownership only of the means of industrial production – but in any event a Marxist political/legal system would not endorse the kinds of private property rights over land and capital resources found in Anglo-American law.[66]

In their handbook *Introducing Liberation Theology*, Leonardo Boff (a leading liberation theologian) and his brother Clodovis Boff state that

> Liberation theology uses Marxism purely as an *instrument*. It does not venerate it as it venerates the gospel. And it feels on obligation to account to social scientists for any use it may make correct or otherwise of Marxist terminology and ideas, though it does feel obliged to account to the poor, to their faith and hope, and to the ecclesial community, for such use.[67]

This ambiguity about Marxism leads to ambiguities about what, precisely, liberation theology says about private property. At the very least, consistent with Marxism, liberation theology criticizes the concentration of ownership of land or other capital resources in individuals or corporations who do not actually produce material goods rather than in the laborers who produce those goods.

64 James Cone, *A Black Theology of Liberation, Fortieth Anniversary Edition* (New York: Orbis, 2011).

65 Karl Marx and Friedrich Engles, "Manifesto of the Communist Party," in *Karl Marx and Friedrich Engels: Collected Works*, vol. 6 (New York: International Publishers, 1976), 498.

66 For a discussion of some of the scholarly debates about Marx's view of private property, see, e.g., George C. Brenkert, "Freedom and Private Property in Marx," *Philosophy and Public Affairs*, 8, no. 2 (Winter 1979): 122–47.

67 Leonardo Boff and Clodovis Boff, *Introducing Liberation Theology* (New York: Maryknoll/Orbis Books, 1987). For a discussion of the ongoing relationship between Liberation Theology and the Roman Catholic Church under Pope Francis, see Jeffrey Klaiber, S.J., "Pope Francis and Liberation Theology," *Political Theology Today* (December 6, 2013), http://www.politicaltheology.com/blog/pope-francis-and-liberation-theology-jeffrey-klaiber-s-j/; "Pope Francis and the Ongoing Dialogue of Liberation Theology," *Political Theology Today* (December 20, 2013), available at http://www.politicaltheology.com/blog/pope-francis-and-the-ongoing-dialogue-of-liberation-theology/.

Since liberation theology first developed in the Latin American context, where poor farmers and migrant workers were being displaced by commercial developers, "land" is a significant theme for liberation theology and praxis. Liberation theologian Miguel De la Torre writes that "[t]he commodification of land – making it into something that can be bought and sold – turns it into a source of power over others and can also turn it into an idol, something to be worshipped."[68] De la Torre argues that "when wealth is concentrated in the hands of a few, democracy is threatened if the privileged few use their property to control the direction and policies of the society."[69] He focuses particularly on the historical origins of property title claims, which in North America are always ultimately rooted in violence and fraud against Native Americans and the forced labor of African slaves. Property rights, De la Torre says, encode a zero-sum game: "[w]hen property (and free markets) secures the liberty of the wealthy class, with the help of the government, it is generally secured at the expense of a marginalized class that becomes increasingly alienated."[70] For De la Torre, the root of Western property law lies in Roman law, incorporated into Christendom as a result of the Constantinian shift, rather than Christian concepts.

Conclusion

As this chapter suggests, there is no single "Christian view" of private property. The Biblical witness and the historic reflection of various Christian traditions on the subject are vast and sometimes inconsistent. The "mainstream" traditional view of historical Christian thought is that private property is useful and good for the ordering of temporal society, and that positive law should protect rights in private property, but also that private property is necessary because of covetousness and sin. Private property would not have been part of the original state of humanity in the Garden, nor will it be necessary in heaven. Given its necessity in the present age, however, it can be enacted in ways that are consistent with Christian charity and with created human dignity. A modern variant of this view, perhaps most evident in the Catholic Encyclical *Rerum Novarum*, seems to go beyond the mainstream traditional view in suggesting a natural right to private property based on something like Locke's labor theory. At the same time, more radical perspectives, both from some corners of Anabaptist thought and from liberation theology, argue for the abolition of private property, or at least for the common ownership of the means of production of capital goods. In these more radical perspectives, common ownership might apply primarily as a rule internal to the Christian community, or, for some forms of liberation theology, this ideal might extend to the broader society through positive law that benefits the poor.

68 Miguel Della Torre, *Doing Christian Ethics from the Margins*, 2nd ed. (New York: Orbis Books, 2014).

69 Ibid.

70 Ibid.

It seems particularly difficult for Christian Anglo-American legal scholars to assess this sprawling milieu in light of our common law concepts of private property. To the extent the common law situates private property in a metaphysical matrix, it tends toward a Hobbsean social contract or Lockean labor theory framing. Even within its varying emphases, Christian thought here at least can remind us that the metaphysics of modern Western property law are embedded in an atheistic narrative of scarcity rather than in the Christian doctrines of creation and grace. As Jeremy Waldron has noted, systems of property rights are necessary only because

> [i]n all times and places with which we are familiar, material resources are scarce relative to human demands that are made on them.... Scarcity, as philosophers from Hume to Rawls have pointed out, is a presupposition of all sensible talk about property.[71]

Waldron further suggests that "[i]f this assumption were ever to fail (as Marx believed it someday would) then the traditional problem of the nature and justification of rival types of property systems would probably disappear."[72]

The Christian doctrines of creation and consummation tell us that scarcity is not the real state of things. In the "Garden" – in creation as God intended it – there is abundance, not scarcity. The creation myths of Western property law, including those of Locke and Hobbes, contradict Christian doctrine. Both Hobbes and Locke thought of nature as inherently scarce and of human competition or human reason as a kind of inherent human dominion over nature. Christian theology views creation as a gift of plenitude and of the original state of human dominion as a form of stewardship over this gift. Moreover, even after the advent of human sin, which does entail violent competition and scarcity, for Christian thought the eschatological goal of redeemed creation is the fullness of the Divine life, plenitude without end. The promise of eschatological fulfillment secured by Christ's resurrection, for Christian thought, diffuses any inclination to anxious accumulation or desperate claims to possession. This promised eschatological fulfillment, likewise, is a gift, initiated and completed by God's grace in Christ. The proper rubric for Christian thought, then, is not "scarcity" but "gift."

At the same time, even in the Garden, there was "work," and work was good. Even in the Garden, humanity was tasked with cultivation and stewardship – with "gardening!" Any garden is potentially subject to a tragedy of the commons, and "stewardship" implies the kind of dominion needed to avoid such tragedies. There is nothing inconsistent about some concept of dominion in the Garden – a dominion clearly given by God to Adam in Genesis 1. The problem, though, is not really "scarcity," because there was more than enough in

71 Jeremy Waldron, *The Right to Private Property* (Oxford: Clarendon Press, 1988), 31.
72 Ibid., 31–32.

the Garden, and there will be more than enough in the coming Kingdom, for everyone's needs, and no one's "needs" will fall outside good, just proportions.

But what about the present time, which is neither in "the Garden" nor in the accomplished eschatological future? For Christian theology, the Kingdom of God has already broken into the present world in Christ. Yet, it is equally true, and painfully obvious, that the eschatological future has not yet fully arrived. How does the "already" of the Kingdom of God arrived in the incarnation, death, and resurrection of Christ relate to the "not yet" of the Kingdom's fullness? This is one of the great points of tension in Christian theology, which directly impacts how we might think about the Church and its relationship to the temporal powers of the world (ecclesiology) and God's work in, through, and outside the Church in the salvation of the world (soteriology). This is precisely the point at which the different streams of Christian thought surveyed in this chapter – Catholicism, the Magisterial Reformation, the Radical Reformation, and Liberationist – begin to diverge. At the same time, all of these various streams of Christian thought recognize that however we might characterize the precise arrangement of spiritual and temporal power in the present age, the preservation of humanity, the goods of culture that still remain, the hope of a better future – all of these, too, are gifts of God's grace.

We find it hard to imagine a world without idolatry and covetousness, where nothing is hoarded and nothing is stolen, but that possibility is the driving force of Biblical imagination. In some way that we may not fully agree upon or understand, our lives now, in this present age, echo the gift of the good creation and participate already in the gift of the coming future of God's reign, even in the face of our own sin. And *this* suspended middle is the space in which we are called to respond now, including through the positive law.[73] All of this means that, for a Christian legal theorist, the role of private property rights in this present Earthly city must remain an interesting problem.

73 I take this phrase from John Milbank, *The Suspended Middle; Henri de Lubac and the Debate Concerning the Supernatural* (Grand Rapids, MI: Eerdmans, 2005).

5 Augustinian property

William S. Brewbaker III

Introduction

Augustine of Hippo (354–430) was a bishop, not a political philosopher. Although his *City of God* is a classic text of the Western political tradition, it is fundamentally a work of apologetics, written to defend the Christian faith against charges that it had brought about the fall of Rome. Unlike many political texts, *City of God* does not attempt to set forth the conditions for a fully just public order; Augustine does not, in fact, believe such an order is possible in this life. However, in the process of explaining why Roman society could not survive, he also explains how humanity's fundamental problem—our proud refusal of divine love—works itself out in our political and legal institutions.

Although Augustine did an enormous amount of writing in addition to the *City of God*, relatively little of what he wrote touched directly upon the institution of private property or the laws that should govern it. To complicate matters further, what he says specifically about property is almost always found when he is giving instruction about some other subject. However, what he does say reveals (or so this chapter will argue) a high degree of continuity between his thinking about property and his thinking about politics more generally. Like government itself, the institution of private property would not exist apart from human rebellion against God. And, like political authority more generally, property law serves the necessary, distasteful, and yet ultimately beneficial purpose of restoring a degree of social order and restraining evil.

Disordered loves

Augustine famously traces the general unhappiness of the human condition back to our disordered loves. What is wrong with the world and we who inhabit it originates in our refusal of God's love in favor of disproportionate love of ourselves and creation.[1] Refusing to find our satisfaction in God, we seek for it in

1 For introductions to Augustine and his political and social thought, see Herbert A. Deane, *The Political and Social Ideas of St. Augustine* (New York: Columbia University Press, 1963); R.W. Dyson, *The Pilgrim City: Social and Political Ideas in the Writings of St. Augustine of Hippo* (Rochester, NY: The Boydell Press, 2001); R.A. Markus, *Saeculum: History and Society in the*

the created order, where it can never be found. When our dissatisfaction persists, we perversely assume that the problem is that we do not yet have enough of the created objects we love, rather than owning up to the fact that we love the wrong things. We may put our hope in our possessions—or sex, or power, or reputation—but if we do, we will never have enough of any of them. But the one who trusts in God finds that he has enough of the good things in creation to be satisfied.

Augustine employs the distinction between *enjoyment* and *use* to illuminate the human person's relation to any particular person or thing in the created order: "[t]o enjoy something is to value it in itself, for itself; to use something is to value it for its instrumental value for another end."[2] Only God is worthy of our enjoyment; all loves of created things must be ordered according to the fundamental enjoyment of God; indeed, our enjoyment of lesser things—even our fellow human beings—must only be "in God":

> When you enjoy a man in God, it is God rather than the man whom you enjoy; for you take joy in Him who will make you blessed, and you will rejoice that you have reached Him in whom you place your hope ....[3]

To say that something or someone should only be used and not enjoyed is not to denigrate it or her; Augustine is not calling on us not to love other people or the good things that we find in the world. He is simply asserting that—for the reasons elaborated above—even good things can become impediments to human flourishing when love for them is not ordered in light of the supreme good, which is God.[4] Money (and other possessions) is to be used as a "means of assisting your pilgrimage, not a means of firing your lust."[5]

Given what has been said so far, it should be no surprise that money and possessions pose special threats to the human person. As one commentator has put it, on Augustine's view

> [t]here is no limit to sinful man's desire for material goods; his life consists in a restless quest for satisfaction by means of one object after another. The moment one desire is satisfied, another rises to demand fulfillment; so there is no rest ... for the anguished soul ... .[6]

Theology of St. Augustine (New York: Cambridge University Press, 1970); Paul Weithman, "Augustine's Political Philosophy," in *The Cambridge Companion to Augustine*, ed. Eleanore Stump (Cambridge: Cambridge University Press, 2001), 234–52.

2 Charles Mathewes, "On Using the World," in *Having: Property and Possession in Religious and Social Life*, eds. William Schweiker and Charles Mathewes (Grand Rapids, MI: Eerdmans, 2004) 189, 202.

3 *On Christian Doctrine*, XXXIII.37 (D.W. Robertson, Jr., trans. 1958).

4 Mathewes, "On Using the World," 201–08.

5 *Tractatus in Ioannis evangelium* 40:10 in Dyson, *The Pilgrim City*, 118; see also *Ep. 153*.

6 Deane, *The Political and Social Ideas of St. Augustine*, 45. Even the poor do not escape. Ibid. at 46. See also *Sermo* 50:2–7.

Human desire for riches persists even though the love of money is the source of a great deal of pain and suffering both to ourselves and to others:

> The rich man is anxious with fears, pining with discontent, burning with covetousness, never secure, always uneasy, panting from the perpetual strife of his enemies, adding to his patrimony indeed by these miseries to an immense degree, but by these additions also heaping up most bitter cares. But that other man of moderate wealth is contented with a small and compact estate, most dear to his own family, enjoying the sweetest peace with his kindred, neighbors, and friends, in piety religious, benignant in mind, healthy in body, in life frugal, in morals chaste, in conscience secure. I know not whether anyone can be such a fool, that he dare hesitate which to prefer.[7]

Material possessions are, for Augustine, both a source of oppression to the weak, and the occasion of shameful desires to the strong. Our desires to inherit property cause us to wish for another's death, our desires to make a profit cause us to wish for someone else's loss; we "wish to be elevated by the fall of others," and we "desire other men to sell their goods so that [we] may buy them."[8] We are like big fish devouring smaller ones, only to be eaten ourselves by a still larger fish.[9]

Our lust for property threatens not only others but also ourselves. Those with money are preyed upon by their friends and enemies.[10] And our love for money threatens to make us enemies of God. Augustine advises that we learn to relinquish the love of anything we "must one day lose and let go of, whether in life or in death" because God may one day call upon us to lose it. If we are unwilling to do so, we may find ourselves hating God for his providence.[11]

Finally, money deceives us and invites us to self-deception. We easily persuade ourselves that we do not love our possessions, but we cannot know how deep our attachment runs until we begin to lose them.[12] Our self-deception is all the more pernicious since material possessions make promises they cannot fulfill: "And this world does not make good what it promises: it is a liar; it deceives you." Not only do we never get everything we want, even when we do get it,

> as soon as [we have] attained to it, it is no longer valued by [us]: other things begin to be desired, other vain things hoped for .... The reason why these things are no longer valued is that they cannot stand, because they are not what He is.... Whatever else you grasp at is miserable, for only He who made you in his own likeness can satisfy you....[13]

7 *De civitate Dei* 4:3 in Dyson, *The Pilgrim City*, 115.
8 Ibid.
9 Ibid.
10 See *Enarrationes in psalmos* 131:18; see also *Sermo* 115:4.
11 *Sermo* 125:11 in Dyson, *The Pilgrim City*, 112.
12 See *De vera religione* 47:92.
13 *Sermo* 125:11 in Dyson, *The Pilgrim City*, 112. Cf., *Enarrationes in psalmos* 39:7.

The ethics of ownership

Augustine's writings concerning the ethics of property ownership must be understood not only in light of his account of the human person's disordered loves, but also in the context of an evolving tradition of Christian reflection.[14] Augustine follows Ambrose and Chrysostom in noting the dangers of property ownership in stark terms, but he nevertheless refuses to follow them in declaring private ownership wrongful per se.[15] While lust for money leads to misery and suffering, "none of this is the fault of gold and silver."[16] Money, he writes, "bring[s] torment to the heart of the miser, but [it] greatly assist[s] the intentions of the benevolent."[17] He also notes specifically that acquiring wealth need not entail sin.[18] Nevertheless, he is clear about the obligations that accompany ownership of property. Although private property may be a permissible civil arrangement, and acquiring property is no sin, "the earth is [still] the LORD's,"[19] and those who own property are in possession of resources that, at bottom, belong to God.[20]

Augustine's affirmative account of what it means to use wealth also draws upon an earlier Christian concept—*communication.*[21] Oliver O'Donovan explains that

> [to] 'communicate' is to hold some thing as common, to make it a common possession, to treat is as 'ours,' rather than 'yours' or 'mine.' The partners to a communication form a community, a 'we,' in relation to the object in which they participate.'[22]

For Augustine, to communicate includes, first and foremost, an ethic of responding to need; those who have resources are to show hospitality to strangers, feed the hungry, clothe the naked, ransom the captives, aid the needy, heal the sick, and so on.[23] This sort of sharing also involves the building of churches and perhaps other public spaces.[24] Significantly, communication blurs the stark lines we moderns tend to draw between private and common ownership.[25]

14 See generally David Opderbeck's fine contribution to this volume. Augustine's writings must be understood in their historical and social context. See generally Peter Brown, *Through the Eye of a Needle* (Princeton, NJ: Princeton, 2012).

15 See, e.g., *Enarrationes in psalmos* 51:10.

16 *Sermo* 50:2–7, in Dyson, *The Pilgrim City*, 122–24.

17 Ibid.

18 *Sermo* 113:4 in Dyson, *The Pilgrim City*, 115.

19 Ps. 24:1 (KJV).

20 See *Sermo* 50:2–7.

21 See *Sermo* 85:4–7; *Sermo* 52:7. Negatively, the wealthy are to avoid the temptation to oppress and defraud others. See *Sermo* 85:4–7.

22 See Oliver O'Donovan, *The Ways of Judgment* (Grand Rapids, MI: Eerdmans, 2005), 242.

23 *Epistulae* 157:4:32–35; *Sermo* 50:2–7.

24 *Sermo* 50:2–7. On the significance of such activities in Augustine's late Roman social context, see Brown, *Through the Eye of a Needle*, 322–58.

25 See O'Donovan, *Ways of Judgment*, 275–76. But see Dyson, *Pilgrim City*, 104–06.

Augustine never specifies a precise benchmark for appropriate giving. Instead he frames his demand for generosity within Christian moral and eschatological narratives. The moral narrative has much to say about appropriate attitudes toward wealth. The starting point is one of correct assessment of the relative value of material goods: you may have come by your material wealth honestly, he says, but "[d]o not call these things riches, for they are not truly so. They are full of poverty, and always liable to accidents."[26] More fundamentally, Augustine counsels against putting one's trust in material wealth; one ought not to rely on riches as security for a happy life or future.[27] Wealth is not something that should be sought after,[28] even by the poor.[29] Rather, one should cultivate contentment with one's material possessions and station in life.[30]

The eschatological narrative calls attention to the future of the world and the church, as well as to the role of Providence in the distribution of material possessions. The Christian is on an earthly pilgrimage that will lead to a heavenly home. Wealth bestowed by God may be a gift that furnishes the donee with the opportunity to please God by doing good.[31] It is a means of providential support for those in need[32] as well as "a means of testing humanity and of punishing greed,"[33] exposing the hearts of those who possess it.[34] Money should be

> the means of assisting your pilgrimage, not ... of firing your lust .... You are passing on your journey, and this life is nothing but a wayside inn. Use money in the way that the traveller at an inn uses table, cup, jug and bed; not intending to stay there, but to leave them behind.[35]

Accordingly, Augustine urges those with more than they need to err on the side of generosity:

> 'Let them be rich in good works, let them distribute easily, let them communicate.' [I Tim 6:17] Must they, then, lose all they have? He said, 'Let them communicate', not 'Let them give everything away.' Let them keep for themselves as much as is sufficient for them; let them keep more than is sufficient: let us give a certain portion of it. How much? A tenth? ... Ask yourselves; consider what you do and what means you have to do it:

26 *Sermo* 113:4, in Dyson, *The Pilgrim City*, 115, 116.
27 See *Epistulae* 157:4:32–35; *Sermo* 125:11.
28 See *Epistulae* 130:2:3; *Sermo* 113:4; *Enarrationes in psalmos* 131:18.
29 See *Sermo* 85:4–7; *Enarrationes in psalmos* 131:19.
30 See *De civitate Dei* 4:3. Poverty is not the same as misery—there are some poor people who are happy and others who are miserable. See *Sermo* 50:2–7.
31 See *Sermo* 50:2–7.
32 See *Sermo* 85:4–7.
33 *Sermo* 50:2–7 in Dyson, *The Pilgrim City*, 122–23.
34 In the case of the greedy, the immediate punishment is the mental torment that accompanies fear of losing what they have. Ibid.
35 *Tractatus in Ioannis evangelium* 40:10 in Dyson, *The Pilgrim City*, 118.

> how much you give, how much you leave for yourselves; what you spend on mercy and what you keep back for pleasure. So, then: 'Let them distribute easily, let them communicate, laying up in store for themselves a good foundation against the time to come, that they may lay hold on eternal life.' [I Tim. 6:19][36]

In Augustine's eschatological narrative, the backdrop of eternity relativizes material goods. In more ordinary times, there may be wealthy Christians "who have decided to keep their riches in order to win merit with God by using them for good works."[37] However, Christians faced with the choice between losing their money and denying the faith must renounce their wealth. In such a case, Christians ought to "hate their riches, ... hate their parents, brothers, children, wives .... [even] go so far as to hate their own life rather than risk being forsaken by a forsaken Christ."[38]

The purposes and content of property law

Up to this point we have been concerned with Augustine's understanding of property as a matter of theology and ethics. Now we turn to his views about the origins of property and property law. One of Augustine's most detailed discussions of private property, and especially property law, appears in *Epistle 153*, written in 414 AD to a Roman magistrate, Macedonius, who had inquired about the then-current episcopal practice of interceding for condemned prisoners. The subject matter of the magistrate's inquiry provides Augustine with an opportunity to explain law's role more generally, and, in the course of doing so, he brings the institution of private property into the picture.

The thrust of Macedonius's complaint involves an appeal to the church's own practice regarding grave sin. Under traditional church practice, a penitent was allowed only one opportunity for formal restoration. Why, Macedonius wonders, "[i]f sin is so strictly forbidden by the Lord, that no opportunity of repentance is granted after the first, how can we argue that any crime of whatever sort should be forgiven?"[39] Augustine provides a lengthy defense of the practice of appealing for clemency in light of this objection.

After responding generally, Augustine responds to a specific charge—Macedonius's complaint that "human behavior has come to this pass that men wish to have the punishment of their crime remitted and at the same time to keep the profit which they gained by their evil deeds."[40] This leads Augustine to

36 *Sermo 85:4–7* in Dyson, *The Pilgrim City*, 120.

37 *Epistulae* 157:4:32–35 in Dyson, *The Pilgrim City*, 121–22.

38 Ibid. Cf., *Sermo* 85:4–7.

39 *Letter* 153, trans. Sister W. Parsons, S.N.D. in *From Irenaeus to Grotius: A Sourcebook in Christian Political Thought*, eds. Oliver O'Donovan and Joan Lockwood O'Donovan (Grand Rapids, MI: Eerdmans 1999), 119, 120.

40 Ibid., para. 20.

address the need for restitution and implicitly brings him to the subject of private property. Augustine categorically affirms the obligation of a thief to make restitution provided the thief has the means to do so.[41]

Augustine's next move, however, takes the reader by surprise. Turning the tables, Augustine suggests that Macedonius's zeal for restitution perhaps does not extend as far as it should. Augustine does not believe that the problem of evil is something that must only be confronted by one group in a society but that can be ignored by a more "righteous" group; everyone must acknowledge his or her own responsibility for the failure of peace and justice that characterizes every society.[42] It follows that not only penitent thieves should make restitution; others, including government officials like Macedonius, as well as lawyers and usurers, should consider their obligations as well!

At last, near the close of the letter, Augustine speaks of private property directly, in what is perhaps the most representative single passage of his writings on the subject:

> And now, if we look carefully at what is written: 'The whole world is the wealth of the faithful man, but the unfaithful one has not a penny' (Prov. 17:6 Septuagint), do we not prove that those who seem to rejoice in lawfully acquired gains, and do not know how to use them, are really in possession of other men's property? Certainly, what is lawfully possessed is not another's property, but 'lawfully' means justly and justly means rightly. He who uses his wealth badly possesses it wrongfully, and wrongful possession means that it is another's property. You see, then, how many there are who ought to make restitution of another's goods, although those to whom restitution is due may be a few; wherever they are, their claim to just possession is in proportion to their indifference to wealth. Obviously, no one possesses justice unlawfully; whoever does not love it does not have it; but money is wrongly possessed by bad men while good men who love it least have the best right to it. In this life the wrong of evil possessors is endured and among them certain laws are established which are called civil laws, not because they bring men to make a good use of their wealth, but because those who make bad use of it become thereby less injurious. This comes about either because some of them become faithful and fervent—and these have a right to all things—or because those who live among them are not hampered by their evil deeds, but are tested until they come to that City where they are heirs to eternity, where the just alone have a place, the wise alone leadership, and those who are there possess what is truly their own.

41 "Often, however, the thief dissipates the goods either by connivance with other offenders or by living an evil life himself, and has nothing left with which to make restitution. To him we certainly cannot say, 'pay back what you took,' unless we believe that he has it and denied it'." Ibid. See also ibid., para. 21 (intercessor who does not force thief capable of making restitution to do so is a party to the theft).

42 See Weithman, "Augustine's Political Philosophy," 237.

> Yet even here, we do not intercede to prevent restitution from being made, according to earthly customs and laws, although we should like you to be indulgent to evil-doers, not to make them take pleasure or persist in their evil, but because whenever any of them do become good, God is appeased by a sacrifice of mercy, and if evil-doers did not find him merciful there would be no good men.[43]

The passage begins with a puzzling quotation: "The whole world is the wealth of the faithful man, but the unfaithful one has not a penny."[44] One would have expected a different biblical starting point, such as, for example, "The earth is the LORD's, and the fullness thereof, the world and those who dwell therein,"[45] or "And all who believed were together and had all things in common. And they were selling their possessions and belongings and distributing the proceeds to all, as any had need."[46] Both statements are invoked with some regularity in Christian thought as counterweights to human pretensions to sovereignty, especially individual sovereignty, over the material world.

Moreover, the meaning of the quotation is itself obscure, even for a proverb. Clearly, the whole world is not owned in any visible way by the faithful person,[47] nor is it the case that the "unfaithful" are uniformly penniless. And yet, the letter in which the statement appears is addressed to a magistrate and is supposed to be relevant to the question of how the law should work. Of what relevance is the proverb for such purposes?

On its face, Augustine seems to be using the proverb to make a psychological claim about the respective attitudes toward money and possessions of (i) those who put their fundamental trust in God and (ii) those who put their trust primarily in possessions. As we have seen, those in the former group feel abundantly provided for even if they are not rich, while those in the latter group experience scarcity at the psychological level regardless of how much wealth they have.

However, Augustine says he is using the proverb to "*prove* that those who seem to rejoice in lawfully acquired gains, and do not know how to use them, are really in possession of other men's property." In other words, Augustine seems to be citing the proverb as an instance of divine law that underwrites a moral, if not a legal, claim about rightful possession of material goods.

The mark of the faithful person is the right ordering of the person's loves. Specifically, as discussed earlier, the faithful person "uses" created goods and "enjoys" God alone. It is thus no surprise that Augustine singles out the distinguishing marks of wrongful possession as "rejoic[ing] in lawfully acquired

43 *Letter* 153, para. 26.

44 Prov. 17:6b (LXX).

45 Augustine elsewhere connects God's ownership of everything with his account connecting property rights and appropriate use. See *Sermo* 50:2–7.

46 Acts 2:44–45 (ESV).

47 Unless Jesus Christ is that "faithful man," in which case Christians believe they are mystically united to him by faith and, in that sense, share in his wealth.

gains" and not "know[ing] how to use them." The unfaithful person delights in the possessions themselves, rather than in their usefulness in loving God and, by extension, neighbor. The person who would make his possessions ends in themselves "has not a penny" in the sense of rightful possession, even if his "gains" are "lawfully acquired."

Even if we are not surprised by Augustine's definition of appropriate use of property, we might still wonder why he would conclude that someone who is overly attached to rightfully acquired property ought not to have it. We do not usually conclude that someone who uses his property in a noxious way (e.g., commits a nuisance) thereby becomes a thief or a trespasser. In our law, and even in our conventional morality, there would seem to be an important distinction between *wrongly possessing* (misusing) "lawfully acquired" property and being in *wrongful possession* of it.

Augustine's answer is that one's "claim to just possession is in proportion to [one's] indifference to wealth." Again, from a contemporary perspective, this claim hardly seems plausible; it is simply not clear what bearing one's attitude toward one's wealth has on one's entitlement to it. Augustine, however, elsewhere defines the virtue of justice as the right ordering of one's loves: "love serving God only, and therefore ruling well all else, as subject to man."[48] Justice is the state of affairs that pertains when an entire community orders its individual and corporate affairs according to the love and service of God.[49] The love of money is both itself disordered and a consequence of humanity's fundamental disorder—its prideful rejection of God in favor of created things.

In a just world, possessions would be used rather than loved (enjoyed), and shared (communicated) based on love for God and neighbor. Justice is what the world looks like when everyone's actions are motivated by ordered loves. In such a world, "rightful possession" could exist, but would not be an especially relevant concept. Wealth would not be regarded as important for its own sake; one's uses of it would be ordered toward the good of others and the community, so the identity of the owner might not make much difference in any event. Not much of any consequence (to such people) would be riding on the question of whether any given thing was common property or private property.

As Augustine is famous for noting, we do not live in such a world. In our world, "money is wrongly possessed by bad men while good men who love it least have the best right to it." And yet, Augustine disappoints us by seeming to propose precisely nothing by way of remedy to this deplorable situation. He simply notes that "[i]n this life the wrong of evil possessors is endured and among them [civil] laws are established, ... because those who make bad use of [property] become thereby less injurious." This happens because either the rich come to faith and become rightful possessors of their property, or, if they do not, the law at least keeps them from devouring the possessions of others. Worse yet,

48 *De Mor. Eccl. Cath.*, XV, 25, in Deane, *Political and Social Ideas of St. Augustine*, 83.

49 See Deane, *Political and Social Ideas of St. Augustine*, 119.

we see in other writings that he seems to acknowledge virtually no limits on the possible content of state-enacted laws governing property ownership and use.[50]

If property and civil authority are tightly linked in virtually all political thought, the link is especially close in Augustine's case. Neither the state nor property is, for Augustine, natural. However, each serves both an ameliorative and a punitive function. Although human beings were inclined toward fellowship and peace prior to the Fall,[51] sin destroyed all that: "Once the nature of man has been corrupted by sin each man seeks to gain possessions and wealth at the expense of others and each seeks to gain mastery over others."[52] Since a society composed of unrestrained individuals seeking to dominate each other could not survive, Augustine sees the state as a merciful ordinance of God, even as the lust for political power is itself an expression of human rebellion.[53] State compulsion is ultimately a blessing in a fallen world, providing relative order and peace. Even a bad state is better than the anarchy that would obtain without it.[54]

If the state is the kind response of a merciful God, preserving his creation even in the midst of its suicidal rebellion, it is also, at the same time, a punishment for that rebellion.[55] The natural freedom and equality that would have obtained among all human beings is replaced with hierarchical human relationships underwritten and enforced by acts of violence.[56] Even those who find themselves in the position of exercising political authority may suffer under its burden,[57] and those who are ruled by them often suffer even more.[58] Indeed, God may providentially order human rule in order to chasten or punish a rebellious society.[59] Even where God's motive is not to punish (and how are we to know?), the unjust actions of a harsh ruler may serve as a test of the righteous person's faith.

Like government, the institution of private property originates in sin and serves both ameliorative and punitive functions. Around 900 years after Augustine wrote about private property, Thomas Aquinas would write that although common property is natural, private ownership is a nonetheless more useful in a fallen world.[60] Augustine never endorses private ownership in these terms, but it is hard to imagine him disagreeing with Thomas's assessment of private ownership's ameliorative effects. Free-riding and quarreling, in particular, are endemic to a fallen world. Nevertheless, as we have seen, Augustine's explanation of why private property is a good institution is a good bit darker than Thomas's: laws protecting property rights keep the rich and powerful from doing even greater

50 See *Epistle*, 93.
51 See Deane, *Political and Social Ideas of St. Augustine*, 78–79, 93 & n.70.
52 Ibid., 93.
53 See generally Dyson, *The Pilgrim City*, at 48–58.
54 Deane, *Political and Social Ideas of St. Augustine*, 144.
55 Ibid., 117.
56 Ibid., 138–39.
57 See *City of God*, Bk.XIX, ch. 6; see also *Ep.* 153 paras. 20, 22.
58 Deane, *Political and Social Ideas of St. Augustine*, 133.
59 Ibid., 145–46.
60 See Thomas Aquinas, *Summa Theologiae* II–II Q. 66.2.

damage to ordinary people in their acquisitive quest. For Augustine, this is a sufficient justification for the protection of private ownership.

As for private property's punitive function, laws protecting private ownership punish those who commit property crimes out of greed and disregard for their neighbor. There is also an indirect punishment inflicted by the institution of private property. As discussed above, riches are potentially a great source of suffering to their owner, threatening her with loss of friendship (of both God and other human beings), self-deception, and inordinate care and worries. And, as with government, property is an occasion for testing of the righteous person's faith; both riches and poverty threaten to subvert the believer's pursuit of eternal goods.[61]

It is worth noting that just about any regime of private property could provide at least some of the benefits Augustine identifies in his discussion of government generally and property law specifically. As long as there are limits on the ways one person can interfere with another's holdings, there will be some constraint of evil, some degree of peace, and some degree of testing for the good and punishment for the wicked. This does not necessarily mean, however, that Augustine is indifferent to the content of property laws that those in power impose.

We know, for example, that Augustine thinks that there are better and worse societies, and that these societies are made relatively better or worse according to the quality of the things they love. Peoples who love better things can expect to have a better state. In addition, Augustine believes in natural law, which he understands chiefly according to the negative version of the Golden Rule: do not do unto others what you would not have others do unto you.[62] The connection between this form of the Golden Rule and Augustine's primary justification of property is easily drawn. The recognition of property rights may serve to protect property in the hands of those who should not own it because they care too much about it, but it also protects the limited holdings of the less powerful against the depredations of their rich counterparts.

Augustinian property law

Might there be features of a real-world property system that could appropriately be called "Augustinian"? Let us, for purposes of argument, accept at face value Augustine's claim that "those who seem to rejoice in lawfully acquired gains, and do not know how to use them, are really in possession of other men's property."[63] Although Augustine clearly would not make obedience to this maxim a condition for the validity of real-world property law, might it play a part in a real-world Augustinian property system? What else might be distinctive about an Augustinian regime of property law?

61 See *Enarrationes in psalmos* 85:3.

62 See *Enarrationes in psalmos* 57:1; *Tractatus in Ioannis evangelium* 49:12; Dyson, *Pilgrim City*, 47–48.

63 See *Letter* 153, para. 26.

Thousands of law students have been introduced to the law of property with an extended study of *Pierson v. Post*.[64] The case involves a contest over the pelt of a fox that had been killed on a "waste land." From a course organization perspective, there are good reasons for starting with a case like *Pierson*. The average person experiences property ownership by first acquiring things, then using them, and finally transferring them. Why not begin with a case about how things are acquired? Better still, why not begin with a case about how to acquire something that nobody else has ever owned? Cases involving the acquisition of wild animals likewise invite consideration of where and how and why property rights might have come into being in the first place.

More recently, *Pierson* has been displaced by *Johnson v. M'Intosh*[65] as the opening chestnut in many Property courses. *Johnson* involves a dispute over a land title acquired from the acknowledged aboriginal owners of the land, the Piankeshaw Indians. The holder of the deed from the Piankeshaw found his title contested by someone who claimed title on the basis of a governmental grant of land (known as a "patent") from the United States. Although the grantee under the federal patent was later in time, and the claim of the Indians to the land was acknowledged by the Court, the patentee nevertheless prevailed, the government's superior claim being grounded in rights of discovery. The case abounds with ironies—chiefly the invocation of the discovery principle *against* the claims of holders who were prior in time! Justice Marshall laments the unjust result in the case, but reluctantly concludes that the law of the conqueror must prevail.

One commentator has described *Johnson v. M'Intosh* as part of the property "anti-canon."[66] As noted above, *Pierson* and similar cases seek to justify (or at least explain) the rules of American property law and the entitlements they generate by finding a basis for them in morality or policy. *Johnson*, however, exposes both the role of raw power in establishing entitlement to property and the particularly disastrous consequences a property law system may have for the powerless.

Even though *Johnson* tends to subvert the traditional justifications for property rights, it nevertheless sits easily within an Augustinian framework. Like the *Johnson* Court, Augustine shows relatively little interest in the question of whether the legal rules governing acquisition of property put it into the "right" hands. We may understand his position a little better if we stop to consider more fully the contours of the traditional Anglo-American approach to property law, where title is typically awarded on the basis of a historical pedigree. Ideally, the chain of title is initiated when previously unowned real or personal property is acquired in a legitimate way—i.e., by creation, capture, or discovery. Once someone is declared the "owner" of the object, she will enjoy more or less complete

64 3 Cai. R. 175, 1805 N.Y.

65 21 U.S. (8 Wheat.) 543 (1823).

66 Stuart Banner, *How the Indians Lost Their Land: Law and Power on the Frontier* (Cambridge, MA: Belknap Press, 2005), 11–12.

freedom to use the property as she sees fit, to transfer it to someone else, and to exclude others from it.

While Augustine holds that property can be (but is not always) acquired in a legitimate way through labor or legally permissible inheritance, the test he suggests for legitimate possession focuses entirely on attitudes toward property and its *use* rather than on the events leading to its acquisition. In this respect, an important parallel exists with Augustine's famous account of the origins of government. In one of the best-known passages in the *City of God*, Augustine asks "Justice removed, then, what are kingdoms except great bands of robbers?"[67] Augustine's question is more subversive than it might appear, since he holds that no real-world government is founded on justice,[68] although there is an earthly justice that appears in better or worse instantiations depending on place and time.[69]

For Augustine, political power comes into existence in the course of divine providence; whatever the defects of a particular regime, its presence is a blessing in the sense that it provides earthly peace (which cannot exist apart from state force) to a larger degree than would be the case in its absence. At the same time, the "blessing" of government may represent God's judgment on a wicked society or a test for the faithful. Augustine's discussion of the origins of government is largely limited to (1) assurance that God has ordained it in some form and (2) a repudiation of the notion that any government we may actually experience is established with true justice in view.

So it is with property in the Augustinian framework. That anyone should come to own any property is a matter of divine providence. Private ownership is, on balance, a blessing in that the rules protecting it keep the holdings of the weak more secure against the depredations of the strong than would otherwise occur. To some degree, at least, it is the instantiation of Augustine's preferred formulation of the natural law: "Do not do to others what you would not have them do to you." In a truly just world, however, those who loved property least would have it, because they could be counted upon to put it to use for the common good, unencumbered by their lust to acquire more of it. What *should* count in determining property rights is not how property was obtained, but what its owner does with it. As noted, this is pretty much the opposite of the usual order of emphasis in canonical American property law, where the question of title is primary and the presumption is against regulating the uses to which an owner can put property that has been lawfully acquired.

The latter point bears some emphasis. Along with *Pierson* and *Johnson*, beginning property students are also likely to encounter William Blackstone's famous definition of property as "that sole and despotic dominion which one man claims and exercises over the external things of the world, in total exclusion of the right

67 *City of God* Bk. IV, ch. 4, R.W. Dyson, trans. (Cambridge: Cambridge University Press, 1998).

68 See Deane, *Political and Social Ideas of St. Augustine*, 119–120. This is true even for a "Christian" state. See ibid. at 121.

69 See ibid. at 125–26.

of any other individual in the universe."[70] Blackstone's statement is, of course, an exaggeration, but it is not an accident that he chooses right and entitlement, rather than limitation and obligation, as the starting point in his discussion of private property. Consider the law of trespass and the right to exclude. The general principle of the law of trespass is that property owners may exclude others from their property, even where the entry might do the owners no harm.[71]

The "right to use" one's lawfully acquired property is similarly robust. To be sure, local communities can enact generally applicable use restrictions as a matter of public law, and landowners can enter into voluntary restrictions with respect to how their real estate will be used. However, the primary universal restriction on land use is found in the law of nuisance, a vague principle requiring landowners not to impose "substantial and unreasonable harm" on their neighbors by virtue of the uses they make of their own property. This principle is arguably less a communitarian norm than a begrudging recognition that neighbors cannot but be affected by other neighbors' decisions about land use.

Use of personal property is even less restricted. One may hoard one's wealth, set fire to it, invest it, give it to poor people or politicians, or lose it in Las Vegas slot machines, to mention but a few options. Public laws may impose some limits on the uses of funds, but these are usually incidental to other primary aims. Inheritance taxes, for example, may limit the ability to pass along wealth at one's death and may also penalize some inter vivos transfers.

We can summarize the preceding discussion of the relative emphases of an Augustinian property framework with that of traditional Anglo-American property law:

Augustinian Property
Fact of possession → Non-interference → "Communicate" or Forfeit

Anglo-American Property
Just Acquisition → Entitlement → Right to Use, Exclude, etc.

Traces of Augustinian property

Notwithstanding the fundamental distinctions between the property norms Augustine endorses and those that seem to animate American property law, it is possible to find points of convergence. This section briefly considers three examples: (1) adverse possession, (2) the law of nuisance, and (3) taxation.

Under the law of adverse possession, title owners can be divested of their property interests on the strength of longtime possession by non-owners. Although adverse possession is not usually justified in Augustinian terms,[72] it contains

70 William Blackstone, 2 *Commentaries on the Laws of England*, vol. 2, Of the Rights of Things (Chicago: University of Chicago Press, 2001[1763]), 3.

71 See, e.g., Jacque v. Steenberg Homes, 563 N.W.2d 154 (Wis. 1997).

72 See Jeffrey Stake, "The Uneasy Case for Adverse Possession," *Georgetown Law. Journal*, 89 (2001): 2419.

trace elements of the Augustinian approach. Where applied, adverse possession amounts to a refusal to look into the precise circumstances under which the new owner's possession of property was obtained.[73] As such, the doctrine is something of an embarrassment to traditional property concepts, and judges and academics have gone to great lengths to attempt to explain it, invoking grounds as various as economic productivity, psychology, and judicial efficiency.

The doctrine is anything but mysterious, however, when considered in Augustinian terms. One need only imagine a legal world in which courts say

> Stop trying to interfere with your neighbor's longstanding possession that has meant so little to you in the past. Why do you care so much? And stop pretending you have been so greatly wronged. Have you wronged no one? How carefully would you like us to look into *your* title?

Augustine's perspective helps us see that opponents of adverse possession trade on a notion of title in which the state is supposedly merely recognizing the title holder's pre-political natural right to property. Augustine will have none of this. To be sure, there are better and worse ways of acquiring property, but, for Augustine, property law is not first and foremost about the instantiation of absolute justice, but about the establishment of relative peace and relative justice. Once adverse possessors establish settled holdings, the non-interference duty applies to them, too. Not only that, adverse possessors are often seen as putting property to beneficial use, at least as compared to the relative indifference manifested by the previous owner.

We can likewise see traces, but only traces, of Augustinianism, in our laws respecting the use of property. The most straightforward private law restriction on use is the law of nuisance. As noted earlier, while the rule requires owners to take account of others' interests in the use of their properties, it is probably more of a concession that uses made by "sovereign owners" will regularly come into conflict than a reflection of the Augustinian idea that land and other wealth are to be put to use by the owner for the common good—i.e., communicated. And, apart from some criminal laws, we rarely see involuntary forfeiture of wealth as a penalty for misuse.

One might also argue that a system of progressive taxation reflects something of an Augustinian approach to the use of wealth. We might assume that someone whose loves are in order would use her wealth to support her family at a reasonable, though not extravagant, level of comfort. Features of the income tax system that shield an initial amount of earned wealth from taxation or tax it at a lower rate can be seen as reflecting a presumption that such "uses"

73 The presence of a good-faith requirement on the part of the adverse possessor in many jurisdictions complicates this description of the doctrine. Indeed, the uneasiness of courts with the doctrine has led many to implicitly inquire into claimants' bona fides even in jurisdictions that supposedly reject a good faith requirement. See R.H. Helmholz, "Adverse Possession and Subjective Intent," *Washington University Law Quarterly*, 61, no. 2 (1983): 331.

are entirely appropriate. Progressively higher rates of tax may be justified once amounts needed for necessities have been met. If one will not voluntarily give one's wealth away or put it to use for the benefit of others, the tax system will help achieve that goal.

Some of the available tax deductions might also arguably reflect the Augustinian principle. We might, for example, understand the deduction for amounts contributed to charity as rewarding those who use their property well—those who make it available for the benefit of the community. Other tax incentives could presumably be seen in a similar light. Supporting a church and feeding the poor are not the only ways, as we have seen, to use one's wealth for the common good. Investments in green technologies or investments that help plant businesses in underserved areas might receive (and under Augustinian principles possibly deserve) favorable treatment. However, we can see the traditional Anglo-American view of property in play in that the most important taxes are levied on income rather than wealth; again, once property is earned and taxed, the remains belong to its owner, who is free to dispose of it at her pleasure.

Conclusion: the perils of Augustinian property

Is it possible to construct a positive program for property law along Augustinian lines? Based on the sketch presented above, such a program would (a) protect private ownership without insisting too strongly on the underlying justice of any particular allocation of holdings, and (b) insist on right use of property as a condition of its continued possession.

The first prong of such a program seems possible. Augustinian property would shift the basis for property rights from the positive goal of purporting to secure the moral justice of the individual owner's claim to the more modest goal of protecting possessors from interference by others. (This flows from Augustine's conception of natural law as embodied in the "negative golden rule" described above.) Indeed, it has been argued that much of traditional property law can be explained by just such a principle.[74]

The second prong—insisting on right use of property as a condition of its continued possession—is much more problematic. By what standard would a decision maker decide which uses fail to take sufficient account of the common good and are therefore impermissible? Who would we want to make such a determination, even assuming a workable standard could be devised? Shouldn't we be worried that the same sins that afflict property holders also afflict those who formulate such standards? And can we take forfeiture seriously as a penalty? If we did, what incentives would be created? Is it possible to have a regime that encourages treating property as an asset destined for the common good without inviting opportunistic behavior on the part of non-owners? In other words, is

74 See, e.g., Thomas W. Merrill and Henry E. Smith, "The Morality of Property," *William & Mary Law Review*, 48, no. 5 (2013): 1849.

legally mandatory communication compatible with Augustine's negative golden rule's command of non-interference?

A careful reader will also have noticed that the characterization of Augustine's test for retaining possession—whether the owner's actions are consistent with communication of the property—is incomplete in at least one important respect. To be sure, Augustine does say "He who uses his wealth badly possesses it wrongfully, and wrongful possession means that it is another's property." However, he also says that rightful possession is a matter of the heart; the people who love wealth the least are the right ones to be in charge of it. As Augustine would be the first to point out, people frequently take externally good actions for bad reasons; it is not given to human beings to discern the motives of their own hearts, much less others'. Thus, the complex task for deciding when someone's use is compatible with pursuit of the common good, and when it is not, is complicated by the question of motivation. The Augustinian judge must acknowledge that she cannot carry out such an inquiry.[75] Again, she cannot see clearly into her own heart, much less others'. A similar challenge confronts the property theorist attempting to discern the possibilities and limitations of Augustinian proposals for property law reform.

75 See *City of God*, Bk. XIX, ch. 6.

6 English property law and Christianity, 1500–1700

R. H. Helmholz

Introduction

At first sight, the notion that there is (or could be) an overtly religious law of property seems little short of ridiculous.[1] Christianity may touch some areas of the law, but surely not the law of real and personal property. Of course it may be granted from the outset that there have long been special areas of property law where the two subjects intersected – consecrated ground, for example. It long came under a special heading in the common law, one that has had rules and consequences different from those applied to most real property.[2] But there is nothing particularly spiritual about protecting a churchyard against trespass or misuse, and today the purpose of this special area of the law seems more like an effort at historic preservation than it does an attempt to advance the goals of the Christian religion. Religion plays little or no part in modern property law.

Scripture, however, sheds a different light on the question of Christianity's possible relevance to property law. Speaking of the knowledge of God that has been imparted to his people, St. Paul reminds us that "we have this treasure in earthen vessels" (2 Cor. 4:7). His statement suggests that there may sometimes be a mixture of these two seemingly disparate elements. The importance of land to the ancient Hebrews, so often and so vividly depicted in the Old Testament (Ps. 83:12), likewise encourages a further look.[3] In the first, St. Paul seems to have held that earth and spirit may exist together within the same container. In the second, the Israelites seem to have treated land as a special part of God's covenant with them. Of course, neither biblical source has an obvious link with the subject of this chapter, the English common law of property. However, Christians have never supposed that the meaning of the Scriptures was exhausted by their relevance to conditions in the Middle East during the first century of the

1 It finds no place in introductory histories of the subject; *see, e.g.*, A.W.B. Simpson, *History of the Land Law*, 2nd ed. (Oxford: Oxford University Press, 1986); Sheldon Kurtz, *Moynihan's Introduction to the Law of Real Property*, 6th ed. (St. Paul, MN: Thompson/West, 2015).

2 *See, e.g.*, Mark Hill, *Ecclesiastical Law*, 2nd ed. (Oxford: Oxford University Press, 2001), 207.

3 *See* Moshe Weinfeld, *The Promise of the Land: The Inheritance of the Land of Canaan by the Israelites* (Berkeley, CA and Los Angeles, CA: University of California Press, 1993), 183.

Christian era.[4] So perhaps a tie might be found between property law and the Christian religion in the former's development over time. At the very least, some passages from the Scriptures encourage investigation. Several law review articles have also suggested this possibility. They called attention to the time when Christianity was itself considered a part of the common law.[5] Also intriguing is the discovery that Sir Edward Coke had himself derived an appropriate precedent for the English term "feoffment" in the gift of Ephron to Abraham described in Genesis 23:17–18. He made this unexpected connection in his *Institutes.*[6] These bits of evidence, inconclusive as they are in themselves, provide an impetus for historical investigation of the subject: the relationship between the Christian religion and the common law of property. Taken together, the bits suggest the possibility that making a fuller examination of the law involving lands and chattels in early modern England might yield some surprising results.

Scope of the investigation

This chapter takes as its subject the possibility that the influence of Christianity is to be found within English property law between 1500 and 1700. In deciding how to proceed with this topic, it seemed sensible to read as many of the cases involving rights in land and chattels from this period of these 200 years as I could within the time at my disposal. Instead of trying to cover the subject over many centuries, I chose to concentrate on a limited period. It appeared to be a more manageable task, and insofar as possible, I wished to avoid the vice of "cherry-picking." The selection of a few famous cases or the citation in the works of one or two particular writers would not be either as informative or as convincing as a study built upon a concentrated study of one area of law among the cases heard in the royal courts in Westminster Hall. This means, however, that the conclusions reached in this chapter are more limited than they would be if an investigation had covered a longer time period or included a fuller range of legal topics. With the exception of working through texts like *Coke on Littleton*, the basic treatise on the land law during this period, this chapter does not look much beyond the case law.

4 *See, e.g.*, the "experiment" offered by Milner Ball, "Biblical Kingdom and American Law," in *The Weightier Matters of the Law: Essays on Law and Religion*, eds. John Witte, Jr. and Frank Alexander (Atlanta, GA: Scholars Press, 1988), 303–14.

5 Stuart Banner, "When Christianity was Part of the Common Law," *Law & History Review* No. 16 (1998): 27–62; Frank Alexander, "Property and Christian Theology," in *Christianity and Law: An Introduction*, eds. John Witte and Frank Alexander (Cambridge: Cambridge University Press, 2008), 205–17; Richard O'Sullivan, *The Inheritance of the Common* Law (London: Stevens, 1950). The place religion in the law of property is, however, barely mentioned in most general works on property theory, as John Brewer and Susan Staves, *Early Modern Conceptions of Property* (London & New York: Routledge Press, 1995).

6 Co. Lit. *9a. *See also* John Fortescue, *De Laudibus legum Anglie*, cc. 1 and 3, ed. S.B. Chrimes (Cambridge: Cambridge University Press, 1949), 2–11.

Investigation of even this limited selection of cases also produces a perplexing problem – deciding what to count as an instance of religious influence on the law. The judges and lawyers during this period in English history were all Christians. They were not at all reticent about saying so. They assumed that their religion was true, sometimes even stating that it was identical with the law of England. Moreover, many of the institutions within which they worked bore an evident religious imprint. The terms during which the courts sat were taken from the Christian calendar, and the oaths that were routine parts of court practice they supervised were purposefully religious in character. I have nonetheless excluded these aspects of the law from this survey. They were routine enough in legal practice not to have called for any real thought about religion (or indeed any thought at all) on the part of the participants. For this survey, ordeals and wager of law have also not counted as religious parts of the law, despite their religious origins. Likewise ignored have been the frequent references to "acts of God" that appear in the reports.[7] The legal distinction between acts of God and acts of men could make a real difference in the outcome of litigation, but it is doubtful that the lawyers who applied the distinction were thinking about religion when they referred to the concept. Also excluded are most cases in which a lawyer or judge based an argument or a decision upon purely moral grounds.[8] Those grounds may have had religious roots, but equally they may not have. It is hard to know. Unless explicitly coupled with religion, this survey excludes appeals to moral concepts like fairness, conscience, or equity.

However, I have not carried this skeptical attitude into the cases in which lawyers and judges specifically invoked a religious authority or made a point buttressed by the Christian religion in arguing and deciding cases. To write these references off as "inconsequential" or as "purely ornamental" risks substituting modern prejudices for the ideas that were characteristic and important during the period. For this reason I have taken them at face value. Finally, although I sought to ignore obviously frivolous or irrelevant references to religion, I have also taken account of arguments based on religion even where they were not in the end accepted by the judges. Since my effort was to understand what part, if any, the Christian religion played in legal practice within the English law of property, the inclusion of even unsuccessful arguments seemed warranted.

Results of the investigation

The results of this survey proved surprising. Many more invocations of religious ideas in the cases exist than most legal histories have allowed. This chapter would not have been written had only a few such invocations been found in the English

7 *E.g. Waller v. Lambe* (1574), 1 And. 21, 123 E.R. 332: "an action of formedon in which the defendant pleaded nonage which was rejected by the court because his entry was "son act demesne de enter en le terre et nemi le act de dieu de getter le terre sur luy."

8 *E.g. Butler v. Baker* (1591), 3 Co. Rep. 25a, 32b, 76 E.R. 684, 701: argument "that equity and equality shall be observed and inequality avoided" in the interpretation of a statute.

reports. Although most legal histories which treat property law say nothing whatsoever about the subject, it turns out that there is actually a good deal that can be said. Many more property cases involving religion appeared in the reports than I myself had expected. In what follows the cases are divided and discussed according to either the source or the nature of the use of religious ideas found within them.

Invocations of scripture in property cases

Examples taken from the Bible, both the New and the Old Testaments, appeared in some quite unexpected places in the case law. Although lawyers do seem to have cited passages from Scripture more commonly in criminal cases,[9] they also did so more widely than is normally assumed in property cases. The common law's claim to exclusive jurisdiction over freehold land was once buttressed, for example, by the authority of Jesus' refusal to become involved in a dispute between brothers over their inheritance (Luke 12:13–14).[10] Since the ecclesiastical courts in England had long exercised a probate jurisdiction over wills and intestate succession, the point drawn from this biblical example was that ecclesiastical courts were exceeding the boundaries established in their own law by meddling incidentally with succession to land, as they sometimes had assumed the right to do. The legitimacy of the English church's testamentary jurisdiction was a contentious one during these years, and this biblical text was regarded as relevant to it. In another case, one involving the requirements for termination or renewal of a lease of land, the words of Jesus, "He who walketh in darkness knoweth not whither he goeth" (John 12:35) also supplied authority for a legal argument.[11] Neither lessor nor lessee could be expected to comply with the lease's terms while they were in the dark about its continuance. That was the passage's point, one lawyer argued. He concluded that because the lease itself contained no definite provision for termination, clear communication of intent to terminate was required. In its absence, no termination was warranted. Similarly, in the famous Case of Mixt Moneys, one lawyer invoked the authority of Jesus' famous statement that his followers must give unto Caesar that which belonged to Caesar (Matt 22:21, Mark 12:17) as a way of establishing the necessity of the prince's authority to render a coin legitimate legal tender.[12] Jesus himself had endorsed the underlying principle raised by the case. Of course, establishing the truth of the Christian religion was not the point of any of these texts. Some of them did

9 See the useful list in *Selected Writings of Sir Edward Coke*, ed. Steve Sheppard (Indianapolis, IN: Liberty Fund, 2003), iii, 1410.

10 Course of Trial of Legitimacy and Bastardy (Castle Chamber 1611), Dav. 51, 54, 80 E.R. 537, 540.

11 *Hill v. Grange* (CP 1556), 1 Plowd. 164, 173, 75 E.R. 253, 267.

12 Case of Mixt Moneys (1604), Dav. 18, 19, 80 E.R. 507, 508; *see also* David Fox, "The Case of Mixt Monies," in *Money in the Western Legal Tradition: Middle Ages to Bretton Woods*, eds. David Fox and Wolfgang Ernst (Oxford: Oxford University Press, 2016), 224–43.

not even touch the main points of dispute in the cases. But they did occupy a place in the law and in legal argument. They were apparently regarded as relevant to interpreting the law.

Passages from the Old Testament were treated as equally relevant in some of the other property cases brought before the King's justices. The words of Solomon in the Book of Wisdom (Sap. 7:10–12) were taken to illustrate the need for the light of reason in statutory interpretation in a case involving a dispute over title to land.[13] Solomon's example was also used to argue (unsuccessfully) that a marriage produced a legitimate child even if it had been contracted by children below the lawful age recognized by English law.[14] A saying attributed to King Solomon in the Scriptures was even used in another case to support an argument in favor of the existence of an implied easement of light and air.[15] And it is worth noting that the phrase sometimes used to describe the role played by English judges – "lions under the throne" – was a reference to the twelve lions keeping guard around the throne of King Solomon (1 Kings 10:19–20).[16] It was famously used with reference to a dispute between Coke and King James I,[17] but its origin (and perhaps its effect) came from its place in the Bible.

Passages from the Old Testament were sometimes used to justify decisions about inheritance of land in cases of partial intestacy, as for example the decision of Moses about inheritance by the daughters of Zelophehad from the Book of Numbers (Num 27:1–11).[18] The fixed rule of English property law that land could only descend to the estate holder's kin upon intestacy was also supported by Biblical citation; the rule that land could not ascend, even to those more nearly related by kinship than descendants was also justified as supported by that same example.[19] The effects of the Statute of Uses of 1535–36 (27 Hen. VIII, c. 10) on land titles in England were also described and justified by evocation of

13 *Partridge v. Strange & Croker* (CP 1553), 1 Plowd. 77, 82, 75 E.R. 123, 130; *see also Earl of Clanrickard et ux. v. Sidney* (1615), Hob. 273, 277, 80 E.R. 418, 423.

14 Kenn's Case (Exch. 1609), Jenk. 289, 145 E.R. 289 ("[S]ome write that Solomon begat Rehoboam at ten years of age").

15 William Aldred's Case (1610), 9 Co. Rep. 57b, 58b, 77 E.R. 816, 821 (Ec. 11:7): "Truly the light is sweet, and a pleasant thing it is for the eyes to behold the sun."

16 *Brownloe v. Michell* (1615), 1 Rolle 288, 289, 81 E.R. 490, 491.

17 Most famously by Catherine Drinker Bowen, *The Lion and the Throne: the Life and Times of Sir Edward Coke* (1552–1634) (Boston, MA and Toronto: Little Brown, 1957). Its provenance was acknowledged by Sir Francis Bacon, "Essays Civil and Moral, no. 56, Of Judicature," in *The Works of Lord Bacon* (London 1837, repr. Holmes Beach, FL: Gaunt, 2000), i, 305.

18 Case of Tanistry (1608), Dav. 28, 35, 80 E.R. 516, 523: "Et cest ordinance accord ove le divine ordinance en le case de Zelophehad." *See also R. v. Boreston & Adams* (1628), Noy 158, 161, 74 E.R. 1119, 1121 (stating that English law of inheritance was fixed "by nature and God's law," also mentioning the example of "the daughters of Zelophead" from Num 27:6 and 36).

19 *See* Ratcliff's Case (1592), 2 Co. Rep. 37a, 40b, 76 E.R. 713, 727. Explaining this strange rule, which excludes direct ascendants but admits collaterals, has been one of the unsolved mysteries of English land law. *See, e.g.*, Frederick Pollock and F.W. Maitland, *History of English Law before the time of Edward I*, 2nd ed., ed. S.F.C. Milsom (Cambridge: Cambridge University Press, 1968), ii, 286–295.

King Nebuchadnezzar's tree in the Book of Daniel (Dan. 4:1–27). In that tree, it was said, "the fowls of the heaven build their nests, and the nobility and gentry of the realm settle and establish their families."[20] Under such a tree-like statute, "a great part of the farmers and lessees of the land do lie for shelter and safety." The point of this surprising comparison was to show that the Statute had come to have many and different effects than those its framers had first intended. Like Nebuchadnezzar's tree, it sheltered many unexpected guests. Their presence had "grown so general" in later usage that it could be said that "they [have] now come to be favoured by the law."[21] The further reaches of their use were controversial no doubt, but at least some lawyers thought that invocation of Nebuchadnezzar's tree would support the legitimacy of extension of the purposes to which the Statute could legitimately be put.

English lawyers used the Biblical examples in a variety of circumstances to justify and interpret English law and customs.[22] The purpose of a statute (4 Hen. VII, c. 24), limiting the time period within which actions to recover real property could be brought, was explained in one case by Justice Dyer as a consequence of following the example of Jesus who "for peace descended from Heaven upon the Earth."[23] The statute's intent was to bring an end to quarrelling over land titles and Dyer thought it should be construed broadly to reach that result. The words of Jesus so suggested. The strange institution of the deodand, the concept by which an animal or inanimate object that had caused the death of a man or woman was forfeit to the Crown, was also said to have been founded "upon the law of God" both in a commentary by Sir Edward Coke and in a case from the Commonwealth period.[24] It was described as the English equivalent of the Biblical ox that gored and hence a legitimate part of English property law. Even more tellingly, in situations where the English law's rules for inheritance of land diverged from principles within natural law, as they did for example in adopting the rule of male primogeniture in the law of succession to land, English lawyers sometimes invoked the Bible to justify this long-standing practice.[25] An accepted principle of medieval jurisprudence held that an "odious" custom – one contrary to natural law – should be abolished, or at least strictly construed. Primogeniture presented a problem, but if it had been established by God himself,

20 *Dillon v. Freine* (Chudleigh's Case) (1589–95), 1 Co. Rep. 120a, 134b, 76 E.R. 270, 304–305, *Berry v. White* (CP 1662) Bridgman O. 82, 90–91, 124 E.R. 480, 485.

21 *Berry v. White* (CP 1662), Bridg. O. 82, 90–91, 124 E.R. 480, 485. *See also* Copyholders' Case (1626), Ben. 187, 190, 73 E.R. 1048, 1050.

22 *See generally*, John Eusden, *Puritans, Lawyers, and Politics in early Seventeenth-Century England* (New Haven, CT: Yale University Press, 1958), 123–26.

23 *Stowel v. Lord Zouch* (1562), 1 Plowd. 353, 368, 95 E.R. 536, 559.

24 *3 Co. Inst. *57*; *R. v. Crosse & Dabbyn* (1663), 1 Sid. 204, 205, 82 E.R. 1058 (citing Exod 21:28). *See also* Anna Pervukhin, "Deodands: A Study in the Creation of Common Law Rules," *American Journal of Legal History* 47 (2005): 237–56.

25 Case de Tanistry, Dav. 28, 36, 80 E.R. 516, 523 (1608); Fortescue, *De Laudibus supra* note 6 c. 40 (citing the example of Abraham, who "gave all his property to his son Isaac").

as the lawyers contended it had, then it passed muster. The Bible was read to make this result palatable.

Knowledge and use of the Church's law in property cases

It has long been thought that the study and use of the canon law in England ceased during the reign of Henry VIII, as demonstrated by the closure of the canon law faculties at Oxford and Cambridge. We know now that this conclusion is misleading.[26] The power and privileges of the papacy were rejected, but the canon law was retained except where it was contrary to English statute law or royal rights. It did acquire a new name: the King's Ecclesiastical Law.[27] Its substance in most matters of private law remained identical to what it had long been.

This retention mattered most in the ecclesiastical courts, of course, but it is still surprising to find that it also mattered in the common law courts. It did so even in cases involving real and personal property. That at least some common lawyers were familiar with the basic documents of the canon law and also some of the treatise literature that went with it is clear. Coke himself acknowledged its relevance.[28] William Lyndwood was the most frequently cited of the medieval canonists – explained no doubt by the specifically "English focus" of his *Provinciale*.[29] However, their knowledge and use of the canon law did not stop there. The *Liber extra* and the great canonists who glossed it – Hostiensis, Innocent IV, Baldus de Ubaldis, Panormitanus, William Durantis, Philippus Francus, Dominicus de Sancto Geminiano – all were cited as of relevance in the English reports in property cases.[30]

It seems particularly surprising to find the canon law being accorded any relevance in the royal courts. In fact, however, its invocation was not uncommon. The canonical view of suicide helps shape the common law on the subject. The property of the *felo de se*, who was thought to be guilty of "an offense against nature, against God, and against the King," passed to the Crown, not to the

26 *See* 25 Hen. VIII, c. 19 (1533), specifying that pending a revision the canon law should remain in force if not contrary to the laws and customs of the realm or the king's prerogatives. The proposed revision was never enacted.

27 *Evans & Kiffin v. Ascuithe* (1627), Palm. 457, 458, 81 E.R. 1169, 1170, by Whitelock and Dodderidge, JJ; *see also* Sir Edward Coke's exposition of the subject in "The King's Ecclesiastical Law," (1509), 5 Co. Rep. 28a, 32b, 77 E.R. 33, 37.

28 E.g. Co. Lit. *95b (of tenure by frankalmoin, that "the common law … taketh knowledge of the ecclesiastical law in that behalf"). *See also* John Dodderidge (d. 1628), *The English Lawyer* (London: Assigns of I. More, 1631), 102–106 (using the canon law to describe the place and status of custom in English law).

29 A good example is *Hilton v. Paul* (CP 1627), Lit. 73, 124 E.R. 143.

30 *See Dickinson v. Greenhall* (1624), 2 Rolle 479, 480, 81 E.R. 928, 929; *Sobrean & Teige v. Kevan* (1619), 2 Rolle 101, 102, 81 E.R. 686, *Jones v. Jones* (1617), Hob. 185, 186, 80 E.R. 332, 333; *Kitchin v. Calvert* (Exch. 1611), Lane 100, 101, 145 E.R. 332, 333; Anon. (1611), Dav. 68, 75, 80 E.R. 552, 559; *Jones v. Boyer* (1610), 2 Brownl. 27, 28, 123 E.R. 795, 796; *Morris v. Webber* (1586), 2 Leo. 169, 172, 74 E.R. 449, 452.

offender's family, a result justified in part by citation of the canon law.[31] The law of the church was also relevant, for instance, where the existence of a valid marriage could determine the outcome of a widow's suit for dower. One operative rule was: "where there is no marriage, there is no dower."[32] Determining how that rule would be applied required some reference to canon law, since the church's law defined what constituted a valid marriage. This was not always a simple question, and the canon law helped to provide an answer to it.

There were other intricate matters of the same sort raised in practice. For example, in determining the scope of a Tudor statute regulating the validity of marriages between persons related by blood or marriage – a question that arose in disputes over inheritance – it was necessary to know, first, what the canon law allowed and, second, what the effect of a Reformation statute (21 Hen. VIII, c. 21) had been. The statute had limited the scope of marriage between kin to unions the law of God had not declared unlawful. Just what that meant was uncertain, but the question required a knowledge of the pre-Reformation canon law.[33] It also required understanding what the Bible held on the subject of unlawful unions, in particular the degrees declared incestuous in the Book of Leviticus. Whenever the definition of an incestuous union became a matter of dispute in the royal courts, the law of the church might be relevant.[34] So it happened that common lawyers and judges sometimes looked at both sources of law, canonical and biblical, when disputes concerning property came before them.[35] Broadly speaking they had recourse to the canonists for the first and theologians for the second, though no firm dividing line between them existed. In a case from the 1670s, for instance, the opinions of John Calvin, Hugo Grotius, Thomas Sanchez (d. 1610), and Johannes Schneidewein (d. 1569) on this point were all introduced to answer the question and interpret the English statute.[36]

Much the same process shaped administration of the common law of tithes. Their payment raised some of the most contentious issues of the time. Best known as a symbol of that disagreement is the question of whether tithes were owed by divine law or only by custom. The role of the learned common lawyer,

31 *Hales v. Petit* (C.P. 1562), 1 Plowd. 253, 261, 75 E.R. 387, 400.

32 Co. Lit. *32a. *See also* Amy Louise Erickson, *Women and Property in early Modern England* (London & New York: Routledge, 1993), 24–26.

33 Co. Lit. *235a; one reason for this was that the pope's power to grant dispensations in matrimonial law was itself limited; see, e.g., D.L. d'Avray, *Papacy, Monarchy and Marriage 860–1600* (Cambridge: Cambridge University Press, 2015), 189–217.

34 *Hill v. Good* (1673), 1 Freem.108, 89 E.R. 80.

35 *See, e.g.*, Williams's Case (CP 1631), Lit. 355, 124 E.R. 282 (Levitical degrees) and *Haines v. Jescott* (1695), 5 Mod. 168, 87 E.R. 587. A similar pattern is found in the cases that dealt with dispensations to hold more than one ecclesiastical benefice, a subject regulated by both English statute and canon law; see, e.g., *Colt v. Glover* (Exch. 1612), 1 Rolle 451, 81 E.R. 600, 601; Case of the Commendam (CP 1611), Dav. 68, 75, 80 E.R. 552, 559.

36 *Hill v. Good* (K.B. 1674), 1 Freem. 152, 153, 89 E.R. 111. See also the report of the same case in Vaughan 302, 314, 124 E.R. 1085, 1092, where the opinion of Martin Luther was also mentioned.

John Selden (d. 1654), in that controversy has long attracted the primary interest of historians.[37] That great question did come up in litigation,[38] but it was confined to the background of most of the tithe cases that came before the royal courts. Front and center in the cases were conflicts between local custom and the formal law of the church on the subject of the amount of tithe owed. The monetary inflation of the period rendered the income derived from many long-established customs inadequate, and those who held the right to tithes sought to upset them in favor of full payment of a tenth part of income derived from the fruits of the earth and the labor of men. This required knowledge of both the status of custom in the common law and the law of tithes as found in the canon law. So we find both being invoked regularly in the reported cases.[39] The law of the medieval church could thus be relevant to the decision of disputes that arose in the King's courts, and although the common lawyers did not always follow it, they often began with it, paying particular attention to it where it did not conflict with their own law.

Invocation of religious principles in property cases

The modern law of real property has not turned its back on principles of morality.[40] What has happened is rather that judges and lawyers have ceased to credit the Christian religion with any part in the process. James Thayer, while a professor at Harvard Law School in the late nineteenth century, wrote that Christianity's only contribution to the common law was to "give the benefit of any doubt to the accused person" in criminal cases.[41] As a description of the situation in today's law of real and personal property, Thayer's assessment may have been correct. Religion seems to have disappeared. But it was not always so. Modern historians have also established that religious ideas once had an effect on the gov-

37 *E.g.* Christopher Hill, *Economic Problems of the Church* (Oxford: Oxford University Press, 1963), 77–131. On Selden's attitude and learning in many areas of law, see Harold Berman and John Witte, Jr., "The Integrative Christian Jurisprudence of John Selden," in *Great Christian Jurists in English History*, eds. Mark Hill and R. H. Helmholz (Cambridge: Cambridge University Press, 2017), 138–61.

38 *See, e.g., Urrey v. Bowyer* (CP 1611), 2 Brownl. 20, 24, 123 E.R. 791, 793.

39 *See, e.g.*, Dickenson's Case (1616), Benl. 163, 73 E.R. 1027, 1028 (accepting those aspects of the canon law of tithes which "ont obteyne le force del ley par usage et length de temps"); *see also Mountford v. Sidley* (1625), 3 Bulst. 336, 81 E.R. 279; Case of Royal Piscary (1610), Dav. 55, 56, 80 E.R. 540, 541 (citing Lyndwood and Thomas Aquinas); *Canning v. Dr. Newman* (1610), 2 Brownl. & Golds. 54, 123 E.R. 811 (citing the decrees of the Fourth Lateran Council of 1215); Dean and Chapter of *Bristol v. Clerke* (1553), 1 Dyer 83a, 84b, 73 E.R. 181, 184.

40 *See* Thomas Merrill and Henry Smith, "The Morality of Property," *William & Mary Law Rev.* 48 (2007): 1849–95; F.E. Dowrick, *Justice according to the English Common Lawyers* (London: Butterworths, 1961), 73–105.

41 Harvard Law School Library, Special Collections, "Thayer Correspondence and Memoranda," vol. 2, s.d. February 28, 1879, quoted in Daniel Coquillette, and Bruce Kimball, *On the Battlefield of Merit: Harvard Law School, the First Century* (Cambridge, MA: Harvard University Press, 2015), 449.

ernment of European nations. The storehouse of ideas found within the medieval *ius commune* was so used, and some of them worked their way into English law. To take only the most clearly investigated example, the principle that what touches all should be approved by all (*Quod omnes tangit ab omnibus approbari debet*), which appears in the Roman law's Codex (Cod. 5.59.5.2) and was endorsed by the canonists, became one foundation for protection against arbitrary taxation imposed by European monarchs.[42] The doctrine was used to establish the necessity of securing the consent of the governed acting through their representatives before they could be taxed. It thus protected rights in property.

The question raised by this topic is whether one can go further. Did something like this same use of Christian moral ideas found in the *ius commune* touch the law of real and personal property in England? The evidence shows that it did. It started at the top. A famous example is the use of Christian principles to guide and control the King and his agents. It reached into feudal law and the royal prerogative. Today, when lawyers describe the King's historic role, they describe him as holding the land of England as the "sovereign lord or lord paramount" of all. He had no superior, and "[t]o this rule there is no exception."[43]

Lawyers four centuries ago would not have said that. They said instead that the monarch did have a superior, namely God.[44] But did this pious rule have any practical consequences? Not an easy question to answer, but what one can say with confidence is that the sovereignty of God was *meant* to have consequences in the world. It was meant, for instance, to set the limits of the King's dispensing power.[45] It was meant to spur him to take action to provide justice to his subjects.[46] It was meant to require him to keep his promises, particularly those he had taken an oath to observe.[47] The judges themselves invoked their own oaths

42 Its development is discussed in Gaines Post, "A Romano-canonical maxim, *Quod omnes tangit*, in Bracton and in early Parliaments," in idem, *Studies in Medieval Legal Thought: Public Law and the State, 1100–1322* (Princeton, NJ: Princeton University Press, 1964), 162–238; and Bruce Brasington, "A Divine Precept of Fraternal Union: the Maxim *Quod omnes tangit* in Anglo-American Thought to the Ratification of the Constitution," in *Bridging the Medieval-Modern Divide: Medieval Themes in the World of the Reformation*, ed. James Muldoon (Farnham: Ashgate Press, 2013), 205–23. Its success in practice proved to be mixed; *see, e.g.*, Thomas Bisson, *Assemblies and Representation in Languedoc in the Thirteenth Century* (Princeton, NJ: Princeton University Press, 1964), 296–99.

43 *See Challis's Law of Real Property*, 3rd ed., ed. Charles Sweet (London: Sweet & Maxwell, 1911), 5.

44 Anon. (1615), 1 Rolle 135, 81 E.R. 385; Henry Finch (d. 1625), *Lawe, or a Discourse Thereof: In Four Books*, Bk. II, c. 1 (London: Miles Fletcher, 1636), 81.

45 *Colt & Glover v. Bishop of Coventry & Lichfield* (1612), Moo. K.B. 898, 902, 72 E.R. 982, 985 (that it did not extend to an exercise of the king's power if "contrary al ley de Dieu"); Anon. (1548), Jenk. 79, 145 E.R. 56.

46 *Case of Duchy of Lancaster* (1562), 1 Plowd. 212, 222, 75 E.R. 325, 338–39 ("considering how that Almighty God hath placed him in the honourable estate of King"). *See also* Ralph Turner, "The Royal Courts Treat Disseizin by the King: John and Henry III, 1199–1240," in idem, *Judges, Administrators and the Common Law in Angevin England* (London & Rio Grande, OH: Hambledon Press, 1994), 251–68.

47 *Willon v. Berkley et al.* (1560), 1 Plowd. 223, 237, 75 E.R. 339, 361.

to God to excuse themselves from executing a questionable order from Queen Elizabeth to admit an unworthy man to an office in the courts at Westminster.[48] Similarly, one of the reasons given to justify the result in *Bushell's Case*, the famous vindication of the power of jurors to return a verdict contrary to judicial instructions, was that jurors had a duty to follow their own consciences.[49] Some of the great moments of English constitutional history have made use of the moral principle that God was the true sovereign of the realm.[50] On a more prosaic level, the presumption that the monarch must have been "deceived" when he had taken an action that was contrary to settled principles of the law of the land allowed cases to be decided aright.[51]

These were great issues, but the role of Christian principles in the case law also extended into some quite humble matters involving land. One of the humblest among them was an invocation of Christ's words describing the Temple at Jerusalem. These words offered a surprising solution to a difficult problem caused by the doctrine of misnomer. The wording in a deed of land naming the intended grantee had not been clear enough to be certain that it qualified as a charitable gift. The grant had not used the intended beneficiary's exact title, and it was questioned whether the words required that its purposes were necessarily charitable.[52] However, the definition given by Jesus – "a house of prayer for all nations" and a place where God was served (Matt 11:17) – seemed ample enough to permit the judges to set aside an objection based on what may have been a simple verbal mistake in naming the beneficiary. The deed's words fit that definition well enough. The scriptural definition of the purposes served by the apparent grantee was wide enough to allow the testamentary gift to be upheld. Today, this apparent deficiency in wording might be disregarded as purely formal or else investigated further to undercover the testator's likely intent. In Jacobean England it was interpreted instead according to a principle found within the Christian religion.

The relaxed approach to the requirements of the land law illustrated by this case extended to several technical questions within the law of real property. A father's agreement to stand seized of a parcel of land to the use of his children ordinarily raised a valid use that was executed by the Statute of Uses. It was effective where a similar agreement with a stranger was not, and this was said to be because "nature, reason, and the law of God countenance and respect the

48 *Cavendish's Case* (1587), 1 And. 152, 155, 123 E.R. 403, 405.

49 *Bushell's Case* (1670), 1 Freem. 1, 3, 89 Eng. Rep. 2, 3.

50 As, for example, the Trial of the Seven Bishops (1688), 12 Howell's State Trials 271, to the effect that the King had no power to suspend the laws affecting religion. See also Paul Halliday, *Habeas Corpus: From England to Empire* (Cambridge, MA: Harvard University Press, 2010), 67–69; Philip Hamburger, *Law and Judicial Duty* (Cambridge, MA: Harvard University Press, 2008), 168–72.

51 *See, e.g.*, *Attorney General v. Bushopp* (1600), 1 Co. Rep. 40b, 50a, 53a, 76 E.R. 89, 114, 120.

52 *Sherborn v. Lewis* (1597), Godb. 120, 75 E.R. 1036; *see also Pits v. James* (1614), Hob. 121, 80 E.R. 271.

love which is between the father and his issue."[53] Similarly, the most common reason attempts to create perpetuities in land were held invalid in the early cases was not that the needs of the market in land required early alienability, but rather that such attempts "fought against God" by supposing that mortal men could control the future to an extent that might deny God's omnipotence.[54]

A further example is that a grant to a specific man and woman "and the heirs of their bodies" ordinarily would have created an estate in fee tail special. It was treated as invalid, however, if the man and woman were married to other persons at the time of the grant. This result was reached not only because it would "introduce dangerous events to inheritances," but also because to have enforced it as written would have contravened a Christian moral principle. It would be said to introduce "a remote and foreign expectancy" that threatened the church's definition of the indissolubility of a lawful marriage.[55] Similarly, one reason given in justification of the English law of coverture that restricted the rights of married women over their own property during their marriage was that "by the law of God she is under the power of her husband."[56] An alternate explanation, one equally tied to religion, was that the man and the women had "become one flesh" in marriage. This meant, it was contended, that they could not be more than one person in the eyes of the law.[57]

Implementation and interpretation of statutes against superstitious uses

Protestant religious principles also worked their way into the case law.[58] The criminal law was the primary means of enforcing religious uniformity in England, as it was elsewhere during this age of the Wars of Religion, but Protestant religious purposes also had real effects – more indirect but still momentous – within the law of real and personal property. Most dramatic in England were the consequences that followed the surrender and dissolution of the English monasteries and other religious houses. Many monks were described as having acted "to the high displeasure of Almighty God [and] the slander of good religion" in one Henrician statute. They had chosen "to rove abroad in apostasy [rather] than conform to the observation of good religion."[59] A drastic remedy seemed

53 *Sharington v. Strotten* (1565), 1 Plowd. 298, 304, 75 E.R. 454, 463. *See also Gerrard v. Worseley* (1577), 1 And. 75, 79, 123 E.R. 361, 364.

54 Anon. (Chan. 1599), Cary 9, 21 E.R. 5; *Floyd v. Cary* (Chan. 1697), 2 Free. Ch. 218, 219, 22 E.R. 1170, 1171.

55 *Hoe's Case* (1622), Winch. 54, 56, 124 E.R. 46, 48.

56 *Haward v. Duke of Suffolk* (1553), 1 Dyer 79b, 73 E.R. 170, 171; *Manby & Richardson v. Scot* (Exch. Ch. 1662), 1 Keb. 482, 83 E.R. 1065.

57 *Manby v. Scott* (1674), 1 Mod. 124, 86 E.R. 781.

58 An illuminating work on this subject, although largely devoted to Continental developments, is John Witte, Jr., *Law and Protestantism: The Legal Teachings of the Lutheran Reformation* (Cambridge: Cambridge University Press, 2002), esp. 168–75.

59 27 Hen. VIII, c. 28 (1535); 31 Hen. VIII, c. 13 (1539).

called for by this diversion from Christianity's true character, and the monastic lands and endowments were surrendered to the Crown as a consequence.[60] The displaced monks were given pensions and their lands put to more profitable uses.

Similar actions were taken against other superstitious uses – as with endowments devoted in perpetuity to the performance of masses for the dead. The so-called Chantry statute from the reign of Edward VI declared that "a great part of superstition and error in [the] Christian religion had been brought into the minds and estimation of men" by these false institutions.[61] The property devoted to saying of masses for the dead in perpetuity would, the statute asserted, be better used for the erection of grammar schools, the augmentation in learning in the English universities, and the better provision of funds for the poor and needy. Repealed briefly during the reign of Queen Mary, most such statutes were brought back into force under Elizabeth I, and they had a long life. It is true that the motives that lay behind these changes have been matters of dispute ever since, but the consequences for titles to land and other endowments that occurred in consequence of the statutes enacted during English Reformation have never been subject to doubt. A massive reordering of titles to land took place.

This was not simply a matter of one group of title holders being substituted for another, though it certainly was that. The effect of the statutes also raised many troublesome legal problems which came before the courts, some of which involved titles to land or to other endowments. A good example is *Holloway v. Watkins*, heard by the Court of Common Pleas in 1604.[62] The Dean and Chapter of York had received a testamentary gift of £400 during the reign of Henry IV (d. 1413) to provide funds for a chantry in York minster. They had received the King's assent under the Statute of Mortmain, and spent that sum to purchase land, subsequently using the rent from the land to pay for a chantry priest according to what they regarded as the testator's intent. Come the Reformation, and the land was seized by the King's agents, acting under the Edwardian Chantry Act. The Act was retrospective in effect. In this case, the lands seized were then conveyed to an individual party by the Crown. However, the Dean and Chapter, thinking that the Act might not have been applicable to these lands, also conveyed it to another purchaser. The question was which of these two grantees had the better claim to the land. The justices held for the grantee of the Dean and Chapter. The reason they gave was that the property purchased with the bequest had been conveyed without formal specification of purpose. Under its own terms, it simply became one of the many possessions of the Dean and Chapter. That they had long used it to support a chantry did not limit what they could do or might do with it in the future, and hence the statute did not apply. It applied only to land specifically conveyed to superstitious uses.

60 The process of surrender and sale is described in David Knowles, *The Religious Orders in England* (Cambridge: Cambridge University Press, 1961–62), iii, 393–401.

61 1 Edw. VI, c. 14 (1547).

62 Cro. Jac 51, 79 E.R. 43; *see also Lancelot v. Allen* (1631), Cro. Car. 248, 79 E.R. 818 (apparently reaching the opposite result); *Waldern v. Ward* (1657), 2 Sid. 46, 82 E.R. 1248.

It may be said that this case and others like it were not really about religion. True enough in a sense, but they would not have occurred without the law's prohibition of the enforcement of superstitious uses. The statutes rested upon a religious movement, and they affected title to land. The most numerous of the ensuing cases found in the English reports were those that involved gifts that were partly superstitious in nature and partly charitable. An Edwardian statute precluded application of the cy pres doctrine to save them, but if a clear division had been made in the grant, only the superstitious part was forfeit to the Crown.[63] That was the sensible result, but it turned out that many more cases were not clear about the division, as where the testamentary direction called for the celebration of masses with any surplus to be devoted to the repair of a parish church,[64] or where it called for payment to the poor who attended a mass celebrated for the soul of the donor,[65] or where the superstitious use was limited in time and followed by a remainder devoted to a valid purpose.[66] Cases like these required the courts to wrestle with religious issues. The fate of grants of lands and chattels used for religious purposes depended upon their conformity with the principle that superstition should be rooted out from the practice of Christianity, and disputes in cases like these led the judges down some uncharted trails. Sir Edward Coke's lengthy opinion in one such case seems to have been the most cited among them,[67] but Lord Ellesmere was not mistaken when he later commented that anyone who read it would "run into a wood or thicket out of which he shall not easily wind himself."[68] The true import of Christianity could be as arguable in the courts as it was among theologians, but religion sometimes furnished a starting point in contested property cases.

Conclusion

The four areas of the law discussed in which Christianity played a conspicuous part do not exhaust the subject. The doctrines and sacraments of the church – baptism and excommunication to take just two examples – could determine the outcome of cases about lands and chattels in the royal courts. The four areas just surveyed are probably enough, however, to demonstrate that English common lawyers recognized that Christianity was sometimes relevant to English property law. It would be incautious to say much more than that. Some lawyers did say more, of course, contending that the laws of England "came as near to the laws

63 *Hart v. Brewer & Harison* (1595), Cro. Eliz. 449, 78 E.R. 688

64 *Pitt v. James* (1620), Palm. 124, 81 E.R. 1009.

65 *Martin v. Chambers* (1662), Latch 38, 82 E.R. 263.

66 *Humphreys v. Knight* (1636), Cro. Car. 455, 79 E.R. 994.

67 *Adams v. Lambert* (1602), 4 Co. Rep. 104b, 76 E.R. 1091.

68 *Lord Chancellor Egerton's Observations on the Lord Coke's Reports* (London: John Nutt, 1710), 21. *See also* Holford's Case (1620), 2 Rolle 205, 206, 81 E.R. 752, 753, in which Sir Edward Montagu, C.J. was recorded as having complained that "un case in ceo in tout appearance contradicts another."

of God as they could."[69] However, it would be pushing the evidence too far to say that English property law was itself based upon the Christian religion on the basis of statements like that one. The common lawyers quoted Virgil's *Aeneid* too,[70] and it would require a stretch to suppose that the poet exercised any real influence on English property law. It should also be added that there were far more reported property law cases between 1500 and 1700 that did not mention Christianity than there were cases that did. All that this survey has shown is that Christianity did sometimes play a conspicuous part in the enactment of English statutes and in the case law involving real and personal property.

There is one additional conclusion derived from the evidence surveyed. It would be a mistake to think of religion's usual influence as if it were a means of amending or resisting the positive law. The English cases do not fit a theme of religious "critiques" of the law. At least in the field of property law, Christianity was used to support or to interpret existing laws and statutes, not to undo or criticize them. Conscientious refusal to obey an unjust law – what we think of as the most common reason for invoking freedom of religion – did not appear in English cases involving real and personal property. Perhaps it did elsewhere, but not within this field of inquiry.

This result may seem disappointing. However, what one can say to the contrary is that religion did play an overt and positive role in the thinking of English lawyers, and it had many uses. What Thomas Shaffer once wrote about the modern American legal academy – that it, "more than any other has systematically discouraged and disapproved of invoking the religious tradition as important or even interesting"[71] – finds no support in the English case law involving property between 1500 and 1700. The reverse is true. During those years – even within a seemingly secular field like this one – the Christian religion occupied a legitimate place in the thought of many English lawyers. It was mixed in with the law of property. Perhaps it was even a bit like the contents in earthen vessels St. Paul had mentioned many centuries before.

69 *Reniger v. Fogossa* (Exch. Ch. 1562), 1 Plowd. 1, 8, 75 E.R. 1, 12. Similar were the opinions of Christopher St. German, in *St. German's 'Doctor and Student'*, eds. T.F.T. Plucknett and J.L. Barton (London: Selden Society 91, 1974), 75 and Michael Dalton, *Countrey Justice* (London: Stationers' Company, 1618), ch. 1.

70 E.g. Co. Lit. *342b.

71 Thomas Shaffer, *American Lawyers and their Communities* (Notre Dame, IN and London: Notre Dame University Press, 1991), 214.

7 The boundaries of dominion

Adam J. MacLeod

Dominion from the beginning

Property ownership is dominion. That is how common law jurists have long thought of it. Dominion in common law is neither a despotic individual right nor a mere concession of privilege from the sovereign. It is not a right to do whatever one wants, no matter the cost to others. And it is not a malleable bundle of legal incidents, which public officials may reasonably alter or detract from at will. Dominion is instead a way in which human beings exercise practical reason in their use and management of things and in their dealings with others with respect to things in the communities of which they are part. Dominion is not just the law of things. It is also a means of being and becoming fully human, perfected in the virtue of practical wisdom, and of doing great good in the world. And it supplies occasion to choose badly, to harm others, and to become vicious. In short, property ownership is morally significant.

In recent decades, the concept of ownership as dominion has almost disappeared from property jurisprudence except as a derelict talisman supposed to represent the individualistic excesses of classical liberalism. But Blackstone's oft-quoted aphorism about the "sole and despotic dominion" does not resemble the complex dominion that Blackstone painstakingly described in the four volumes of his *Commentaries*. Blackstone insisted that the "despotic dominion" ideal which "so generally strikes the imagination" is precisely *not* the true "original and foundation" of private property. No, God's delegation of authority to mankind is "the only true and solid foundation of man's dominion over external things, whatever airy metaphysical notions may have been started by fanciful writers upon this subject."[1]

1 William Blackstone, *Commentaries on the Laws of England*, vol. 2, *Of the Rights of Things* (Oxford: Oxford University Press, 2016 [1766]), 2. After reading Blackstone's extensive and complex description of property rights and duties in the rest of the *Commentaries*, one could not maintain the view that the aphorism was meant by Blackstone to describe actual dominion as found in human law. See Carol M. Rose, "Canons of Property Talk, or Blackstone's Anxiety," *Yale Law Journal*, 108 (1998): 601, 603–06.

The student of the common law reading this passage will already have read Blackstone's Introduction to the first volume of the *Commentaries*, in which he explained that the lawmaking authority which God delegates to his human creatures is constrained by natural law, the first principles of critical morality often associated with the Christian philosopher Thomas Aquinas (common law jurists sometimes call it the law of reason), and by divine law, which is found in the Hebrew and Christian Scriptures. This chapter draws upon those same resources.

Liberal elements also pervade the *Commentaries*, as they suffuse common law generally. But common law liberty is not license. In his first volume, Blackstone famously cited Locke and listed property among the absolute rights of Englishmen.[2] But this meant simply that "no freeman shall be disseised, or divested, of his freehold, or of his liberties, or free customs, but by the judgment of his peers, or by the law of the land," and that an owner could not be required to yield his goods or land to the king or the public without compensation.[3] It does not mean that property rights are absolute. To the contrary, God shaped dominion to fit human reason, and He shaped human beings to make them fit for the office of dominion. Whatever is forbidden by reason and revelation is not within the liberties and powers of dominion. The Hebrew and Christian scriptures which Blackstone cited say that God created the world and then conveyed dominion over it to Adam and Eve.[4] Blackstone and other common law jurists maintain that this conveyance is the origin and foundation of property ownership, which remains constrained by God's prior right.[5]

Blackstone took the architecture of dominion not from liberal political philosophers such as Hobbes and Locke but from earlier common law jurists such as Matthew Hale. Thus, the rights of property are limited by maxims and doctrines, such as nuisance and waste; rules, such as the rule against perpetuities; and judgments, especially of civil juries in cases of conflict; all of which mark the outer boundaries of the owner's liberty to use, manage, and dispose of his things. And the estates of ownership are plural and cooperative, facilitating the exercise of dominion not only by individuals but also by groups, such as families, universities, business owners and their customers, and other associations of people who plan and work together to achieve common goods.

Dominion thus both secures and bounds liberty. It is an office uniquely suited to human beings as discerning, reasoning, deliberating, choosing, and planning moral agents. Humans shape dominion. And dominion shapes humans. It partly determines human choosing and acting, and thereby shapes human character in the order of the will. In particular, the structure of dominion's rights and

2 Blackstone, I, 122–25.

3 Ibid., 138–39.

4 Gen 1:1–31.

5 *See*, e.g., Blackstone, *Commentaries*, II, 2–3.

duties—its legal reasons for action—determines in part the practical reasoning of those who interact with property, both owners and non-owners.

This concept of ownership is richer than the more recent idea of property as an individual right, though it also entails unique challenges. In its egalitarian form as plural estates and interests of ownership, dominion both requires and fosters a people capable of ordering the world. That exercise requires liberty. Yet liberty can be abused. And its abuse harms both the material well-being of the abused and the practical reasonableness of the abuser. Abuse of liberty pits one against one's neighbor and diminishes one's ability to be an order-creator. As a consequence, the liberty at the core of dominion must be bounded in such a way as to constrain liberty without destroying it. The common law resolves this dilemma by bounding dominion with the law of wrongs. The law of wrongs constitutes dominion as it simultaneously secures it from outside infringement and restrains its harmful exercises.

The boundaries of dominion are variable. The law of wrongs is partly determined according to laws that could not reasonably be otherwise given the nature we have. Yet dominion is in most respects under- or un-determined. This opens the opportunity to exercise practical reason in the settling and specification of property's norms and institutions. Property is constituted first by boundaries which develop and constitute the most important given aspect of our nature—the capacity-become-ability to choose and act for reasons—and secondarily by boundaries that we ourselves create as we develop that aspect. Insofar as the law of wrongs does not specify all rights with the same degree of conclusiveness and generality, it can meet the multiple needs of dominion. It can satisfy natural justice, secure natural and civil rights, including others' domains of liberty, and meet other requirements of practical reasonableness.

This chapter concerns only the shape of dominion. It is not intended to resolve the debate whether private acquisition or collective ownership is more justifiable, in general and all things considered. That debate does not bear directly on what follows (though what follows has obvious implications for that debate). Even in a Communist country, humans have duties of abstention with respect to things they do not own. Dominion has proven to be ineradicable from human society. Whether many people exercise it over small shares or a few people exercise it over the whole, someone must decide what to do with the tangible and intangible assets we have available to us.

Not-so-despotic dominion

Fitting human nature

God granted dominion to Adam and Eve. The Hebrew scriptures describe these two, alone among the animals, as beings created in the image of God. The central tradition of Christian thought adds that Adam and Eve bear God's image by virtue of their radical capacity to speak and reason and thus to order actions to their proper ends, a capacity that when cultivated flowers into that virtue known to ancient minds as wisdom.[6] In more recent jurisprudence, this excellence has become known as practical reasonableness.[7] Greek and Roman philosophers also noticed these godly capacities. So, Cicero remarked on the "creature of foresight, wisdom, variety, keenness, memory, endowed with reason and judgment, which we call man," who alone of all living creatures "participates in reason and reflection," a divine capacity "which, when it has developed and become complete, is rightly called wisdom."[8]

The work of exercising dominion is the job of the one who excels in the virtue of practical wisdom. Because dominion involves specification of reasons, only one who first has ordered his deliberations concerning good ends is suited to the office of dominion-holder. Dominion begins with mastery of oneself. Humans are the authors of their actions, creators of new states of affairs, by virtue of their free choices. They are authors of *good* states of affairs by virtue of their exercise of reason. Summarizing Aquinas' account of this tradition, John Finnis says that "one's deeds (acts, actions) are really human only if one is fully in charge—ruler, master, owner {dominus} of them."[9] The object of dominion is not mere freedom from coercion. It is to choose well.

The faculty of practical reason is not the virtue of practical reasonableness, only its potential. Practical reason must be perfected. And its perfection is difficult because practical reason is complicated. To order the world fruitfully requires skillful and wise engagement with the world. The world is a complex place. And practical reason must be both backward- and forward-looking. Reason is constrained by what is given, especially our nature and the rules of logic. Yet it brings about order by bringing about what is undetermined, what can come to be only if we choose it and pursue it by effective means.

Aquinas identified four orders upon which reason operates—the orders of nature, logic, free will, and technique.[10] In the first order, the order of nature,

6 An ecumenical account of this tradition is found in Dylan Pahman, *Foundations of a Free & Virtuous Society* (Grand Rapids, MI: Acton Institute, 2017), 1–20. Of course, some Christians have held other views of what it means to be created in the image of God. But for present purposes, whether the human capacity for practical reason is the respect in which we resemble God or is merely an aspect of the nature He bestowed on us is not important.

7 John Finnis, "Grounding Human Rights in Natural Law," *American Journal of Jurisprudence*, 60 (2015): 199, 205–13.

8 Cicero, *The Republic and the Laws*, trans. Niall Rudd (Oxford: Oxford University Press, 1998), 104–05.

9 John Finnis, *Aquinas: Moral, Political, and Legal Theory* (Oxford: Oxford University Press, 1998), 20. This idea of dominion is captured well by Servais Pinckaers' phrase, "freedom for excellence." Servais Pinckaers, O.P., *The Sources of Christian Ethics*, trans. Sr. Mary Thomas Noble, O.P. (Washington, DC: Catholic University of America Press, 1995). Pinckaers contrasts freedom for excellence with "freedom of indifference," which is not analogous to the common-law category of matters of indifference. In context, it seems to mean freedom exercised without regard to what is true and right and good.

10 See Thomas Aquinas, *Commentary on Aristotle's Nicomachean Ethics*, trans. C. J. Litzinger (Notre Dame: Dumb Ox, 1993), 1–2; Finnis, *Aquinas*, 20–23; Adam J. MacLeod, *Property and Practical Reason* (Cambridge: Cambridge University Press, 2015), 91–107.

reason perceives and discerns what is objectively true of the world as given to and received by us. For example, reason can discern that price is a function of supply and demand. In the second order, the order of language and logic, reason distinguishes and names what it finds to be true. For example, reason can distinguish between "mine" and "yours." In the third order, that of the will, reason deliberates and acts for possible ends through the exercise of free choice. For example, a reasonable person can choose to give money to another person, though she has no duty to do so, solely for the reason of the other's well-being. And finally, in the fourth order, reason brings new orders into the world by innovating and building devices and artifacts to improve life. For example, humans invented alternating current and the light bulb. We also create law.

As an artifact of law, dominion over property exists in the fourth order. But it cannot be constructed to suit the beings who occupy it unless it is suited to perfection in all four orders. For human beings exist and exercise practical reason in all four orders. The one who exercises the power to choose is the crown of all creation, the very being whom God made in His own image, Adam and Eve. For their sons and daughters, choosing and acting can cause order in the world. And it can cause chaos.

The stakes are high not only for the world of material and intellectual resources but also for ourselves. The exercise of the power to choose changes the one who exercises it in the third order, the order that "reason in deliberating establishes in the operation of the will."[11] Intentional action shapes the actor's will in the mold of those motivations to which the will is directed. The voluntary choice of reasons found the chosen reasons in one's character.[12] For better and worse, our habits and dispositions are not stable. They are constituted over time according to the reasons that we establish in our wills by deliberate choice and action. One who covets tends to become covetous. Some actions are intrinsically wrong; one should never be willing to do them. However, one who gives freely becomes charitable. Some actions are intrinsically good; one must be free to do them in order to internalize them as ends toward which one's will is inclined.

Like other laws, property norms can determine in part the shape of the wills and characters of human beings who exercise and encounter them. For property norms are reasons for action. They are the sort of reasons that function by blocking from our deliberation other possible reasons and by directing us toward particular ends, by particular means. The reasons that property norms deflect from the will and those that they require to be acted upon have third-order, moral effects on those who are governed by property law.

So, any institution of property faces twin, opposing dangers. If ownership does not entail liberty and power to shape the norms of property then people are deprived of opportunities to become practically reasonable people, more fully

11 Aquinas, *Commentary*, 2.

12 John Finnis, *Collected Essays of John Finnis, vol. II: Intention & Identity* (Oxford: Oxford University Press, 2012), 37–38; John Finnis, *Collected Essays of John Finnis, vol. I: Reason in Action* (Oxford: Oxford University Press, 2012), 237–43.

human. And defective or arbitrary property laws can badly damage the practical reasonableness of those governed by law. However, too much liberty, or the wrong kinds of liberties generate opportunities to cause lasting self-harm in the way that matters most to us as humans, the shape of our character. Virtue requires liberty. But liberty is occasion for vice.

A bounded office of liberty

The question who succeeds to Adam's and Eve's office of dominion has often been a point of difficulty, as dominion over things was at times tied to the dominion of the crown over the kingdom. The early American view was expressed by Jefferson, who argued that the crown's claim was a usurpation, for the "Saxon ancestors" from whom the common law descends "held their lands, as they did their personal property, in absolute dominion, disencumbered with any superior." In Jefferson's account, William the Conqueror introduced feudal land holdings to English soil, and those estates that he dispensed to his agents remained the exception to the general "Saxon laws of possession, under which all lands were held in absolute right." Since America was never conquered by William, it is governed by the Saxon doctrine of radically independent title.[13]

Pollock and Maitland, whose account is a work of scholarship rather than advocacy, thought the early English conception of dominion more complicated, for "it has to assume so many shades of meaning." All land must be held of the king; "otherwise he would not be king of all England. To wish for an ownership of land that shall not be subject to royal rights is to wish for the state of nature." But the medieval conception of rights as distinct things allowed English jurists to separate ownership of the land, which vests in the tenant, from ownership of the seignory—the service owed—which is owned by the lord. Thus, "an owner is none the less an owner because he and his land owe services to the king or to some other lord."[14] Dominion over the resources of the world was distinct from a king's dominion over his subjects at least as early as Bracton, and the Roman and civilian distinction between dominium directum—the lord's right of disposition—and dominium utile—the vassal's right to use—"is quite alien to the spirit of English law."[15] In this sense, the king's *dominium* over land is no different in kind from the rights of private landholders.[16]

13 Thomas Jefferson, *A Summary View of the Rights of British America* (1774), http://avalon.law.yale.edu/18th_century/jeffsumm.asp.

14 Frederick Pollock and Frederic William Maitland, *The History of English Law before the Time of Edward I*, vol. 2 (Indianapolis: Liberty Fund, 2010) (2nd ed., 1898), 3–6.

15 Ibid., vol. 2, 6 note 9. In another footnote, Pollock and Maitland discussed Bracton's double use of "dominus" to mean both chief lord ("capitalis dominus") and true owner ("verus dominus"). They observe that the English language of Bracton's day had not the word "ownership." Ibid., 4 note 4. Nevertheless, Bracton and his contemporaries "ascribed to the tenant in demesne ownership and nothing less than ownership." Ibid., 6.

16 Ibid., vol. 1, 538–41.

The two most influential property theorists of the early modern period, Matthew Hale and John Locke, both expressly severed the concept of dominion of title from the dominion of man over man, and gave it an egalitarian employment.[17] Hale connected dominion to "propriety," which he identified with the right to use resources for profitable ends.[18] Locke wrote of "Adam's propriety, or private dominion," which he distinguished from a "power over men,"[19] the patriarchal right to rule which Robert Filmer had grounded in Adam's "command" over the world.[20]

Hale's account, which Blackstone later followed and adapted both in its general structure and in many of its particulars,[21] is especially instructive. Writing a decade before Locke, Hale traced "the originall Dominion and propriety of all things" from "Almighty God" to God's human creatures. God "hath given the profitable use of all things in this lower world to mankind."[22] He expressed doubt that natural property rights could be grounded in a state of nature "because most of the methods of acquisition of property seems to be by institution." He conceded that the first person to appropriate out of the common stock might justly claim priority of title under a "secondary Law of Nature." His claim is "superadded to that primitive right in common... somewhat by his industry." Yet title requires some specification and settlement in human customs and laws.[23]

Nevertheless, natural law itself both justifies and limits some rights of private ownership. Hale assumed for the sake of argument "that antecedently to civill institutions, where by the Rules and Laws of Property are settled, there is no means peculiarly to appropriate any thing to any man." Yet even before political society and positive law got going, "there are certaine rights of Natural Law and Justice instituted by almighty God and obliging every person of Mankind."[24] For even in that condition of "indeterminate property" prior to conventional rights, all are governed by (a version of) the Golden Rule, "not to do to another what a Man would not have done to himself," and by the Second Great Commandment, to love one's neighbor as oneself. These laws entail certain categorical limitations on one's freedom to act with respect to things. Natural justice both forbids wrongful invasion of another's possession and requires an exception

17 I am grateful to James Stoner and S. Adam Seagrave for these observations on Hale's and Locke's meanings.

18 Matthew Hale, *Of the Law of Nature*, ed. David S. Sytsma (Grand Rapid, MI: Christian's Library Press, 2015) (1670), 89–102.

19 John Locke, *Two Treatises of Government and a Letter Concerning Toleration* (Stilwell, KS: Digireads.com, 2005) (1689), 13–22.

20 Robert Filmer, *Patriarcha, or the Natural Power of Kings* (1680), http://oll.libertyfund.org/titles/filmer-patriarcha-or-the-natural-power-of-kings.

21 John Finnis, *Collected Essays of John Finnis, vol. IV: Philosophy of Law* (Oxford: Oxford University Press, 2012), 189–210.

22 Hale, *Law of Nature*, 90.

23 Ibid., 89–90.

24 Ibid.

to exclusive possession in cases of necessity to save a human life.[25] Natural law determines an incipient right to exclude and an incipient necessity doctrine.

Indeed, though human law supplies "specification" and "determination" to natural duties variously, "according to the variety of Circumstances,"[26] Hale thought that the nature of human relations *requires* ownership. Hobbes' idea that fear primarily moves humans into society "is but a narrow and weak conjecture." Citing Aristotle, Hale insisted that humans enter society because they love it and find it reasonable and useful to their well-being. Here and elsewhere, Hale contrasted the common law, resting on reason which must be completed and perfected by experienced judgment, to Hobbes' "doctrine of sovereignty" and the "resulting arbitrariness of the command theory of law implicit in that doctrine."[27]

Thus, in Hale's conception of dominion, the divisions and distinctions of property law are determined according to considerations of practical wisdom. Human society requires norms to govern the use of things. And insofar as those norms must be congruous to human nature, they must be consonant with reason. Though the "full complement" of property laws is not settled and specified until after the settlement of government, "the distinction of property began early in the world, and that by a kind of natural congruity and propension to which men were inclined." The reasons Hale identified for the pre-political division into private estates, and the rejection of "Plato's Community," are recognizable as incipient statements of what we now know as the tragedy of the commons and the moral hazards of free riding.[28]

Hale's concept of dominion is neither an individualistic state of nature, in which each is free to order his actions without asking leave of any other, nor a sovereign-command system, in which liberty is merely the absence of law, contingent upon the sovereign's forbearance. What emerges from his sketch is the image of a few, immutable structural elements and considerable open space between them. Most rights and duties are specified by those who exercise dominion as they go about their business according to the customs and practices of their communities.[29]

In short, the natural law of property ownership is partly determined. In this, Hale followed Aquinas' distinction between human laws that are derived from natural law by logical deduction, such that only one correct norm can be specified within reason, and those that are promulgated through the more creative

25 Ibid., 90–93.

26 Ibid., 91–92.

27 Robert Lowry Clinton, *God & Man in the Law* (Lawrence, KS: University Press of Kansas, 1997), 99–100.

28 Hale, *Law of Nature*, 98–101.

29 So powerful are custom and usage in the specification of the common law that an ancient statute can be repealed by contrary usage, and general and particular customs and statutes enacted before the "Time of Memory" all have their legal force as a result of usage, though common law courts supply their particular obligations. Matthew Hale, *The History and Analysis of the Common Law of England* (1713), 2–4, 23–30.

means of determination, on which reasonable minds might come to various conclusions.[30] Blackstone later adopted this distinction when he contrasted natural duties and *mala in se* wrongs with those aspects of municipal law that are matters of indifference.[31]

In matters of indifference, those who exercise dominion have freedom and responsibility to specify the first principles of practical reason as rights and duties of property ownership. That freedom is constrained by practical reason itself, which determines some duties completely and conclusively and others partly and categorically. The fully determined duties of natural law are drawn more or less directly out of first principles, and violations of such duties are *mala in se* (wrongs). The non-owner's duty not to steal or trespass and the owner's duty not to exclude one whose life is in jeopardy are inherent in dominion because human beings are the kind of beings they are. Trespass doctrine, with its categorical duty not to break the close without permission and its categorical right to enter to save a life, is more or less determined by first principles.

Apart from those rights and duties, the norms of property are contingent upon custom, convention, private ordering, legislative promulgation, and the other means by which people make law to govern human affairs. Whether hunters and hikers have a right to pass over land is to be resolved according to local custom. What purposes are valid reasons for entry by consent is a question to be resolved according to the purposes for which leases and licenses are created. What counts as a reasonable use which affects the owner's neighbor is a question for a jury. What uses will be permitted in state-owned common areas is a question for the state as owner. And so forth.

The common law of property ownership bears out Hale's speculative reasoning. English jurists reflected Hale's concern for the fully determined duties of the law of love at critical moments in the development of property law, though not always, not perfectly, and sometimes only after correction. For example, in the late eighteenth and early nineteenth centuries, landowners developed the practice of setting spring guns to shoot trespassers and poachers.[32] In the landmark decision *Ilot v. Wilkes*, King's Bench ratified the practice.[33] But Parliament enacted a law prohibiting the setting of spring guns. And in the pivotal case *Bird v. Hoolbrook*, decided shortly thereafter, the Court of Common Pleas accepted Parliament's instruction.[34] The court sustained an action against Holbrook, whose spring gun injured a young man who entered Holbrook's garden to retrieve a pea hen. The court reasoned that Parliament's enactment, which was prospective with respect to spring guns set with notice, was declaratory of the common law rule that spring guns are not to be set without notice. The court

30 Thomas Aquinas, *Treatise on Law* (Washington, DC: Regnery, 1996), 78–79.

31 Blackstone, *Commentaries*, I, 53–55.

32 *Compare* Richard A. Posner, "Killing or Wounding to Protect a Property Interest," *Journal of Law & Economics*, 14 (1971): 201, 209–12; *with* Finnis, *Philosophy of Law*, 340–51.

33 (1820) 106 Eng. Rep. 674.

34 *Bird v. Holbrook* (1825) 130 Eng. Rep. 911.

distinguished *Ilot* on the ground that Wilks had posted notice of his spring gun, while Holbrook had not.

In his opinion, Chief Justice Best located the declaratory aspect of the rule in a Christian moral absolute.

> It has been argued that the law does not compel every line of conduct which humanity or religion may require; but there is no act which Christianity forbids, that the law will not reach: if it were otherwise, Christianity would not be, as it has always been held to be, part of the law of England. I am, therefore, clearly of opinion that he who sets spring guns, without giving notice, is guilty of an inhuman act, and that, if injurious consequences ensue, he is liable to yield redress to the sufferer.[35]

Common law also bears out Hale's observation that most property norms are contingent upon human customs, choices, and laws. The history of common law recorded not only by Blackstone but also by Gray, Pollock and Maitland, Hogue, Plucknett, Kurtz and Moynihan, Simpson, and Helmholz is the history of the settlement and specification of property norms before the advent of the regulatory and administrative state.[36] The work of specifying dominion's boundaries is performed by plural institutions, such as the family, the jury, and trade in the market; through plural means of promulgation, such as custom, conveyance, license, and judicial discernment of the logic of and reasons for rules; with legislation used either to declare pre-existing norms or to correct some deficiency by changing the law in a particular respect. All of this is supposed in principle to be the working out of, and consistent with, what reason commends.

Settling boundaries, specifying rights

Declaring and making determinate

Dominion is constituted by its boundaries. In common law jurisprudence, wrong remediation just is right specification. It is not right creation, and common law is not judge-made law. The legal realists missed what Hart noticed, that adjudication entails that at least some legal norms pre-exist their declaration in

35 Ibid., 916.

36 John Chipman Gray, *The Rule against Perpetuities* (Boston, MA: Little, Brown and Company, 1886); Frederick Pollock and Frederic William Maitland, *The History of English Law before the Time of Edward I* (Indianapolis: Liberty Fund, 2010) (2nd ed., 1898); Arthur R. Hogue, *Origins of the Common Law* (Indianapolis: Liberty Fund, 1986); Theodore F.T. Plucknettt, *A Concise History of the Common Law* (Indianapolis: Liberty Fund, 2010) (5th ed., 1956); Sheldon F. Kurtz, *Moynihan's Introduction to the Law of Real Property*, 6th ed. (St. Paul: West Academic, 2015); A.W.B. Simpson, *A History of the Land Law*, 2nd ed. (Oxford: Oxford University Press, 1986); R.H. Helmholz, *The* ius Commune *in England: Four Studies* (Oxford: Oxford University Press, 2001).

judgment.[37] The right must pre-exist the wrong, else the wrong is not intelligible as a wrong, that is, as the deprivation of somebody's right.

Nevertheless, the right emerges to view as it is settled and specified in adjudication. Many formalists missed (Hart did not) what the legal realists noticed, that law—especially unwritten law, but also legal text—is partly indeterminate. The process of adjudication is an exercise in identifying, clarifying, and giving legal effect to reasons that were known in common law jurisprudence as "rights" and "rules," and which are more precisely identified by Joseph Raz's helpful analytical term, exclusionary reasons for action.[38] Exclusionary reasons operate in practical reasoning by excluding from deliberation various motivating reasons for or against an action or omission. They can exclude more or less comprehensively. They can be completely exclusionary—peremptory, conclusive, exceptionless—by ruling out all reasons that might be marshaled against an action or omission that the legal reason requires. Or they might rule out some *categories* of motivating reasons but not others.[39]

The common law idea of the declaratory aspect of law, which precedes the actions of legislative and judicial officials, is thus neither mysterious nor especially conceptually challenging. One need not even believe in natural law to perceive it. Any pre-political source of authority will suffice to settle and specify rights. And because rights and duties can be and are settled and specified by custom, license, contract, jury verdicts, and other pre-positive common law institutions, officials can be duty-bound to treat those rights and duties as exclusionary reasons for their official actions. And insofar as some of those rights and duties are fully exclusionary, official duties to act according to law can be exceptionless.

Yet we ought to avoid the opposite danger of claiming too much efficacy for vested private rights.[40] Exclusionary reasons are more or less determinate, according to the categories of motivating reasons that they exclude. The duty to exclude oneself from another's property is more determinate than the duty not to make an unreasonable use one's own property. And neither of those duties is exceptionless in an abstract and general sense, as are the duties not to enslave and to provide notice of spring guns one has set.

Three modes of specification

Common law structures dominion to account for the difference between absolute and categorical prohibitions, without which a society cannot function, and matters of indifference, where norms are at least partly indeterminate except in

37 H.L.A. Hart, *The Concept of Law*, 3rd ed. (Oxford: Oxford University Press, 2012), 124–54.

38 Joseph Raz, *The Morality of Freedom* (Oxford: Oxford University Press, 1986), ch. 7; Joseph Raz, *Practical Reason and Norms* (Oxford: Oxford University Press, 1999), 35–48, 73–89; Joseph Raz, *Practical Reasoning* (Oxford: Oxford University Press, 1978), 128–43.

39 MacLeod, *Property and Practical Reason*, 184–96.

40 Adam J. MacLeod, "Of Brutal Murder and Transcendental Sovereignty: The Meaning of Vested Private Rights," *Harvard Journal of Law & Public Policy*, 41 (2017): 253.

particular judgments. It also draws upon plural sources of authority, not only positive law but also custom, conscience, private ordering, and civil juries. By these means it responds to the requirements of practical reason, which must bring correct and conclusive judgment to bear upon matters of absolute and categorical wrong, and must also allow freedom for deliberation and development of the virtues in response to questions of indifference.

The common law of property has three modes of right and wrong specification, by which it addresses different degrees of specificity and conclusiveness to different property wrongs, and thereby to property rights. In the first mode, it prohibits absolute wrongs—e.g. slavery, setting spring guns without notice—without exception and conclusively. In the second mode, it defines categorical wrongs—e.g. trespass, conversion, infringement—so as to exclude from deliberation and justification all but discrete categories of first-order reasons, such as strict necessity to save a human life. And in the third mode, it leaves to common law institutions—e.g. custom, licenses, bailments, juries, legislatures—judgment concerning those context-dependent wrongs that require resolution case by case, such as nuisance, waste, and other harmful acts and omissions that are unlawful only when performed unreasonably but should be generally prohibited for prudential reasons. These modes can be perceived in the law of property, both separately and in combination.

In the first mode, the common law imports an exceptionless duty of abstention directly from some pre-political sources of law. This mode is responsible for excluding from deliberation those motivations for action that are inconsistent with a virtuous society and damaging to individual character. A binding, conclusive prohibition against an intrinsic wrong, coupled with the threat of legal disabilities and other sanctions, is designed to supplant in the deliberations of citizens the various motivating reasons they might have to commit intrinsic wrongs. In many cases, it deflects the temptation to do a grave wrong for the sake of some putatively greater good. Wrongs are often committed for, or rationalized on the basis of, good reasons. But the choice of evil means to achieve good ends is no less deforming of character than a choice to pursue evil ends by efficient means. An exceptionless prohibition deflects the temptation by excluding from deliberation those good reasons for evil actions and replacing them with a conclusive exclusionary reason: don't do it. Or else.

The duty not to set a spring gun is one of these exceptionless prohibitions. Another example is found in the doctrine of Free English Soil, which provides that any slave who steps foot on English soil or an English warship instantly becomes a free man.[41] This entails that everyone else has an absolute duty not to possess, buy, or sell him and could be liable for battery if they tried to do so by coercion. The right to own a slave could not be found in the rights of the common law. So, where slavery was practiced in English and Spanish colonies in

41 *Somerset v. Stewart* (1772) 98 Eng. Rep. 499; *Forbes v. Cochrane* (1824) 107 Eng. Rep. 450; 2 B. & C. 448. See generally, Justin Buckley Dyer, *Natural Law and the Antislavery Constitutional Tradition* (Cambridge: Cambridge University Press, 2012), 37–73.

North America, the right to buy and sell slaves had to be created by positive law, either by local custom or by statute or both. This meant that when the positive law creating slavery was revoked, by legislation in England's colonies and by the 13th Amendment in the United States, all of the rights to buy and sell slaves vanished.[42] Slaveholders and their customers had no right to obtain compensation for the loss of their slaves because slavery is an intrinsic wrong.

In the second mode of specification, rights and duties are categorical but not absolute and exceptionless. This categorical mode of specification responds to the human needs for information-cost efficiencies and for liberty of choice and action.[43] From an economic perspective, we need simple duties of abstention to govern most of our interactions with things because we very seldom have more than scant information about others' plans of action for things. From a moral perspective, we need freedom from interference by others and liberty from constraint by government in order to exercise practical reason. So, even where one has no absolute liberty or immunity, one should have liberties and immunities that impose on others a prima facie duty of non-interference, or some other abstention.

Categorical duties supply both needs. Walking home from work, I pass thousands of owned resources—cars, trucks, bicycles, homes, signs, playgrounds, businesses, schools, and places of religious assembly. My categorical duties not to enter or possess without permission, not to interfere with others' use, and not to use my own resources to injure others' property conclusively direct my practical deliberations and simultaneously guard the liberties and immunities of those people. And the duties perform all that work without requiring any knowledge about the people themselves or their actions.[44]

The clearest example of categorical specification is the right to exclude others from property one owns and the correlative duty every one of us has to exclude ourselves from things that we do not own. This duty-right correlative is categorical rather than exceptionless or peremptory because it applies regardless what motivations the non-owner might have for entering for possessing the thing but it also admits into deliberation certain discrete categories of motivating reasons on the basis of which entry is not trespassory; the action is justified. I must not enter. But if I see a human being in grave danger and the only way to save that person is to enter or use a resource without permission, the law says that I have no duty to abstain.

Here, as elsewhere, Blackstone provided the canonical account. Trespass is prima facie any action that breaks the close. But an entry is justifiable—is not trespass—even without consent, if the entrant acts for one from among enumerated categories of first-order reasons. Most obviously, under the doctrine of necessity, which Hale thought fully specified by natural law even before political

42 *Buckner v. Street*, 4 F. Cas. 578 (E.D. Arkansas, 1871).

43 Thomas W. Merrill and Henry E. Smith, "The Morality of Property," *William & Mary Law Review*, 48 (2007): 1849.

44 J.E. Penner, *The Idea of Property in Law* (Oxford: Oxford University Press, 1997), 75–76; MacLeod, *Property and Practical Reason*, 41, 205–10.

community, a purpose to save a human life is one such reason. Other purposes which justify entry include to exercise a general public accommodation license, to serve judicial process, to hunt "ravenous beasts of prey," and, if one is poor, to glean after harvest.[45] Local customs also abrogate the general duty of self-exclusion for certain purposes, as for hunting in South Carolina[46] and for hiking in Scotland.[47] These categories of reasons justify entry. Reasons that are not within the discrete categories of justifying reasons do not justify entry, and are deflected from a non-owner's legal reasons by the duty of self-exclusion from things one does not own. The non-owner is not permitted to justify entry or possession on the ground that her plan for use or management of the thing is more reasonable than the owner's, or will benefit a larger number of people, or is better for the resource itself, or… She knows what she must do.

Absolute duties, such as the duties not to enslave and set spring guns, and categorical duties, such as the duty not to trespass, direct people toward practically reasonable choices and actions by directing them away from vicious and unlawful choices and actions. They impose duties of abstention and thus can be generalized as multital rights, good against the world. But insofar as most choices and actions with respect to things involve action, they cannot be universalized the way that absolute and categorical norms can. They are either undetermined or underdetermined by the first principles of practical reasonableness. They must be settled and specified in discrete contexts as paucital jural relations according to all the facts and requirements of practical reason that pertain in the case.

Most of the rights and duties governing property in the common law are therefore neither absolute nor categorical. These fall into the third mode of specification, the mode for determining matters of indifference. This is the mode in which private ordering and self-governance shape the law of property. It is where liberty of action is greatest and where one finds the greatest opportunities to plan and act, to cooperate positively with others, and to become excellent in bringing about and ordering the common good. This is not a freedom to be sole and despotic. It is instead a liberty to make law to govern oneself in community in acts of cooperation with one's neighbors.

In this mode, owners and their fellow citizens have great freedom to specify rights and duties governing property in any number of reasonable ways. In short, humans and groups of humans make their own private law. And the common law provides many very sophisticated tools for the job. Every leasehold for possession of an apartment, every bailment created for repair of an automobile, every public accommodation license exercised by a customer who walks into a department store or bakery or barbershop is the artifact of an act of law-making and of judgment. In short, it is the creation of human dominion. In each of these

45 Blackstone, *Commentaries*, III, 212–13.

46 *McConico v. Singleton*, 9 S.C.L. 244 (Constitutional Court of Appeals of South Carolina, 1818).

47 Alan Blackshaw, "Implied Permission and the Traditions of Customary Access," *Edinburgh Law Review*, 3 (1999): 368.

cases human beings cooperate in specifying rights and duties of property by their deliberate actions. They are exercising practical reason. And if they act consistently with the legal reasons they have made for themselves, they will realize the good of practical reasonableness.

Even in the third mode, liberty is somewhat bounded. For example, common law judges defer to the intentions of grantors, testators, and donors in their specification of rights and duties, but limit the variety of possible configurations of property incidents according to the numerus clausus principle.[48] Freedom to use property is also partly bounded. In determining the boundaries of use rights, common lawyers work from maxims, intermediate premises which reflect ancient practical wisdom.[49]

These limitations reflect Aquinas' insight that even in matters of indifference those who make laws are not free to act arbitrarily but are constrained by certain, given first- and second-order realities, such as the laws of physics and economics. Aquinas used the analogy of an architect, who has freedom to shape and adorn the house, but who also must make the house amenable to human use.[50] So, the doors must be large enough for humans to pass through, and the load-bearing walls must hold the weight of the roof, and the design must in other respects meet given demands, which the architect is not free in reason to disregard.

Like real property, intellectual property law also employs all three modes of specifying wrongs and rights. Certain intentional actions, such as spiteful harm to another's productive employments, are absolutely forbidden under the ancient rule of *Keeble v. Hickeringill*,[51] which American courts have adopted.[52] The duty not to destroy another's invention nor deprive him of the fruits of his intellectual labor out of malice, with no object in view other than to cause him harm, is an absolute, exceptionless reason for action. One may compete with a neighbor and even do him injury without liability, if one is pursuing a rival plan of action directed toward some intelligible good. But one may not prevent him from appropriating the fruits of his innovation out of spite.

The prohibition against spiteful injury is grounded in both third- and fourth-order considerations. It excludes entirely from a person's deliberation and choice, and therefore from his character in the third order, the most corrosive of all motivations, the desire to cause harm or loss to one's neighbor. And it helps

48 See Thomas W. Merrill and Henry E. Smith, *The Oxford Introductions to U.S. Law: Property* (New York: Oxford University Press, 2010), 108–09.

49 J. Stanley McQuade, "Ancient Legal Maxims and Modern Human Rights," *Campbell Law Review*, 18 (1996): 75.

50 Aquinas, *Treatise on Law*, 79.

51 *Keeble v. Hickeringill* (1707) 88 E.R. 945 (King's Bench).

52 E.g. *Burke v. Smith*, 37 N.W. 838 (Mich. 1888). Called the "American rule," this version of abuse of rights doctrine applies only where the actor's *sole* motivation is to cause harm. Compare *Sundowner, Inc. v. King*, 509 P.2d 785 (Idaho 1973) with *Chesley v. King*, 74 Me. 164 (1882).

to preserve trust, which is necessary for a functioning marketplace of ideas and innovations, a fourth-order institution.

American courts have located the foundation of this rule in the second great commandment, the injunction to love one's neighbors as oneself,[53] the same law of love in which Matthew Hale located the foundations of natural property rights. The duty comes into human law because of the third-order implications for judges, who cannot in conscience allow themselves to become instruments of spiteful harm. For a judge to provide the remedy requested by a wrongful claimant, or to fail to provide a remedy for someone harmed by a wrongful exercise of liberty, would be for the judge to declare a wrong to be a right.[54]

In the second mode we find duties not to appropriate the fruits of another's intellectual labor. These duties are categorical and somewhat context-dependent rather than fully determined once for all purposes and against all persons. Some have called the rights correlating with such duties "quasi-property rights" to distinguish them from in rem exclusion.[55] But they are no less property for presenting different facets to different audiences in different contexts.

Patent infringement doctrine develops out of the second mode of specification. It exhibits the same structure of practical reason as trespass to real and personal property. Any act of using, making, offering, or selling a patented invention—any action which breaks the close of the patent—is infringement prima facie.[56] But the action is not infringement if done to satisfy curiosity. In that case, the actor's reason for using or making is experimental. Experimental reasons constitute a discrete category of reasons that are not ruled out of deliberation by the otherwise-conclusive duty not to use or make the patented invention, and which justify use.[57]

The second, categorical mode of specification can also place non-normative limitations on an owner's right. For example, title in a trademark follows priority of use in commerce. Yet at common law, the right is defined locally or regionally rather than once for all in the abstract. Thus, the first user within a regional market cannot be enjoined on behalf of a prior user from a different region. Priority is determined by the purpose for trademark protection, which is to secure the association between the mark and the source of the goods or services. Where a mark is used in two different markets with different meanings, the reason for trademark protection does not justify an injunction.[58]

53 See e.g. *Barger v. Barringer*, 66 S.E. 439, 442 (NC 1909); *Commonwealth v. VonBestecki*, 30 Pa. D. & C. 137, 141–44 (Pa Ct Common Pleas 1937).

54 *Burke v. Smith*, 37 N.W. 838, 842 (Mich. 1888). This is because courts must not "permit themselves to be used as instruments of inequity and injustice." *Henningsen v. Bloomfield Motors, Inc.*, 161 A. 2d 69, 86 (N.J. 1960).

55 *International News Service v. Associated Press*, 248 U.S. 215 (1918).

56 *Hilton Davis Co. v. Warner-Jenkinson, Co., Inc.*, 62 F.3d 1512, 1527 (Fed. Cir. 1995), rev'd on other grounds, 520 U.S. 17 (1997).

57 *Whittemore v. Cutter*, 29 F. Cas. 1120 (C.C.D. Mass. 1813); *Sawin v. Guild*, 21 F. Cas. 554 (C.C.D. Mass. 1813); *Madey v. Duke University*, 307 F.3d 1351, 1360–63 (Fed. Cir. 2002); 35 U.S.C. §271(e).

58 *United Drug Co. v. Theodore Rectanus Co.*, 248 U.S. 90 (1918).

Most of intellectual property law is practiced in the third mode of specification, the domain of private ordering. Inventions and copyrights can be licensed, assigned, mortgaged, and contracted for in much the same way as tangible resources, and trademarks can be conveyed with the business enterprises to which they are appurtenant. Intellectual property law thus opens up new horizons of opportunities for people to collaborate on the basis of creation and discovery, even those who are land poor and politically powerless.

The use and management of intellectual resources is often just as complicated and collaborative as dominion over material resources, if not more so. Thus, the law of intellectual property often combines the modes of wrong specification. For example, the doctrines of unfair competition and misappropriation combine categorical norms with private ordering. As another example, while the law of patent infringement employs categorical norms at the liability stage, it brings in context-dependent considerations such as willfulness, independent invention, and persistence after notice at the remedial stage.

By categorically prohibiting those wrongs that would cause moral harm or destroy trust, and by leaving other acts of commercial interference outside the scope of the law of wrongs in the domains of conveyance and contract, the law of intellectual property strikes a balance between the requirements of commercial morality and the liberty to exercise reason. It maintains this balance insofar as it maps over the common law boundaries of dominion.

Conclusion: eternal implications

The Christian account supplies a profound meaning to property dominion. The exercise of dominion endures in the human being who exercises it. The reflexive aspect of one's actions—character, virtues, and vices—is the part of one that lasts. Unless one repents of one's prior commitments, which repentance becomes increasingly difficult as one becomes more habituated to a commitment, one constitutes one's identity in a permanent disposition. And if the Christian story is true, this course is set not only within time but for eternity. For according to the Christian story, human beings, who bear the image of God in respect of their capacity to choose and act, also bear His image in that they are eternal beings.

In the Christian account, those who take on new life in Christ and endure to the end will exercise dominion for all eternity, participating in the rule of God's eternal kingdom. "Do you not know that we are to judge angels?" Saint Paul asked the Corinthian Christians. "How much more, then, matters pertaining to this life!"[59] One might think of dominion on earth as a tryout for that lasting dominion.

59 1 Cor. 6:3 (ESV). Reacting to an early draft of this paper, Gerald McDermott informed me that to "judge" in this passage likely means to rule as the judges of Israel did in the Old Testament period before the kings.

8 Housing and hope

Private property and Catholic social teaching

Paula A. Franzese and Angela C. Carmella

Introduction: private property and the social mortgage

Many social and economic conditions plague societies and demand our attention and action, particularly at a time when disparities in income are increasing. This chapter presents three that relate to housing. First is the unsafe and uninhabitable properties that pervade the rental market in poorer communities. Second is the lack of affordable housing, which impacts both the poor and the middle class. Third is the failed promise of authentic neighborhoods that are conducive to sustained relationships. Property law, as well as the incentives it creates, affects landlords, developers, and homeowner associations in ways that can ameliorate or worsen these conditions. The intent of this chapter is to provide examples of reform efforts in each of these areas that are consistent with the lessons of Catholic social thought and channel private law decisions in ways that are consistent with the common good.

Property—and the connection between our material world and human dignity—has long been a topic for theological reflection.[1] Catholic social thought about private property always starts with the "universal destination" of created goods.[2] The earth's abundance must be used to ensure that the needs of all are met, and private property is critical to that task. Only through human work—with the use of our freedom and agency and our capacity for reason—will the resources of nature be turned into goods for use and enjoyment. Through work and the ownership of its fruits, we are able to provide for ourselves and our families, to serve ourselves and others.

Private property, then, is a "good" that protects human dignity, promotes responsible actions, and reinforces a stable and secure family life. The Catholic social teachings have encouraged private ownership of property, declaring it to

1 Leo XIII, *Rerum Novarum*, encyclical letter, Vatican website, May 15, 1891, secs. 6, 8. http://w2.vatican.va/content/leo-xiii/en/encyclicals/documents/hf_l-xiii_enc_15051891_rerum-novarum.html.

2 Pontifical Council for Justice and Peace, *Compendium of the Social Doctrine of the Church* (Washington, DC: United States Conference of Catholic Bishops, 2017), sec.177; Edward A. Hartnett, "Catholic Social Teachings on Property," 2001 Law Professors' Christian Fellowship (unpublished manuscript on file with authors).

be "a natural right which the state cannot suppress." But the teachings also declare that private property is under a social mortgage, meaning that private property has a fundamentally social function, that it "naturally entails a social obligation."[3] In essence,

> [w]hatever the forms of property may be ... attention must always be paid to this universal destination of earthly goods. In using them, therefore, man should regard the external things that he legitimately possesses not only as his own but also as common in the sense that they should be able to benefit not only him but also others.[4]

The most recent pronouncement on property and its limits is Pope Francis' call for urgent attention to the stewardship of the earth, given the way in which the abuse of "our common home" has come to harm both the environment and the poor and vulnerable. Francis encapsulated nearly a millennium of church teaching on private property in this paragraph:

> Whether believers or not, we are agreed today that the earth is essentially a shared inheritance, whose fruits are meant to benefit everyone. For believers, this becomes a question of fidelity to the Creator, since God created the world for everyone. Hence every ecological approach needs to incorporate a social perspective which takes into account the fundamental rights of the poor and the underprivileged. The principle of the subordination of private property to the universal destination of goods, and thus the right of everyone to their use, is a golden rule of social conduct and "the first principle of the whole ethical and social order." The Christian tradition has never recognized the right to private property as absolute or inviolable, and has stressed the social purpose of all forms of private property. Saint John Paul II forcefully reaffirmed this teaching, stating that "God gave the earth to the whole human race for the sustenance of all its members, without excluding or favoring anyone." These are strong words. He noted that "a type of

3 John XXIII, *Mater et Magistra*, encyclical letter, Vatican website, May 15, 1961, secs. 19, 112. http://w2.vatican.va/content/john-xxiii/en/encyclicals/documents/hf_j-xxiii_enc_15051961_mater.html.

4 Second Vatican Council, "Pastoral Constitution on the Church in the Modern World, *Gaudium et Spes*, 1965," sec. 69, http://www.vatican.va/archive/hist_councils/ii_vatican_council/documents/vat-ii_cons_19651207_gaudium-et-spes_en.html.

> The exercise of solidarity within each society is valid when its members recognize one another as persons. Those who are more influential, because they have a greater share of goods and common services, should feel responsible for the weaker and be ready to share with them all they possess.

John Paul II, *Sollicitudo Rei Socialis*, encyclical letter, Vatican website, December 30, 1987, Sec. 39. http://w2.vatican.va/content/john-paul-ii/en/encyclicals/documents/hf_jp-ii_enc_30121987_sollicitudo-rei-socialis.html.

> development which did not respect and promote human rights—personal and social, economic and political, including the rights of nations and of peoples—would not be really worthy of man." He clearly explained that "the Church does indeed defend the legitimate right to private property, but she also teaches no less clearly that there is always a social mortgage on all private property, in order that goods may serve the general purpose that God gave them." Consequently, he maintained, it is not in accord with God's plan that this gift be used in such a way that its benefits favor only a few.[5]

The reader may wonder why the Church would even have teaching about private property and economic issues more generally. Its social teachings began in 1891 with a critique of labor conditions and gross disparities in wealth and power, with the intention of being a moral voice for humanity against crushing economic and political forces. The Church's social and economic concerns rest in its sacramental consciousness: the belief that Jesus' incarnation, death, and bodily resurrection locate God's love and concern squarely in the material world. Because the Word became flesh, things of the earth can carry the mystery and power of God, and the focus of our Christian service is to love one another and bring about a just social order. The exhortation "to dwell among [the people]"[6] is at the core of Catholic social teachings. It is there that we find Christ.

When we cultivate proximity to one another we more fully understand that we do not live solely for ourselves. We are each connected to the larger tapestry of our collective humanity and shared dignity. We are responsible for and to each other. Our inextricable interconnectedness teaches us that what we do for others cannot help but redound to our own benefit. What is more, what we do *to* others we do to ourselves.

The call to proximity asks that we use our empathetic pathways to compassionately connect with the experiences and suffering of others, so that we might do what we can to ease that suffering.[7] In that task, it is important that we pay particular attention to the plight of the marginalized, the poor, the forgotten, and the misunderstood. When we cultivate proximity to the roads traveled by others, we come to know our neighbor not as "the other" but instead *as us.*

Everyone has a story to tell and something to teach us. By listening to those stories we learn that we share a common humanity and an intrinsic worth. Most essentially, we see that the burdens of our own travails do not relieve us of the responsibility to respond with an open heart to the suffering endured by others. There is no pain on earth that does not yearn for a benevolent witness. We are

5 Francis, *Laudato Sí*, encyclical letter, Vatican website, May 24, 2015, sec. 93. http://w2.vatican.va/content/francesco/en/encyclicals/documents/papa-francesco_20150524_enciclica-laudato-si.html.

6 Exod 29:45; 2 Cor. 6:16 Revised Standard Version.

7 Paula A. Franzese, "The Power of Empathy in the Classroom," *Seton Hall Law Review*, 47, no. 3 (2016): 693.

asked to be that witness so that we might be moved to help ease that pain. At its best, the work of justice provides relief from despair, restores agency to the voiceless, and narrows the gap between what is and what ought to be. Dwelling amidst the people with the increased understanding that proximity brings, our work as lawyers helps us and the people we serve to see that "love is the motive and justice its instrument."[8]

This notion of proximity reflects the Church's teaching on the dignity and social nature of all human persons. Dignity is a transcendental characteristic possessed by each of us, to be recognized and respected in all concrete historical situations. Sociality means we become fully ourselves within and through community with others. All rights, civil and material, come from our inherent dignity, and all societies must create the conditions needed for the realization of those rights for all. Indeed, to be vindicated those rights call for and depend on a good education system, accessible health care, housing, employment, decent working conditions, a just wage, and private property (subject to social duties).

The social teachings provide no blueprint for achieving the common good but call on all private actors in civil society as well as governments to work toward these goals. In that task, special attention must be paid to the poor and vulnerable because the common good must attend to the humanity of all. The "preferential option for the poor" is offered as a demand of justice, not an act of charity. A key value of Catholic social teaching is the preferential option for the poor, which teaches that the "quality of justice is best measured by how the poor and most vulnerable are faring."[9] Thus, private property is always a qualified right: property must be used in ways that recognize the moral claims of others in society.

American property law presumes a private property system and protects the interests of owners. Landlords, developers, and homeowner associations enjoy substantial legal protections for the properties they rent, develop, and control. Yet property laws are also capable of guiding these private actors in ways that respect the human person, whose healthy development depends upon life in family, community, and neighborhood. In Catholic social thought, private actors are responsible for promoting the common good; the state coordinates private efforts in this regard but does not usurp them.

The principle of subsidiarity locates and protects problem-solving and community-building at the local level. But the state steps in to regulate or change the incentives where private efforts are insufficient and especially when they are contrary to the common good. Consistent with this Catholic social vision, laws that affect the condition of housing, the access to housing and neighborhoods, and the neighborhood environment can be crafted to support human dignity,

8 Patrick Granfield, "An Interview with Reinhold Niebuhr," *Commonwealth*, 85, no. 16 (Dec. 16, 1966): 1935–1965.

9 United States Catholic Conference, "Homelessness and Housing, A Human Tragedy, A Moral Challenge," (March 24, 1988): 639, http://www.usccb.org/issues-and-action/human-life-and-dignity/housing-homelessness/upload/homelessness-and-housing.pdf.

development, and solidarity. This is precisely how law can reflect the social mortgage. By contrast, the social mortgage is compromised by laws and policies that exclude whole segments of the population from the promise of opportunity and a safe, welcoming place to call home.

Channeling private law decisions to promote the common good

Affordable and safe shelter

The lack of affordable housing is a constant concern for far too many American families. The amount that a household can pay for housing determines both the quality of the dwelling and the choice of community or neighborhood.[10] At the time we write, the majority of low-income renters spend over 50% of their income on rent, with many spending in excess of 70%.[11] And a full one-third of Americans struggle to get by on a daily basis.[12] Nationwide, two-thirds of renting families below the poverty line receive no housing assistance.[13] Yet, the number of government housing vouchers continues to decrease and the striking gap between those of little or no means and those of vast wealth continues to widen.[14]

Sociologist Matthew Desmond, who has studied eviction, poverty, and affordable housing, notes that "the high cost of housing is consigning the urban poor to financial ruin." He explains that society has "ushered in a sad and unreasonable moment in the history of the United States if thousands of poor families are dedicating upward of eighty and ninety percent of their income to rent." [15] Tenants are being evicted at astonishingly high rates. Because of the vast volume of evictions seen in housing courts, judges often do not have the time to distinguish between tenants who are victims of uninhabitable premises and those who neglected to pay the lease, thus grouping all tenants together irrespective of their reason for being in housing court in the first place.[16]

10 Jacqueline Luffman, "Measuring housing affordability," *Perspectives on Labour and Income*, 7, no. 11 (November 2006).

11 Matthew Desmond, "Unaffordable America: Poverty, housing, and eviction," *Fast Focus: Institute for Research on Poverty*, 22, no. 22 (March 2015): 2.

12 Greg Kaplan, Giovanni L. Violante, and Justin Weidner, "The Wealthy Hand-to-Mouth," *National Bureau of Economic Research*, No. w20073 (2014).

13 Desmond, "Unaffordable America," 2. "Public Policy Forum at Drew Tackles Eviction Crisis," Drew University, last modified November 7, 2017, http://www.drew.edu/news/2017/11/07/public-policy-forum-at-drew-tackles-eviction-crisis.

14 Richard Fry and Rakesh Kochhar, "America's Wealth Gap between Middle-Income and Upper-Income Families Is Widest on Record," *Pew Research Center*, 17 (December 17, 2014): 1840–1860.

15 Mathew Desmond, "Eviction and the reproduction of urban poverty," *American Journal of Sociology*, 118, no. 1 (July 2012): 122.

16 Emily Badger and Quoctrung Bui, "In 83 Million Eviction Records, a Sweeping and Intimate New Look at Housing in America," *New York Times*, April 7, 2018, https://www.nytimes.com/

Catholic social teachings exhort us to correct this untenable state of affairs. Indeed, the Church recognizes several aspects of human identity as essential and not optional: "the protection of human dignity and human rights, the provision of a deep sense of meaning for every human activity, and the promotion of the human family." It is not surprising that rights to housing, along with food, health care, education, and a healthy economy, are part of "the common good." The Church's core mission is focused upon the welfare of humanity, so it is vital that there be equal attention paid to "justice, liberation, development and peace."[17]

Pope Francis has called land and housing a "sacred right" that stems from the "social teaching of the Church," explaining that family and housing go "hand in hand" and that for a house to be a home, it requires a community dimension, since it is "precisely in the neighborhood where the great family of humanity begins to be built." The Pope expressed dismay at the fact that housing is denied to thousands, including children, "who are called inelegant names such as 'street people' or 'without fixed abode' or 'urban camper'."[18] Without a safe and sustainable roof over one's head, all aspects of one's life suffer.

The United States Conference of Catholic Bishops has referred to the global issue of homelessness as a "human tragedy" and a "moral challenge." The housing crisis does not only manifest itself in the vast lack of safe and habitable dwellings, "but also implicates other values that directly impact those who are rendered homeless." Homelessness and the lack of adequate housing are "destroying lives, undermining families, hurting communities, and weakening the social fabric of our nation." Traditional Catholic teaching views housing not as a "commodity" but as a "basic human right," which is grounded in Catholicism's conviction of society's responsibility to protect the life and dignity of each person and ensure that human life is enhanced. As Pope John Paul II so aptly stated, a "house is much more than a roof over one's head" but is a "place where a person creates and lives out his or her life."[19]

But for all too many, sadly this is not a reality. Instead, the so-called "American dream" of owning a decent, stable home has turned into a nightmare. The many who cannot afford housing fall along a vast spectrum of circumstances—from young people whose jobs do not pay enough for them to afford to live in reasonable proximity to their places of work to senior citizens who are suffering

---

interactive/2018/04/07/upshot/millions-of-eviction-records-a-sweeping-new-look-at-housing-in-america.html.

17 Angela C. Carmella, "A Catholic View of Law and Justice," in *Christian Perspectives on Legal Thought*, eds. Michael W. McConnell, Robert F. Cochran Jr., and Angela C. Carmella (New Haven, CT: Yale University Press, 2001), 256–266.

18 Francis, "Address to the Participants in the World Meeting of Popular Movements," Vatican website, October 28, 2014, http://w2.vatican.va/content/francesco/en/speeches/2014/october/documents/papa-francesco_20141028_incontro-mondiale-movimenti-popolari.html.

19 Catholic Conference, "Homelessness and Housing," 639–42. There is a "national disgrace of widespread homelessness… and the broader housing crises that undermines the life and dignity of so many." *Id.* at 639.

from pension cuts and can no longer afford rent payments. Several factors, including unemployment, low salaries, gentrification, rural exodus, industrialization, and an accelerated population growth, have led to grossly inadequate and insufficient stocks of affordable housing.[20]

Property has a "specific social function," and should be "subordinated to the right to common use." Housing is not simply a "market commodity." It is a human right. Hence, a host of public and private actors must work together to ensure that there is "just distribution of housing," and, what is more, the opportunity for those of all socio-economic levels and backgrounds to be homeowners. Housing is more than a mere room with four walls and a roof. In addressing the housing problem, the Pontifical Commission writes that "the right to shelter also implies the notion of security" and urges society to implement rent policies and local planning in order to allow the entire community to coalesce.[21]

There are many parallels between biblical teachings and the goals of affordable housing, of helping the marginalized, remediating exclusion, and ensuring access for all. There is an intimacy between the family and the house, and the Church notes that "God himself wanted his people to build him a 'house' ... which he deigned 'to dwell' and 'to make his name dwell there'."[22] Pope Francis has said, "[w]e can find no social or moral justification, no justification, no justification whatsoever, for lack of housing." The Pope explained that

> [t]he Son of God came into this world as a homeless person. The Son of God knew what it was to be a homeless person, what it was to start life without a roof over his head. We can imagine what Joseph must have been thinking. How is it that the Son of God has no home? Why are we homeless, why don't we have housing?[23]

He added, "[t]hese are questions which many of you may ask daily. Like St. Joseph, you may ask: Why are we homeless, without a place to live?"

The problems

Two trends have been heralded as responsible for the steady rise in homelessness over the past several decades—a decrease in affordable rental units and an

20 Ibid., 642 (The shattering of the American dream of homeownership has been described "from an ethical point of view," as "a scandal.")

21 Holy See, "Charter of the Rights of the Family," Vatican website, October 22, 1983, http://www.vatican.va/roman_curia/pontifical_councils/family/documents/rc_pc_family_doc_19831022_family-rights_en.html.

22 Ibid.

23 "'No justification whatsoever' for lack of housing, pope says," Catholic News Service, last modified September 24, 2015, http://www.catholicnews.com/services/englishnews/2015/no-justification-whatsoever-for-lack-of-housing-pope-says.cfm.

increase in systemic poverty.[24] Diminishing federal and state rental assistance programs are simply unable to keep up with the staggering demands for affordable housing. At present, waiting lists for subsidized units can extend up to five years.

Tenants able to secure subsidized housing often endure deplorable living conditions, fraught with insurmountable health and safety hazards. Countless instances of abuse have been documented, ranging from bedbug infestation to mold to the absence of heat in the winter, the lack of running water, and inadequate plumbing. Landlords in the business of leasing government-subsidized affordable rentals often continue to receive sizable federal and state subsidies even for units grossly unfit for basic dwelling. In that way, so-called slumlords are without the incentive to repair and rehabilitate dilapidated units as they continue to profit at the expense of tenants who cannot afford alternatives. Dr. Martin Luther King, Jr. noted aptly that "Every condition exists simply because someone profits by its existence. This economic exploitation is crystallized in the slum."[25]

While there are legal mechanisms in place to assure habitability and prevent wrongful evictions, the overwhelming majority of low-income tenants are unaware of those safeguards and without counsel to achieve their vindication. One of those safeguards, the implied warranty of habitability, is an implicit promise that every residential landlord makes to provide tenants with premises suitable for basic human dwelling. This warranty can be asserted affirmatively in a claim against the landlord or defensively in the course of an eviction proceeding. Yet, the warranty is grossly underutilized, on both the local and national level. But in those few instances where it is raised (in the rare case that the aggrieved tenant has legal representation), it does work, prompting courts to compel landlord compliance with applicable standards for habitability.[26] That fact makes plain that access to counsel matters, and that a right without a means for its realization is hollow.

The vast preponderance of aggrieved tenants facing eviction and its devastating consequences are without legal representation. Unrepresented tenants are at extreme disadvantages without the "specialized knowledge" that attorneys bring to the courthouse. A mere 7% of unrepresented tenants were reinstated in their apartments after an eviction proceeding.[27] In housing court, the difference

24 "Why Are People Homeless?" National Coalition for the Homeless, last modified July 2009, http://www.nationalhomeless.org/factsheets/why.html.

25 Matthew Desmond, *Evicted: Poverty and Profit in the American City* (New York: Broadway Books, 2017), 305.

26 Paula A. Franzese, Abbott Gorin and David Guzik, "The Implied Warranty of Habitability Lives: Making Real the Promise of Landlord-Tenant Reform," *Rutgers Law Review*, 69 no. 1 (2016): 1.

27 Steven Gunn, "Eviction Defense for Poor Tenants: Costly Compassion or Justice Served?" *Yale Law & Policy Review* 13 no. 2 (1995): 414. ("Only twelve percent of the legal services tenants who related settlement agreements with their landlords defaulted, while thirty-four percent of the unrepresented tenants defaulted.")

between a victory and a defeat can turn on something as simple as the questions the judge poses to a tenant: judges usually inquire whether tenants have paid the rent, but very rarely ask tenants if there was a defense to non-payment.

For a tenant to appear in court without legal representation requires that she navigate on her own a procedural labyrinth rife with sand traps for the unwary. Her very appearance in court likely requires her to take time off from work, lose wages, and secure additional child care. A tenant living paycheck to paycheck cannot afford those costs. What is more, to successfully contest an eviction action requires substantive knowledge of the law and familiarity with the defenses available for nonpayment of rent when the premises are unsafe and unsound. It requires the effective assistance of counsel.

As a result of the vast range of housing court inequities, evicted tenants are left to the calamitous effects of displacement. There is a harmful relationship between health outcomes—such as asthma, malnutrition, and lead poisoning—and household conditions—such as rodent infestations, lead paint, broken appliances, and building code violations.[28] Free legal counsel must be afforded to low-income tenants facing eviction. Across the board, tenants who are represented by an attorney are far less likely to suffer eviction than those without legal representation.[29] But without legal assistance, tenants find themselves consigned to the insecurity and hardship that comes when one is without a sustainable and livable dwelling.

To compound the harms suffered by tenants with little choice but to endure unsound living conditions, tenants who withhold rent to direct those sums to on-site abatement of the problems or to compel landlord remediation of the defective conditions find themselves summarily evicted. Tenants named in an eviction action are often relegated to damning registries or "blacklists" of undesirable tenants.[30] Those lists do not indicate anything about the surrounding circumstances that resulted in the given tenant's not paying rent. They do not provide the final disposition of the action and do not even indicate when the named tenant has prevailed in the matter. They do not afford the adversely affected tenant the opportunity to clear her name, respond or correct errors in the listing.[31] Yet, a tenant whose name appears on the list will be denied

28 "Housing Displacement and Health," *Regional Public Health* (September 2011): 4. ("Evidence suggests that housing displacement and subsequent relocation is a traumatic experience with considerable short term and long-term health costs.")

29 Desmond, "Eviction and the Reproduction of Urban Poverty," 123.

30 Julie Satow, "On the List, and Not in a Good Way," *New York Times*, October 16, 2014, https://www.nytimes.com/2014/10/19/nyregion/a-tenant-blacklist-culled-from-tedium.html?_r=0.

31 Anne Machalinski, "The Dreaded Tenant Blacklist: What You Need to Know," *Brick Underground*, October 23, 2017, https://www.brickunderground.com/blog/2014/05/tenant_blacklist. ("[F]or tenants, the major issue is that the information is incomplete. The blacklist doesn't provide any context for the case, such as who sued whom, the winning party, or whether there was a settlement.") Instead of a formal appeals process to remedy errors or explain misleading information, renters are limited to attempting to explain, on their own, to a potential landlord why she was placed on the report.

future rental opportunities, stigmatized and excluded from the promise of fair housing.[32]

For example, Yanira Cortes, a mother of four young children, lives in subsidized housing in Newark, New Jersey. Her apartment is infested by rats, roaches, and mold. Her complaints to the landlord have gone unheeded. Finally, when the premises' bathroom ceiling collapsed, she withheld rent as allowed by law and was promptly sued for eviction. As a result, she found herself placed on a tenant blacklist that sunk her chances of finding another apartment. In her words, "Now when I try to apply to other places, they tell me, 'You went to court for an eviction, you're a bad tenant'."[33]

Call to service

Various entities and agencies must coalesce in order to recognize a "constitutional right to shelter."[34] There is more than a lack of sufficient available affordable housing; there is also an overabundance of housing that is neither decent nor safe and instead oftentimes completely uninhabitable, with "infrahuman living conditions."[35] Because of this, there are both quantitative and qualitative aspects to the housing problem. The Church often analogizes Christ's struggles with those who are currently suffering in uninhabitable living conditions. The Church aspires for people to see the face of Christ in the poor, as the "first human problem Christ faced on earth was a lack of shelter."[36] But all too often, the poor are forgotten, relegated to the margins of society and forced to face their struggles alone.[37] Catholic social teaching seeks to reverse this by encouraging everyone to feel the pain and desperation faced by those who are without a home or living in uninhabitable premises, unfit for human dwelling.[38]

32 Teri Karush Rogers, "Only the Strongest Survive," *New York Times*, November 26, 2006, http://www.nytimes.com/2006/11/26/realestate/26cov.html.

> 99 percent [of landlords] flat out reject anybody with a landlord-tenant record, no matter what the reason is and no matter what the outcome is, because if their dispute has escalated to going to court, an owner will view them as a pain.

33 Ms. Cortes' story, together with the stories of other similarly situated tenants, is chronicled in Paula A. Franzese, "A Place to Call Home: Tenant Blacklisting and the Denial of Opportunity," *Fordham Urban Law Journal*, 45, no. 3 (2018): 673.

34 S. Lynn Martinez, "An American Vision: The Right to Shelter," *In Public Interest*, 12 (1992): 1.

> Naturally, the right to temporary shelter is a band-aid on an open sore. However, once established, this reform may lead to another right which should have existed all along: the right to clean and safe, affordable and habitable permanent housing."

35 "What Have You Done to Your Homeless Brother?" Feast of the Holy Family, last modified December 27, 1987, http://theolibrary.shc.edu/resources/homeless.htm.

36 Catholic Conference, "Homelessness and Housing," 639.

37 Dorothy Day, "Poverty and Precarity," *The Catholic Worker*, May 1952, http://www.catholicworker.org/dorothyday/articles/633.html. ("We must talk about poverty because people lose sight of it, can scarcely believe that it exists.")

38 Dorothy Day, "Poverty and Destitution," *The Catholic Worker*, April 1966, http://www.catholicworker.org/dorothyday/articles/838.html. ("The pain, the anguish, the sin and despair,

The Church urges society to be "haunted by the tragic reality of so many without decent housing" as "it is a sign of serious social neglect and moral failure." In combining its own goals with those of the state and government, it emphasizes that a "great and good nation cannot turn away as people wander our streets looking for a decent home."[39] The Church is concerned with the lack of decent housing for those who cannot afford otherwise, explaining that adequate housing is vital in order for a person to achieve individual, familial, and societal fulfillment and that a mission of the Church is to make society more humane.[40] When a person does not have safe housing, his or her very dignity is threatened. The Church and external agencies are to work in conjunction in order to provide shelter to homeless families, educate and strengthen community development, and partner with legislative bodies that are developing housing policies that favor the poor.

Still, despite its best efforts and goals, Catholic social teaching is cognizant of the fact that charitable efforts alone are not a substitute for "public policies that offer real opportunities and dignity for the poor." The United States Conference of Catholic Bishops proposes several goals for national housing policy, including preservation, production, participation, partnership, affordability, and opportunity.[41] It takes a progressive stance on this matter and a range of others including gun control, health care, minimum wage standards, and immigration reform.[42] But the right to housing is not a partisan issue and transcends party lines and labels. Yet, many who seek to defend the dignity of others can find themselves caught in political crosshairs or swayed by political affiliations that frustrate the collective aims of decent housing for all.[43]

Christ must be seen in the "despised, the poor, the weak, and the 'useless'" and "God himself and God's absolute demand for justice and love" should be seen in each and every person. Society must answer the call to protect the poor in order to overcome social, political, and economic injustices.[44] These teachings call for a "new heaven and a new earth, wherein justice dwelleth."[45] The preferential option for the poor is an imperative if justice is to be served.[46] As lawyers, we are uniquely situated to wield the powerful instrument of the law for the

the remorse, at not living as one knows one should live, as a human being should live, fully and abundantly!")

39 Catholic Conference, "Homelessness and Housing," 639.

40 "What Have You Done to Your Homeless Brother?"

41 Catholic Conference, "Homelessness and Housing," 639.

42 Eddie Zakreski, "The Democrats, Catholics, God and Caesar," *The Wall Street Journal*, March 29, 2018, https://www.wsj.com/articles/the-democrats-catholics-god-and-caesar-1522345432.

43 Cardinal Timothy Dolan, "The Democrats Abandon Catholics," *The Wall Street Journal*, March 22, 2018, https://www.wsj.com/articles/the-democrats-abandon-catholics-1521761348.

44 Carmella, "A Catholic View of Law and Justice," 275.

45 Dorothy Day, "Aims and Purposes," *The Catholic Worker*, February 1940, http://www.catholicworker.org/dorothyday/articles/182.html (quoting from Rev. 21:1).

46 Carmella, "A Catholic View of Law and Justice," 275.

common good and to use our expertise to be catalysts for meaningful reform, so that the promise of that "new heaven and earth" can be realized.

Catholic Social Teaching has implications for many aspects of property law, concerning both the availability and the quality of housing. These final two sections consider an example of each: first, the New Jersey Supreme Court's effort to make neighborhoods more inclusive; and second, the importance of regulating homeowners' associations so as to build community.

The promise of inclusion and inclusionary zoning

In 1975, the Supreme Court of New Jersey issued a groundbreaking decision, *Mount Laurel I*, and officially declared that the state constitution required the state to regulate land use for "developing municipalities" in order to provide low and moderate income housing. The New Jersey legislature in turn created the Council on Affordable Housing (COAH), which was tasked with defining housing regions within the state, establishing the present and prospective state and regional need for affordable housing, and promulgating guidelines to assist municipalities within each region to determine their "fair share of [that] region['s] housing need." The goal was to eliminate exclusionary zoning—"local land-use controls that have the effect of excluding most low-income and many moderate-income households from suburban communities and, indirectly, of excluding most members of minority groups."[47] COAH was disbanded after failing to meet a judicially imposed deadline for establishing new housing guidelines, thus placing the task of enforcing the *Mt. Laurel* mandate in the hands of certain designated judges.

There have been mixed reactions to the legislature's mandate that municipalities must require the development of affordable housing for poor and middle-class families left behind by tides of gentrification and upscale development.[48] The *NIMBY* syndrome, or "not in my backyard," is often invoked in the effort to block access to those of low income within a given township's borders. A significant part of the resistance to inclusionary housing is predicated on fear of "the other" and, in particular, misperceptions about the consequences of inclusionary housing. Many equate such development with a parade of dire conditions such as increased crime, drugs, blight, higher taxes, and diminished property values. But compelling empirical study tells us that those fears yield to fact and that inclusion redounds to the benefit of *all* residents. In the town of Mt. Laurel itself, where the New Jersey Supreme Court's mandate to provide affordable housing

47 Daniel Mandelker and Roger Cunningham, *Planning and Control of Land Development* (Charlottesville, VA: Michie Co., 1985), 304.

48 Salvador Rizzo, "N.J. Supreme Court: Towns Must Have Affordable Housing," *NorthJersey.com*, January 18, 2017, http://www.northjersey.com/story/news/new-jersey/2017/01/18/nj-supreme-court-ramps-up-towns-affordable-housing-obligations/96712760/.

was abided, the inclusion of low-cost housing had no adverse effects on more well-off residents, and crime rates dropped while property values rose.[49]

Mt.Laurel's main goal is inclusionary zoning—preventing the exclusion of the perceived "other" and instead allowing for those of varying income levels to co-inhabit the same communities. Catholic social teaching aims to advance inclusion among those of differing economic backgrounds. Even though the state only provides a baseline framework regarding how municipalities must act, Catholic teaching supports "active government involvement in housing."[50] "Solidarity" means "thinking and acting in terms of community" as the "lives of all take priority over the appropriation of goods by a few." The Pope speaks about marginalization and how cities "abandon a part of themselves to marginal settlements on the periphery," and has called it "painful" to hear of the "cruel" images of "violent evictions, bulldozers knocking down the tiny dwellings, images just like from a war."[51]

Pope Francis has explained that "the line to follow is neither eradication nor marginalization but urban integration" through a form of "cosmetic architecture," thus supplanting projects that "aim to varnish poor neighborhoods, prettify the outskirts and daub make-up on social ailments instead of curing them by promoting genuine and respectful integration." In making this claim, the Pope has urged all neighborhoods to have adequate infrastructure that will allow for all families to have housing, thus creating bonds and unity.[52] Churches must work in connection with community groups, the private sector, and state and local governments to recognize those struggling with securing housing as "part of the human family, as part of us."[53]

Famed Catholic social activist and advocate for the poor Dorothy Day writes that "Christ comes to us each day ... each time we look into the face of our brother who is poor."[54] By doing for the neediest and by seeking basic assurances for others that we would seek for ourselves, we advance the aims of proximity and narrow the growing divide between those of immense means and those of far less means.[55] Father Greg Boyle has stated that the closest that he

49 Douglas S. Massey et al., *Climbing Mount Laurel: The Struggle for Affordable Housing and Social Mobility in an American Suburb* (Princeton, NJ: Princeton University Press, 2013), 1 (noting the salutary effects of affordable housing development in Mt. Laurel township); David Kirp, "Here Comes the Neighborhood," *New York Times*, October 19, 2013, https://www.nytimes.com/2013/10/20/opinion/sunday/here-comes-the-neighborhood.html.

50 Carmella, "A Catholic View of Law and Justice," 269.

51 Francis, "Address on Popular Movements."

52 Ibid.

53 Catholic Conference, "Homelessness and Housing," 639.

54 Dorothy Day, "Poverty Is the Face of Christ," *The Catholic Worker*, December 1952, http://www.catholicworker.org/dorothyday/articles/641.html.

55 Dorothy Day, "The Mystery of the Poor," *The Catholic Worker*, April 1964, http://www.catholicworker.org/dorothyday/articles/189.html.

> The mystery of the poor is this: That they are Jesus, and what you do for them you do for Him. It is the only way we have of knowing and believing in our love. The mystery of poverty is that by sharing in it, making ourselves poor in giving to others, we increase our knowledge of and belief in love.

has gotten to Christ is when he is standing with those who find their needs ignored.[56] Father Boyle explains that the measure of compassion is in being willing to empathize with those who are marginalized.[57] He clarifies that "kinship" is the key to creating peace, justice, and equality.[58] Christ walked and slept among the poor,[59] and Christian criteria teach that integrating oneself into the social process assists the development and social integration of those otherwise relegated to the fringes of society.[60]

Putting community back into common interest communities

We are living in our own atomized, customized spheres. The two Americas—the sharp and indivisible lines between those of great wealth and those without—have infected countless spheres of daily interaction. Common interest communities are but a manifestation and a metaphor for our times.[61]

Common interest communities (CICs) are real estate developments or neighborhoods that consist of individually owned lots or units that are burdened by servitudes

> (1) to pay for the use of, or contribute to the maintenance of, property held or enjoyed in common by the individual owners, or (2) to pay dues or assessments to a homeowners association that provides services or facilities to the common property or to the individually owned property, or that

56 "The Calling of Delight: Gangs, Service, and Kinship," On Being, last modified November 22, 2017, https://onbeing.org/programs/greg-boyle-the-calling-of-delight-gangs-service-and-kinship-nov2017/

> I haven't found anything that's brought me more life or joy than standing with Jesus, but also with the particularity of standing in the lowly place with the easily despised and the readily left out, and with the demonized so that the demonizing will stop, and with the disposable so that the day will come when we stop throwing people away. And I find the fullness of life in trying to, as best I can, in my own way, to stand there.

57 Ibid. ("[T]he measure of our compassion lies not in our service of those on the margins, but in our willingness to see ourselves in kinship. And so that means the decided movement towards awe, and giant steps away from judgment.")

58 "Gregory Boyle: Save the World or Savor It?" Faith & Leadership, last modified February 23, 2016, https://www.faithandleadership.com/gregory-boyle-save-world-or-savor-it

> We've become focused on peace, justice and equality, when the truth is, none of those things can happen unless there's some undergirding sense that we belong to each other, that we're connected, that we matter. But the good news is, if we focus on kinship, the byproduct of that effort is peace, justice and equality.

59 Dorothy Day, "Room for Christ," *The Catholic Worker*, December 1945, http://www.catholicworker.org/dorothyday/articles/416.html.

60 "What Have You Done to Your Homeless Brother?"

61 Paula A. Franzese, "Privatization and Its Discontents: Common Interest Communities and the Rise of Government for the "Nice," *Urban Law*, 37 no. 3 (2005): 337 (describing how common interest communities' patterns of excessive regimentation erode neighborliness and a shared sense of community).

> enforces other servitudes burdening the property in the development or neighborhood.[62]

Estimates state that one in five Americans lives in some form of homeowner-association (HOA) controlled dwelling, with figures in some states showing that even more than half of all homeowners live in a CIC.

Relying on the phenomenon of privatization to shift from government provision of essential services to private provision of those services, these literally and metaphorically walled-off enclaves can allow those of greater means to essentially secede from the world outside the walls.[63] "Fortress America" risks denying proximity to those whose experiences, identities, and circumstances deserve our attention and care. It can impede the work of empathy and instead feed the indifference that isolation when coupled with privilege can breed. In turn, those outside the walls remain out of sight, out of mind, and further marginalized.

In *Laudato Sí*, Pope Francis noted that

> [i]n some places, rural and urban alike, the privatization of certain spaces has restricted people's access to places of particular beauty. In others, 'ecological' neighborhoods have been created which are closed to outsiders to ensure an artificial tranquility. Frequently, we find beautiful and carefully manicured green spaces in so-called 'safer' areas of cities, but not in the more hidden areas where the disposable live.[64]

Within the gates and walls, CICs use a wide array of rules contained in what is called a declaration of covenants, conditions, and restrictions (CC&Rs) to privately control land use. The rules are characterized as a means to preserve property values, order, security, and aesthetic appeal. The mechanisms for rule enforcement vary in each community, as does the very efficacy of the given rules-based regime. Some CICs provide convenience, stability, and order. In other venues, excessive reliance on rules to control the range of residents' individual autonomy creates inefficiency, misunderstanding, and heightened acrimony. There, zealous rule enforcement transforms the relevant inquiry of neighborly relations from "*how are you doing?*" to "***what** are you doing?*"

CIC templates must be reframed to restore and reinforce norms of basic trust, community, and neighborliness. By contrast, today disgruntled residents have described their common interest communities' system of governance and regulation as petty, tyrannical, and authoritarian. Litigation follows.[65]

62 Restatement (Third) Of Prop.: Servitudes § 1. 8 (2000).

63 Paula A. Franzese, "Does It Take a Village – Privatization, Patterns of Restrictiveness and the Demise of Community," *Villanova Law Review*, 47, no. 3 (2002): 553.

64 Francis, *Laudato Sí*, sec. 45.

65 Franzese, "Does It Take a Village," 562–63.

The concept of the connected community is part of the American dream, a highly sought-after emblem that increases social capital and encourages civic accountability. In countless contexts, we have seen the erosion of shared values and common purpose. Community has yielded to the anonymity of virtual, online connection, which is a poor substitute for real face time. The lures of anonymity render social media anything but. When societal bonds deteriorate, democracy withers. In many ways, CICs are a mirror for a larger crisis of community.

As they currently stand, distressed CICs often lack transparency, and create barriers to residents receiving requisite information. As a direct result, boards are often unresponsive, evasive, or prefer roundabout means of communication with residents. Board members are uneducated on their fiduciary responsibilities, taking their positions without proper training and without implementing an appeals process for aggrieved tenants. The CC&Rs put into effect often do not reflect an adequate consensus of residents and many times are not fully advertised to prospective residents. To make matters worse, residents view the CC&Rs as fixed and immutable, and often selectively enforced, many times in discriminatory manners based upon board member preferences.[66]

Proposed change

The current homeowner association system focuses upon regimentation and punishment instead of on the power of social trust and community. The promise of social capital must be predicated on a legal foundation that includes eliminating developer-imposed servitudes and granting statutory rights to CIC residents. In doing so, there must be the implementation of an affordable alternative dispute resolution process and ways to guarantee transparency.

Traditional CIC models must be reconfigured. Excessive reliance on restrictive covenants must yield to a manageable set of scaled-down baseline rules that residents can live with but not come to resent. More organic norms of neighborliness should be given the opportunity to develop and grow, thereby obviating the need for aggressive regimentation and rule enforcement. Governing boards must be made subject to a meaningful set of checks and balances to avoid corruption and arbitrary, selective, or overzealous enforcement of the rules that do apply.

Call to service

In many ways, HOAs are the epitome of private law, created by homeowners and administered by homeowners, rather than imposed by the state. This can create both benefits and pitfalls. Catholic notions of community rest heavy upon

66 Paula A. Franzese and Steven Siegel, "Trust and Community: The Common Interest Community as Metaphor and Paradox," *Missouri Law Review*, 72, no. 4 (2007): 1111.

the love of neighbor and justice being intertwined, upon the inherent dignity and sociality of human persons. Love implies an "absolute demand for justice, namely a recognition of the dignity and rights of one's neighbor."[67] The idea of neighborliness and cultivating proximity to others stems directly from the Catholic social teaching that because we are "'meant to live with others and to work for one another's welfare,' a positive conception of society emerges, one that safeguards human dignity through the specification of correlative rights and duties universal to all."[68] The individual's role in the greater society is integral; citizens of common interest communities must take on increased involvement in their own communities and work with relevant boards and homeowners' associations. The tradition of communal living and religious communism should be embraced by communities seeking to foster neighborliness and assistance between those living in the same community. Instead, poverty isolates people from each other.[69] Catholics "see a social person embedded in relationships" and find that we become a full-fledged person only within and through community.[70] By creating transparency and connectivity in these communities, we are one step closer to this vision.

Conclusion

There are consequences when the divide between the "us" and the "them" widens and whole segments of society become marginalized, disenfranchised, and invisible. We can and must do better for those forced to endure unsafe and unlivable dwellings and the toxic consequences of housing displacement. Everyone deserves a safe place to call home. The promise of inclusion can and must be made real, to ordain meaningful opportunity for those of low and moderate income to share in the benefits of communities otherwise closed to them. Community must be restored to common interest communities to make real the promise of social trust.

Catholic social teachings provide an important foundation upon which to rest the aims of inclusion, equal opportunity, neighborliness, and justice. The compassionate lens of Church doctrine helps to put into sharper focus the imperative that we allay the suffering experienced by those excluded from the promise of sustainable, peaceful dwelling. In so doing, we achieve even more than success. We achieve significance.

67 Third International Synod of Bishops, "Justitia in Mundo 1971," in *Catholic Social Thought: The Documentary Heritage*, eds. D. A. O'Brien and T. A. Shannon (Maryknoll, NY: Orbis Books, 1992), 520.

68 Carmella, "A Catholic View of Law and Justice," 263.

69 Dorothy Day, "Poverty Is the Face of Christ," *The Catholic Worker*, December 1952, http://www.catholicworker.org/dorothyday/articles/641.html.

70 Carmella, "A Catholic View of Law and Justice," 263–64.

Part III
Contracts

9 Christian contract law and the morality of the market

A historical perspective

Wim Decock

Introduction

The concept of "Christian contract law" comes with a troubled past. A standard part of the first-year law experience includes exposure to the notion that moral values and legal rules are to be neatly distinguished from one another. "The coercive power of the state, exercised or brandished, makes the difference between the pious hopes of morality and the grim certitutes of law," as Michael Barkun, a political scientist, once summarized the positivistic creed underlying modern legal systems.[1] Even more so, the thought of judges taking into account exclusively religious arguments, or of religious authorities enacting rules that are enforceable in courts of law, is alien and even hostile to the modern mindset. The separation of church and state, or for that matter, of religious beliefs and legal norms, is a fundamental tenet of Western legal systems since the nineteenth century. As a consequence, the notion that Christianity could have to do anything with law appears like a contradiction in terms. John Austin (1790–1859), one of the most influential theoreticians of legal positivism in the Anglo-Saxon world, allegedly claimed that "an exception, demurrer or plea founded on the law of God was never heard in a Court of Justice, from the creation of the world down to the present moment."[2] This chapter will nevertheless show that legal

1 Michael Barkun, *Law without Sanctions. Order in Primitive Societies and the World Community* (New Haven, CT, London: Yale University Press, 1968), 8, also cited in Wim Decock, *Theologians and Contract Law: The Moral Transformation of the Ius commune (c. 1500–1650)* (Leiden/Boston, MA: Brill/Nijhoff, 2013), 86.

2 According to Herbert L.A. Hart, "Positivism and the Separation of Law and Morals," *Harvard Law Review*, 71 (1958): 593–629 (616) and Alan Watson, *Failures of the Legal Imagination* (Philadelphia, PA: University of Pennsylvania Press, 1988), 122. However, it is worthwhile noting that the passage attributed to John Austin does neither figure in the original, 1832 London edition of his *The Province of Jurisprudence Determined*, nor in the second, posthumous 1861 London. Hart refers to the 1954 Library of Ideas edition, p. 185, which takes as a starting point the fifth, London 1885 edition of Austin's lectures, which was never seen by John Austin himself, but "revised and edited by Robert Campbell with the assistance of the notes taken by John Stuart Mill of the original lectures." In any event, Hart's citation has been copied by countless scholars, and it may reflect the spirit of Austin's positivism, irrespective of the original content of his lectures.

positivism is not a good guide to understand the historical foundations of Western law, especially in the field of contracts.

Christians, contract law, and the morality of the market

The fact that we have been accustomed to think of morality, law, and religion separately does not mean that Western law does not bear any historical relationship to moral and religious culture, quite the contrary. If anything, John Austin would not have had to reject the use of religious arguments in court so emphatically, if his opinion had already been common currency in nineteenth-century Britain. In the passage quoted above, he was obliged to oppose the contrary view advocated by William Blackstone (1723–1780), an icon of the British Enlightenment. Faithful to a centuries-old tradition in European jurisprudence,[3] Blackstone adhered to the view that the civil laws could be invalidated by contrary natural laws, which he considered as God's dictates.[4] In recent decades, recognition of the religious foundations of Western legal culture has received strong impetus by the work of Harold Berman (1918–2007), the late Harvard law professor, and of John Witte Jr., his intellectual heir at Emory's Center for the Study of Law and Religion. Berman's book *Law and Revolution: The Formation of the Western Legal Culture* (1983) has had a tremendous impact on the way scholars across the world have come to acknowledge the Christian element in the historical development of both the common and the civil law traditions.[5]

In the field of contract law, in particular, the Christian origins of modern law have been laid out in great detail by James Gordley in his *Philosophical Origins of Modern Contract Doctrine* (1991). In a world that was not yet characterized by the modern division between state and church, it was not only the civil lawyers who specialized in Roman law and statutory law, but also the experts in canon law, that is, the law of the Church, who were responsible for shaping contract doctrine, along with Christian theologians. While Roman law had a lot to say about specific contracts such as sale and lease, what it had to offer was a collection of cases and precedents, without much in the way of systematic reflection or principles. As Gordley has shown, medieval canon lawyers and scholastic theologians in the sixteenth and seventeenth centuries combined the technical vocabulary of Roman contract law with evangelical principles and Aristotelian-Thomistic virtue ethics. As a result, they came up with general principles such as good faith in contracts, the bindingness of bare agreements, and the principle of fair bargaining.

3 R. H. Helmholz, *Natural Law in Court: A History of Legal Theory in Practice* (Cambridge, MA: Harvard University Press, 2015).

4 William Blackstone, *Commentaries on the Laws of England*, vol. 1, book 1, section II, p. 41, Philadelphia, 1893 [1753], http://files.libertyfund.org/files/2140/Blackstone_1387-01_EBk_v6.0.pdf.

5 Thomas Duve, "Law and Revolution – Revisited," *Rechtsgeschichte – Legal History*, 21 (2013): 156–159.

The medieval and early modern canonists and theologians – often referred to simply as the "schoolmen" or the "scholastics"[6] – would not have defined themselves as legal theorists. They were pragmatic thinkers, involved in the business of counseling and confessing merchants, bankers, and princes.[7] As a result, the treatment of contract law in the works of medieval and early modern canon lawyers and theologians cannot be severed from their concern with the morality of the marketplace. Confessors needed to evaluate the righteousness and sinfulness of individual Christians' behavior, especially in day-to-day transactions in the marketplace such as money exchange, commercial loans, and credit sales.[8] To better understand the moral issues involved in those transactions, theologians and canonists analyzed business transactions through the lens of contract law. It offered them a technical framework to determine rights and obligations of contracting parties with a high degree of precision. It is certainly not a coincidence that one of the first treatises on contracts in the Western legal tradition was written by Peter of John Olivi (ca. 1248–1298), a Franciscan theologian and counselor of merchants in Southern France.[9] After studying in Paris with Thomas Aquinas, Olivi taught at the Franciscan convent in Narbonne, where he also became one of the principal confessors to the new urban class of prosperous businessmen. His treatise on contracts, dealing mostly with the law of sales, money-lending, and restitution, grew out of his combined experience as a lecturer and an adviser in the marketplace. Sylvain Piron, a French historian, has convincingly shown that Olivi delivered a remarkably liberal account of contract law, where the free will of the contracting parties occupied a central role.[10] His analysis of specific commercial and financial contracts was pervaded by a spirit of liberalism that fully acknowledged the economic value of capital and industry.

A Plethora of sources – waiting for further analysis

Peter of John Olivi's *Treatise on Contracts* remained unknown until the late 1970s, when Giacomo Todeschini and other Italian and French scholars discovered the text and soon realized that it deserved a place of honor in the history of

6 John T. Noonan, *The Scholastic Analysis of Usury* (Cambridge, MA: Harvard University Press, 1957), 48.

7 Nicole Reinhardt, *Voices of Conscience. Royal Confessors and Political Counsel in Seventeenth-Century Spain and France* (Oxford: Oxford University Press, 2016).

8 Michael Thomas D'Emic, *Justice in the Marketplace in Early Modern Spain. Saravia, Villalón and the Religious Origins of Economic Analysis* (Lanham: Lexington, 2014).

9 Peter of John Olivi, *A Treatise on Contracts*, critical edition and commentary by Sylvain Piron, trans. Ryan Thornton (from Latin) and Michael Cusato (from French) (Saint-Bonaventure: Franciscan Institute Publications, 2016).

10 Sylvain Piron, *Parcours d'un intellectuel franciscain. D'une théologie vers une pensée sociale: l'oeuvre de Pierre de Jean Olivi (ca. 1248–1298) et son traité 'De contractibus'* (Paris: EHESS, 1999), unpublished PhD thesis. *See also* Juhana Toivanen, "Voluntarist Anthropology in Peter of John Olivi's *De contractibus*," *Franciscan Studies*, 74 (2016): 41–65.

economic thought.[11] As a matter of fact, they found that Olivi's work had been a major source of inspiration for Bernardine of Siena (1380–1444) and Antonine of Florence (1389–1459) – two late medieval theologians whose moral support for the spirit of commercial enterprise was even recognized by Max Weber (1864–1920), the famous legal historian and sociologist, in *The Protestant Ethic and the Spirit of Capitalism.* Bernardine of Siena and Antonine of Florence are just two among the more famous medieval theologians who dealt with issues at the crossroads of market morality and contract law. Since the thirteenth century, hundreds of treatises on sale, money-lending, and restitution were written by canonists and scholastic theologians at universities and convents across Europe, the enormous depth of which has been revealed to us in a merely fragmentary way, despite the seminal investigations by eminent scholars such as Odd Inge Langholm and Lawrin Armstrong.[12]

Something that has consistently surprised researchers examining the source material is that they reveal a great compatibility between everyday market behavior and the moral-legal framework developed by medieval Christian thinkers.[13] This sense of surprise is due to many reasons, but not in the least to the huge impact of Weber's *The Protestant Ethic*, a reductionist interpretation that has exerted undue influence on the popular imagination.[14] Yet, the spirit of entrepreneurship and capitalism did certainly not have to wait for ascetic Protestant sects to find legitimation in Christian writings on contracts and commerce.[15] The apotheosis of the canon law and scholastic theology of contract came in the sixteenth and seventeenth centuries, against the background of the first wave of globalization, the rise of inter-continental trade networks, and the emergence of financial capitalism. Catholic theologians and canon lawyers across Europe wrote vast treatises on commerce and contracts that were even more ambitious in scope than their late medieval predecessors. They also contained unprecedented acceptance of new commercial and financial practices in the marketplace.[16] Incidentally, while the Catholic theologians in the sixteenth and seventeenth

11 Giacomo Todeschini, *Un trattato di economia politica francescana: il 'De emptionibus et venditionibus, de usuris, de restitutionibus' di Pietro di Giovanni Olivi* (Rome: Istituto Storico Italiano per il Medioevo, 1980).

12 Odd Inge Langholm, *Economics in the Medieval Schools: Wealth, Exchange, Value, Money and Usury According to the Paris Theological Tradition, 1200–1350* (Leiden/Boston, MA: Brill, 1992); Lawrin Armstrong, *Usury and Public Debt in Early Renaissance Florence: Lorenzo Ridolfi on the Monte Comune* (Toronto: Pontifical Institute of Medieval Studies, 2003).

13 James Davis, *Medieval Market Morality. Life, Law and Ethics in the English Marketplace, 1200–1500* (Cambridge: Cambridge University Press, 2012), 411–413.

14 A discussion of the Weber thesis would largely exceed the limits of this paper. A good starting point is Peter Ghosh, *Max Weber and the Protestant Ethic: Twin Histories* (Oxford: OUP, 2014).

15 Giacomo Todeschini, *Ricchezza francescana. Dalla povertà volontaria alla società di mercato* (Bologna: Il Mulino, 2004); Paolo Prodi, *Settimo non rubare. Furto e mercato nella storia dell'Occidente* (Bologna: Il Mulino, 2009); Sylvain Piron, *L'occupation du monde* (Brussels: Zones Sensibles, 2018).

16 For concrete examples, see Wim Decock, "Lessius and the Breakdown of the Scholastic Paradigm," *Journal of the History of Economic Thought*, 31 (2009): 57–78; Wim Decock, "In Defense of Commercial Capitalism: Lessius, Partnerships and the Contractus Trinus," in *Companies and*

centuries were more prolific than ever writing about business and contracts, Protestants started to advocate the idea that religious authorities should leave legal and political matters to the jurists and concentrate exclusively on spiritual matters. Against the Catholics, Protestant jurists such as Charles Dumoulin (1500–1566) in France and Alberico Gentili (1552–1608) in England urged theologians "to keep silent about matters outside their province" – a warning that has often been interpreted as the beginning of the modern age, since it emphasized the separation between law and religion that a modern jurist or theologian is still familiar with. But, again, this statement should not lead us into the temptation of neglecting the profound contribution of theologians and Church lawyers to the development of contract law in the pre-modern era.

Hundreds of treatises *On Contracts*, *On Justice and Right*, *On Laws*, and similar subjects rolled from printing presses in Antwerp, Ingolstadt, Leuven, Madrid, Mainz, Paris, Rome, Salamanca, Venice, and many other cities.[17] Except for big names such as Francisco de Vitoria (1483/1492–1546), Domingo de Soto (1494–1560), Luis de Molina (1535–1600), and Leonardus Lessius (1545–1623), they have received only scarce attention by modern jurists and economists, undoubtedly because the majority of them were never translated into modern languages. It deserves mentioning that the outburst of voluminous treatises on legal subjects written by scholastic theologians and canonists was not limited to mainland Spain, even if early modern scholasticism has largely become associated with the so-called "School of Salamanca," since the University of Salamanca played a paramount role in disseminating the scholastic revival movement across the globe.[18] The first huge treatise *On contracts* in the early modern scholastic tradition was published in 1502 by Conrad Summenhart (1455–1502), a German theologian at the University of Tübingen, and the apex of the tradition was reached with the publication in 1646 of a four-volume work on both general contract law and special contracts by Pedro de Oñate, a Jesuit theologian who spent his career in South America. A practical consequence of this is that the next paragraphs will not be able to discuss all these authors or go into the details of scholastic contract law, let alone discuss their analysis of specific contracts or dozens of cases occurring in the marketplace. References to primary sources and Latin citations will be kept to a minimum, but can be checked in the secondary literature.[19]

Bare agreements and promissory morality

The sheer volume of the primary source material, combined with the so-called "dialectic" nature of scholastic culture – which left room for "dialogue" and a

Company Law in Late Medieval and Early Modern Europe, eds. Bram Van Hofstraeten and Wim Decock (Louvain: Peeters, 2016), 55–90.

17 An overview of the most important sources is included in Wim Decock and Christiane Birr, *Recht und Moral in der Scholastik der Frühen Neuzeit* (Berlin: De Gruyter, 2016).

18 Marjorie Grice-Hutchinson, *The School of Salamanca: Readings in Spanish Monetary Theory (1544–1605)* (Oxford: Clarendon, 1952).

19 Especially in Decock, *Theologians and Contract Law*, passim.

multitude of divergent opinions to co-exist – makes generalizations hazardous. Yet, a commonly accepted principle of Christian contract doctrine from the late Middle Ages onward was that bare agreements are binding by virtue of mutual consent alone. Moreover, from the late sixteenth century onward theologians started to articulate the notion of contract through the concept of "promise," which first only meant gratuitous promises or, alternatively, the offer made by the promisor, but eventually denoted the entire agreement. Binding promises or contracts were analyzed as the combination of an offer (or promise in the strict sense of the word) and an acceptance. The following paragraphs will give a brief introduction to the development of these two general principles in pre-modern Christian contract doctrine.

The principle that agreements are binding by virtue of consent alone reaches back to the classical period of canon law (ca. 1100–1300). Canon law in this period touched the lives of virtually everyone and dealt with almost every possible subject that a modern jurist would expect today to fall within his exclusive competence, including contracts.[20] The principle that agreements, however naked, are binding was formulated by Huguccio, one of the leading canonists at the university of Bologna in the late twelfth century.[21] It is also known as the principle of consensualism. Agreements are enforceable by virtue of mutual consent alone. The motivation behind the rule was religious in nature, since Huguccio argued that God made no distinction between what a Christian says and what he swears (Mt 5:37: "let your word be 'yes, yes' or 'no, no'"). Therefore, a contracting party who does not respect the agreement commits a sin. Concerned as they were with the salvation of souls, subsequent canonists and theologians unanimously adopted the principle that all bare agreements are binding, to prevent the debtor from sinning. In the ecclesiastical courts, a creditor could file a claim against a debtor who failed to fulfill his contractual obligations by virtue of the mutual consent underlying the contract. Unlike in the Roman law tradition, or in the medieval civil courts, the canon law largely ignored formality requirements and the existence of specific writs or legal remedies. What mattered to the canon lawyers was substance, not form, since God's eyes saw all the evidence.

From the early sixteenth century onward, the consensualist principle developed by the canonists was gradually adopted by the civil courts, too, as kings sought to restrain the power of the Roman Catholic Church and concentrate jurisdictional power in their own hands. They borrowed judicial precedents and legal doctrines from the canon law tradition.[22] The explanation why this happened was made explicit by Matthew Wesenbeck (1531–1586), a major jurist from the Catholic Southern Netherlands who went on to teach at the Lutheran University of Wittenberg: "each time we are dealing with the protection from

20 James Brundage, *Medieval Canon Law* (London and New York: Longman, 1995); Richard H. Helmholz, *The Spirit of Classical Canon Law* (Athens, CA: University of Georgia Press, 1996).

21 Decock, *Theologians and Contract Law*, 123.

22 Laurent Waelkens, *Amne adverso. Roman Legal Heritage in European Culture* (Louvain: Leuven University Press, 2015), 111–113.

sin and a matter of conscience, even in the civil court the canon law has to be observed."[23] This is clear evidence not only of the persistence of substantive doctrines of canon law in Protestant lands, but also of the profoundly religious considerations about the law of contracts even in the work of a "pure" jurist, of Lutheran convictions, in the early modern period. Even in the Protestant tradition, juridical and theological thinking remained closely intertwined, if only because the civil authorities were expected to lay down laws according to Christian principles. For example, the Augsburg Confession of 1530, one of the first texts to outline the major points of the Lutheran faith and its consequences for civil and ecclesiastical governance, considered the civil authorities as part of the divine order. Laws enacted by civil authorities required absolute obedience from the citizens, unless that would have obliged them to commit a sin. To use the words of Harold Berman, the fact that Luther and his followers consigned law to a secular realm under civil authority does not mean that law and religion became mutually irrelevant.[24]

In the meantime, the Catholic theologians, for whom law was clearly not consigned exclusively to the secular realm, further refined the conceptual framework for analyzing contracts, developing a general law of contract centered around the notion of "promise."[25] Previously, the notion of "promise" had been mainly used to refer to a gratuitous promise or a gift, which was motivated by gratitude or liberality. Whether those promises were binding was a matter of controversy that goes beyond the scope of this chapter.[26] The notion of "promise" could also refer to the "offer" made in an agreement by the promisor. But in the work of Jesuit theologians such as Lessius and Oñate, "promise" additionally became a generic concept to articulate the basic structure behind all kinds of contracts, namely the combination of offer and acceptance. "Every binding agreement is composed of promise and acceptance," Oñate explained,[27] "just as a physical thing is composed of matter and form, or a human being of soul and body." Observing that "promise" had now also simply become synonymous with "contract," he went on to specify that "if promise is understood in the second manner [*sc.* as a combination of offer and acceptance], then it does not differ from contract, just as a man does not differ from the combination of his soul and body." The principle that all binding agreements are the result of a combination of offer

23 Decock, *Theologians and Contract Law*, 157.

24 Harold Berman, *Law and Revolution II: The Impact of the Protestant Reformations on the Western Legal Tradition* (Cambridge, MA: Harvard University Press, 2003), 72.

25 Decock, *Theologians and Contract Law*, 176–214.

26 On the status of lucrative contracts, *see* Decock, *Theologians and Contract Law*, 174–176. A seminal attempt to argue that donations were fully fledged contracts was made by Conrad Summenhart, who was followed by Fortunius García, Lessius, and Oñate. They argued that lucrative contracts are also true contracts because they are composed of offer and acceptance, which are the necessary elements to form a binding contract. Their main opponent was Domingo de Soto, who argued that gifts were the fruit of the virtue of liberality and were therefore excluded from the rules of commutative justice.

27 *See* Decock, *Theologians and Contract Law*, 178 (citing Oñate).

and acceptance became almost universally accepted by the Catholic theologians. The binding status of specific types of unilateral promises, for instance offers for public building projects, known in Roman law as *pollicitationes civitati*, led some theologians to nuance that standpoint, but generally they agreed that an offer could not bind the promisor until it had been accepted.[28]

In the Protestant tradition, the conceptual shift from contract as "agreement" to contract as "promise" was taken up by influential Calvinist natural lawyers such as Hugo Grotius (1583–1645) and Lutheran theologians such as Johann Adam Osiander (1622–1697). In his work *On the Law of War and Peace* (1625), Grotius developed a general law of contract against the background of a chapter on promises, just as Lessius had done a few years before.[29] Occasionally, Grotius referred to early modern Catholic theologians and canonists such as Martín de Azpilcueta (1492–1586), Diego de Covarrubias y Leyva (1512–1577), and Tomás Sánchez (1550–1610) in his text. In similar fashion, Protestant theologians such as Osiander borrowed extensively from the Catholic theologians in their treatment of contractual issues in works on moral theology.[30] In a chapter of his *Theology by Cases* (1680), Osiander elaborated upon the notion of promise, emphasizing the need for promises to be accepted in order to become binding. He extensively borrowed from theologians such as Sylvester Mazzolini da Prierio (1456–1523), a Dominican theologian and author of one of the most important manuals for confessors in the Catholic tradition.

The early modern Christian doctrine of contracts was committed to the notion that the enforceability of contracts resulted from the moral obligation to keep promises. In this regard, modern promissory theories of contract resemble those of the early modern theologians, even if modern jurists such as Charles Fried refer to Kantian philosophy rather than early modern scholasticism as the foundation of their promissory account of contract law.[31] However, one should be clear about the "legal" character of the "moral" obligation to keep promises in the scholastic tradition. The modern distinction between law and morality is unhelpful in reading the early modern sources, since, as has been highlighted earlier, canonists and theologians conceived of "morality" in remarkably juridical terms.[32] Even conscience was thought of as a juridical space, a tribunal or forum (*forum internum*, *forum conscientiae*), where man's conduct was judged according to objective standards by confessors trained not only in biblical studies but also in the law.[33] A much better guide to understand the discussions

28 Decock, *Theologians and Contract Law*, 187–192.

29 Martin Hogg, *Promises and Contract Law: Comparative Perspectives* (Cambridge: Cambridge University Press, 2011), 128.

30 Paolo Astorri, *Lutheran Theology and Contract Law in Early Modern Germany (ca. 1520–1720)* (Paderborn: Ferdinand Schöningh, 2019), 220–222.

31 Charles Fried, *Contract as Promise: A Theory of Contractual Obligation*, 2nd ed. (Oxford: Oxford University Press, 2015).

32 Decock, *Theologians and Contract Law*, 69–86.

33 Wim Decock, "Confessors as Law Enforcers in Mercado's Advice on Economic Governance (1571)," *Rechtsgeschichte – Legal History*, 25 (2017): 103–114.

about the bindingness of contracts in the sources from the sixteenth and seventeenth centuries is Thomas Aquinas's (1225–1274) virtue ethics. Thomas made a distinction between two kinds of debt, namely moral debt and legal debt. Legal debt is the object of the virtue of justice in exchange, while moral debt is governed by virtues that are similar, but not identical to the virtue of justice, such as piety, fidelity, and honesty.

The principle that promises create not only moral debt but also legal debt was supported by most early modern canonists and theologians. They rejected the opinion that contracts were binding merely by virtue of honesty, fidelity, or the moral duty to speak the truth. The promisor deliberately binds himself to the promisee in order to give or to do something, Lessius explained, thereby conferring a right to the promisee to enforce the promise.[34] All contracts are therefore binding as a matter of justice in exchange. Grotius followed Lessius in adopting this "juridical" conception of promising, conceiving of perfect promises in terms of the transfer of rights and the alienation of a part of the promisor's liberty. Lessius, Grotius, and their colleagues would have agreed that promises were morally binding, too, because it was morally necessary to speak the truth and to be honest, but that was not the main point of their legal reasoning, which started from a juridical analysis of the relationship between promisor and promisee. "Promising is not merely a matter of truth, but of commutative justice," Domingo de Soto emphasized.[35] In doing so, he wanted to distance himself from the contrary opinion of Thomas Cajetan (1469–1534), an authoritative Dominican theologian in the early sixteenth century, who had argued that a contracting party was bound to keep his promises only as a matter of honesty, truth, or faith.[36]

Freedom of the will and legal security

The turn toward an open and consensualist doctrine of contract, articulated around the notion of "promise," reached a climax in treatises on justice, law, and contracts written by Jesuit theologians in the first half of the seventeenth century. They fully endorsed the evolution of the doctrine of contract in the canon law tradition since the principle that all agreements are binding by virtue of consent alone guaranteed one of the values they esteemed most: freedom – a word they designated with the Latin term *libertas*. According to Oñate, who saw free will as the basis of the entire doctrine of contract, the consensualist principle and the promissory theory allowed the contracting parties to fully exercise their freedom of action. "Liberty has very wisely been restored to the contracting parties," he explained in his four-volume treatise on contracts,

34 Decock, *Theologians and Contract Law*, 210–211.

35 *See* Decock, *Theologians and Contract Law*, 200 (citing Domingo de Soto).

36 James Gordley, *The Philosophical Origins of Modern Contract Doctrine* (Oxford: Clarendon, 1991), 73.

> so that whenever they want to bind themselves through concluding a contract about their goods, this contract will be recognized by the civil or the ecclesiastical court before which they will have brought their case, and it will be upheld as sacrosanct and inviolable.[37]

Oñate's exposition on the enforceability of accepted promises abounds with references to the "will" and to verbs expressing that will. Oñate also emphasized the connection between the law of goods and contract law, conceiving of contracts as the instrument to transfer property rights. In Oñate's eyes, private property and freedom of contract were two sides of the same coin: "Man would not be the true and perfect owner of his goods unless he could dispose of them by contractual agreement when he wanted, with whom he wanted, in whatever way he wanted."[38] Strong property rights necessitated freedom of contract. Oñate was not alone in making that explicit connection. Molina, a Jesuit famous for his treatise *On Justice and Right*, of which the second volume is entirely dedicated to contract law, explained at the beginning of his treatment of contracts that his aim was to demonstrate how property rights are transferred by virtue of the will of the contracting parties.[39] Gregorio de Valentia (1549–1603), a fellow Jesuit teaching in Ingolstadt, talked about the individual's "right to love his own goods."[40] Juan de Mariana, a Jesuit famous for his scathing critique of absolutist kings, was highly suspicious of laws and policies that might violate the property rights of the citizens, considering monetary debasement without consent of the people as a form of disguised robbery by the government.[41]

The central value of the individual's intent in the theologians' conceptualization of contractual obligation facilitated the emergence of a Christian contract doctrine centered on autonomy of the will, but it also raised numerous questions. For example, what is the legal status of fictitious promises or contracts in which the underlying intent of the parties is doubtful? If the will of the parties is the ultimate criterion to interpret contracts, judges, or, for that matter, confessors, may have difficulties in upholding a contract to which one of the parties did not want to be bound entirely. For example, what if a man promised to marry a girl just to be able to have sexual intercourse with her, but actually did not intend to be bound by his promise? In dealing with this issue, theologians such as Lessius developed the so-called "reliance theory" of promising, arguing that the will was still the main criterion, but that the promisee's reliance on the promisor's declaration should be protected. Deceit could not be tolerated.

37 *See* Decock, *Theologians and Contract Law*, 163 (citing Oñate).

38 *See* Decock, *Theologians and Contract Law*, 170 (citing Oñate).

39 *See* Decock, *Theologians and Contract Law*, 164 (citing Molina).

40 Decock, *Theologians and Contract Law*, 595.

41 W. Decock, "Quantitative Easing Four Centuries Ago: Juan de Mariana's *De monetae mutatione* (1609)," in *Texts and Contexts in Legal History: Essays in Honor of Charles Donahue*, eds. J. Witte Jr, S. McDougall, and A. di Robilant (Berkeley, CA: Robbins Collection, 2016), 365.

"Faith in contractual affairs would crumble," Lessius warned,[42] "if promisors could free themselves of their obligation simply by saying that they had made a fictitious promise."

Another issue that was complicated by the emphasis on the will concerned the doctrine of changed circumstances. For centuries, Christian contract law took for granted that contractual obligation would be frustrated by a significant change in the contextual circumstances of the contract, for instance if war broke out, or if one of the contracting parties was confronted with health issues.[43] The early modern theologians took this idea from Thomas Aquinas and the medieval canon lawyers, who introduced the idea that there is an "implied term" or "tacit condition" in every agreement. This tacit provision means that the agreement will no longer be binding if the context in which the agreement was made changes considerably. One of the most radical formulations of this principle was offered by the Jesuit Manuel de Sá (1528–1596), who argued that "in a general obligation, even if strengthened by an oath, those things which you did not intend are not included," specifying that "those things seems to be all the things to which you would not have bound yourself if you had then thought about them."[44] Lessius explained that the will does not cover what is unknown, concluding that ignorance about a future change in circumstances could be considered as a kind of mistake that had vitiated the contract from the beginning.[45] Even Oñate, who went further than anyone else in advocating the autonomy theory of contract, considered the principle of changed circumstance as a universally applicable principle and the supreme expression of equity (*epikeia*):[46]

> Just as under those changing circumstances *epikeia* is to be applied to the laws and constitutions of the princes, so will it be equitable to apply *epikeia* to the promises made by private persons. For promises are like laws which private persons impose upon themselves.

The fact that the doctrine of implied terms posed a threat to legal security went not unnoticed to most Christian jurists and theologians. The issue was addressed explicitly in Juan de Lugo's (1583–1660) treatise *On Justice and Right*. Lugo pleaded for a maximum restriction of the use of the "tacit condition," expressing fears that all contractual exchange would become unstable if the principle of changed circumstances was adhered to without reserve. In the course of refuting the doctrine of implied terms, he referred to business interests and the "security of contract."[47] Consent to onerous contracts must be unconditional. Such contracts must have the stable and indissoluble character of marriage contracts,

42 *See* Decock, *Theologians and Contract Law*, 195 (citing Lessius).
43 Gordley, *The Philosophical Origins of Modern Contract Doctrine*, 90–91.
44 *See* Decock, *Theologians and Contract Law*, 202 (citing Manuel de Sá).
45 Decock, *Theologians and Contract Law*, 203.
46 *See* Decock, *Theologians and Contract Law*, 207 (citing Oñate).
47 Decock, *Theologians and Contract Law*, 320–321.

Lugo argued, urging contracting parties to think twice before they engaged themselves. It deserves mentioning that Lugo also provided one of the most nuanced accounts of a Christian approach toward debt collection. Although it would take us too far afield to discuss debt collection in Christian contract doctrine, there was general consensus that the general principle of the bindingness of agreements by virtue of mutual consent opposed a laxist attitude toward bad debtors.[48] Debt cancellation or debt relief was not thought of as an adequate way to address the problem of bad debt. Balancing the rights of the creditors and the obligations of the debtors, the canonists and theologians generally saw deferral of repayment as the most fair solution. Lugo fully recognized that courts had good reasons to enforce contracts in the strictest of ways, not least to prevent moral hazard. At the same time, he appealed to higher principles such as charity and "a kind of natural law equity" to urge Christian judges and Christian creditors to make all efforts to prevent poor and destitute debtors from collapsing into what he called the "abyss of despair."[49]

Fairness in exchange, equality, and charity

We have been accustomed to conceive of contractual freedom and of fairness in exchange as two entirely opposite principles. The nineteenth-century developments toward a positivistic doctrine of law, briefly referred to in the introduction, played an important role in shaping that modern view. Will theorists of contract in the nineteenth century referred to the will as the central element of contract precisely to reject moral notions of justice or morality. According to Justice Joseph Story's famous adage, "whether bargains are wise and discreet, or profitable or unprofitable, are considerations, not for courts of justice, but for the party himself to deliberate upon."[50] They wanted parties to stick to their contracts, regardless of how unfair and unbalanced the bargains turned out to be.[51] A will theorist such as Sir Frederick Pollock (1845–1937) associated the notion of justice in exchange with a return to the natural law paradigm of contract which had certainly prevailed in the past but which he did not recommend for modern industrial society.[52] His admonishment that ethical considerations should remain "outside the province of jurisprudence" recalls John Austin's plea for the separation of law and morality in *The Province of Jurisprudence Determined* to which we referred earlier.

In Christian contract doctrine, however, the opposition between freedom and fairness is a false one. The reason lies in a proper understanding of the notion of autonomy of the will. In the eyes of the canonists and the theologians, contracts

48 For further exploration of this topic, *see* Wim Decock, "Law, Religion and Debt Relief: Balancing Above the 'Abyss of Despair' in Early Modern Canon Law and Theology," *American Journal of Legal History*, 57 (2017): 125–141.

49 Decock, "Law, Religion and Debt Relief", 134–136.

50 *See* Decock, *Theologians and Contract Law*, 507 (citing Justice Joseph Story).

51 Michael Lobban, "Contract." in *The Oxford History of the Laws of England*, vol. 12: 1820–1914: *Private Law* (Oxford: Oxford University Press, 2010), 297.

52 Gordley, *The Philosophical Origins of Modern Contract Doctrine*, 216.

were tantamount to private laws which the parties created and imposed upon themselves. In creating those private laws, they exercised "auto-nomy" in the etymological sense of the word.[53] The metaphor of contracts as laws privately imposed by contracting parties upon themselves has a long history that reaches back to Roman law.[54] It gained enormous significance in the early modern scholastic period. "A promise is a private law chich the promisor imposes upon himself and through which he binds himself," Lugo explained.[55] At the same time, Lugo and his colleagues were unanimous to acknowledge that the universe of laws from which individuals derived rights and incurred obligations was wider than the laws they issued themselves. That universe of laws also contained binding norms promulgated by civil government, by ecclesiastical authorities, by the voice of God as revealed in the Bible, or by dictates of nature. Between these laws, a clear hierarchy existed which, in the theologians' eyes, indisputably followed from the social nature of man and his relation to God. The latter assumption, indebted to Aristotelian philosophy as much as to Biblical anthropology, is crucial to understand the unproblematic co-existence of the emphasis on fair bargaining and freedom of contract in Christian contract doctrine of the Middle Ages and the early modern period. This still holds true for natural lawyers such as Hugo Grotius, who thought that man was subject to the natural law principle of justice in exchange because God created man with a rational and social nature.[56] It is that assumption, however, which the nineteenth-century will theorists abandoned. Niklas Luhmann (1927–1998), a German sociologist of law, inferred from this observation that modern contract law has become incompatible with Christian contract law of the pre-modern era.[57]

A good illustration of the unproblematic co-existence of principles of contractual freedom and fairness in exchange in Christian contract doctrine can be found in Oñate's work. While praising the fact that canon law and theology had restored freedom to the contracting parties by elevating their wills to the guiding principle of contract law, he also recalled the moral embeddedness of bargaining:

> Natural law ordered that natural equity be observed in contracts. It prescribed, not only that you should not do unto others what you would not have them do unto you, but also that equilibrium be observed between the objects of these exchanges, as is required by commutative justice.[58]

Every single word in this passage would deserve a detailed commentary, but suffice it here to say a couple of words about the notion of "equilibrium" or

53 The word "autonomy" combines the Greeks words for "self" (autos) and "law" (nomos).
54 Paul J. du Plessis, "The Roman Concept of 'Lex contractus'," *Roman Legal Tradition*, 3 (2006): 69–94.
55 *See* Decock, *Theologians and Contract Law*, 178 (citing Lugo).
56 Gordley, *The Philosophical Origins of Modern Contract Doctrine*, 123.
57 Decock, *Theologians and Contract Law*, 507.
58 *See* Decock, *Theologians and Contract Law*, 512 (citing Oñate).

"equality" in contracts.[59] Christian contract doctrine puts a lot of emphasis not only on the Golden Rule (Mt 7:12), but also on the notion that contracts should be balanced, that bargains should be fair, and that there should be an even relationship between what is given and what is received in a transaction. As Joel Kaye, a medieval historian, has rightly observed, writers in the scholastic tradition "universally identified the process of economic exchange as a process of equalization, which, is to say, a process of achieving a just balance between exchangers."[60] Contracts were conceived of as instruments to advance the interests or "utility" of all parties involved, which meant that bargains must be equalized if they suffer from gross disparity or one-sidedness.[61]

The idea of equalization was articulated through Aristotle's doctrine of justice in exchange and the concomitant notions, developed particularly by scholastics such as Thomas Aquinas, of just pricing and restitution.[62] Within the context of this chapter, it is not possible to go into the details of the theory of just pricing. Nevertheless, it matters to realize, first of all, that the notion of the "just price" should not be mistaken for some kind of metaphysical value inherent in all objects. It also does not refer to the so-called "labor theory of value," which holds the just price should reflect the labor which an individual seller suffered to markets his goods. The just price, also designated as the "equal price," was a price that signaled a balanced or equalized transaction. One of the clearest expressions of the market-friendly nature of the concept of just pricing can be found in a text by Diego de Covarrubias y Leyva, one of the most prominent canonists in sixteenth-century Spain.[63] He explained that reaching a just price did not depend on considering the ontological nature of the merchandise or the expenses which the merchant had incurred. The just price did not consist in one specific price, either, but rather covered a broad range of prices that reflected the merchandise's utility according to the common estimation in the market – "even if it were insane," Covarrubias added.[64] If a Flemish merchant incurred more costs than the average businessman on his way to Spanish markets, he could only charge the common estimation of his goods in the local market. Alternatively, if a merchant noticed that his good sold much dearer in another place, or that his expenses were lower than that of his rivals, he was allowed to speculate on that information and make profits.[65] Covarrubias and other scholastics conceived of

59 For a more extended treatment of fairness in exchange, containing references to further literature, *see* Decock, *Theologians and Contract Law*, 507–604.

60 Joel Kaye, *A History of Balance, 1250–1375: The Emergence of a New Model of Equilibrium and Its Impact on Thought* (Cambridge: Cambridge University Press, 2014), 20.

61 Decock, *Theologians and Contract Law*, 509–510.

62 James Gordley, "Equality in Exchange," *California Law Review*, 69 (1981): 1587–1656.

63 Richard H. Helmholz, "Diego de Covarrubias y Leyva," in *Great Christian Jurists in Spanish History*, eds. Rafael Domingo and Javier Martínez-Torrón (Cambridge: Cambridge University Press, 2018), 174–190.

64 *See* Decock, *Theologians and Contract Law*, 521 (citing Covarrubias).

65 See the famous case of the "Merchant of Rhodes", discussed in Decock, "Lessius and the Breakdown of the Scholastic Paradigm".

the market as a contest, in which merchants should be allowed to play the market game.[66] This was one of the basic intuitions from which they assessed the morality of bargaining in the marketplace.

A second observation regarding the doctrine of just pricing is that it served practical interests. It provided confessors a concrete criterion to assess the justice of transactions in the marketplace. Once the just price of goods, or rather once the range of balanced bargains had been determined – for the just price allowed for a certain "latitude"[67] – the confessor could decide whether the penitent had committed a violation against the principle of fairness in exchange. Under such circumstances, the penitent would be obliged "to make restitution," which is tantamount to saying that the contract must be equalized. One of the main tasks of confessors was, indeed, to urge penitents to make restitution of illicit gains, or, more broadly, to undo any violation of the principle of equilibrium in exchange. Following a highly influential passage from a letter of Saint Augustine, the act of restitution was considered a prerequisite for the remission of sin. It found its way into the canonical tradition and became the background theory for all theologians' engagement with the morality of the market.[68] Not making restitution of ill-gotten gains was considered as theft, thus constituting a violation of the Decalogue. Through restitution, violations of property rights were undone, and the equilibrium in between things restored. As the first Roman Catechism (1566) specified, confessors could not absolve the penitent unless restitution was made of the harm caused by him (e.g., by exploiting a dominant position, charging excessive interest, or selling toxic financial products).[69]

As Paolo Astorri has shown, Protestant theologians preserved the idea that contracts must meet the requirements of justice in exchange and make restitution to equalize unbalanced agreements. The doctrine of restitution nevertheless lost part of its practical significance for them.[70] Even more so than concentrating on justice in exchange, they insisted that all contracts should be permeated by the spirit of charity. The precept of equality in exchange was regarded as a species of the more universal Christian duty to be charitable toward the neighbor. In this regard, Astorri has observed a kind of altruistic shift away from the concern of merchants with gaining their own salvation, by not indulging in unfair bargaining, to the active promotion of the other contracting party's interest.[71]

66 Decock, *Theologians and Contract Law*, 592–594.

67 Leonardus Lessius, *On Sale, Securities and Insurance*, trans. W. Decock (introd.) and trans. N. De Sutter in *Sources in Early Modern Economics, Ethics, and Law* (Grand Rapids, MI: CLP Academic, 2016), 10, 17.

68 Decock, *Theologians and Contract Law*, 516–517.

69 Decock, "Confessors as Law Enforcers in Mercado's Advice on Economic Governance (1571)," 108.

70 This is to do with the Lutheran doctrine of justification by faith. The Lutherans did no longer accept the Catholic doctrine that salvation can be obtained through works (including restitution) imposed upon the penitent by the confessor; see Astorri, *Lutheran Theology and Contract Law (ca. 1520–1720)*, 249–252.

71 Astorri, *Lutheran Theology and Contract Law (ca. 1520–1720)*, 309–311.

Clearly, in the work of the Lutheran theologians, Christian contract doctrine became less minimalistic than in the work of the Catholic moral theologians. Christians were now stimulated to show gratitude for the salvation received by God by virtue of faith alone through caring for the interests of their contracting parties. In respecting the principle of commutative justice, Christians performed an act of charity toward their neighbor, which they owed because of their duty of obedience to God.

Contractual freedom and the morality of the marketplace

The development of a substantial, Christian doctrine of contract was not the fruit of a mere academic interest that theologians and canonists took in the subject. Rather than defining themselves as theoreticians, they were engaged in the practical business of solving cases of conscience, especially in the marketplace. Contemporary jurists often referred to Catholic theologians as the best experts on the technicalities of financial contracts, since they were known to engage in conversations with men of practice on a daily basis. Empirical evidence or "experience" was a normative argument frequently used by Molina, Lessius, and Lugo, for instance in discussing the nature of interest as a price for money.[72] On account of their analytical skills in understanding the functioning of markets, which preceded their normative judgments, Joseph Schumpeter (1883–1950) has credited them with the title of "forefathers of modern economic science."[73] The academic attention traditionally given to the scholastic usury doctrine has obscured the fact that theologians and canonists discussed many other types of contracts than money-lending in the strict sense of the word. In reality, discussions about bonds, annuities, credit sales, foreign exchange transactions, corporate financing, and investment vehicles received much more attention. If anything, as Joel Kaye observed, "the early solidification of the Church's condemnation of usury had the effect of forcing scholastic moralists, legal scholars, and theologians to become expert in the ways of the marketplace."[74]

To illustrate the close connection between the turn toward a principle of contractual freedom and the practical solution of cases of conscience in the early modern marketplace, the next paragraphs will offer a brief sketch of how Catholic theologians assessed the legitimacy of a new investment vehicle and corporate financing technique that was widespread in sixteenth-century Europe and the

72 Toon Van Houdt, "Money, Time and Labor. Leonardus Lessius and the Ethics of Lending and Interest Taking," *Ethical Perspectives*, 2 (1995): 11–27; Wim Decock, "Leonardus Lessius y el valor normativo de 'usus et consuetudo mercatorum' para la resolución de algunos casos de conciencia en torno de la compra de papeles de comercio," in *Entre hecho y derecho: tener, poseer, usar en perspectiva histórica*, eds. Marta Madero and Emanuele Conte (Buenos Aires: Manantial, 2010), 75–94.

73 Joseph A. Schumpeter, *History of Economic Analysis* (New York: Oxford University Press, 1954), 111.

74 Kaye, *A History of Balance*, 22.

Americas: the so-called "triple contract."[75] The "triple contract" was an intellectual construct to capture the following practice: merchants borrowed money from investors for the sake of a business venture and promised those investors that they would return the invested money at the end of the project while also paying dividends on an annual basis. Clearly, this was an alternative way of lending money at interest to businessmen. To capture the practice in legal terms, it was analyzed as a combination of three contracts, viz. a partnership contract (because both parties confer something for the purpose of setting up a common venture), an insurance contract (because the merchant promises the investor to return the capital at the end of the venture), and a sales contract (because the merchant promises to pay a fixed annual price to the investor – the dividend – in exchange for the right to reap the remainder of the profits generated by the common venture). As John T. Noonan has noted, discussions about this contract are much more important to understand the Christian approach to the market in the sixteenth century than standard debates about interest titles in loans or the usury prohibition.[76]

A key step in justifying the practice of "triple contracts" was the breakthrough of freedom of contract. Traditionalists, on both the Catholic and the Protestant side,[77] opposed the practice since they considered the simultaneous conclusion of those three contracts between the capital investor and the entrepreneur as illicit. This objection did no longer convince Christians such as John Eck (1486–1543), the arch-enemy of Luther and a personal advisor to the Fugger banking family, and Lessius, a Jesuit theologian and the principal confessor to merchants in the Antwerp market. They argued that, from the point of view of the virtue of justice in exchange, it did not matter with whom the contract was concluded. One could enter into any contract with the partner of one's choice as long as there was voluntary consensus. Once freedom becomes the starting point of contract law, it becomes futile to maintain that the investor can conclude an insurance contract only with a third party and not with his business partner. Moreover, freedom of contract frustrated the "essentialist" analysis of partnership contracts as necessarily including exposure to risk for both partners. This static view of partnership contracts was outdated, according to Eck and Lessius. They argued, instead, that the essential feature of a partnership contract was that two or more parties agreed to confer something for the sake of a common enterprise. Once that condition was met, the distribution of risk could be the object of free bargaining. Moreover, everybody was free not to enter into a partnership

75 The following paragraphs are largely borrowed from the Calihan lecture "Knowing before Judging: Law and Economic Analysis in Early Modern Jesuit Ethics," delivered in Rome on November 29, 2017 and published in the *Journal of Markets and Morality*, 21 (2018): 309–330.

76 Noonan, *The Scholastic Analysis of Usury*, 249.

77 W. Decock, "The Catholic Spirit of Capitalism? Contrasting Views on Profit-Making through Capital Investment in the Age of Reformations," in *Law and Religion: The Legal Teachings of the Protestant and Catholic Reformations*, eds. Wim Decock, Jordan Ballor, Michael Germann, and Laurent Waelkens (Göttingen: Vandenhoeck & Ruprecht, 2014), 22–44.

contract without also entering into an insurance contract. The capital guarantee, too, was a matter of free individuals concluding an additional insurance contract by their mutual consent. As long as the fund provider paid the merchant a just price for that insurance service, contractual freedom did not lead to a violation of the principle of commutative justice.

Conclusion

It is natural to take the law of one's own time and country as a norm, and, hence, to consider it as "normal."[78] As this chapter has tried to show, however, if carried to excess, this tendency leads to an impoverished understanding of the historical roots of Western contract law. To assess the morality of the marketplace, Christian theologians and lawyers in the Middle Ages and the early modern period brought to bear their knowledge of virtue ethics and the Bible on commercial transactions and contract law. As a result, over a period of more than five centuries, a detailed, Christian doctrine of contracts was developed in commentaries on canon law texts and in voluminous works *On Justice and Right*, *On Contracts*, *On Restitution*, etc. Imbued with the credo of nineteenth-century legal positivism, a modern lawyer might not expect to find such an elaborate treatment of both general contract law and specific contracts in the writings of theologians and jurists belonging to the Church. It may even come as a bigger surprise that their thought, influenced as it was by Aristotelian moral philosophy and evangelical principles, evolved toward a contract theory centered around the notions of freedom, autonomy, and the individual will. For several reasons, this past engagement with contract doctrine may resemble a foreign country where people did things differently, as the British novelist Leslie Poles Hartley famously said. However, reading the scholastics' expositions on promissory morality or observing their sensitivity to economic issues, a modern audience may be prompted to agree with William Faulkner that "the past is not dead, it is not even past." Christian contract doctrine as developed from the twelfth through the seventeenth century showed a remarkable ability to accommodate the rise of individual autonomy and the entrepreneurial spirit. Moreover, within a Christian universe, where man was essentially thought of as a social and religious being, it did not consider those values as incompatible with the principles of fair bargaining and evangelical charity.

78 Decock, *Theologians and Contract Law*, 86.

10 Private law in Christian perspective

The example of Dooyeweerd on contracts

David S. Caudill

Introduction

> Dooyeweerd…may be said to have the ambivalent honor of being a grand system builder in an age when systems are viewed with some suspicion…. The comprehensiveness of [his] philosophy is part of its grandeur but also a stumbling block to many interested in familiarizing themselves with it.[1]

In this book exploring the potential connections between private law and Christianity, it is helpful to consider the work of Herman Dooyeweerd (1894–1977), a Dutch university professor who was trained in law but went on to develop generally the foundations of a distinctly Christian philosophy—the "Philosophy of the Law-Idea." Assessments of Dooyeweerd's significance as a philosopher, you might surmise if you have never heard of him, vary. According to the author of an intellectual biography of Dooyeweerd, it is too early to write the history of twentieth-century Dutch philosophy, but "Dooyeweerd will surely be assigned a generous place within it."[2] After all, there is in Canada a "Dooyeweerd Centre for Christian Philosophy," actively ensuring that Dooyeweerd's writings are translated into English.

> And what is more, those who have made this philosophy their own have brought it to life in society. They have institutionalized it, have trained teachers, have enriched a university [i.e., Vrije Universiteit-Amsterdam], and founded a scholarly periodical [*Philosophia Reformata*]. And the Philosophy of the Law-Idea has struck a responsive chord in the world of Reformed Protestantism far beyond the borders of the Netherlands.[3]

1 R.D. Henderson, "Illuminating Law: The Construction of Herman Dooyeweerd's Philosophy 1918–1928," Ph.D. diss. (Vrije Universiteit Amsterdam, 1994), 13.

2 Marcel E. Verburg, *Herman Dooyeweerd: The Life and Work of a Christian Philosopher*, trans. and eds. Herbert Donald Morton and Harry Van Dyke (Jordan Station, Ontario: Paideia Press, 2015), xii.

3 Michael John Petry and Jan Sperna Weiland, "Voorwoord," in *Herman Dooyeweerd, Grenzen van het theoretisch denken*, ed. Marcel E. Verburg, vol. 20 of *Geschiedenis van de wijsbegeerte in*

However, some would say that, like Thomism, "its capacity to convince those who do not share its philosophical points of departure is minimal."[4] I suspect the late Herman Dooyeweerd would disagree, insofar as he did not see himself as engaged in sectarian theology or Biblical exegesis for the benefit of believers—rather, he was engaged in conventional, mainstream social, political, and legal argumentation. Yes, he had a perspective, but for Dooyeweerd and his followers, everyone does.

> De facto what we find in theoretical learning is a plurality of particularistic perspectives; but we are not to rest content with fractured actuality....Bodies of learning shaped by different worldviews are not incommensurable on account of being so shaped.[5]

In short, Dooyeweerd is not a *Christian* scholar if that is supposed to be an indication of some unique *bias* among other scholars—he is just a scholar, and like every other scholar in the marketplace of ideas, he has a worldview. However, Dooyeweerd's Christian faith was certainly the starting point for his philosophical system. And even though he hoped that his views on private law and legal relationships would be compelling to others irrespective of their religious or non-religious beliefs, the fact remains that the foundations of his philosophy are oriented to the Biblical framework of creation, fall, and redemption in Christ. That orientation guided his reflections on what would be the best—the most just and workable—legal doctrines (including the law of contracts), for *everyone*, in a pluralistic society.

The philosophy of the law-idea

> The place of the jural aspect in the order of the [15] aspects [of being]... reveal[s] itself only by way of a precise analysis of the constant modal structure of law....
>
> The modal meaning of the jural norm is contained within...article 1275 of the [Dutch] Civil Code: All contractual undertakings to do some positive act or refrain from acting are satisfied by the payment of costs, damages, and interest where the party from whom performance is due fails to carry out his or her obligations.[6]

Most readers of this chapter, unless they are familiar with the neo-Calvinist movement in the mid-twentieth-century Netherlands, would find the foregoing

---

Nederland, ed. Michael John Petry and Jan Sperna Weiland (Baarn: Ambo, 1986), 8–0.

4 Ibid., 8.

5 Nicholas P. Wolterstorff, "Abraham Kuyper," in *The Teachings of Modern Christianity on Law, Politics, and Human Nature*, eds. John Witte and Frank Alexander (New York: Columbia University Press, 2006), 304–05.

6 Herman Dooyeweerd, *Encyclopedia of the Science of Law*, Vol. 1, ed. Alan Cameron, trans. Robert D. Knudsen. (Lewiston, NY: Edwin Mellen Press., 2002), 197–98.

passage to be enigmatic (just as first-time readers of the texts of any number of philosophers might react). Note that Dooyeweerd, a professor of jurisprudence and "old Dutch law" at the Vrije Universiteit Amsterdam from 1926 to 1967[7], first identifies law or legality as one of the central, "constant" structures of God's creation; and then he elucidates its essence with a conventional Dutch statute: damages will satisfy a contractual obligation which has been breached. The first move is that of a Christian philosopher generally, insofar as Dooyeweerd attempted to identify *every single* structure of the creation, and law (the "jural") was one of those structures; the second move is that of a lawyer, focusing on his own legal training (his doctoral dissertation was on constitutional law)[8]. The two moves are, however, related—*every single* structure of the creation (e.g., business, politics, legal processes and institutions, art, biology) involves normative "laws," such that conventional legal processes and institutions are only one "aspect" of what Dooyeweerd called the "cosmonomic idea" (usually referred to as "the law-idea"). And if "cosmonomic" suggests only laws of nature, it bears mention that, for Dooyeweerd, the "law sphere" ordering our legal system or business or politics or art is not so different from the "law sphere" of biology!

> By "law sphere" I understand a cluster of laws, which distinguishes itself from others by a particular sovereign quality. Hence, the arithmetic laws lie in one law sphere. So similarly do the geometrical, the physical, the biotic, the psychic, the logical, the social, the historical, the aesthetic, the economic, the juridical and the ethical laws, etc....[9]

This passage confirms—a point to which I will return—that there are two senses of law in Dooyeweerd's thought: (i) the legal processes and institutions that we call law, and (ii) the normative laws that can be identified within every aspect (or "mode of being," or "modal structure") of the creation, including the laws of nature in biology or the laws of economics—and, of course, including legal processes and institutions as one of those aspects of the creation.

When Bruno Latour, the French sociologist of science and technology, recently published his magnum opus *An Inquiry into Modes of Existence*[10]—identifying 15 such modes—students and disciples of Dooyeweerd must have noticed. Over 80 years ago, Dooyeweerd himself identified 15 "modes of being" in his own four-volume magnum opus, *De wijsbegeerte der wetsidee* (1935–1937).[11] Both

7 Verburg, *Herman Dooyeweerd*, 90, 457.

8 Verburg, *Herman Dooyeweerd*, 15.

9 Herman Dooyeweerd, "Het Juridisch Causaliteitsprobleem in Het Licht der Wetsidee," *Antirevolutionaire Staatkunde*, 2 (1928): 21–121. Quotation in text translated in Henderson, "Illuminating Law," 167.

10 Bruno Latour, *An Inquiry into Modes of Existence: An Anthropology of the Moderns*, trans. Catherine Porter (Cambridge, MA: Harvard University Press, 2013).

11 Literally, "the philosophy of the law idea," but it was translated into English in two volumes entitled *A New Critique of Theoretical Thought* (1953–1958). Latour's 15 "ways of being" are Reproduction; Metamorphose; Habit; Technics; Fiction; Reference; Politics; Right; Religion;

thinkers were ambitiously attempting a comprehensive account of, well, nearly everything—a "grand theory," as it were. In Latour's case, the goal was to understand modernity; in Dooyeweerd's case, the goal was both to "give the Christian worldview a place in the modern world," and to offer an "understanding [of] the nature, scope, and limitations of the law...."[12] (Dorrestijn 2015). Dooyeweerd's inquiry into law as a discipline, and its relationship with other disciplines ("sciences," in European parlance), necessitated for him a grand theory:

> In order to attain knowledge of the internal connection of the science of law with the other sciences it is necessary to undertake an investigation of the internal structure of the *entire extent of human knowledge* so that, in terms of its place within this *totality*, we can deduce the inner structure of the science of law.[13]

In any event, understanding the complexities of either Latour's or Dooyeweerd's project requires a substantial commitment on the part of the reader, which means that it is difficult to introduce a systematic thinker like Dooyeweerd (or Latour) in a brief chapter addressing only a minor focus—namely contract law—in his theoretical investigations.

Nevertheless, it is significant that Dooyeweerd (in the epigraph) chose a fairly standard contract doctrine as exemplary of the "jural norm." He both (i) identifies the jural or legal "aspect" as one of 15 aspects of reality in which all things participate (e.g., a rose is *biological*, but is *economic* when it is sold, *legal* when it is regulated, *linguistic* when it is discussed), and (ii) explains that the modal structure of any aspect must be revealed in analysis, because each has a unique meaning and normative *purpose*—a "leading function" in neo-Calvinist terminology. The meaning of *law* is captured, Dooyeweerd notes, in the way that an obligation can be satisfied by either performance or damages. That is an example of law's purpose—to govern legal relationships by doctrinal guidelines; other modal structures (biological, economic, linguistic) have different meanings and

---

Attachment; Organization; Morality; Network; Preposition; and Double-click. Dooyeweerd's 15 modal aspects of being are Quantitative; Spatial; Kinematic; Physical; Biotic; Psychical; Logical; Historical; Linguistic; Social; Economic; Aesthetic; Legal (or jural); Ethical; and Pistical. Relevant to this chapter, Dooyeweerd used the example of a contract, the leading aspect of which is legal, which shares in all the other aspects, to illustrate those aspects: there is a *numerical* aspect to two contracting parties, who are in particular (*spatial*) places, and there is *movement* of money and goods; the parties are *human* beings who declare their *will* to contract after a *logical* thought process, and their transaction reflects the historical development of *law*, is expressed in *language*, and is governed in part by *social* customs, *economic* structures, a certain *aesthetic* harmony, a *moral* (i.e., not immoral) purpose, and a set of pre-theoretical assumptions that function like a *religion*. *See also* Dooyeweerd, *Encyclopedia*, 17–20.

12 Steven Dorrestijn, "Hoe techniek kruist met ethiek, politiek en religie: Bij Latour en Dooyeweerd" (The Crossings of Technology with Ethics, Politics, and Religion: On Latour and Dooyeweerd), *Denkwijzer*, 15, no. 2 (July 2015): 12–17.

13 Dooyeweerd, *Encyclopedia*, 11–12 (emphasis added).

purposes than legal processes and institutions. Moreover, the scientific inquiry or discipline focused on a particular aspect cannot "be reduced or explained in terms of another" aspect (e.g., law cannot be reduced to or fully explained in terms of morality or economics, even though both are related to law in the "mutual coherence" of all the aspects).[14]

As suggested above, two different understandings of law are in play in Dooyeweerd's systematic philosophy. In addition to (i) the processes and doctrines of the legal system as a development of the "jural" aspect, (ii) each of the aspects is "ruled by its own type of laws."[15] There are "laws" of nature in biology, "laws" of economics, and so forth. Borrowing from the Calvinist Abraham Kuyper's notion of sphere sovereignty (which was for Kuyper an argument for the independent authority of church, state, school, and family as to matters within each's "sphere of competence"), Dooyeweerd suggested that each aspect of *reality* is a sovereign "sphere" or domain with distinctive norms, "because of divine command."[16] Thus Dooyeweerd's "philosophy of the law-idea" (originally called "the Philosophy of the *Cosmonomic* Idea") refers to "a biblically anchored idea of law and its correlate, the creaturely *subjectum*, as its basic philosophical idea."[17] This latter project is not legal theory *per se* (i.e., law and legal processes and institutions represent only one aspect of reality), but rather a theological commitment to the idea of a normative *creation* governed by "laws" or norms in each of its aspects.

Christian legal theory in Dooyeweerd

> Ethical and juridical norms...are not posited by reason itself; rather, the essence of the legal order and moral order is normative on grounds of the divine authority that instituted it. Thus understood, law [cannot] derive its normative meaning...from the state....[18]

Before turning to Dooyeweerd's reflections on private law and the law of contracts, the focus of this chapter, some general remarks about his approach to Christian legal theory are in order. First, even though Dooyeweerd believed that the meaning of law is a matter of divine authority and not state authority, one would not characterize his orientation as theocratic, either in terms of (i) privileging Christianity (he finds "objectionable [the] idea that the Christian State

14 Henderson, "Illuminating Law," 33.

15 Ibid., 40.

16 Ibid., 36–40.

17 Herman Dooyeweerd, "Introduction by the Editor in Chief," *Philosophia Reformata*, 38, no. 1 (1973): 9.

18 Herman Dooyeweerd, "De Leer der rechtssoevereiniteit en die der staatssoevereiniteit in haar consequenties voor de verhouding van Overheid en onderdanen" (The Theories of Sovereign Law and State Sovereignty and their Consequences for the Relationship between government and Subjects), trans. Herbert Donald Morton and Harry van Dyke (A. Kuyper Foundation white paper) (unpublished manuscript, October 1923), 5.

ought to have an ecclesiastical character")[19] or in terms of (ii) basing contemporary law on Scripture verses (such as Proverbs 22:26: "Be not one of those [puts] up security for debts"). "In Dooyeweerd's view, Scripture informs us that legal norms exist, though the norms themselves may not be derivable simply by looking at Scripture."[20] Dooyeweerd adopted Kuyper's notion of the state as *secular*, in the sense of its contrast to the church as *confessional*—civil society in Calvinist thought was not to be a confessional regime.[21] Dooyeweerd's vision of politics is therefore democratic and pluralistic, and decidedly *modern*; following Weber, Dooyeweerd argued that the historical differentiation of social formations—distinct social spheres of human activity—was necessary for a genuinely free society.[22] Primitive cultures, governed by a single social collectivity, offered neither civil legal freedoms nor private property rights. James W. Skillen's work on pluralism in the USA reflects Dooyeweerd's influence when he recognizes

> the legitimacy of government protecting each citizen's civil rights and developing the commonwealth for the good of all while at the same time acknowledging that many other kinds of social authority exist beyond the boundaries of government…[T]he government's responsibility to promote the common good…ought to take into account, and do justice to, that full range of differentiated institutions and communities.[23]

Dooyeweerd was following Abraham Kuyper, who believed that civil society should be comprised of diverse and independent "spheres" of authority that require state protection (but not its centralized planning)—Kuyper explained that just

> as we speak of a 'moral world,' a 'scientific world,' a 'business world,' [or] the 'world of art,' so we can more properly speak of a 'sphere' of morality, of the family, of social life, each with its own domain.[24]

Second, and somewhat counter-intuitively given his rejection of theocratic ideals, Dooyeweerd did not believe that the state was ever neutral ("The State can be no more neutral…than science"[25])—pre-theoretical commitments (that function like a religion, even among secularists) on the part of government

19 Herman Dooyeweerd, *New Critique of Theoretical Thought*, vol. 1 trans. D.H. Freeman and W.S. Young, vols. 2–3 trans. D.H. Freeman and H. de Jongste, vol. 3 trans H. de Jongste (Phillipsburg, NJ: Presbyterian and Reformed Publishing Company, 1969), III 502.

20 Henderson, "Illuminating Law," 45.

21 Abraham Kuyper, "Sphere Sovereignty," in *Abraham Kuyper: A Centennial Reader*, ed. James D. Bratt (Grand Rapids, MI: Eerdman's Publishing Company, 1998), 197.

22 Wolterstorff, "Abraham Kuyper," 314.

23 James Skillen, *Recharging the American Experience: Principled Pluralism for Genuine Civic Community* (Grand Rapids, MI: Baker Books, 1994), 65.

24 Wolterstorff, "Abraham Kuyper," 292, 314; Kuyper, "Sphere Sovereignty," 461, 467.

25 Dooyeweerd, *New Critique*, III 503.

leaders are unavoidable; therefore, appeals to some sort of neutral, objective public reason or to common sense are unrealistic. Even as a doctoral student, Dooyeweerd

> was already thinking in terms of the dependence of thought...upon certain religious a priori ideas....[He assumed] that there are other than rational factors which affect or co-determine the internal operation of reason....[26]

Later, as an intellectual historian, he asserted that the "autonomy and neutrality of philosophical thought had to be recognized as a fundamental error."[27]

If, for example, the state reflects Christian ideals, the fact that all citizens are not Christians does not affect their relationship with the legal system or their benefits (or burdens) from that system. As to the Netherlands and its law of contracts,

> we live in a Christian land where legal conceptions have been influenced in great measure by Christian ideas. Completely independent of the question whether the contracting parties personally adhere to Christian beliefs, the agreement which they conclude is thoroughly bound to [the] connection between law and faith.[28]

In other words, our legal system will always reflect some "faith" in a set of pre-theoretical or "religious" principles. The contractual agreement between two non-Christians in a "Christian land" ends up being based on biblical principles—"the principle of contractual freedom, with the simultaneous binding of every contract to a lawful cause,[29] stems from the canon law of the Roman Catholic Church which based this principle on the Holy Scriptures."[30] Likewise, the "interpretation of such concepts as 'good faith' [, which is required of all contracts under Article 1374 of the Dutch Civil Code,]...has also undoubtedly been strongly influenced by Christian conceptions and concerns."[31] And yet,

26 Henderson, "Illuminating Law," 24. Henderson is here citing an article written by Dooyeweerd as a student, "Fr. van Eeden and Neo-Mysticism," August 20, 1915, *Orgaan van het Studenten Corps aan de Vrije Universiteit.*

27 James Skillen, "Philosophy of the Cosmonomic Idea: Herman Dooyeweerd's Political and Legal Thought," *The Political Science Reviewer*, 32, no. 1 (Fall 2003): 320.

28 Dooyeweerd, *Encyclopedia*, 19–20.

29 Ibid., 19. Dooyeweerd illustrates the concept of "lawful cause" in the Dutch Civil Code, which is similar to the prohibition of illegal contracts, or contracts against public policy, in the common law:

> Let us suppose that a person promises another a sum of money for spreading false rumors in the stock market by which means the first hopes to personally benefit. The other party agrees to this proposition. There is therefore mutual agreement. But such an agreement has an "immoral cause," and for this reason is legally void.

30 Ibid., 20.

31 Ibid., 19.

a Christian legal theorist is not engaged in *adding* a pre-theoretical commitment to an otherwise neutral or "rational" legal system!—the legal system, in neo-Calvinist thought, will always reflect pre-theoretical commitments from some "faith" tradition, whether an overtly religious tradition or a secular faith in a set of values or assumptions about the world that are matters of belief and not matters of proof. In that sense, there is nothing unique about *Christian* legal theory—it is simply *legal theory* in competition with other legal theories that are no less faith-based than the theories promoted by Christians.

Third, Dooyeweerd's oeuvre is highly theoretical—a philosophical project of which legal theory is only a part—and therefore quite undeveloped in terms of practical legal insights. When Dooyeweerd completed his law degree, he held several positions as a practitioner—a civil servant in the national tax service, then a city attorney for a year, then a legislative aide in the Department of Labor—but he was committed to theoretical research and writing: "Since finishing my doctorate in 1917, I have spent all of my free time on methodological and philosophical legal studies."[32] He soon left law practice and became a law professor and a prolific scholar, but his field of inquiry was jurisprudence, and he paid relatively little attention either to the lawyering practices of the legal profession, or the doctrines, statutes, and judicial opinions of Dutch law.

Fourth, and closely related to Dooyeweerd's theoretical orientation, Dooyeweerd frequently illustrates his theoretical principles with practical legal examples, many of which are from the field of contract law. The examples, however, are striking, both because (i) they are rarely complex—they read like an introduction to contract law for first year law students in the USA—and appear especially simple in the context of a highly complex, even esoteric, systematic philosophy; and (ii) they do not appear to be "Christian" in any direct sense of the term. Perhaps because Holland is a "Christian land," Dooyeweerd neither criticizes nor commends as appropriately "biblical" the contract doctrines to which he refers—it is as if he might only be critical if he was living in a primitive, undifferentiated society without freedom of contract:

> In the most primitive phase of Roman and German law, the contract, as a source of legal relationships relating to property, was unknown. Here only a delict [i.e., an obligation arising from a wrong, similar to a tort in the common law] created juridical relations between members of the tribe.[33]

Indeed, when Dooyeweerd wrote his dissertation on the Dutch constitution, for the law faculty at the (Calvinistic) Vrije Universiteit Amsterdam, he made "no

32 Herman Dooyeweerd to J.J.C. van Dijk, 1922, in G. Puchinger, "Dr. Herman Dooyeweerd," in *Perspectief, Feestbundel van de jongeren bij het, vijfentwintig jarig van de Vereniging voor Calvinistische Wijsbegeerte*, ed. W.K van Dijk (Kampen: Kok, 1961), 47–52.

33 Dooyeweerd, *Encyclopedia*, 17.

special references to the content of his Christian faith, nor does he say anything at this time about offering a Christian view of his subject."[34] Even in his later work, Dooyeweerd proceeds as if he is doing legal theory generally, and not theology or biblical exegesis; for example, when he discusses the limitations on state authority with respect to contracts, there is a "religious" character to his analysis, but it is not unique for that reason, because all theory is faith-based—the uniqueness is his particular belief that in a just state, "all of the differentiated institutions and organizations of society" should flourish.[35] And even that belief, based on biblical principles, is offered and justified as good for everybody from any background; so while it can be traced to the theoretical reflections of a Christian, that need not be mentioned in a *policy* argument for freedom of contract. Likewise, Dooyeweerd's passing remark that "Young children…cannot legally bind themselves," the commonly accepted doctrine of minors, is offered as an illustration of how contract law in the "jural" sphere is related to the psychical (or psychological) sphere:

> A valid declaration of will…can only be expressed in a jural fashion by responsible persons, and responsibility in a jural sense is unbreakable connected with a normally developed life of feelings and imagination.[36]

The theory of the 15 aspects (illustrated here in the connection between the jural and the psychical) can be traced to the reflections of a Christian philosopher, but the contract law regarding minors is not discussed as a Christian law.

This approach provides a model for Christian theorizing about law. Dooyeweerd welcomes the differentiation of Western society "as a *deepening* and *unfolding* of the meaning of law."[37] We are beyond Biblical times; we have transcended Roman law and feudal regimes, as well as nineteenth-century individualism and twentieth-century totalitarianism, and our contemporary legal systems will reflect that progress. If we want a Christian theory of law,

> Scripture does not provide us with a body of indubitably known propositions by reference to which one can govern all our acceptance and nonacceptance of theories….[T]he Bible cannot function as a black book of theories for the Christian scholar….[We arrive] at the data…by using the same strategies as everyone else.[38]

34 Henderson, "Illuminating Law," 25.

35 Skillen, "Philosophy of the Cosmonomic Idea," 352.

36 Dooyeweerd, *Encyclopedia*, 18.

37 Herman Dooyeweerd, *The Relationship between Individual and Community in the Germanic Conception of Property*, trans. D.F.M. Strauss (De verhouding tusschen individu en gemeenschap in de Romeinsche en Germaansche) (1938), 54.

38 Nicholas P. Wolterstorff, *Reason Within the Bounds of Religion* (Grand Rapids, MI: Eerdmans, 1976), 58, 74, 76.

We do, however, have a worldview—everyone does, but ours is unique—that provides us with religious control beliefs, which in turn lead us to reject or accept certain assumptions, based on Christian ideals, for example, of freedom and responsibility.[39] However, all Christians do not agree on theoretical matters, so "the" Christian perspective on law is simply not available. Other than our unique control beliefs, therefore, Christian theories of law are just like any other theories of law with which we compete—they look at the same data, and then they theorize under the influence of control beliefs, which everyone has, religious or not—there is no unbiased, neutral position from which to reflect on law.

Contract law in Dooyeweerd

> In answering [the question of whether investigating law is a matter of speculative thought or an inquiry grounded in the structure of the life of law itself,] we do not wish to commence with profound philosophical and epistemological considerations, but rather give a brief account of the multifacetedness of an ordinary activity in daily life.[40]

The transaction in a cigar shop

One of Dooyeweerd's discussions of the law of contract is not presented as a guide to contract doctrine, but as an illustration of how each of the 15 modes or aspects of being is both independent—sovereign, with each's own norms—and interrelated, in what Dooyeweerd call "mutual coherence," such that everything in the world is both identifiable and "qualified" by a particular aspect (a contract is primarily a "jural" object) even as everything participates in all of the aspects of reality (i.e., a contract "participates" in all 15 aspects). Dooyeweerd, who enjoyed cigars, begins his "brief account of the multifacetedness of an ordinary activity in daily life" by stating, "I enter a store and purchase a box of cigars."[41] Lawyers, he explains, recognize that event as "a jural transaction, as a legal agreement, out of which flows mutual rights and juridical obligations for the buyer and the seller."[42]

> [L]et us suppose that the buyer had specified a box of 25 authentic Havanas of good quality and, with the owner's consent, had only paid one dollar for it. In such a case suspicion immediately arises in the jurist's mind as to whether the agreement was a genuine one. Is it a true commercial agreement, or do we have a disguised gift, a sham transaction?

39 Ibid., 64, 66, 70, 73.
40 Dooyeweerd, *Encyclopedia*, 13.
41 Ibid.
42 Ibid.

> Or if no gift is intended, is the entire matter suspect? Has the store owner obtained the cigars honestly? Does the agreement indeed have a "lawful cause"?[43]

Unlawful cause is then illustrated by the example of a party paying another to spread false rumors in the stock market; their agreement is void because Article 1374 of the Civil Code, to which this transaction is subject, explicitly states that an agreement must be brought into existence 'in good faith'."[44] Moreover, Dooyeweerd reminds readers that an agreement obtained by deceit is invalid, but the primary reason for this stock market hypothetical is (i) to place the transaction into the jural sphere, and (ii) to show that it is not isolated because it is "unbreakably connected" to another aspect of reality, the moral sphere, the location of notions of deceit and good faith.[45]

Dooyeweerd then shows that the transaction has even more aspects; the price of the cigar suggests an economic aspect. And we also find in

> the Civil Code an entire heading devoted to the 'interpretation of contracts.' The jurist, qua jurist, thereby comes into immediate contact with the lingual aspect of the transaction, and it is plain from the outset that the entire jural configuration of the commercial agreement can only exist on the basis of linguistic forms of expression....[46]

And there is a historical aspect to the transaction:

> [T]he positive juridical content of the agreement, as well as usage, wherever recognized in the Civil Code, has a close connection with the modern stage of cultural development. The form of the contract itself has its own legal history and can only be understood scientifically in connection with it.[47]

The analysis continues with identifications of the mathematical and spatial aspects (two different parties in a particular place), the psychical aspect of willing parties who want something, and so on for all 15 spheres of reality.

43 Ibid., 15. The editor's note in Dooyeweerd, *Encyclopedia* at 15, confirms that "lawful cause" (*causa*) has no precise equivalent in the common law, except insofar as contracts can be declared void as against public policy:

> At the time when Dooyeweerd was writing, *causa* was a requirement of all contracts under the Dutch Civil Code [Article 1356]. The requirement has now been abandoned. Common law jurisdictions...still retain the requirement of "consideration" which is a more narrowly economic concept than the continental *causa*.

44 Ibid., 19.

45 Ibid.

46 Ibid., 17.

47 Ibid.

Limits of the competence of the state

Private law develops within a state, and whether

> codified by the legislator or...formed by the courts..., it is by its inner nature a legal sphere bound to the body politic. And the original competence of its formation cannot belong to any other organized community but the state....But the internal spheres of...specific kinds of private law, qualified by the non-juridical leading function of the societal relationship to which they belong, remain exempt from the competence of the state.[48]

Dooyeweerd illustrates this theoretical notion, the limits of state interference (not with respect to *all* private law, but clearly with respect to private *contracts*), with the Dutch Code of Commerce in 1838, which set forth a "compulsory definition of commercial acts and of the occupation of merchants which restricted the objects of commerce to movables."[49] But this state law wrongly left out real estate brokers who did not deal in "movables":

> Here we meet with a clear encroachment on the part of the civil legislator upon the internal sphere of competence of commerce and industry. We have seen that civil law....lacks any specific qualification of a non-juridical character. It is consequently beyond the civil legal power of the legislator to determine the inner sphere of activity of commerce and industry....[50]

The law was eventually repealed; note that the point of Dooyeweerd's exposition is not really to educate us as to a law that mistakenly left out brokers, but to educate us as to the boundaries of state power with respect to the private law of business associations.

On the classifications of private law

Apart from the competence of the state to create and enforce both (i) public law, including constitutional law, administrative law, and criminal law and procedure, and (ii) private, civil state law governing inter-individual relationships, such as the statutes and common law governing contracts, there are two types of *non-state* law in Dooyeweerd's legal theory, including (iii) non-state laws of communal associations (e.g., church laws, internal corporate law) and (iv) non-state, non-civil law, which includes contracts between parties. These categories of law can best be illustrated in the following table:

48 Dooyeweerd, *New Critique*, III 451.
49 Ibid., III 692.
50 Ibid., III 693.

State Law		*Non-State Law*	
Public Law (e.g., Constitutional Law, Law of Nations, Administrative Law, Criminal Law/ Procedure)	Private Law: *Three Types* (1) Civil Law (e.g., State Law governing inter-individual relationships)	(2) Communal Associations (e.g., internal law of churches or corporations)	(3) Non-civil Law (e.g., **contracts, commercial customs**)

Note the references to (1) civil commercial law, which might be a type of statutory law governing contracts, and to (3) the non-civil commercial law of free social intercourse (freedom of contract), which might include customs that have become binding.[51] For example:

> In article 1375 of the Civil Code, the jurist finds a reference to 'usage' which, in addition to the express stipulations of the transaction itself and the requirements of 'fairness' and the 'law,' determines the extent of the responsibilities and rights of the contracting parties.[52]

Social customs have no legal meaning, but if one becomes "usage" it has a legal meaning:

> [U]nder normal economic conditions, [consider] the commercial custom of not demanding payment from a sound trader immediately upon the delivery of the goods. It is apparent that this custom is primarily a social one; it is initially a rule of courtesy. But it is not out of the question that in various lines of business this custom might have taken on such established forms that it would also have to be taken into account juridically in determining the extent of mutual rights and responsibilities of the contracting parties.[53]

In another formulation:

> Think of the transgression involved in breaching a requirement of discipline in wearing a particular kind of clothing, or a requirement in the army to salute in a certain way. In a jural sense, these fall into the category of an unlawful act, but undoubtedly they primarily involve transgressing the rules of social intercourse.[54]

51 Dooyeweerd, *Encyclopedia*, 199.
52 Ibid., 16.
53 Ibid.
54 Ibid.

The dress code may be a non-state rule "of greater or lesser formality functioning within some sphere of social life, but not originating in state law,"[55] while the social obligation to salute may actually originate in state law. Both transgressions are unlawful "in a jural sense," because the term "unlawful acts" includes "both breaches of state and nonstate law...."[56] The point, however, is to oppose the false identification of all private law as civil law: private "law encompasses many spheres of law which do not display a civil legal character."[57] Hence there are limits on the competence of the state to govern civil matters, i.e., through "private" laws governing inter-individual relationships, thereby leaving a sphere of *non*-civil private law for contracts. In short, for an easy example, while the state can prohibit fraudulent contracts, the state cannot impose payment terms on parties to a contract—there must be limits on the state to ensure the freedom of citizens to form mutually advantageous contracts.

Dooyeweerd is, in his schema above, rejecting both extreme individualism and extreme collectivism, and instead balancing the two—there is room in his schema for public law and (1) private civil law, on the one hand, governing legal rights and relationship, but there is also room for (2) freedom of association and (3) freedom of contract (the so-called categories of non-state law). The state, that is, alternatively protects from each other *and* leaves alone to flourish both individuals entering into contracts and communities in their activities (families, schools, churches, labor unions).

Conclusion: Dooyeweerd for our times

> [C]ivil law protects the individual against infringements by collective and communal organs—including that of the state[,but civil law] needs the counter balance of the social legislation of the state guided by the public idea of communal law, which opposes the power usurpations of private individuals or organized communities. [And civil law also] needs the counter balance of private communities which ought to protect their inner spheres against usurpation by the state.[58]

Dooyeweerd did not write a book setting forth a Christian set of laws of contracts for contemporary society; even his *Encyclopedia of the Science of Law* is a theoretical project, using certain contract doctrines or statutes as mere examples, as he sets forth a more general Christian legal theory. He does offer a taxonomy of three different types of private law, but he does not offer a Christian theory of *contract* law. This is not, however, a criticism, because he clearly offers a potential and compelling foundation for a Christian contract theory. That foundation combines several *images*: (i) a pluralistic society with Christian influences

55 Ibid., n.1 (*Editor's note*).
56 Ibid.
57 Dooyeweerd, *The Relationship between Individual and Community*, 13.
58 Ibid., 12–13.

in the form of policies for everyone; (ii) no expectation that appropriate laws for modern society are found in the Scriptures, and (iii) a balance between individualistic freedom and public (or civil) law interests. If we consider the current controversy in modern commercial law, a real-world example, over whether the government can restrict the production and sale (to willing buyers) of flavored cigars, Dooyeweerd would likely balk at the loss of individual freedom for adults, but out of Christian love, he would likely be convinced by arguments that public health risks to children should outweigh that freedom. Significantly, it also seems likely that someone *without* Dooyeweerd's Christian faith could settle on those same three *images* above, casually (i) accepting the historical and contemporary (if popular) influences of Christianity on law, and also (ii) agreeing with Dooyeweerd's analysis of the flavored cigar prohibition. I do not think Dooyeweerd would see anything wrong with that—when asked, in a television interview at the age of 79 (four years before his death), what the philosophy of the law-idea would look like in 50 years, Dooyeweerd answered, "It's possible that it will have disappeared. And I would not mind that, if it had indeed done its work."[59]

59 Verburg, *Herman Dooyeweerd*, 483.

11 Revisiting unconscionability

Reciprocity and justice

C. Scott Pryor

Introduction

The defense of unconscionability in contract law was revitalized with the adoption of the Uniform Commercial Code (UCC) in the 1960s. Yet the UCC left unconscionability undefined.[1] Since then American courts have struggled to articulate a predictable standard by which to apply it. Drawing from the opinion of J. Skelly Wright in *Williams v. Walker-Thomas Furniture*,[2] courts and commentators frame unconscionability in terms of procedural ("absence of meaningful choice") and substantive ("contract terms which are unreasonably favorable to the other party"). It remains unclear, however, what exactly deprives a contract party of meaningful choice or what makes a contract term unreasonably favorable.

Over 500 years of painstaking Christian legal analysis stands in sharp contrast with contemporary vagaries of procedural and substantive unconscionability. From the late 1000s through the 1600s and beyond, theologians and clergy, jurists and judges, as well as lawyers and contract parties would have understood what made a contract unconscionable: a substantial deviation from market price. Comparison of the contract price to the market had the virtues of clarity and predictability. Such a narrow focus of inquiry also freed unconscionability from the danger of judicial subjectivity. For over half a millennium, unconscionability was not the length of the chancellor's foot; it was gross over- or underpayment *as measured by the market.*

The reason for a doctrine like unconscionability is the ground for society itself: reciprocity. Humans are both finite and social. Society cannot exist without

1 U.C.C. § 2–302. Unconscionable Contract or Clause.

> (1) If the court as a matter of law finds the contract or any clause thereof to have been unconscionable at the time it was made the court may refuse to enforce the contract, of it may enforce the remainder of the contract without the unconscionable clause, or it may so limit the application of any unconscionable clause as to avoid any unconscionable result.

James J. White, *Uniform Commercial Code* (St. Paul, MN: American Law Institute & Uniform Law Commission, 1997).

2 *Williams v. Walker-Thomas Furniture*, 350 F.2d 445 (D.C. Cir. 1965).

exchange and parties to exchanges might well suppose that they're getting as much as they give. That has never always been the case since the entrance of sin into the world. Nonetheless, the biblical witness and the subsequent Christian moral tradition made clear what had only been implicit in the classical world: contract parties should do no harm. Under what circumstances *the law* should take account of an unbalanced exchange raised a different question although for centuries few in the West doubted that at some point any legal system should remedy a contractual disparity.

The measure of unconscionability is the ground for law itself: justice. The purpose of contract law in biblical, Roman, medieval, and early modern times was to neither increase social welfare nor enhance personal autonomy. The end or *telos* of law was justice. Both the Bible and the classical tradition taught that justice was foundational to human society. And for over half a millennium in the West, justice for contract law was framed as rough equality in exchange. Drawing on internal and external resources, it was a Christian society that developed a clear and predictable doctrine of unconscionability. Cutting themselves adrift from those resources, contemporary versions of unconscionability are neither clear nor predictable. Yet, because equality in exchange is based on reciprocity and measured by justice, its revitalization can resonate with those who would reject an overtly Christian account.

The ancient roots of unconscionability

Biblical Israel

Torah—the law (or teachings) comprising the first five books of the Hebrew Scriptures—has little to say about contract law. Examples of bargaining and related formalities include Genesis 23:8–16 (Abraham's purchase of a tomb for Sarah) and Genesis 31:43–54 (settlement of a dispute between Laban and Jacob). The only specific exchanges that receive attention in biblical law are what today would be understood as bailments for hire (Exodus 22:7–15), repayment of loans (Leviticus 25:25ff; Deuteronomy 15:1–6; Deuteronomy 24:10–13), and payment of wages (Deuteronomy 24:14–15). There is no general contract law in the Bible.

This lack of biblical specification for contract law does not mean there was none. As theologian Jonathan Burnside explains, "Our sense that law in biblical Israel was fragmentary and incomplete may be more apparent than real. Simply because a rule is not mentioned in biblical law does not mean that it did not exist."[3] From this lack of biblical specificity we can, however, infer that within the bounds of reciprocity and justice, a legal system is free to frame its own contract law.

3 Jonathan Burnside, *God, Justice, and Society: Aspects of Law and Legality in the Bible* (Oxford: Oxford University Press, 2011), 18.

More significant for unconscionability is that Torah presents two fundamental principles that are crucial to contract law: the virtues of fidelity and fairness. The biblical record has much to say by way of example and precept about the importance of performing what was promised. The Hebrew Scriptures use the term ndr (vow) to describe a unilateral promise to God.[4] Examples include Hannah's prayer for the birth of a child (1 Samuel 1:11) and David's prayer for a place to build the temple (Psalm 132:2–5). If God accepts the "offer" and answers the prayer the person making the vow must, of course, pay or perform as promised (Deuteronomy 23:21–23).[5]

If a vow brings to mind an offer of a unilateral contract, then b+r't (covenant) is the biblical term that covers a variety of bilateral agreements including international treaties (1 Kings 5:12; Ezekiel 17:11–21), a declaration of the relationship between a king and his subjects (2 Samuel 5:3), the marriage relationship (Malachi 2:14), and an agreement settling a dispute (Genesis 21:27–31). While b+r't is broader than the contemporary understanding of contract, it is the word that persons in the ancient biblical world would have used for a simple contract.

Like vows, the obligations of a b+r't were to be performed. God directed Abraham and later Israel to "keep my covenant" (Genesis 17:9; Exodus 19:5). God, of course, remains faithful to his obligations (Deuteronomy 7:9). And God's people would be condemned for not keeping theirs (Deuteronomy 28:15ff.). The fundamental obligation of covenantal fidelity should extend to interpersonal relationships (Jeremiah 9:4–6).

Just as Torah emphasizes the virtue of fidelity, it also prohibits various vices that could arise in the practice of exchange. The meanings of the Hebrew terms gnb (steal), kjv (deal falsely), vqr (lie), uvq (oppress), and gzl (rob) extend beyond a one-to-one correspondence with a single English word. As used in the commandment forbidding theft (Exodus 20:15), gnb focuses on secretive theft but was also used more broadly of deceit (Genesis 31:20). To deal falsely (kjv) and to oppress (uvq) are joined in Leviticus 19:11 and 13 as the sorts of actions that should never characterize God's people: "You shall not steal, nor deal falsely, nor lie to one another .... You shall not oppress your neighbor or rob him ...."[6] In other contexts, oppression describes various forms of injustice by which the rich in Israelite society oppressed the poor.[7] An exchange of substantially unequal values could fall within the scope of oppression.

4 *See* Willem A. VanGemeren, ed., ***New International Dictionary of Old Testament Theology and Exegesis*** (Grand Rapids, MI: Zondervan Publishing House, 1997), 3:38 ("With one exception . . . vows made by Israelites in the OT were directed at Yahweh").

5 Even vows could be set aside in the limited situation of one made by a dependent woman (Num 30:3–15). Moreover, a votary could commute a specific obligation with the payment of 120% of the value of a devoted object (Lev 27).

6 ***The Holy Bible: Revised Standard Version*** (New York: Oxford University Press, 2008). All other quotes from the Bible are from ***The Holy Bible: English Standard Version*** (London: Collins, 2010).

7 *See* VanGemeren, ***Old Testament Theology and Exegesis***, 557–58 ***supra*** note 4.

> [This group of words] frequently describe various forms of social injustice by which the rich in Israelite society oppressed the poor. . . . It is significant that in a number of usages

What should a judge in ancient Israel have done when faced with the tension between the virtue of fidelity and the vice of contractual oppression? Would a contract have been enforced notwithstanding its unfair terms, or would it have been set aside in the interest of substantive justice? While no example of biblical case law frames this precise issue, the description of the vocation of judge in the Wisdom texts emphasizes doing justice above all (Job 29:7–17). The refrain of judgment and justice in Deuteronomy 16 makes it clear that justice provides the form for judicial activity:

> 18You shall appoint judges and officers in all your towns that the LORD your God is giving you, according to your tribes, and they shall judge the people with righteous judgment. 19You shall not pervert justice. You shall not show partiality, and you shall not accept a bribe, for a bribe blinds the eyes of the wise and subverts the cause of the righteous. 20Justice, and only justice, you shall follow, that you may live and inherit the land that the LORD your God is giving you.

While no single Hebrew word corresponds to unconscionability, Torah's prohibition of a variety of practices that could work to the disadvantage of a contract party warranted an equally wide variety of contract defenses.

Equally relevant to the understanding of ancient Israel about justice in contracts was the context in which biblical law was to be applied. Burnside explains that

> Israel is called not merely to a covenantal relationship with God but also, and as a consequence to, right relationships within the body of the people—hence the law of Leviticus 19:17–18, which includes the command to "love your neighbor as yourself" (19:18). [B]iblical law is concerned with promoting the quality of relationships in biblical society.[8]

Relationships consistent with biblical law were righteous, and righteousness in ancient Israel was understood as the pattern of life that should come to

of uvq and its derivatives is explicitly indicated in the context (Deut 24:14; Jer 7:6; Amos 4:1). People most likely to be mistreated and socially oppressed were those without adequate defence of their rights, viz., the widow, orphan, sojourner, and the poor. Uvq and its derivatives thus have strong overtones of "extortion" and "despoliation": they are often accompanied by the verbs gzl and lqj; see Lev 6:2, 4 [5:21, 23]; Deut 28:29, 33; 1 Sam. 12:3–4. The oppressor robs the oppressed in different ways: by using false scales and doing fraudulent trade (Hos 12:7[8]); by holding back the laborer's wages (Jer 22:13); by bribery, usury, and profit at the expense of the poor and the foreigner (Ezek. 22:12, 29).

For a discussion of the rabbinic analysis of contractual oppression see Sharhar Lifshitz, "Oppressive-Exploitive Contracts: A Jewish Law Perspective," *Journal of Law and Religion*, 23, no. 2 (2007–2008).

8 Burnside, *God, Justice, and Society*, 26–27 *supra* note 3.

expression in social relationships. Reciprocity was to characterize Israel's society.[9]

Not only was life in ancient Israel under Torah to be relational, Israel was to serve as witness to its neighbors. As theologian Christopher J.H. Wright observes:

> God's purpose [for Israel] ... was ... to create a new community of people who in their social life would embody those qualities of righteousness, peace, justice and love that reflect God's own character and were God's original purpose for humanity.[10]

In brief, Israel's living witness to fidelity and fairness would reveal human society as it was meant to be.

The New Testament witness

Describing the transition of God's redemptive actions from a geographically localized and a largely homogeneous ethnic community, the writings of the New Testament represent the culmination of God's redemptive purposes to which Torah had alluded. The writings of the New Testament recast the whole of Torah through the life, death, resurrection, and ascension of Jesus. As Philip Turner explains, "It is Christ who fulfills Israel's destiny, and the life of Christ's body, the church, is continuous with that of Israel."[11] While no longer tethered to the historical-cultural specifics of biblical law, Christians were equally called to live in relationships characterized by reciprocity and justice. As they had for Israel, fidelity and fairness were to identify the Christian community. The continuing significance of fidelity receives support in James 5:12 ("[L]et your 'yes' be yes and your 'no' be no, so that you may not fall under condemnation"), which in turn summarizes the words of Jesus

9 *See* ibid., 27:

> This concern for right relationships is reflected in the Hebrew term *tsedaqah* ("righteousness" . . .). . . . Tsedaqah is the goal of *mišpāt* (justice), and both "justice and righteousness" (*mišpāt vtsedaqh*) are major concerns of the prophets . . . . Israel's righteousness is to be seen in her relationship with God, the nations, and at the level of relationships between individual Israelites.

See also Raymond Westbrook and Bruce Wells, *Everyday Law in Biblical Israel* (Louisville, KS: Westminster John Knox Press, 2009), 108. "[T]he primary interest of the biblical law codes, as indeed of the prophets, in the law of contracts is in measures of social justice to temper their harsh application to the poor and weaker members of society."

10 Christopher J.H. Wright, *Old Testament Ethics for the People of God* (Downers Grove, IL: InterVarsity Press, 2004), 51.

11 Philip Turner, *Christian Ethics and the Church: Ecclesial Foundations for Moral Thought and Practice* (Grand Rapids, MI: Baker Academic, 2015), 62.

from the Sermon on the Mount.[12] Ephesians 4:1–3 emphasizes reciprocity and James 2 makes clear that members of the nascent Christian community were to treat each other fairly

> [1]My brothers, show no partiality as you hold the faith in our LORD Jesus Christ, the LORD of glory. [2]For if a man wearing a gold ring and fine clothing comes into your assembly, and a poor man in shabby clothing also comes in, [3]and if you pay attention to the one who wears the fine clothing and say, "You sit here in a good place," while you say to the poor man, "You stand over there," or, "Sit down at my feet,"[4]have you not then made distinctions among yourselves and become judges with evil thoughts? ...[6]But you have dishonored the poor man.

In other words, members of the community of believers were not to practice oppression. While neither Jesus nor the New Testament writers developed an ethical system from which civil law can be deduced, the New Testament writers had much to say about how the believers' new lives in Christ should manifest themselves. Their community was the context in which fidelity and fairness could be seen by their unbelieving neighbors.

The community-centered focus of the New Testament should not be understood to limit social virtues to the church. As Turner puts it, "an ethical focus on the common life of the church does not exclude but leads to a profound concern for the common life of society."[13] So we read in one of the earliest New Testament letters: "[A]s we have opportunity, let us do good to everyone, and especially to those who are of the household of faith" (Galatians 6:10). By both their intercession for civil rulers (1 Timothy 2:2–3) and their example, the writers of the New Testament held out the hope that Christians could influence the larger society (Colossian 4:5–6) and ultimately civil government (1 Peter 2:13–15). Justice and mercy, ultimately reconciled in Christ, provided the framework within which the focus of the legal system on justice is reinforced.

Sharing in Jesus' anointing, Christians have a part to play in exemplifying and thus preserving a just social order until the consummation of the ages. As the Church proclaims that God's judgment on Christ was just, it cannot help but intimate that civil judgment also should be just. Given that reciprocity and justice are aspects of the created social order, warrant exists for a legal rule remedying an unjust transaction with a doctrine like unconscionability.

Yet the emphasis of Torah and the New Testament on relational righteousness raises a fundamental problem: since contemporary nations are not in covenant with God, how can a legal doctrine rooted in the relational nature of biblical law be extended to twenty-first-century America and beyond?

12 *See* Matt 5:34–37.

13 Turner, *Christian Ethics and the Church*, 202 *supra* note 11.

Classical Greece and Rome

A brief excursion to Aristotle

The Western theological and legal traditions synthesized the teachings of both the biblical text and the Roman law through the lens of Greek philosophy. More than a millennium after he wrote it, Aristotle's *Nicomachean Ethics* was used for analyzing, synthesizing, and applying the teachings of the Bible and the deposit of Roman law. Book V of Aristotle's *Nicomachean Ethics*, where he focuses on the virtues of justice and liberality, proved instrumental for developing a Christian jurisprudence of unconscionability.

Under the rubric of corrective justice, Aristotle identified the circumstances where an existing distribution of goods was unjustly disrupted. Injustice of this sort could occur either by an involuntary transaction (a crime or tort) or in a voluntary transaction of exchange. How could a voluntary exchange be unjust? To answer this question Aristotle identified the virtue of commutative justice. For one to engage in a just exchange, commutative justice required equality.[14] Thus, the one who profited by an unequal exchange was an unjust person and the one who lost had been wronged.

Aristotle's remedy for injustice in either an involuntary or voluntary exchange was straightforward: take the unjust gain from the wrongdoer and restore it to the one who was wronged.[15] Yet at this point an important question suggests itself: why doesn't the mere voluntariness of an exchange suffice for establishing its justice? Or, to put it anachronistically, why wasn't Aristotle a neo-classical economist? Aristotle scholar Ronna Burger explains why voluntariness was not a replacement for justice in exchange:

> [Since for Aristotle] corrective justice only rectifies an unjust exchange, there must be a prior principle of what makes a just exchange, and that seems to be the role of *reciprocity*. Though it is not a matter of distributive justice, it shares in the principle of proportionate equality; and it is that principle, Aristotle adds, that holds the city together (emphasis added).[16]

14 Aristotle, Lesley Brown, and W. D. Ross. *The Nicomachean Ethics* (Oxford: OUP Oxford, 2009). eBook Collection (EBSCOhost), EBSCOhost (accessed May 16, 2018), 84.

> Of particular justice and that which is just in the corresponding sense, . . . and (B) one is that which plays a rectifying part in transactions between man and man. Of this there are two divisions; of transactions . . . (2) others involuntary— . . . (*a*) some are clandestine, such as theft . . . and (*b*) some are violent, such as assault . . . ."

15 Ibid., 87.

> Now the judge restores equality; it is as though there were a line divided into unequal part, and he took away that by which the greater segment exceeds the half, and added it to the smaller segment. And when the whole has been equally divided, then they say they have "their own"—i.e. when they have got what is equal.

16 Ronna Burger, *Aristotle's Dialogue with Socrates: On the "Nichomachean Ethics"* (Chicago, IL: University of Chicago Press, 2008), 99.

Aristotle believed that the bonds of social and political community are necessary for human flourishing. Political community, in turn, can exist only when there is exchange among its members. Exchange, however, would be stifled without some assurance of reciprocity. Equality in exchange is thus foundational to social life and injustice—inequality in exchange, a failure of reciprocity—threatens the fabric of society. Simple consent is thus subordinate to the common good of a society. Justice is more important than autonomy. A flourishing civic life depends on reciprocity.[17]

The legacy of Roman law

Over the course of it many centuries' growth in the republic and then the empire, the mass of accumulating Roman law resisted theorization. As legal historian Harold Berman explained, "Roman law consisted of an intricate network of rules, yet these rules were not presented as an intellectual system but rather as an elaborate mosaic of practical solutions to specific legal questions."[18] Roman law ultimately found unity through codification. Reaching its culmination with the Code of Justinian in 534, codifications of Roman law were commissioned and, in Justinian's case, the results were declared to be the only source of law.[19] And, as we shall see, this codification (which, along with a commentary on the Code and a textbook for law students, was known as the *Corpus iuris civilis*) had ramifications many centuries after the fall of the Roman Empire.

The origin of what later in medieval times came to be called the remedy of *laesio enormis* ("great harm") is found in Book IV, title 44 of the Code of Justinian. Quoting an advisory opinion of earlier co-emperors in a particular case, Code 4.44.2 provided a remedy for certain sellers of land who received less than half the value of property sold.[20] The seriously shortchanged seller could rescind the transaction (and return what had been paid) unless the buyer paid the full value of the property. The Code, however, left several questions unanswered: does the power to rescind extend only to sales of real estate? And what of buyers who overpay; can they demand refunds?

17 As did life in the Christian community. See 2 Cor. 8.12–15 where Paul enjoins the Christians living in Corinth to support their needy fellow-believers in Jerusalem:

> For if the readiness is there, it is acceptable according to what a man has, not according to what he has not. For I do not mean that others should be eased and you burdened, but that as a matter of equality your abundance at the present time should supply their want, so that their abundance may supply your want, that there may be equality. As it is written, "He who gathered much had nothing over, and he who gathered little had no lack."

18 Harold J. Berman, *Law and Revolution: The Formation of the Western Legal Tradition* (Cambridge, MA: Harvard University Press, 1983), 150.

19 *See generally* Barry Nicholas, *An Introduction to Roman Law* (Oxford: Oxford University Press, 1962), 38–45.

20 *Code of Justinian*, trans. Samuel Parsons Scott (Cincinnati, OH: Central Trust, 1932), 4.44.2.

Interestingly, Code 4.44.2 was inconsistent with earlier codifications of Roman law, none of which had provided for relief for mere inadequacy of price.[21] Perhaps this section demonstrated the ameliorating influence of Christianity on strict Roman contract law.[22] Whatever its origin, there is little evidence that Code 4.44.2 had much practical effect until the rediscovery of the entire *Corpus iuris civilis* in Italy in the eleventh century.

The mediaeval trunk of unconscionability

The early scholastic synthesis

In 1080, long after the collapse of the Roman Empire in Western Europe, scholars at the University of Bologna rediscovered the complete text of the *Corpus iuris civilis.*[23] With this "new" text, the study of law first became part of the curriculum in a Western university. The rediscovered *Corpus iuris civilis*, the Scriptures, and the works of Aristotle[24] together formed the foundation of the new field of legal science. As should be familiar to first-year American law students, the medieval legal curriculum was based on texts. As Berman explained, this medieval method of combining Roman law, the Scriptures, and Greek philosophy came to be known as scholasticism. Not only was scholasticism text based, it had a distinctive analytic methodology that should also seem familiar:

> [Scholasticism], which was first fully developed in the early 1100s, both in law and theology, presupposes the absolute authority of certain books, which are to be comprehended as containing an integrated and complete body of doctrine; but paradoxically, it also presupposes that there may be both gaps and contradictions within the text: and it sets as its main task the summation of the text, the closing of gaps within it, and the resolution of contradictions.[25]

Early scholastic jurists applied Aristotle's dialectic method to synthesize Roman law—including Code 4.44.2—at a high level of abstraction and then applied the result to contemporary situations. "At a very early date," writes James Gordley, the initial scholastic jurists extended the logic of Code 4.44.2 "to sellers as well

21 *See generally* Kenneth S. Cahn, "The Roman and Frankish Roots of the Just Price of Medieval Canon Law," in *Studies in Medieval and Renaissance History* (New York: AMS Press, 1969), 6:6–12.

22 See H.F. Jolowicz and Barry Nicholas, *Historical Introduction to the Study of Roman Law* (Cambridge: Cambridge University Press, 1972), 508–09.

23 *See* Randall Lesaffer, *European Legal History: A Cultural and Political Perspective* (Cambridge: Cambridge University Press, 2009), 253.

24 Early medieval access to Aristotle came through translations of a few of his works by Boethius (480–524) as well as the *Isagoge* of Porphyry (234–305), which was an introduction to another of Aristotle's works.

25 Berman, *Law and Revolution*, 131 *supra* note 18.

as buyers and to parties to analogous contracts."[26] The expanded remedy for unbalanced transactions is still known by its Latin name—*laesio enormis*—in countries in the civil law tradition. More importantly, what began as an object of academic study eventually became reality as over the succeeding centuries large parts of Western law became rationalized in Roman law terms.[27]

Later scholastic developments

A few centuries later, with the translation into Latin of the complete *Nicomachean Ethics* in 1240, Aristotle's analysis of justice as virtue provided late medieval scholastic jurists with a new text by which to amplify their conclusions.[28] The early scholastics had not needed Aristotle's notion of justice as virtue to create the remedy of *laesio enormis*. Yet Aristotle's notion of commutative justice allowed their successors to provide a deeper explanation for why this doctrine should be the law. As Gordley summarizes the late-medieval understanding: "An unjust [above-market] price violated 'natural equity'."[29] Natural equity was the way a late-medieval jurist would refer to commutative justice. Commutative justice—equality in exchange—entailed the conclusion that "when each party gives in order to receive something in return, neither is unjustifiably enriched because they trade at a price that preserves equity or equality."[30] Thus by 1300, elements of Roman law, biblical morality, and Aristotle's formulation of commutative justice had been combined to create not only a remedy for an unbalanced exchange but a legal theory for why this should be so.

Early modern growth of unconscionability

Constraining creativity

Trade and commerce within Western Europe picked up in the thirteenth century. Growth in commerce was matched by the growing sources for theology and law with the reception of new texts from the shrinking Byzantine Empire. While the substance of *laesio enormis* did not change, jurists worked to explore ramifications of unconscionability in a world of increasing commercial activity.

26 James Gordley, *The Philosophical Origins of Modern Contract Doctrine* (Oxford, England: Clarendon Press, 2011). eBook Collection (EBSCOhost), EBSCOhost (accessed May 16, 2018), 65.

27 *See* Berman, *Law and Revolution*, 131 *supra* note 18.

> [T]he revival of the study of Roman law of an earlier time led to the analysis of current legal problems. Roman law served at first as an ideal law, a body of legal ideas, taken as a unified system; current legal problems, previously unclassified and inchoate, were analyzed in its terms and were judged by its standards.

28 *See generally* James Gordley, *Foundations of Private Law: Property, Tort, Contract, Unjust Enrichment* (Oxford: Oxford University Press, 2006), 7–14.

29 Gordley, *Philosophical Origins*, 56 *supra* note 26.

30 Gordley, *Philosophical Origins*, 67 *supra* note 26.

The use by sellers of "fine print" to avoid liability for *laesio enormis* is an example of that sophistication as well as an occasion to see how Christian jurists responded.

In the *Nicomachean Ethics*, Aristotle had identified a second virtue relevant to a flourishing society: liberality.

> Now virtuous actions are noble and done for the sake of the noble. Therefore the liberal man ... will give for the sake of the noble, and rightly; for he will give to the right people, the right amounts, and at the right time ...[31]

Liberality—gift-giving—is not framed in terms of justice because it concerns an unequal but *appropriate* reallocation of goods. Gift-giving is not a matter of reciprocity but of generosity, a virtue esteemed in both the Old and New Testaments (Proverbs 11:24–25; 1 Timothy 6:17–18).

A gift that expects nothing in return is by its nature is unequal and thus the remedy of *laesio enormis* would not avoid an agreement to make a gift. Liberality was a virtue, not a vice, and in the civil law tradition, unlike the common law, a promise to make a gift could receive legal enforcement. By the sixteenth century, sellers saw in the enforceability of gift promises a means to avoid the risk that a court might apply *laesio enormis* to avoid a sales contract. By adding a term to a contract that any part of the price that exceeded the market value was actually a gift, sellers hoped to insulate the transaction from critical judicial review. As Wim Decock explains, this effort to avoid *laesio enormis* was met with disapproval. After all,

> [i]n a sale there is no reason to believe that the parties intend to make a donation. The intention of the contracting parties is directed towards obtaining a mutually advantageous sale contract, there is nothing they want less than to make a gift.[32]

Notwithstanding the presence of a term providing that any overpayment was a gift, its presence in a contract of sale created a strong presumption that neither party actually intended to make a gift. Such a term, the jurists concluded, should be ignored.[33] The contextual application of commutative justice to a specific situation was justice applied. And justice was the reason for the law.

31 Aristotle, *Nicomachean Ethics*, 67 *supra* note 14.

32 Wim Decock, *Theologians and Contract Law: The Moral Transformation of the Ius Commune* (Leiden: Martinus Nijhoff Publishers, 2013), 557 (summarizing conclusion of Spanish jurist Diego de Covarrubias (1512–1577)).

33 Along similar lines, Portuguese jurist Arias Piñel (1515–1563) argued that even actual "[k]nowledge of the true price should not be a ground to relinquish the remedy [of *laesio enormis*]." Ibid., 584.

The irrelevance of the Reformation

For the Protestant reformers, the doctrine of justification by faith alone represented one of the most significant breaks with the Roman church. The Protestant understanding of justification did not, however, sever the connection between law and the way Christian believers were to live (commonly called "sanctification"). Protestants understood sanctification as the process by which the believer's life is gradually conformed to the image of Christ. While Protestants believed that sanctification did not count toward one's ultimate standing before God, they also taught that sanctification was inextricably bound to God's work of justification.[34] The Protestant reformers and the theologians who followed them discussed sanctification under the rubric of the Ten Commandments with specifications drawn from the rest of the Scriptures. The commandment against theft became the locus for their moral theology of contracts.

Protestant theologians and confessional statements also demonstrate the continuing vitality of the principle of equality in exchange. Thus, at the outset of the Reformed tradition, John Calvin (1509–1564) addressed matters of commutative justice when he excoriated a variety of illegitimate transactional practices. Informed by the civil law, Calvin supported a robust notion of equality in exchange:

> We cannot by evil devices deprive anyone of his possessions without fraudulently setting aside God's dispensation. Now there are many kinds of thefts. One consists in violence, when another's goods are stolen by force and unrestrained brigandage. A second kind consists in malicious deceit, when they are carried off through fraud. Another lies in a more concealed craftiness when a man's goods are snatched from him by seemingly legal means.[35]

The Westminster Larger Catechism, concluded in 1646, was a joint venture of English Puritans and Scottish Presbyterians. The catechism's formulation of what sins are encompassed by the commandment against theft is clear: both reciprocity and fairness in exchange are required by God and thus burden a Christian's conscience.

Unfaithfulness in contracts spoke of course to the virtue of fidelity and injustice in contracts was understood in terms of commutative justice.[36] Even if the

34 *See, e.g., Calvin: Institutes of the Christian Religion*, ed. John T. McNeill, trans. Ford Lewis Battles (Philadelphia, PA: Westminster Press, 1960), 593. "For when this topic [justification] is rightly understood it will better appear how man is justified by faith alone, and simple pardon; nevertheless actual holiness of life, so to speak, is not separated from free imputation of righteousness."

35 *Calvin: Institutes*, 408–09.

36 William Ames, *Conscience with the Power and Cases Thereof* (Amsterdam: Walter J. Johnson, Inc., 1975), 233, 236.

> Those civil laws which confirm a contract made by circumvention, so it be under half of the just price, are permissive only to diminish strifes, and do not justify the contract, but leave

common law did not formally recognize unconscionability, the consciences of Protestants and Catholics in England certainly did.

Seventeenth-century Protestant jurists on the Continent also taught that moral theology remained relevant to the law. Jurists Hugo Grotius (1583–1645) and Samuel Pufendorf (1632–1694) accepted the notions of reciprocity and equality in exchange and the significance of the legal doctrine of *laesio enormis*. Grotius, a Dutch Protestant, restated the commonplaces of his Catholic contemporaries.[37] At the end of the same century the Lutheran Pufendorf elaborated on the principle of equality in exchange:

> For since I have need of contracts to obtain things which I could not by law require of another, and so it is in him to decide whether or not he will give them to me … it follows that no one is believed to want to transfer anything by another by a contract save in so far as he feels that he will, in return for his contribution, receive as much for his part.[38]

Thus at the close of the seventeenth century, Christian Europe, Protestant and Catholic alike, held that equality in exchange was inextricably caught up into the moral and legal understandings of contract.[39] Justice in exchange was not an altruistic appeal to love one's fellow contract party but was tethered to something more prosaic. Equality measured by the market aimed to prevent contract parties from harming each other. And doing no harm was the baseline of reciprocity which in turn was (and is) a requisite for a flourishing society.

Missing or hidden? England's branches of unconscionability

The significance of the absence of the doctrine of equality in exchange in the English legal tradition should not be overstated. On the one hand, "it is almost impossible to find even a reference to the principle of equality in exchange … in the cases decided from the time the doctrine of unconscionability originated

---

> it to be judged in the Court of Conscience, by the law of nature, and the Divine law. … The common rate of the market, and of wise and good men is to be followed. For this rate hath the force of tacit law, and excludes the danger of any deceit to the damage of another.

Although Ames (1567–1633) had left England for the Netherlands in 1610, his moral theology was consistent with those who drafted the Westminster Larger Catechism.

37 Hugo Grotius, *The Rights of War and Peace, Including the Law of Nature and of Nations*, trans. A.C. Campbell (New York: M. Walter Dunne, 1901), 148–50.

38 Samuel Pufendorf, "De Jure Naturae et Gentium Libri Octo," in *The Classics of International Law*, ed. James Brown Scott (Oxford: Clarendon Press, 1934), 708.

39 *See* Harold J. Berman, *Law and Revolution, II: The Impact of Protestant Reformations on the Western Legal Tradition* (Cambridge, MA: Belknap Press of Harvard University Press, 2003), 164. Disputes about just price, which in pre-Reformation Europe had been fought in ecclesiastical courts, "now became, especially in Protestant lands, the responsibility chiefly of the princes, enforced mainly through secular legislation and secular judicial and administrative sanctions."

through the end of the eighteenth century."[40] Even without using the expression, however, the concept of equality in exchange can be found at various points through the course of English legal history. Its apparent absence had more to do with the diversity of jurisdictions in England than a rejection of the principle itself.

There was a working system of ecclesiastical (church court) adjudication in England until after Henry VIII severed the English church from Rome. These courts would have applied their canon law to contract cases and not surprisingly, canon law recognized *laesio enormis*. Moreover, ecclesiastical courts in England had an active contract docket.[41] Contract parties could stipulate orally or in writing to submit disputes to the church courts applying canon law.[42] And English litigants regularly did so until the 1530s.[43]

Moving from ecclesiastical courts to the courts of equity and picking up in the fifteenth century, English Courts of Chancery deployed a notion of the fairness. Perhaps drawing from the principles embodied in the canon law,[44] the Chancellor permitted mortgagees to avoid forfeitures of interests in land created by mortgages. The common law courts could not address the injustice of even a day-late tender of payment by a mortgagor because they had no way of ameliorating the strict effect of this (or any other) condition. Yet by the early seventeenth century, the Chancellor would permit relief from forfeiture if a mortgagor tendered the amount due within a reasonable time after the due date.[45] Judges in Chancery did not ground their decisions on "equality of exchange." Instead they used expressions like "unreasonable, unjust, unequitable or unconscientious, hard and unequal"[46] to describe unenforceable results. Such expressions suggest that equality in exchange was lurking not far beneath the surface. Rooted in Christian conscience, the remit of the courts of equity, as English legal historian

40 Gordley, *Philosophical Origins*, 149 *supra* note 26.

41 *See* R.H. Helmholz, *Canon Law and the Law of England* (London: Hambledon Press, 1987), 283–84.

> *Fidei laesio* reached (or retained) a high level of use in the late fifteenth century. By the second decade of the sixteenth century, there had been a marked decline, but breach of faith causes was still being heard. By the 1550s and 1560s the Church's jurisdiction over these causes was gone.

42 *See* Berman, *Law and Revolution*, 245 *supra* note 18. "[T]he ecclesiastical courts sought and obtained a large measure of jurisdiction over economic contracts between laymen, where the parties included in their agreement a 'pledge of faith' . . . ."

43 *See generally* William Stubbs, "The History of Canon Law in England," in *Select Essays in Anglo-American Legal History* (Boston, MA: Little, Brown, and Co., 1907), 1:248, 272–74.

44 *See generally* A.W.B. Simpson, *A History of the Common Law of Contract: The Rise of the Action of Assumpsit* (Oxford: Clarendon Press, 1987), 396–402.

45 *See generally* Charles J. Reid, Jr., "The Seventeenth-Century Revolution in the English Land Law," *Cleveland State Law Review*, 43, no. 2 (1995): 293–96.

46 Gordley, *Philosophical Origins*, *supra* note 26, at 149–150.

John Baker explains, "did not come to destroy the law, but to fulfill it by ordering what conscience demanded."[47]

Even a common law court, bound by the formal limits of the writ system, on one occasion directed the jury to find against a plaintiff seeking enforcement of a contract for an exorbitant price for a horse.[48] The general unwillingness of the common law courts to address substantive unfairness can be explained by the bifurcated nature of common law adjudication. Courts ruled on issues of law raised in the relevant writ while juries addressed the facts. Thus, until the nineteenth century, it was jurors, not the court, who were to exercise their consciences in an action for damages for breach of contract:

> The [common law] judges sought refuge from the agony of decision—and the perils of undue influence—by umpiring the ancient game strictly according to the rules .... Conscience belonged to the realms of fact rather than law, for whereas judges were sworn to do justice according to law, jurors were charged to give a true verdict according to their conscience.[49]

As James Whitman reports, instructions to jurors in the sixteenth century focused on their consciences: "'[D]o in this matter as God will give you grace, according to the evidence and your conscience'; '[D]oe that which God shall put in your mindes to the discharge of your consciences'."[50] The conscience of jurors was not an amalgam of free-floating moral intuitions. It was the faculty by which moral truths filtered through the law would be applied to the facts of a case. And until modern times the faculty of conscience would have been trained in terms of Christian moral doctrine.

The absence of *laesio enormis* in English law does not mean that commutative justice had no place. Multiple jurisdictions—ecclesiastical, equitable, and legal—each with its own mode of adjudication and with its own body of procedural and substantive law, meant that sometimes commutative justice functioned openly, at other times obliquely, or perhaps entirely hidden in a jury's general verdict. In any event, it seems unlikely that those exercising their consciences could have failed to consider commutative justice given its pervasive place in English (and American[51]) moral theology.

47 John H. Baker, *The Oxford History of the Laws of England. Vol. VI, 1483–1558* (Oxford: Oxford University Press, 2003), 42.

48 James v. Morgan, 1 Lev 111 (1663).

49 Baker, *Laws of England,* 47 *supra* note 47. For contract cases recognizing a remedy for too- hard bargains see Val Ricks, "Consideration and the Formation Defenses," *Kansas Law Review*, 62, no. 2 (2013): 330–33.

50 James Q. Whitman, *The Origins of Reasonable Doubt: Theological Roots of the Criminal Trial* (New Haven, CT: Yale University Press, 2008), 153.

51 *See* Charles Hodge, *Systematic Theology* (New York: Scribner, 1872–1873), 3:436:

> It may be said that there is no fixed standard of value to the man who demands it . . . [that] if a man perishing of thirst is willing to give his whole estate for a glass of water, it would be right to exact that price . . . . Such conduct every man feels would be worthy of execration.

Unconscionability's blight

Anglo-American courts in the nineteenth century rejected a stand-alone doctrine of equality in exchange. Subordinating equality in exchange to the doctrine of consideration meant that nineteenth-century contract law treatises mentioned unconscionability only in connection with equitable remedies,[52] and even there some expressed doubt.[53] The equality of an exchange was for the parties to determine, not the court or even the jury.[54]

As Morton Horwitz has explained, "By 1820 ... [in America] law was no longer conceived of as an eternal set of principles expressed in custom and derived from natural law."[55] Substituting policy in place of a formal connection to justice, American courts and jurists found no warrant for the principle of fairness in exchange apart from grants of equitable relief.[56] Adding insult to ignorance, the omission of unconscionability from the first Restatement of Contracts underscored a long century of desuetude.[57]

Unconscionability's new growth

Unconscionability returned to American contract law after decades of bare survival with the adoption of the Uniform Commercial Code. The late law professor Arthur Leff has told the story of how in the early 1940s Columbia law professor Karl Llewellyn inserted a version of unconscionability in his initial draft of what became Article 2 of the UCC.[58] Subsequent drafts of the UCC identified unconscionability with failure to read a term or having failed to bargain for it. By 1949

> The fact is that things have an intrinsic value, however determined, which cannot be enhanced because our suffering fellow-men may be in pressing need of them.

52 *See, e.g.*, Joseph Story, *Commentaries on Equity Jurisprudence* (Boston, MA: Little & Brown, 1843), 261. The author explains that equity would not set aside a contract for inadequacy of price unless coupled with other evidence of "imposition, or some undue influence."

53 *See* Frederick Pollock, *Principles of Contract at Law and in Equity* (Cincinnati, OH: Robert Clarke & Co., 1885), 176. The author doubts that courts of equity should take inadequacy of consideration into account even for specific performance.

54 *See, e.g.*, C.G. Addison, *Addison on Contracts* (Boston, MA: Soule & Bugbee, 1883), 1:31. "If parties choose to enter into unwise and improvident bargains, they must abide by the consequences of their own rashness and folly . . . ."

55 Morton J. Horwitz, *The Transformation of American Law*, 1780–1860 (Cambridge, MA: Harvard University Press, 1977), 30.

56 *See* ibid., 261–62.

> During the first half of the [nineteenth] century, legal writers and judges were largely successful in banishing fair price conceptions from the law of contract and in shifting the focus of contract law to the determination of where there had been a 'meeting of mind.'

57 *See generally Restatement (First) of Contracts* (St. Paul, MN: American Law Institute, 1932). Although the first Restatement avoided any reference to unconscionability, it preserved the rationale and result of an unbalanced transaction (without the label) when it came to specific performance.

58 Arthur Allen Leff, "Unconscionability and the Code—The Emperor's New Clause," *University of Pennsylvania Law Review*, 115, no. 4 (February 1967): 487–496.

the meaning of unconscionability had swung to unbalanced contract terms. And then in 1952 (and ever since) the UCC has fudged with the bare term "unconscionability" and a comment that defines unconscionability in terms of itself.[59]

Unconscionability has provided twentieth- and twenty-first-century contract parties with mixed success.[60] That success, however, has not come with clarity or predictability. Legal opinions applying unconscionability have had a difficult time explaining it. Thus in the 1969 case of *Jones v. Star Credit*,[61] the trial court concluded that a contract obligating the buyer of a freezer to pay three times its market value was unconscionable. Yet the court lamented that, "deciding the issue is substantially easier than explaining it." The court framed its conclusion in terms of substantive unconscionability—although it couldn't explain precisely why three times the market value was unconscionable—plus the buyer's poverty, shoehorned into the category of procedural unconscionability. Using a buyer's poverty as a convenient trope for procedural unconscionability led J. Skelly Wright to identify unconscionability as one element of the "law of the poor."[62] Eventually this class-based characterization contributed to the lessening of unconscionability's effectiveness as the 1960s-era War on Poverty fell from political favor.[63] Constrained by the early two-pronged approach, most courts have held that gross price disparity does not make a contract unconscionable without some sort of procedural unconscionability.[64]

Further reducing the place for unconscionability, scholars influenced by neo-classical economics—law and economics—have provided a rationale for ignoring price disparity altogether. Since, the story goes, contract parties are best suited to valuing the relative utility of their current resources, avoiding a contract because the price paid turns out to be greater than the market's estimation rewards regret. And "if regret is allowed to undo decisions," asserts Richard Posner, "the ability of people to shape their destinies is impaired."[65] Whether the purpose of contract law should be to maximize welfare—"shaping destinies"

59 James J. White, *Uniform Commercial Code* (St. Paul, MN: American Law Institute & Uniform Law Commission, 1997), § 2–302, Off. Cmt. 1. "The basic test is whether, in the light of the general commercial background and the commercial needs of the particular trade or case, the clauses involved are so one-sided as to be unconscionable under the circumstances existing at the time of the making of the contract."

60 *See* Susan Landrum, "Much Ado About Nothing? What the Numbers Tell Us About How State Courts Apply the Unavoidable Doctrine to Arbitration Agreements," *Marquette Law Review*, 97, no. 1 (Fall 2013): 780–801. The author analyzes cases from 20 states and concludes that the overall rate of appellate holdings of unconscionability was 23% but that rate varied substantially from state to state.

61 Jones v. Star Credit, 298 N.Y.S.2d 264 (1969).

62 *See* Anne Fleming, "The Rise and Fall of Unconscionability as the 'Law of the Poor,' " *The Georgetown Law Journal*, 102, no. 1 (November 2013): 1385 (quoting from letter of Wright to William E. Shipley).

63 *See generally* ibid.

64 *See, e.g.*, *Whirlpool Corp. v. Grigoleit Co.*, 713 F.3d 316 (6th Cir. 2013).

65 Richard A. Posner, *Economic Analysis of Law*, 7th ed. (New York: Aspen Law & Business, 2007), 7.

in Posner's turn of phrase—or effecting justice is a question that neo-classical economic analysis cannot answer except by presupposing the former. Framing human nature in terms more robust than individual instrumental behavior returns us to reciprocity. Framing human ends in terms more significant than welfare maximization returns us to justice. Both of which return us to the classical Christian notion that contracts exist to enable reciprocity and that contract law should recognize a baseline of fairness in exchange.

Conclusion

This genealogy of the birth, growth, blight, and revitalization of unconscionability demonstrates at least two truths. First, no matter its current configuration, unconscionability is an unmistakably *Christian* doctrine of law. Unconscionability represents, in James Smith's expression, one of the "craters" of the gospel[66] in the contemporary legal world. In the middle of his three-volume work of political theology Oliver O'Donovan explains that

> What has become clear ... from half a century of research in political history, is that the roots of this new organisation of political priorities [the contemporary liberal order] run deep into the centuries that preceded it, not only through the late scholastics who are recognisably forebears of the Reformation, but through the earlier scholastics back into the Carolingian and patristic eras; and not only through theologians and their disputations but through the various concrete forms of life in the Christian community: corporations, monastic communities, canon law, penance and so on.[67]

Unconscionability did not, of course, spring fully formed from the pages of Scripture. Its tap root can be found in Torah that, combined with the philosophy of Greece and the law of Rome under the tutelage of the Church, gave the Western legal tradition two important insights: that the form of law is justice and that inequality in exchange is injustice.

Second, shorn of any recollection of its historical roots, contemporary legal thought finds itself the heir of a rule of contract law without any clear idea of why the law should be or how it can be applied. Reciprocity finds in contemporary individualism sandy soil from which to draw sustenance. Justice, without a norm by which to be measured, becomes little more than an intuition. Yet reciprocity *is* the ground of human society and justice *is* the norm that norms all law. Whether recognized or repressed, the basis and measure of unconscionability remain part of the law written on the heart. Tracing the history and lineaments of unconscionability should give those who acknowledge the truths of God's

66 James K.A. Smith, *Awaiting the King: Reforming Public Theology* (Grand Rapids, MI: Baker Academic, 2017), 91.

67 Oliver O'Donovan, *The Desire of the Nations* (Cambridge: Cambridge University Press, 1996), 226.

revelation in Scripture, as well as in keen observations of the world, confidence to assert the doctrine of unconscionability when the occasion demands.

Such confidence opens the door to explore ramifications of inequality in exchange beyond classical *laesio enormis.* Even recognizing the limits of the abilities of judges and juries, and after placing some responsibility for an unequal bargain on the disappointed party, avoiding only purchases for more than twice the market value or sales for less than half represents a very wide berth for freedom of contract. The limits of institutional competence can be narrowed in the era of "big data." It may even be true that over time efficient markets will balance the gains of trade among buyers and sellers notwithstanding non-salient boilerplate. Yet in the interim, those gains can be evaluated in light of justice.

Nothing in this chapter answers the question of whether this or that particular transaction is unconscionable. What should be learned is that the struggle for contractual justice was and is a real one and that the classical Christian tradition provides a powerful platform from which to seek the just result.

12 Christianity, freedom, and the doctrine of consideration

Val D. Ricks[1]

Government and law should maximize people's freedom to do all the good they can, including to serve Christ—that should be law's objective.[2] This is a way to state as a general maxim or normative principle what I believe scripture teaches and is confirmed by my experience trying to live the Gospel and serve as a legal scholar.

This principle draws support from Paul's first letter to Timothy (2:1–4 (NIV)):

> I urge, ... first of all, that petitions, prayers, intercession and thanksgiving be made for all people—for kings and all those in authority, that we may live peaceful and quiet lives in all godliness and holiness. This is good, and pleases God our Savior, who wants all people to be saved and to come to a knowledge of the truth.

But the whole content of the principle is not contained within this passage. Rather, the principle draws both support and content from other passages and broader knowledge of the Gospel, government, law, and human nature.[3] I intend to sketch the principle's premises here, then measure the contract doctrine of consideration against it.

This sketch comes with a two-fold caveat. First, it is impossible in this short space to do more than give an outline and point to broader sources. The reader should expect an incomplete description.

Second, I will employ the language of certain sources. I begin with the New Testament but draw on two other sets of writings. One is *Dignitatis Humanae*, the Second Vatican Council's Declaration on Religious Freedom, which is searchable online. The second and more complete set is the work of John Courtney Murray (1904–67), an American Jesuit priest and theologian who wrote

1 The author thanks Teresa Stanton Collett for recommending Murray's work many years ago.

2 Val D. Ricks, "Contract Law and Christian Conscience," *BYU Law Review*, 993 (2003): 993.

3 I first learned the central principle and ideas in this essay from Sections 98:4–10 and 101:76–80 of *The Doctrine & Covenants of the Church of Jesus Christ of Latter-Day Saints*. *See* Ricks, "Contract and Conscience," 1038–42.

carefully and movingly about law, government, and the American experience.[4] The outline of my sketch comes from one of Murray's last public speeches.[5]

A Christian view of law

The Christian experience

To understand a Christian view of law, one must first believe or at least appreciate some things that a Christian believes about the world and being human. The world we know is "fallen." In part, this means that while women and men desire to do good and can see and understand a much better world, they find themselves incapable of reaching it. Their hearts are flawed and their minds and bodies distracted and tired and worn by life. The world's fallenness is evidenced by its impermanence. Things built here do not last. Life itself, as well as success in wealth, honor, or power, is temporary, like Ozymandias's kingdom.[6] And even success in those things cannot satisfy us. The Christian freely admits that life here leaves us yearning for something more, something else.

The Christian faith is experienced—a Christian is a person who has had a certain kind of experience while living in this fallen world. This experience comes by faith in Christ, but it also produces faith in Christ. The experience is described variously by Christians, but it is contact with the divine.[7] The experience changes the person. The change happens mostly in the heart and mind and so is hard to pin down in words, but the experience is always positive. Its effects are far-reaching. This experience changes the meaning of the fallen world—not always at once, as often more and greater experiences follow. Whereas to a person without this experience the temporal world may seem to be all there is, now new possibilities open up. There is more hope, more peace. Relationships with others become better, more fulfilling. Doing good becomes easier. One can see, believe, and even know that some things we experience in this world do not change and decay as time moves on, but instead continue for eternity. The experience persuades the person that God exists and loves us enough to come down to us, be with us, and lift us up. Life is still a struggle, but it is now more meaningful, sometimes filled with meaning, and contains a promise of peace, love, and joy.

The change is so rejuvenating and so positive that the Christian gives her heart and dedicates her life to it. She begins to serve God and other people, whom she begins to see as sisters and brothers. She seeks to share with them what she has found, persuaded that, if God loves her and can and will lift her

4 I will in particular draw from the writings included in John Courtney Murray, *Religious Liberty: Catholic Struggles with Pluralism*, ed. J. Leon Hooper, S.J. (Louisville, KY: Westminster/John Knox Press, 1993).

5 *See* John Courtney Murray, "Arguments for the Human Right to Religious Freedom," in Murray, *Religious Liberty*, 229–44.

6 Percy Bysshe Shelley, *Ozymandias* (1818).

7 By way of illustration, consider Matt 16:17; John 3:5, 14, 15:1–8; 1 Cor. 2 & 4:20; 1 John 4.

up, God can and will lift up each person similarly, and they can begin to see and feel that same hope, peace, and love.

And law?

Human dignity: law's incompetence in matters of ultimate importance

What does human law have to do with this? Law has nothing directly to do with it.

"Law is ... a coercive discipline ultimately effective ... through force and fear."[8] Law is more than this, of course. To be law, this force or threat of force must be regularized, mostly discernable in its patterns, and equally applied.[9] But law is at root violence.

To a Christian, law must have a limited use. Whatever else the Christian experience is, it is not the result of force. God loves us; His first command is that we love him. God commands us next to love one another. Love is not coerced. Christ died to "draw all" to him, to win our souls with love. God's power makes us "free,"[10] and "man's response to God in faith must be free: no one therefore is to be forced to embrace the Christian faith against his own will." "[N]o one is to be coerced into faith," as if that were possible: "The act of faith is of its very nature a free act." "[I]t is upon the human conscience that these obligations [to serve God] fall and exert their binding force."[11]

God's respect for our freedom—for us as willing, choosing, and loving beings, able to take responsibility—is part of what *Dignitatis Humanae* calls human "dignity." Murray elaborates,

> [H]uman dignity demands that in [t]aking this fundamental religious option and in carrying it out through every type of religious action, whether private or public, in all these aspects a person should act by his own deliberation and purpose, enjoying immunity from all external coercion so that in

8 John Courtney Murray, "Leo XIII and Pius XII: Government and the Order of Religion," in Murray, *Religious Liberty*, 66–67; *see also* John Courtney Murray, "The Issue of Church and State at Vatican Council II," in Murray, *Religious Liberty*, 212 ("Government is a power whose mode of action, like that of law, is ultimately coercive"); *see also, e.g.*, Robert Cover, "Violence and the Word," *Yale Law Journal*, 95 (1986): 1601 ("Interpretations of law also constitute justifications for violence which has already occurred or which is about to occur").

9 *E.g.*, "The Rule of Law," Stanford Encyclopedia of Philosophy, June 22, 2016, https://plato.stanford.edu/entries/rule-of-law/.

10 *See* John 3:16, 1 John 4:10 (God's love); Matt 22:36–40, Mark 12:28–34, Luke 10:25–28 (command to love God); Matt 22:36–40; Mark 12:28–34; Luke 10:25–28; 1 John 4:7–12 (command to love others); John 12:32 ("draw all"); John 8:31–36, Rom. 8:2, Gal 5:1 (that God makes us free).

11 *Dignitatis Humanae,* chs. 1, 2, 10, 12 (1965); *see also* ibid., chs. 2–4 (extending this freedom to educational, cultural, charitable, and social organizations); *see also* ch. 5 (extending this freedom to the family).

> the presence of God he takes responsibility on himself alone for his religious decisions and acts.[12]

"[T]his doctrine of freedom," *Dignitatis Humanae* concludes, "has its roots in divine revelation"—

> [Christ] bore witness to the truth [cf. John 18:37], but He refused to impose the truth by force on those who spoke against it. Not by force of blows does His rule assert its claims [cf. Matt 26:51–53; John 18:36]. It is established by witnessing to the truth and by hearing the truth, and it extends its dominion by the love whereby Christ, lifted up on the cross, draws all men to Himself [cf. John 12:32].

Murray elaborates,

> The primordial demand of that dignity, then, is that man acts by his own counsel and purpose, using and enjoying his freedom, moved, not by external coercion, but internally by the risk of his whole existence. In a word, human dignity consists formally in the person's responsibility for himself and, what is more, for his world. So great is his dignity that not even God can take it away—by taking upon Himself or unto Himself the responsibility for his [the human being's] life and for his fate. This in the Christian tradition ... is the dignity of the person conceived, fashioned in the image of God.

The Christian view of human dignity forbids that law try to do what God refrains from doing: "This demand of both freedom and responsibility is the ultimate ontological ground of religious freedom." Because coercion cannot bring love, "[i]t is beyond the competence of civil government and beyond the rightful power of human law to coerce or constrain the citizen to make acts of religious faith or worship."[13]

Society's goal

Human dignity mandates that the good of each human being be the purpose of society. Human dignity, knowledge of God's love for all people, and love for others require that Christians help each human being and human society toward what is good, toward flourishing.

Murray put this somewhat obscurely:

> Now, from the ... ontological principle (the dignity of the human person), there follows a second principle, the social principle .... The social principle

12 Murray, "Human Right," 240.
13 Murray, "Human Right," 238, 240; Murray, "Order of Religion," 55.

> states that the human person is the subject, foundation, and end of the entire social life.

Murray at times suggests that the social principle can be thought of as the common good:

> The common good includes all the social goods, spiritual and moral as well as material, which man pursues here on earth in accord with the demands of his personal and social nature. The pursuit of the common good devolves upon society as a whole.[14]

This description of the social principle is reminiscent of John Finnis's theory of basic goods,[15] and I have come to think of the social principle in those terms.

Finnis's list of "basic aspects of [human] well-being" includes life, knowledge, play, aesthetic experience, sociability, practical reasonableness, and religion. What makes these basic?

> First, each is equally self-evidently a form of good. Secondly, none can be analytically reduced to being merely an aspect of any of the others, or to being merely instrumental in the pursuit of the others. Thirdly, each one, when we focus on it, can reasonably be regarded as the most important.

What makes them aspects of human well-being? Each is "an aspect of authentic human flourishing" and, expressed as a principle, "formulates a real (intelligent) reason for action." Each "seems to promote persons and bring them together," and those serving these ends can "never finish doing what can be done to serve them."[16]

Finnis explained how these become the common good:

> [E]ach is in principle good for any and every person, and each has been, is being, and can be participated in, instantiated, actualised, realised in the life of inexhaustibly many persons. But each of these basic human goods is also an aspect of a common good in a related but significantly different sense. For each can be an aspect of the flourishing of a group, a community, big or small, formal or informal, and can be a reason for that community or group to act in the way that groups do: by the more or less coordinated conduct

14 Murray, "Human Right," 238; John Courtney Murray, "The Problem of Religious Freedom," in Murray, *Religious Liberty*, 145.

15 John Finnis, *Natural Law and Natural Rights*, 2nd ed. (Oxford: Oxford University Press, 2011): 81–97.

16 John Finnis, "Human Acts," in II John Finnis, *Intention and Identity: Collected Essays* (Oxford: Oxford University Press, 2011): 140 & 140 n.13.

> which their members choose to engage in for the sake of some purpose shared with the other members of the group.[17]

Murray is careful to specify, however, that the social principle must include the truth about humans known empirically and also by revelation. He proposes that at its center is

> the human person itself, really existing, in the presence of its God and LORD, in association with others in this historic world, but in such wise that it transcends by reason of its end both society and the whole world. The human person exists in God's presence as a moral subject bound by duties toward the moral order and toward the historical order of salvation established by Jesus Christ.[18]

Murray is mindful of both humans' social nature and the need for rules for understanding one another, living together in peace, and getting along, but he emphasizes that at root humans have a moral nature:

> The human person exists with others in society as a moral-juridical subject furnished with rights that flow directly and altogether from human nature, never to be alienated from that nature. The juridical order cannot be sundered from the moral order, any more than the human person can be halved.[19]

In practical terms, this view of the common good allows each individual and community a wide range of particular instantiations of each basic good, or of mixes of them. Basic goods are seven, and billions of people seek them, each in circumstances that are unique. So Chinese art will provide aesthetic experience and religion differently than, say, Navajo art, but both may serve the common good in those ways and probably in other ways. And each Chinese artist and appreciator of art will differ from each other in the good created. Knowledge of art is good in a way different from knowledge of science or technology, yet each knowledge is justifiably sought. As guides to conduct, *ex ante*, these forms of good therefore predict very little about what the common good will look like as actualized by any particular individual or group; *ex post*, however, the forms justify a great and wide range of individual and group conduct as productive of good and common good.

In practical terms for the Christian, the social principle means, on the one hand, that society should find room for Christians to follow Christ. This is no small thing. The Christian life will include prayer, church attendance, scripture

17 John Finnis, "What Is the Common Good, and Why Does It Concern the Client's Lawyer?" *South Texas Law Review*, 40 (1999): 42–43.

18 Murray, "Human Right," 238.

19 Ibid.

study, proclaiming the Gospel, and charitable works. But the commands of our God are greater than these. His grace changes everything we do. Christ commanded his disciples to follow him—to become like him. He was meek, merciful, a peacemaker, slow to anger, sexually pure, reverent, and loved his enemies. He did good deeds in secret, fasted and prayed earnestly in secret, asked us to forgive everyone, and sought to serve God, trusting that God would care for him. He set aside personal comfort, fear, and the things of the world to serve his Father and humankind.[20] The religion of a person like this is hardly limited to obviously religious acts. "Whereas the obligation of worship is occasional, the obligation of service is constant. It is also comprehensive."[21] It encompasses all of life and becomes the motivation for every effort.

For such a person, choices are strongly influenced and sometimes dictated by that person's understanding of God's will for her or him. These include especially major choices such as whom to marry, how many children to have and care for, how to educate those children, how to earn a living, where to live, how that life is lived, and what to do with time and other resources not spent directly in service to others. In all these things, the Christian seeks to live a life approved by God. All these are matters of faith to one degree or another, and part of living our religion. This truth must be part of the social principle.

However, the social principle must include room also for those who understand God and what is good very differently than the Christian understands, and even room for those who reject God and believe they have found good elsewhere. Respect for human dignity requires that humans not be coerced in these matters of seeking good. Again, particular instantiations of basic goods and of the common good will have near-infinite variety, and the life of a Christian is but one instantiation (or many—as many as there are Christians, perhaps). Human dignity requires freedom to seek other instantiations. Christ himself did not coerce. He taught "truth in love" and protected the sacredness of holy things with at least a threat of violence, but he allowed even those who would persecute believers to do so. In a world in which many call "evil good, and good evil,"[22] what is good and what is not can be extremely confusing, and not all seek good with equal determination, farsightedness, and so on. Human dignity must allow for all sincere attempts to do good, no matter how misguided. Murray reasons that even

> [t]olerance of evil may be wisdom and virtue, as it is with God. It may not be simply a lesser evil but a means to a higher good, again as it is with God.

20 *See* Matt 16:24, Mark 8:34, Luke 9:23 (follow him); Matt 5:48; 2 Cor. 3:18; Gal 4:4–7; Eph 4:13–15; 1 John 2:3–6, 3:2–3 (become like him); Matt 5–7; Matt 4:1–11.

21 Murray, "Order of Religion," 55.

22 Eph 4:15 ("truth in love"); Matt 26:52–53; *cf.* Matt 5:10–12 ("Blessed are those who are persecuted because of righteousness" (NIV)); Mark 11:15–17 (casting money changers from the temple), John 2:13–16 ("Making a whip of cords, he drove all of them out of the temple" (NRSV)); Isaiah 5:20 ("evil good, and good evil").

> ... It is ... false to assert, as a matter of absolute and unconditional principle, that religious and moral aberrations ought always to be suppressed when it is possible to suppress them. God Himself does not adopt this norm of action.[23]

Rather, God gives humankind, God's children, their choice; the social principle, based as it is on human dignity given by God, requires that we respect each other and allow each other freedom to do good as we each believe it, whether we agree with each other or disagree.

Freedom: a limitation on law's role

Following on these two principles, Murray posits a third, the "principle of the free society."

> This principle affirms that man in society must be accorded as much freedom as possible, and that that freedom is not to be restricted unless and insofar as necessary. By necessary I mean the restraint is needed to preserve society's very existence or ... necessary for preserving the public order in its juridical, political, and moral aspects.

Murray returned to this formulation often: "As much freedom as possible, as much government as necessary"; "as much freedom as possible, as much coercion as necessary."[24] In positive form, this is the principle expressed in the first line of this chapter, that government and law should maximize freedom to serve in very deed as a disciple of Christ—to do all the good we can. Dallin Oaks explained similarly, "[T]he most desirable condition for the effective exercise of God-given moral agency is a condition of maximum freedom and responsibility."[25] I have called this principle salvific freedom in other writings.

It is not libertarianism. The principle as expressed bears superficial resemblance to maxims of libertarianism, but whereas libertarians respect other people as sentient beings,[26] the principal of salvific freedom respects God and God's creations made in God's image. Whereas libertarians hope to do as they please to seek happiness within the limits of respecting others' similar rights, the end

23 Murray, "Order of Religion," 107.

24 Murray, "Human Right," 239; Murray, "Order of Religion," 81 (attributing the thought to Leo XIII, *Rerum Novarum* (1891)); Murray, "Church and State," 154.

25 Dallin H. Oaks, "The Divinely Inspired Constitution," in *The Spirit of America* (Salt Lake City, UT: Bookcraft, 1998): 11, 20–21.

26 *E.g.*, "Libertarianism," Stanford Encyclopedia of Philosophy, September 5, 2002, rev. July 1, 2014, https://plato.stanford.edu/entries/libertarianism/ ("agents are, at least initially, *full self-owners*"); David Boaz, "Key Concepts of Libertarianism," *Cato Institute*, January 1, 1999, https://www.cato.org/publications/commentary/key-concepts-libertarianism, accessed July 12, 2018 ("[L]ibertarianism proposes a society of liberty under law, in which individuals are free to pursue their own lives so long as they respect the equal rights of others").

of salvific freedom is responsibility to God and freedom to become and to do good—as Murray puts it, so that "*in the presence of God* [the human] takes responsibility on himself alone for his ... decisions and acts." "Human society is not an ultimate end in itself; it is called upon to serve the ultimate ends of the human person, whose destiny is eternal."[27] The scope of freedom of action ensured under these two theories may overlap to some degree, but the two differ in emphasis and scope because their purposes and justifications differ. Moreover, as we see in Murray's elaboration of a fifth principle, *infra*, the role of government with respect to freedom is not merely negative.

Equal application

The three principles we have discussed lead to a fourth—equal application of the laws:

> Parallel with the third principle, a fourth issues from taking the first two, the ontological and the social, together. The principle is juridical and maintains that all citizens enjoy juridical equality in society. This principle rests upon the truth that all persons are peers in natural dignity and that every human being is equally the subject, foundation, and end of human society.[28]

The political principle: protection of rights

Lastly, Murray posits a role for government and law in positive terms:

> Finally, there follows a fifth principle, the political principle[:] .... "To protect the inviolable rights proper to human beings and to ensure that everyone may discharge his duties with greater facility—this is the paramount duty of every public power." This constitutes for the public power its first and principal concern for the common good—the effective protection of the human person and its dignity. This definition of the paramount function of public power rests clearly upon the first four principles.

This duty is active protection of freedom—"[t]o protect the inviolable rights proper to human beings."

Murray expands in other passages. Note in particular that this freedom includes more than simple freedom of religion. It includes freedom to do the will of God in all relevant ways—to do good:

> [T]he function of human law is to assure those minimal conditions of actualized morality within society which are necessary for the coexistence

27 Murray, "Human Right," 240 (emphasis added); Murray, "Order of Religion," 75; *see also* Murray, "Religious Freedom," 145.

28 Murray, "Human Right," 239.

> and cooperation of the citizens toward the common good of justice and peace.
>
> [T]he function of government appears as the protection and promotion, not of religious truth, but of religious freedom as a fundamental right of the human person. This is a secular function, since freedom in society—notably religious freedom—is a secular value, as are the values of justice and love or civic friendship. All three of these values are rooted in the truth about the human person, which is the truth upon which the whole social and political order rests.
>
> It means also the assurance that the members of the Church as a spiritual community will have possession of their native freedom to live as Christians and citizens, to do the will of God within society without having obstacles put in their way. This latter freedom ... creates a demand on government and on other social orders that they should provide proper conditions of social welfare and economic prosperity.[29]

Murray's language is general and abstract, but the theory clearly mandates practical results. It is a theory of human freedom expansive enough to ensure robust religious freedom for those whose faith touches everything, or it is a theory of religious freedom expansive enough to ensure human freedom with respect to everything that might be touched by faith. This freedom extends to all the ends God wills for his children. Pope John Paul II, in the Encyclical Letter *Centesimus Annus*, wrote that it included

> the right to life, an integral part of which is the right of the child to develop in the mother's womb from the moment of conception; ... the right to develop one's intelligence and freedom in seeking and knowing the truth; the right to share in the work which makes wise use of the earth's material resources, and to derive from that work the means to support oneself and one's dependents .... In a certain sense, the source and synthesis of these rights is religious freedom, understood as the right to live in the truth of one's faith and in conformity with one's transcendent dignity as a person.

Or, as Michael McConnell wrote, "To the extent that God's will affects all of life, then the principle of freedom must apply to all of life."[30] A similar sentiment is the very American prayer for our country that God "[c]onfirm ... liberty in law!"[31]

29 Murray, "Human Right," 239 (attributing the quoted material to Pius XII and John XIII); Murray, "Church and State," 206; Murray, "Order of Religion," 58, 79 (internal quotations omitted).

30 Michael W. McConnell, "Old Liberalism, New Liberalism, and People of Faith," in *Christian Perspectives on Legal Thought*, ed. Michael W. McConnell, Robert F. Cochran, Jr. and Angela C. Carmella (New Haven, CT & London: Yale University Press, 2001), 14.

31 Katherine Lee Bates, "America the Beautiful," in *America the Beautiful and Other Poems* (New York: Thomas Y. Crowell Co., 1911): 3, https://catalog.hathitrust.org/Record/006634139.

Because the political principle is built on the first four principles, and particularly on human dignity, it must protect those who seek good that a Christian might not recognize and in ways with which a Christian might not agree, even ways that appear evil to the Christian. Murray notes,

> Public order, whose care devolves upon the state, is a narrower concept [than the common good]. It includes three goods which can and should be achieved by the power which is proper to the state—the power inherent in the coercive discipline of public law. The first is the public peace, which is the highest political good. The second is public morality, as determined by moral standards commonly accepted among the people. The third is justice, which secures for the people what is due to them.

Sometimes "the legalization of evil is necessary."

> [F]reedom under law is the basic rule of jurisprudence, which runs thus: 'Let there be as much freedom, personal and social, as is possible; let there be only as much restraint and constraint, personal and social, as may be necessary for the public order.'[32]

Summary

In summary, the theological normative principle for human law outlined here—that government and law should maximize people's freedom to do all the good they can, including to serve Christ—rests on five sub-principles:

1. The dignity of each human being requires that they be free to choose whether and how they will serve God and do good, free from all external coercion.
2. The goal of society is the flourishing of each human being personally, socially, and morally. Together with (1), this goal requires that each human being be free, individually as well as in concert with others, to seek what is good and to serve God as she sees fit.
3. Human beings in society must have as much freedom as possible, with law imposed on them only when necessary for preserving public order in its juridical, political, and moral aspects.
4. Each human being is to have juridical equality, meaning that each is equal under the law.
5. The role of law is to protect the freedoms of human beings so that each person may do as much good as she will, personally, socially, and morally, and with greater facility. The law will do this by ensuring public peace, public morality, and justice.

Now to apply it.

32 Murray, "Religious Freedom," 145–46; Murray, "Order of Religion," 64.

An application: the doctrine of consideration

A gulf separates this lofty, general, normative principle and theory about human nature and law, on the one hand, and an examination of the common law doctrine of consideration, on the other. To apply this theological principle about law, the theorist will have to engage the particular facts to which the doctrine of consideration is applied and ask whether the application of the consideration doctrine is justified according to the theory.

Whether the doctrine of consideration is justified will depend not on deduction but on practical reasonableness. Human flourishing and the public order are not abstractions, and the legal cases that the consideration doctrine resolves present real human needs.

> By reason of the very nature of law, the issue of the ideal never arises. The function of law ... is to be useful to men. Necessity or usefulness for the common good—these are the norms of law.[33]
>
> Legal questions therefore depend for their right solution, not only upon general principles of the moral and theological order, but also upon an intermediate set of norms, the norms of jurisprudence and political wisdom. The goodness of human law is judged by a moral and theological norm; it is also to be judged by a juristic norm, the exigencies of the common good in determinate circumstances.[34]

Law should be "proportioned to the necessities of the situation, as created by contingent fact."[35] Our analysis, then, will not be abstract at all. It will be an examination of moral and doctrinal wisdom applied to the exigencies of the common good as they arise in actual cases involving promises.

Our conclusions therefore cannot be determined in advance, or abstractly by deduction. Only by looking at laws in operation in actual cases can the laws' consistency with these principles be determined; as facts change, the justifying must be done anew; and as our views of the facts differ and our understandings of human flourishing differ in emphasis, so we should expect a range of legal conclusions to be justifiable at any given time under these principles.

The general rule is not to enforce promises

Contract law has large aspirations, and the consideration doctrine manages a relatively small corner of them. Contract law intends to be a general theory of promise enforcement under the law, and consideration is commonly thought to be the door or gateway to legal enforcement, so that only a promise made with consideration is enforceable. But this general statement is an exaggeration.

33 Murray, "Religious Freedom," 140.
34 Murray, "Order of Religion," 59.
35 Ibid., 82.

What actually occurs is that the plaintiff presents to the court a claim and perhaps evidence that a promise was made and breached. But promise and breach alone have never been enough to warrant a court's attention; if promise and breach alone are presented to the court, the court will not even hear the case—the court will not ask the defendant to respond to the complaint and will deny relief even if the defendant never appears in court. Contract law simply does not as a general matter recognize promises as legal acts. Is this state of the law consistent with Murray's theory, outlined above?

It is. This may be surprising. One might expect that a normative principle emphasizing freedom would encourage promise enforcement, and it does. After all, promises are generally voluntary acts. The law's conferral of a right to make a legally binding promise generally *enlarges* freedom: not only can human beings make promises, but they can also make legally binding promises. This enlarged capacity can give a promise greater value; a promise can be more useful if it is legally binding.

Yet, the normative principle maximizing freedom to do good, when applied to individual promises in contexts that arise daily, has a much more discerning effect. The normative principle includes the "principle of the free society," which is that people "must be accorded as much freedom as possible" and only "as much government as necessary." In many cases, this means that no law can form at all, even the private law that can arise from individual volitional acts. Accordingly, the law ignores most of the numerous promises people make. Consider some examples.

The most important promises a person can make are to God. These promises have eternal consequences. According to our normative principle, the law should have no role in them at all. To involve the courts in promises made to God would impose coercive force on a fundamentally religious decision. As noted, Murray reasoned that

> through every type of religious action, whether private or public, in all these aspects a person should act by his own deliberation and purpose, enjoying immunity from all external coercion so that in the presence of God he takes responsibility on himself alone for his religious decisions and acts.[36]

The employment of human law to enforce promises made to God would override that immunity from external coercion. Even that the person once promised fealty to God does not make a decision to breach any less a religious decision; freedom to decide only one way is not freedom at all. Also, no enforcement could occur without a judicial determination of the content of the promise—at the least what it means to promise to God—and this move would make a judge arbiter of religious acts and doctrine and thus undermine religious freedom.[37]

36 Murray, "Human Right," 240.

37 Courts have also reached a similar conclusion. *See Kedroff v. St. Nicholas Cathedral*, 344 U.S. 94 (1952).

Besides these, many other important promises are not enforced by contract law. Marriage vows—the promises couples make at the altar—are not generally enforced as contracts. If marrying couples want a contract, they must do more than merely promise at the altar. Likewise, oaths of office given by public servants are not enforced as contracts, and neither are jury or witness oaths (though a witness's breach of an oath to tell the truth may be a crime). Contract law rightly ignores these promises. Contract law leaves people to be good—or not.

Many promises we make are merely social promises: "I will be there at 6." "I will sing with the choir." "I will come to your graduation." The law also should not enforce these promises, for several reasons. First, social relationships are founded in voluntary friendship and love, but law is the threat of violence. Violence is inconsistent with the care that holds us together as friends. We enjoy social relations with each other in part because participation is chosen, not required by the state. Second, we should have law only as necessary, and law is not necessary here. The common social sanctions attendant to normal friendly relationships provide sufficient incentive to give us freedom to seek all the good we can in these matters. If I arrive after 6, I should have a good explanation. If I do not, you will not trust either my explanation or my commitment to our relationship. If my promise-breaking causes you enough distrust or trouble, you may not invite me again. I will miss you, and count our friendship as a loss. This entirely solves the problem. This social dynamic is sufficient to allow us to form friendships and enjoy the company of those we care for. Legal enforcement of merely social promises is not necessary to the public order. Third, legal enforcement of merely social promises would create a disincentive to friendship, and I may befriend others only cautiously. If you sue me when I am late for dinner, my relationship with you and perhaps many others will be too costly to maintain. Fourth, getting the courts involved would be a waste of scarce judicial resources. Courts are paid for by the public with limited funds; the public has more pressing needs than the enforcement of social promises.

Perhaps most fundamentally, a Christian recognizes that human beings are able to grow and change as they receive grace. They grow in moral acuity.[38] Moreover, we live in a fallen, changing world. Though a promise is frozen in time, time does not stop, and as circumstances change, people's needs also change. So, for instance, all decent people recognize situations in which forgiveness of breach of promise would be morally required. If I am not there at 6 because I rode with my spouse to the emergency room at 5:30 in an attempt to save her life, your anger at my tardiness will be cruel and insensitive. The need to allow a change of mind is recognized in contract law that allows damages as

38 On this topic, see, for example, the unfortunately named article by Aditi Bagchi, "Contract and the Problem of Fickle People," *Wake Forest Law Review*, 53 (2018). Bagchi's topic is the good of change in moral agents and how that value conflicts with the assumption of continuity that underlies the value of promising. Ibid., 2–6. A proper moral theory of promising should accommodate both values.

a remedy rather than ordering specific performance, but it is also recognized in not imposing a legal remedy at all unless significant need for one exists.[39]

The law requires a reason to enforce

The general rule

So the law appropriately declines to enforce every promise. Then when should the law consider enforcing a promise? When that is necessary, says our theory, to preserving our freedom to flourish—to do all the good we can. The "political principle," as Murray calls it, requires the positive protection of these freedoms necessary to flourishing.

This political principle requires some protection of economic rights as a practical matter. As Murray said,

> It means also the assurance that the members of the Church as a spiritual community will have possession of their native freedom to live as Christians and citizens, to do the will of God within society without having obstacles put in their way. This latter freedom ... creates a demand on government and on other social orders that they should provide proper conditions of social welfare and economic prosperity.[40]

It is hard to think of a greater obstacle to freedom than economic dependency or deprivation. Control of economic resources "is the control of the means for [many] ends. And whoever has sole control of the means must also determine which ends."[41] Deprivation shrinks capacity; conversely, control of economic resources expands capacity, allowing one to do more and greater good.

The positive role of government and law, then, includes maintaining, as Murray put it, "proper conditions of social welfare and economic prosperity." John Paul II's *Centesimus Annus* included in the list of proper freedoms "the right to share in the work which makes wise use of the earth's material resources, and to derive from that work the means to support oneself and one's dependents."

Without contract law, which gives us a right to make and to ask others to make legally enforceable promises, few would trust others outside of their immediate social circles sufficiently to trade with them. Performing a service for a promise to pay afterward, or delivering goods for a promise to pay on delivery, is an expensive investment and requires trust. Contract law boosts our trust in others by ensuring that we will have a legal remedy for breach of such promises. The legal proceedings and remedy give moral support to breach victims and impose a

39 It is also recognized in the law's unwillingness to let us bind ourselves to certain promises that are too harmful to ourselves, such as selling ourselves into slavery or agreeing not to work for anyone in the future except our current employer. Ibid., 10.

40 Murray, "Order of Religion," 79.

41 Friedrich Hayek, *The Road to Serfdom* (London: G. Routledge & Sons, 1944), 95.

costly hassle on breaching parties. The system thus encourages trusting behavior on which economies can thrive.

In practical terms, then, as the law does not enforce all promises, what plus promise and breach must a plaintiff allege to get a court to hear her case? Consideration is the most commonly accepted additional factor added to promise and breach that courts consider adequate to justify entertaining the plaintiff's petition, though it is not the only one.[42]

This is consideration doctrine: a promise must be made for a consideration. "To constitute consideration, a performance or a return promise must be ***bargained for***," meaning "sought by the promisor in exchange for his promise and ... given by the promisee in exchange for that promise."[43] Though the test asks what the parties "sought," it does not consider anyone's merely internal motives: "[T]he law is concerned with the external manifestation rather than the undisclosed mental state: it is enough that one party manifests an intention to induce the other's response and to be induced by it and that the other responds in accordance with the inducement." To the judge, then, it must appear plausible from objective facts that (i) a promise induced and was induced by (ii) another's promise or performance; that is enough.

Various benefits flow from the law's focus on exchange. First, please note that this standard is particularly important to the poor. Almost everyone has something to barter, even if it is only time and some work. The legal standard for entry to the court does not depend on some prior status or title; it does not require any property; it requires only that one can offer something someone else would want in exchange. It is ultimately as broad a rule for economic and social opportunity as one could create. It gives its benefits to anyone willing and able to work. On its face, it treats us all equally in terms of opportunity, as juridically equal.

Second, a system of voluntary exchange including promises also allows those who can participate fully in such a system to obtain what they need and want better than any other system of allocating resources. Experience teaches that this method cannot be the only method of resource allocation (and other methods exist—inheritance, gift, and government redistribution, for instance), but it justifiably plays a prominent role. If resources are allocated not by us, as our choices and the values we place on resources determine, then by whom? And by whom especially if our goal is to facilitate the good of each individual and the common good?

42 Others include promissory estoppel, American Law Institute, *Restatement of the Law, Second, Contracts* (St. Paul, MN: American Law Institute Publishers, 1981): § 90; certain formalities, *SKF USA, Inc. v. Workers' Comp. Appeal Bd.*, 714 A.2d 496 (Pa. Commw. Ct. 1998) (a seal or a formal statement); the promisee's good faith in seeking the promise, American Law Institute and National Conference of Commissioners on Uniform State Laws, Uniform Commercial Code (St. Paul, MN: West, 2009): § 2–209; or the parties' pre-existing relationship, *see Spry v. Pruitt*, 54 So.2d 701, 705–06 (Ala. 1951); *Watkins & Son v. Carrig*, 21 A.2d 591, 592–94 (N.H. 1941); Uniform Commercial Code § 2–209. Like consideration, each of these factors provides adequate justification to only a small subset of promises.

43 This paragraph's quoted language appears in American Law Institute, *Restatement (Second)*, § 71 & cmt.b (emphasis added).

Certainly not the government, at least not in most cases. The government is relatively ignorant of what individual people want, and this makes resource allocation by individual choice nearly always preferable to allocation by government choice. By "relative ignorance" I mean that, as between the government and an individual, the individual knows more about what the individual needs and wants. The individual's needs probably change in real time. I think it clear that individuals will always know *more* about their own goals and how they may best do good with what they have than the government can know. So my knowledge of my families' needs allows me to choose a better automobile for us, from those available,[44] than the government could choose. And I can seek a job that allows me to keep my faith, serve others, and also be a good father; I do not believe a government employment board would have done the same. My labor and funds are better allocated by me than by the government. (In the United States, at least, government allocation of resources often comes in the form of cash equivalent rather than any specific resource, and individuals choose at least in part how that cash is spent; in that respect, the US government recognizes the wisdom of letting individuals allocate as they see fit.)

As between the government and me, I am more likely to allocate resources to those causes I believe are good. Contract law's subservience to the rule "as much government as necessary" but not more allows me and all of us greater freedom to serve God or do some other good in which we believe. Letting the government control such matters would take our power to choose good away from us, mostly and in some situations completely. I make no claim that individuals will always choose good, or a good that others agree with. But our general normative principle gives individuals the first choice, absent cause to take it from them. That allows individuals to be responsible to God for their actions, and this is a goal of salvific freedom.

Lastly, by facilitating voluntary exchange, contract law encourages resources to move to those who value them more than those who convey them. Exchange in this way helps draw more value from the resources available to us, perhaps the most value of any system of allocation.

The rule applied

In application, the consideration doctrine is in almost all cases justified and uncontroversial because the doctrine requires a showing of real loss by a party who acted in reliance on the promisor's promise, a promise given to induce that

44 The government's stepping in with safety standards for all automobiles is in part an enforcement of automakers' promises to sell a "car." *See, e.g.*, American Law Institute and National Conference of Commissioners on Uniform State Laws, Uniform Commercial Code (St. Paul, MN: West, 2009): § 2–314. But the government also mandates certain safety features and standards. *See* Charles J. Kahane, *Lives Saved by Vehicle Safety Technologies and Associated Federal Motor Vehicle Stds., 1960 to 2012—Passenger Cars and LTVs*, at https://www-esv.nhtsa.dot.gov/Proceedings/24/files/24ESV-000291.PDF. Such standards can be justified as ensuring the public safety necessary for maximal peace and freedom.

very reliance. For instance, if the parties have exchanged a performance for a promise, then one party has already performed in exchange for the promise. A promisor said, "If you, Performer, do X [build my house, paint my car, represent me in this litigation], I, Promisor, will pay you $__." The promise is not enforceable until consideration exists—in other words, until Performer performs the bargained-for service. Once the service has been performed, Promisor ought to pay for it. The law threatens Promisor with violence because Promisor's promise and breach have caused Performer a real loss for which Promisor ought to pay. Promisor and Performer together agreed when the deal was made that the value of the performance was what was promised, so enforcement of the promise by a remedy based on that promise or its value is probably most just. Without the law's enforcing such deals, fewer strangers would do business with each other.

Most contracts do not take the form of a trade of performance for promise; most take the form of a trade of promises, but the law reaches the same result. Each party promises a performance. When parties trade promises of performances, one party must perform first.[45] After that party has performed, and the other has not, the party who has performed is in the same position as Performer in the last paragraph.

When consideration is absent because no bargained-for performance or promise occurred, courts generally do not take up the plaintiff's case unless the plaintiff presents some other good reason for legal enforcement—some additional factor beyond mere promise and breach that makes the plaintiff's case worth hearing. For instance, nearly 100 years ago, Professor Samuel Williston surmised that if (i) a promisee relied on a promise as a promisor should reasonably have expected would occur, and (ii) that reliance justified enforcing the promise, then courts should proceed with the plaintiff's promise and breach case and may grant a remedy.[46] Most states have adopted this theory, which has been called "promissory estoppel."[47] It is, similar to consideration, a factor in addition to promise and breach that justifies a legal remedy.[48]

Gift promises—promises without necessity

When a court finds that no additional factor justifying enforcement exists and rejects a plaintiff's claim, it is finding not just a lack of bargain but a lack of

45 *See, e.g.*, American Law Institute, *Restatement (Second)*, § 234. Cases in which neither party performs before suit is brought are exceedingly rare in practice. I have addressed them elsewhere. *See* Val Ricks, "Consideration and the Formation Defenses," *The University of Kansas Law Review*, 62, no. 2 (2013): 340–43.

46 The American Law Institute, *Commentaries on Contracts: Restatement No. 2* (Philadelphia, PA: The American Law Institute, 1926): 14–20 (commentary of Samuel J. Williston, reporting authorities from his treatise, I–V Samuel J. Williston, *The Law of Contracts* (New York: Baker, Voorhis & Co., 1920–24)).

47 Marco J. Jimenez, "The Many Faces of Promissory Estoppel: An Empirical Analysis under the Restatement (Second) of Contracts," *UCLA Law Review*, 57 (2010): 669; Eric Mills Holmes, "Restatement of Promissory Estoppel," *Willamette Law Review*, 32 (1996): 263, 514 ("all American jurisdictions adopt and apply a theory of promissory estoppel").

48 *See supra* note 42 for a list of other factors that courts have approved.

ground for litigation. In short, the judge sees no good reason to impose law. The judges impose law only when necessary, and this is as the theory of law outlined above directs.

Sometimes courts, when finding that nothing was exchanged for a promise, say that a promise was merely a gift, and "gift promises" are not enforced. "Gift promise" denotes that nothing is given in exchange for the promise, but this is too simple a statement. If a so-called gift promise was given to induce another's reliance on the promise, and succeeded in inducing such reliance, the promise may well be enforceable under the doctrine of promissory estoppel.[49] Promissory estoppel is an expansive doctrine that gives courts discretion to enforce those relied-on promises when they believe that such promises should in justice be enforced.[50] The law can be applied when necessary, exactly as our theory requires. But courts do not call promises enforceable under the doctrine of promissory estoppel "gift promises." The condemning label "gift promise" means not just that nothing was given in exchange but that the law will not enforce at all.

But without some additional factor present, the gift promise probably should not be enforced, for several reasons. Most obviously, there is no direct harm, and more particularly no economic harm, to anyone from the promise's breach. Trust between the parties is weakened, but this alone is an insufficient reason for enforcement. Legal enforcement of promises is hardly the only possible social consequence from breach of promise. Usually, many of the factors present in social promise situations are also present in gift promise cases. Many such cases, perhaps most, are among family members whose relationship should be one of love and caring, not force and violence, even the sparing violence of the law. The same can be said of promises to give a gift to charity. Unless someone is directly harmed by the breach, these relationships are better handled informally for many of the same reasons informal social promises are not enforced.

Even more importantly, Christians recognize that people can change in good ways. There should be space for repentance. If the promisor of a gift later regrets the promise (realizing that the gift would harm the donee, or enable the donee to harm himself; or realizing that the donor cannot afford the gift, having misread her own needs), then good moral reasons justify a breach. Even without the good moral reasons, the promisor should be allowed the legal space to change her mind if no one will be harmed in a way that should require government action. God allows the promisor to harden her heart, and the law should, too, absent some necessity. The law's refusal to enforce mere gift promises leaves these moral decisions in the minds and hearts of human persons made in the image of and responsible to God. That is where such decisions belong.

49 *See, e.g.*, *Harvey v. Dow*, 962 A.2d 322 (Me. 2008) (holding a gift promise from parents to daughter enforceable under promissory estoppel after daughter built a house in reliance); *Satcher v. Satcher*, 570 S.E.2d 535, 538–40 (S.C. App. 2002) (promise of grandfather to grandson that certain farmland with home would be grandson's at grandfather's death enforced pursuant to promissory estoppel).

50 The last element of promissory estoppel is that "injustice can be avoided only by enforcement of the promise." American Law Institute, *Restatement (Second)*, § 90(1).

Consideration succeeds, but with a caveat

The consideration doctrine is for all of these reasons consistent with the theological principle of human law outlined in this chapter. But I offer a caveat: like all legal doctrines, the doctrine of consideration can be misused. I offer two examples.

First, courts sometimes abuse the doctrine by finding an objective bargain where the facts do not warrant it, imposing a contractual obligation on grounds that consideration exists when it does not.[51] This abuse of the consideration doctrine takes away freedom to do good and imposes on a party an obligation or a harm to which the party has never agreed.

For instance, generally in the United States employment is presumed to be at will. This means that either the employer or employee may terminate employment at any time, for any or no reason. However, at-will employment may be displaced by a contract for something else. An employer may promise employment for a term, or not to fire an employee except for cause, and if such a promise is given for consideration, it becomes binding.

Late in the last century, when what later became human resources departments within businesses were less well trained, sometimes human resource managers would promulgate handbooks or policies that promised employees something more than at-will employment: to be fired only for cause, to be re-assigned before being laid off, etc. When these promises were tested in court, courts inferred consideration for them in the work employees performed after learning about these promises. This was a fair inference (though not necessarily the only inference). Such promises were made to induce employees to work harder and with greater loyalty, and they probably had this effect. When employees were fired in violation of these promises, courts often held employers liable for breach.

Later, seeing the costs of such promises, businesses tried to remove them. Many businesses offered additional benefits in place of them and obtained employees' written consent. But some did not. Instead, they merely announced that the promise would end. When employees tried to enforce the promises notwithstanding the announcement, many courts ruled that the change was ineffective because consideration and assent could not be inferred.[52] This was correct. Inferring that continued work after the removal of employment benefits was induced by the *removal* of the benefits is not a fair inference.

Many courts, however, claimed that if a promise followed by employees' continued work could create a contract, the removal of a promise followed by employees' continued work could unmake the contract. The continued work showed that employees assented, these courts surmised, and also provided consideration for the change.[53] This inference is unwarranted. The cancellation of

51 *Durand v. SSA Terminals*, LLC, No. A116884, 2009 WL 321214 (Cal. Ct. App., 1st Dist., Feb. 9, 2009) (inferring consideration without justification).

52 *E.g.*, *Demasse v. ITT Corp.*, 984 P.2d 1138, 1144–48 (Ariz. 1999) (discussing cases).

53 *E.g.*, *Asmus v. Pacific Bell*, 96 Cal. Rptr. 179, 185–88 (Cal. 2000).

a valuable and binding promise to employees does not induce them to work and does not induce loyalty; it has only the effect of making the employment less valuable. The inference that employees continued working in assent to and induced by the change is not plausible, but this is what courts held.

Now this false inference of consideration is creeping into the law. Contracts which are ongoing and structured (as is employment) as a promise in exchange for a performance can be modified by the promisor without regard to the substance of the change, and the other party's continuing to perform after the modification constitutes acceptance and consideration regardless of the change's effect. This means that the promisor can change its own contractual obligation merely by giving notice to the other party. Of course, such a power can be granted by the agreement of the other party;[54] what is new is courts' declarations that all agreements structured this way allow immunity from breach claims and complete control of the terms by one party whether the other party assents or not. So, a promise of job security that changes at-will employment can be discarded by a simple notice to employees. Terms of an investment account can be changed at will by the investment custodian without the other party's consent, merely by notice. Purchasers of products who have paid and already taken delivery are bound by terms the seller throws in the box to be discovered by buyers later.[55]

The use of consideration doctrine to justify such a result runs counter to the normative principle of freedom we have introduced. In such cases, the law fails to protect the freedom of one of the parties to do good. Instead, the rights of the parties to a contract are reduced to status: the performing party has whatever rights the promising party says, no matter what original bargain was struck. Some contract law doctrines limiting what can be bargained for—unconscionability and some public policies—doctrines rarely used by courts and costly to litigate—constitute the only limit on the promising party's power.

It may be possible to justify such fictional assent and inducement under some normative principle, but not the normative principle we have been considering. Utilitarianism may justify it, because the power allocated to promisors in such relationships may create societal benefits (in efficiency, lower product costs, etc.) that exceed the costs to individual performers. But utilitarianism, which seeks the greatest aggregate good for the greatest number, is entirely at odds with the theological principle of law set forth in this chapter, which requires that the law treat each human being as made in the image of God, equally—not balance what is good for one against harmful results to others.

54 Credit card and cell phone agreements often provide such a power to the issuing bank and provider, respectively.

55 *See, e.g.*, *Asmus*, 96 Cal. Rptr. at 179; *Durand*, 2009 WL 321214, at *1 (employment); *Pollok v. Vanguard Group*, Inc., 774 Fed. App'x 407, 409 (2019) (investment account); *Taylor v. Samsung Electronics America*, No. 16 C 50313, 2018 WL 3921145 (N.D. Ill. Aug. 16, 2018) (binding a cell phone user to a dispute resolution clause placed in the cell phone box after the sale occurred, merely because the cell phone user (who was not the buyer) used the phone, and reviewing like cases).

Second, it is an abuse of the consideration doctrine to treat it as more than it is. It does not define the borders of promise enforcement; it is merely one reason for legally recognizing a promise as prima facie enforceable. And just as consideration cannot justly be the sole additional factor able to support suit for breach of promise, so exchange cannot justly be the government's sole method of allocating resources or supporting economic prosperity. Some individuals are unable in certain contexts fully and freely to exchange, and some individuals will be unable to offer much or anything in exchange, either for a time or permanently. The government tasked with proper conditions of social welfare and economic prosperity cannot support only people who can help themselves through exchange. The law should provide a way by which those who cannot take advantage of that system can also flourish. For these reasons, the law offers defenses to promises given in defective exchanges,[56] specially regulates certain kinds of contracts,[57] and provides a "safety net," as we sometimes say, of laws and policies aimed at promoting flourishing other than by exchange. The political principle requires that government and law address all conditions necessary to maintain the public order for all human beings subject to it, so that each and all can flourish. What specifically this mandate requires for such of our brothers and sisters who cannot participate in exchange would take us well outside the doctrine of consideration and of contract law and this study.

56 *See* Ricks, "Formation Defenses."

57 For instance, special regulation applies to consumer transactions, sales of securities, insurance, plea-bargaining, bankruptcy, various agreements regarding family obligations, and agreements between fiduciaries and beneficiaries.

13 Privatization and pluralism in dispute resolution

Promoting religious values through contract

Michael A. Helfand

Religious dispute resolution under public law

When many U.S. lawyers first encounter the concept of religious dispute resolution, their minds travel to categories of public constitutional law. This reaction is far from surprising. Numerous, and primarily Christian, denominations resolve internal disputes by submitting them to established church courts. For example, the United Methodist Church maintains a formal judicial system which, among other issues, adjudicates claims filed against pastors and members.[1] Similarly, the Presbyterian Church (U.S.A.) provides its members with a "judicial process," serving as "the means by which church discipline is implemented within the context of pastoral care and oversight."[2] Along the same lines, the Roman Catholic Church's canon law system covers a wide variety of substantive matters, including "virtually every aspect of ecclesiastical life for the Catholic Church's

1 The United Methodist Church, *The Book of Discipline of the United Methodist Church, 2016* (Nashville, TN: United Methodist Pub. House, 2016), ¶ 362

> Whenever [a local pastor, an associate member, a probationary member, or a full member], including those on leaves of all types, honorable or administrative location, or retirement, is accused of violating this trust, the membership of his or her ministerial office is subject to review.

General Council on Finance and Administration of the United Methodist Church, *Administrative and Judicial Procedures Handbook* (Nashville, TN: United Methodist Pub. House, 2017), 2, https://www.gcfa.org/media/1274/ajp_handbook_revjune2017.pdf (explaining that the Methodist judicial system provides for a "Biblical understanding of justice and process").

2 Presbyterian Church (U.S.A.), *The Constitution of the Presbyterian Church (U.S.A.), Part II, Book of Order 2011–2013* (Louisville, KY: Office of the General Assembly, 2011), § D-2.0100; Steven R. Hadley, "Handbook of American Church Courts," *Whittier Law Review*, 22, no. 1 (Winter 2000): 251, 309–14 (observing that "the 'Rules of Discipline' section of the *Book of Order* literally read[s] like the Federal Rules of Civil Procedure"); *see also* Presbyterian Church (U.S.A.), *Book of Order*, *supra*, §§ D-3.0101–3.0106 (describing jurisdiction in the judicial process); ibid. §§ D-5.0100–D5.0206 (describing obligations and authority of permanent judicial commissions). The decisions rendered by the permanent judicial commission of the General Assembly are available online at http://oga.pcusa.org/section/committees/gapjc/permanent-judicial-commission-decisions/.

congregations in almost every corner of the world."[3] Other prominent examples of Christian denominations employing church courts in the United States abound.[4]

And for nearly a century and a half, courts have afforded the internal dispute resolution processes of church courts the deference required by prevailing interpretations of the First Amendment. This framework of deference draws from a long-standing constitutional doctrine, often referred to as the "church autonomy doctrine," which requires courts, "whenever the questions of discipline, or of faith, or ecclesiastical rule, custom, or law have been decided by the highest of these church judicatories," to "accept such decisions as final, and as binding on them, in their application to the case before them."[5] While initially merely a doctrine of federal common law, the Supreme Court has subsequently recast the church autonomy doctrine as drawing from the First Amendment.[6]

In seeking to identify the doctrinal link between the church autonomy doctrine and the First Amendment, courts have vacillated between the two religion clauses. Thus, at times, the Supreme Court has characterized the doctrine in free exercise terms, explaining that the constitutional principle of church autonomy "radiates a spirit of freedom for religious organizations, an independence from secular control or manipulation, in short, power to decide for themselves, free from state interference, matters of church government as well as those of faith and doctrine."[7] In recent years, however, courts have focused more and more on the Establishment Clause roots of the doctrine, highlighting that the deference afforded by the internal dispute resolution processes within religious institutions stems from overarching concerns that judicial intervention in such matters would impermissibly entangle courts in religious matters that are beyond their constitutional purview.[8]

3 Brief of Religious Tribunal Experts Amici Curiae in Support of Petitioner at 15–16, *Hosanna-Tabor Evangelical Lutheran Church and School v. EEOC*, 565 U.S. 171 (2012) (No. 10-553); *see also* Hadley, "Handbook," 318–23. For additional background on the sources of canon law, *see* Libero Gerosa, *Canon Law* (London: Continuum, 2002), 49–60 (discussing the sources and formation of canon law). *See generally* R. H. Helmholz, *The Spirit of Classical Canon Law* (Athens: University of Georgia Press, 1996) (describing the "origins of a system of canon law").

4 *See* Hadley, "Handbook," 259–317 (describing the church courts of Seventh-Day Adventist, Baptist, Churches of Christ, Episcopal, Jehovah's Witnesses, Church of Latter-Day Saints, Lutheran, Methodist, Nazarene, Orthodox, Pentecostal, and Reformed denominations); Brief of Religious Tribunal Experts Amici Curiae in Support of Petitioner at 5–24, *Hosanna-Tabor*, 565 U.S. 171 (No. 10-553) (describing the internal dispute resolution process of various religious communities and denominations).

5 *Watson v. Jones*, 80 U.S. 679, 727 (1871); *see also Bryce v. Episcopal Church in the Diocese of Colo*, 289 F.3d 648, 655 (10th Cir. 2002) ("This church autonomy doctrine prohibits civil court review of internal church disputes involving matters of faith, doctrine, church governance, and polity").

6 *Kedroff v. St. Nicholas Cathedral of Russian Orthodox Church*, 344 U.S. 94 (1952).

7 *Kedroff*, 344 U.S. at 116.

8 *See, e.g.*, *McClure v. Salvation Army*, 460 F.2d 553, 558 (5th Cir. 1972).

This doctrinal ambivalence reflects, to some extent, a theoretical debate as well. Some scholars have grounded the church autonomy doctrine in a dual-sovereignty approach to religious institutions—that is, religious institutions are constitutionally granted inherent sovereignty over their own internal affairs[9] so that they can develop religious doctrine and practice in an environment free from government interference and influence.[10] This sovereigntist view is often linked to James Madison's famous articulation in his *Memorial and Remonstrance against Religious Assessments*: "We maintain therefore that in matters of Religion, no man's right is abridged by the institution of Civil Society and that Religion is wholly exempt from its cognizance."[11]

A second prominent theory argues, contra the sovereigntist approach, that courts must defer to the internal dispute processes within religious institutions not because the constitution affords them inherent autonomy or authority,[12] but because courts are constitutionally prohibited from resolving questions of faith and religious doctrine. On this theory, judicial deference to religious institutions is simply a by-product of the "adjudicative disability" of courts—that is, courts cannot resolve disputes within religious institutions because they lack the constitutional competence to resolve disputes that implicate religious doctrine or practice.[13] In this way, the second account of judicial deference to religious dispute resolution derives from the broader "religious question" doctrine, which understands the Establishment Clause to prohibit "civil courts [from] adjudicat[ing] disputes turning on church policy and administration or on religious doctrine and practice."[14]

9 *See, e.g.*, Paul Horwitz, "Act III of the Ministerial Exception," *Northwestern University Law Review Colloquy*, 106 (2011): 156, 161–62. This approach links up with the "church autonomy" body of scholarship. *See, e.g.*, Richard W. Garnett, "Do Churches Matter? Towards an Institutional Understanding of the Religion Clauses," *Villanova Law Review*, 53, no. 2 (2008): 273, 288; Thomas Berg, Kimberlee Wood Colby, Carl H. Esbeck, and Richard W. Garnett, "Religious Freedom, Church-State Separation, and the Ministerial Exception," *Northwestern University Law Review Colloquy*, 106 (2011): 175–90; Gregory A. Kalscheur, "Civil Procedure and the Establishment Clause: Exploring the Ministerial Exception, Subject-Matter Jurisdiction, and the Freedom of the Church," *William and Mary Bill of Rights Journal*, 17, no. 1 (October 2008): 43, 48–49; *see also* Mark DeWolfe Howe, "Political Theory and the Nature of Liberty," *Harvard Law Review*, 67, no. 1 (November 1953): 91, 94.

10 *See, e.g.*, Paul Horwitz, "Churches as First Amendment Institutions: Of Sovereignty and Spheres," *Harvard Civil Rights-Civil Liberties Law Review*, 44, no. 1 (Winter 2009): 79, 87.

11 James Madison, "Memorial and Remonstrance against Religious Assessments," in *The Separation of Church and State: Writings on a Fundamental Freedom by America's Founders*, ed. Forrest Church (Boston, MA: Beacon Press, 2004), 64.

12 Ira C. Lupu and Robert W. Tuttle, "The Distinctive Place of Religious Entities in Our Constitutional Order," *Villanova Law Review*, 47, no. 1 (2002): 37, 78–79.

13 Ira C. Lupu and Robert W. Tuttle, "Courts, Clergy, and Congregations: Disputes between Religious Institutions and Their Leaders," *Georgetown Journal of Law & Public Policy*, 7, no. 1 (Winter 2009): 119, 122; *see also* Ira C. Lupu and Robert W. Tuttle, "Sexual Misconduct and Ecclesiastical Immunity," *Brigham Young University Law Review*, 2004, no. 4 (2004): 1789, 1815.

14 *Natal v. Christian & Missionary Alliance*, 878 F.2d 1575, 1576 (1st Cir. 1989).

On either theory—whether based on inherent sovereignty or adjudicative disability—courts must remain "hands off";[15] that is, they must resist adjudicating the dispute and dismiss the case on First Amendment grounds.[16] Maybe the most prominent example where courts, as a matter of constitutional law, refuse to adjudicate is the "ministerial exception," which is the constitutional doctrine that exempts religious institutions from liability under various anti-discrimination statutes when such liability stems from the hiring and firing of ministers.[17] In cases where a minister challenges the legality of a house of worship's decision to terminate his or her employment, courts refuse to adjudicate the case.

The application of the ministerial exception often manifests the theoretical divisions described above. For some, the reason courts ought to abstain from resolving these cases touches on the deference courts ought to give the unique relationship between a minister and house of worship, captured at times in judicial language describing this relationship as the institution's "lifeblood."[18] For others, this judicial abstention in cases of the ministerial exception is related instead to the fact that such cases often implicate religious questions that courts are incompetent to resolve.[19] Accordingly, where—for example—a minister is terminated for cause, courts typically dismiss the case because assessing the institutional claims of "cause" will invariably require judicial assessment of the religious misconduct at stake; and that inquiry will invariably entail judicial evaluation of whether the minister is sufficiently fulfilling the religious functions demanded by his or her position.[20]

Regardless of the background theory, the typical framework through which courts conceptualize dispute resolution within religious institutions is the prism of public law. Public law demands that courts remain on the sidelines in such cases either as a function of a quasi-sovereignty granted religious institutions or because cases would require resolution of questions beyond a court's constitutional competence. In turn, the internal dispute resolution process within religious institutions is granted some degree of space to resolve disputes in accordance with shared religious rules and values.

15 *See* Kent Greenawalt, "Hands Off! Civil Court Involvement in Conflicts over Religious Property," *Columbia Law Review*, 98, no. 8 (December 1998): 1843.

16 *See generally* Michael A. Helfand, "Litigating Religion," *Boston University Law Review*, 93, no. 2 (March 2013): 493–562.

17 42 U.S.C. § 2000e-2 (2018); *see also Hosanna-Tabor*, 565 U.S. at 186–90 (noting the uniform acceptance of the "ministerial exception" among the federal courts of appeals).

18 *McClure*, 460 F.2d at 558.

19 *See generally* Ira C. Lupu and Robert W. Tuttle, "The Mystery of Unanimity in *Hosanna-Tabor Evangelical Lutheran Church & School v. EEOC*," *Lewis & Clark Law Review*, 20, no. 4 (2017): 1265, 1299–1304.

20 *See, e.g.*, *Leavy v. Congregation Beth Shalom*, 490 F. Supp. 2d 1011, 1026 (N.D. Iowa 2007); *Kraft v. Rector, Churchwardens & Vestry of Grace Church*, no. 01-CV-7871 (KMW), 2004 U.S. Dist. LEXIS 4234, at 22–23 (S.D.N.Y. Mar. 15, 2004); *Friedlander v. Port Jewish Ctr.*, 347 F. App'x 654 (2d Cir. 2009).

This space, however, should not be confused with legal enforcement. To the contrary, the public law approach to religious dispute resolution adopts what Ralf Michaels has described as an approach of deference, which "recognizes the normative autonomy of communities (and even of non-communities) and protects them from state regulation and interference by granting them a private space."[21] In so doing, the state does not grant these forms of private ordering recognition as law, "[r]ather, the state refrains from interfering."[22] This distinction may have some significant consequences.

First, it means that possession is not just, as the legal idiom goes, nine-tenths of the law; it may very well be ten-tenths. To see why, consider the following hypothetical. Imagine a church that terminates its pastor for inadequate sermons.[23] But—because the church has the minister on automatic bill pay—it accidently deposits two additional paychecks into the pastor's bank account. The pastor believes he is legally entitled to these paychecks, along with many more in the future on the theory that the church has breached his contract (he assumes, of course, that his sermons were quite good). Under the public law umbrella, if the pastor files suit in court against the church, the court will presumably dismiss the case because underlying the breach of contract claim are religious questions that the court lack the authority to resolve.[24]

But recognizing that a court is likely to dismiss the pastor's suit doesn't quite resolve the case. Would the pastor have to return the paychecks erroneously deposited in his account? To the extent a court takes the religious question doctrine as demanding a judicial "hands off" posture,[25] there is good reason to think that

21 Ralf Michaels, "The Re-State-Ment of Non-State Law: The State, Choice of Law, and the Challenge from Global Legal Pluralism," *Wayne Law Review*, 51, no. 3 (Fall 2005): 1209, 1233.

22 Ibid.

23 *See, e.g.*, *El-Farra v. Sayyed*, 226 S.W.3d 792, 795 (Ark. 2006) (affirming a summary judgment against an Islamic minister who had been terminated based on the quality of his sermons).

24 *See e.g.*, *Friedlander*, 347 F. App'x at 655 (dismissing rabbi's breach of contract claim because

> review of [the rabbi's] claims in this case would require scrutiny of whether she should have, *inter alia*, read more extensively from the Torah at certain services, prepared students for their Bar or Bat Mitzvah more adequately, performed certain pastoral services that were not performed, or followed the Temple's funeral service policies. A reviewing court would also be required to assess whether any failures rose to the level of "gross misconduct or willful neglect of duty" under the relevant employment contract. We agree with the district court that such review would involve impermissible judicial inquiry into religious matters.);

El-Farra, 226 S.W.3d at 795–96

> [A]ppellant's claims that there are no ecclesiastical issues involved and that he is not seeking reinstatement but only damages do not persuade us that the circuit court erred in finding it had no subject-matter jurisdiction. Appellant is suing for breach of contract. Regardless of the remedy he is requesting—and in this case he is seeking the traditional remedy of damages as opposed to specific performance—the court must review whether the grounds for termination were "valid grounds according to Islamic Jurisdiction." It is our opinion that any determination of this claim would involve ecclesiastical issues.

25 *See supra* note 15.

not only would the church not be required to reinstate the pastor—or, for that matter, pay him damages for breach of contract—but that the pastor would also not be required to return the extra paychecks. To see why, simply consider that the only way for the court to determine that the pastor is not entitled to those paychecks is to adjudicate the underlying breach of contract claim. If the pastor is correct that the church breached his contract, he is legally entitled to the paychecks; if the pastor is incorrect, then the church is entitled to the return of those paychecks; and the only way a court can determine whether the pastor is correct or incorrect is by resolving a prohibited religious question. Thus, in the words of Ira Mark Ellman, "[a] true 'hands-off' approach would have the court refuse to entertain the case at all, leaving the parties where the court found them."[26] In our fact pattern that would mean the church need not pay damages to the pastor, but also the pastor need not return paychecks to the church. These two outcomes are, on one level, legally inconsistent. But under public law's abstention paradigm, they both make sense. Public law, on this account, does not enforce the dispute resolution process within religious institutions. It remains hands off, leaving the parties without an actual resolution of the underlying claims.[27]

Now there may be reasons to resist this conclusion. If a court were to view the religious question through a dual-sovereignty paradigm—where religious institutions have inherent sovereignty over their own internal affairs[28]—one can imagine a court deferring to the outcome of the church; thus, if the church concluded that the pastor failed to fulfill his religious duties, a court might defer to that determination.[29] In turn, it might require the pastor to return the erroneously deposited paychecks.

But a quasi-sovereignty paradigm generates its own set of challenges. Deferring to the internal decision-making and dispute resolution processes within religious institutions makes it difficult to identify limits to this deference. Linking

26 Ira Mark Ellman, "Driven from the Tribunal: Judicial Resolution of Internal Church Disputes," *California Law Review*, 69, no. 5 (September 1981): 1378, 1409–10.

27 *See* Greenawalt, "Hands Off!" 1843–1907.

28 *See supra* notes 9–11 and accompanying text.

29 *See, e.g.*, *Natal*, 878 F.2d at 1578

> We, like plaintiffs, are obligated to accept the Church's decisions "on matters of discipline, faith, internal organization, or ecclesiastical rule, custom, or law." Serbian Eastern Orthodox Diocese, 426 U.S. at 713. . . By its very nature, the inquiry which Natal would have us undertake into the circumstances of his discharge plunges an inquisitor into a maelstrom of Church policy, administration, and governance. It is an inquiry barred by the Free Exercise Clause. For this reason, and because the coplaintiff has also failed to state an actionable claim, the decision and judgment below must be *affirmed*.

see also El-Farra, 226 S.W.3d at 796

> Finally, the courts have held that the First Amendment protects the act of decision rather than the motivation behind it; therefore, whether the termination of appellant was based on secular reasons or Islamic doctrine, this court will not involve itself in ICLR's right to choose ministers without government interference.

the deference afforded religious dispute resolution to a form of institutional sovereignty would seem to countenance few—if any—exceptions. As Richard Schragger and Micah Schwartzman have argued,

> The strong form of sphere sovereignty claims that churches have a special, unique, and exclusive mission to preach the Word, to convert the unconverted, and to glorify God. This is the nature of the jurisdictional claim at its heart, and stated in its baldest form, it seems to countenance very few limits on church immunity. The stakes are too high.[30]

Indeed, if the internal dispute resolution process within religious institutions is afforded deference for reasons of quasi-sovereignty, thereby placing such religious institutions beyond the authority of the state, it is difficult to see what legal principles could be marshaled to place limits on religious institutional authority. And given that there are certainly some claims where we might expect some legal limits on the authority of religious institutions,[31] a sovereignty approach seems to prove too much to serve as a viable framework.

This same problem also plagues public law theories that ground deference in the constitutionally limited competence of courts. On these accounts, religious dispute resolution is granted deference not because of some inherent autonomy granted to religious institutions, but because adjudicating at least some religious claims would require courts to resolve questions of religious doctrine—questions that courts lack the constitutional competence to resolve.[32] The challenge, however, is that refusing to interrogate claims that implicate religious standards creates a legal space where government cannot adequately protect the interests of citizens from serious harms. For example, if a religious institution breached its fiduciary duty to one of its members—for example, where the internal dispute resolution process within a religious institution failed to adequately prevent a religious leader from engaging in sexual misconduct—courts would remain constitutionally disabled from addressing the underlying claims. In the words of two leading scholars, "the Establishment Clause forbids a state from using the civil law to impose a normative vision of the structure of religious organizations."[33]

30 Richard Schragger and Micah Schwartzman, "Against Religious Institutionalism," *Virginia Law Review*, 99, no. 5 (September 2013): 917, 946.

31 *See* Michael A. Helfand, "How to Limit Accommodations: Wrong Answers and Rights Answers," *Journal of Law, Religion and State*, 5, no. 1 (November 2017): 1–24 (discussing, and criticizing, the attempt use of RFRA as a defense to physical violence by a group of rabbis seeking to force husbands to grant their wives religious divorces); Michael A. Helfand, "Implied Consent to Religious Institutions: A Primer and a Defense," *Connecticut Law Review*, 50, no. 4 (December 2018): 877, 894–97 (discussing claims related to sexual misconduct by religious leaders).

32 *See supra* notes 12–14 and accompanying text.

33 Lupu and Tuttle, "Sexual Misconduct," 1844; *see also* ibid., 1845 ("Because such duties of loyalty to all adherents of the faith effectively dictate the mechanisms of control over clergy, and effectively compel a particular organizational response to victims of clergy misbehavior,

This is not to say that public law cannot provide a workable framework for providing space to the religious dispute resolution process. I have, in other contexts, attempted to provide an alternative implied-consent grounding for the constitutional protections afforded by the internal dispute resolution process within religious institutions.[34] But the foregoing identifies some of the core shortcomings of leveraging public law to provide space for religious dispute resolution. Judicial abstention from intervening in a religious institution's dispute resolution system may facilitate the internal adjudication of disputes in accordance with a church's religious rules and values, but—under a pure hands-off paradigm—the church's resolution of those disputes may not be judicially enforced on their terms. Instead, it creates a plaintiff-loses system where possession may be privileged by constitutional rules that simply require courts to remain hands off.

Moreover, the hands-off posture of courts struggles to provide any limitations on the authority of religious institutions when functioning in their dispute resolution capacity. This unregulated space for religious dispute resolution raises worries whether the parties to the process are all guaranteed the types of protections they might presume, or desire, when resolving disputes in accordance with shared religious rules and values. In this way, public law's approach to religious dispute resolution—an approach predicated on either theories of judicial abstention or quasi-institutional sovereignty—raises significant questions as to whether many of the prevailing approaches to public law's treatment of religious dispute resolution provide the optimal framework for ensuring that parties can resolve disputes in accordance with shared religious rules and values.

Religious dispute resolution under private law

Public law is not the only mechanism to create legal space for religious dispute resolution. Private law provides an alternative. Maybe most directly, parties—both individuals and institutions—seeking to resolve disputes in accordance with shared religious rules and values can leverage the contemporary framework of U.S. arbitration law to achieve their objectives through contract.[35] But impor-

---

imposing these duties tends to unconstitutionally establish a legally preferred structure of denominational life").

34 Helfand, "Implied Consent," 877–926; Michael A. Helfand, "Religious Institutionalism, Implied Consent, and the Value of Voluntarism," *Southern California Law Review*, 88, no. 3 (March 2015): 539–86; Michael A. Helfand, "Religion's Footnote Four: Church Autonomy as Arbitration," *Minnesota Law Review*, 97, no. 6 (June 2013): 1891–962; Helfand, "Litigating Religion," 493–562.

35 Indeed, there has been a recent increase in scholarly investigation of religious arbitration. *See, e.g.*, Farrah Ahmed and Senwung Luk, "How Religious Arbitration Could Enhance Personal Autonomy," *Oxford Journal of Law and Religion*, 1, no. 2 (October 2012): 424–45; Amanda M. Baker, "A Higher Authority: Judicial Review of Religious Arbitration," *Vermont Law Review*, 37, no. 1 (Fall 2012): 157–238; Nicholas Walter, "Religious Arbitration in the United States and Canada," *Santa Clara Law Review*, 52, no. 2 (2012): 501–70; Michael C. Grossman, "Is This Arbitration? Religious Tribunals, Judicial Review, and Due Process," *Columbia Law Review*,

tantly, the private law framework, embodied in religious forms of arbitration, is grounded in fundamentally different legal mechanisms—mechanisms that may, in a variety of cases, provide an alternative set of legal outcomes for both individuals and institutions pursuing religious dispute resolution.

Religious forms of arbitration are borne out of attempts to graft religious rules and values on a process of dispute resolution that is both recognized and enforced by U.S. law. Thus, if arbitration represents the voluntary submission of a dispute to a neutral third party for binding resolution,[36] religious arbitration represents the submission of that dispute for binding resolution to a *religious* authority for binding resolution in accordance with *religious* law.[37] By so doing, parties to religious arbitration manifest their intention not simply to resolve a dispute, but to live out shared religious aspirations in the context of dispute resolution.

To achieve these objectives, religious arbitration agreements typically contain two central provisions: choice-of-law provisions that identify the body of religious law that will govern the dispute and an arbitration provision that identifies the religious institution or religious authorities that will be tasked with applying the relevant body of religious law to the case before them.[38] In the United States, the most prominent use of religious arbitration occurs within the three Abrahamic faith communities—Jewish, Islamic and Christian.[39]

107, no. 1 (January 2007): 169–209; Caryn Litt Wolfe, "Faith-Based Arbitration: Friend or Foe? An Evaluation of Religious Arbitration Systems and Their Interaction with Secular Courts," *Fordham Law Review*, 75, no. 1 (October 2006): 427–70; Michael J. Broyde, Ira Bedzow, and Shlomo C. Pill, "The Pillars of Successful Religious Arbitration: Models for American Islamic Arbitration Based on the Beth Din of America and Muslim Arbitration Tribunal Experience," *Harvard Journal on Racial & Ethnic Justice*, 30 (Spring 2014): 33–76; Michael J. Broyde, "Jewish Law Courts in America: Lesson Offered to Sharia Courts by the Beth Din of America Precedent," *New York Law School Law Review*, 57, no. 2 (2012–2013): 287–312.

36 To be sure, the Federal Arbitration Act famously does not provide a definition of "arbitration," an omission that has some important legal consequences. Michael A. Helfand, "Arbitration's Counter-Narrative: The Religious Arbitration Paradigm," *Yale Law Journal*, 124, no. 8 (June 2015): 2994, 3023–42.

37 I have elsewhere explored the unique context of religious arbitration, its relevance for conceptualizing alternative forms of alternative dispute resolution and some of the legal issues raised by applying the current legal framework in the context of religious arbitration. *See* Michael A. Helfand, "The Future of Religious Arbitration in the United States: Looking Through A Pluralist Lens," in *Oxford Legal Handbook on Global Legal Pluralism*, ed. Paul Schiff Berman (New York: Oxford University Press, 2020) 901; Helfand, "Arbitration's Counter-Narrative," 2994; Michael A. Helfand, "Between Law and Religion: Procedural Challenges to Religious Arbitration Awards," *Chicago-Kent Law Review*, 90, no. 1 (2015): 141–62; Michael A. Helfand, "Religious Arbitration and the New Multiculturalism: Negotiating Conflicting Legal Orders," *New York University Law Review*, 86, no. 5 (November 2011): 1231–305; Yaacov Feit and Michael A. Helfand, "Confirming Piskei Din in Secular Court," *Journal of Halacha & Contemporary Society*, 61 (Spring 2011): 5–27.

38 *See* Helfand, "Arbitration's Counter-Narrative," 3015 & n.80.

39 For an extended discussion of religious arbitration in the U.S. Jewish and Islamic communities, *see* Helfand, "Arbitration's Counter-Narrative," 3014–19.; Helfand, "Religious Arbitration," 1247–52).

Of the three, the Jewish *beit din* or rabbinical court is likely the most prominent;[40] as an institution, it appears to have the longest track-record in the United States, with examples of such proceedings dating back at least to the nineteenth century,[41] and currently such rabbinical courts continue to operate across the United States, particularly in large metropolitan areas.[42] While the use of Islamic arbitration appears far less prevalent, there have been a number of attempts within the Muslim community in the past three decades to begin building a larger and more uniform Islamic arbitral system in the United States.[43] And a number of Islamic organizations have developed protocols, rules and procedures for use by Islamic arbitration panels in the United States.[44] Finally, a number of Christian communities also make use of religious forms of alternative dispute resolution.[45] Although Christian dispute resolution often tilts toward non-binding forms of mediation, it also includes options for binding arbitration.[46] Indeed, members of Christian communities interested in Christian dispute resolution can contact a range of Christian dispute resolution service providers.[47]

What all three communities share in common is their use of private law to facilitate religious dispute resolution. This happens at two stages of the dispute resolution process. The first is at the agreement stage where, as noted above, parties incorporate religious objectives into an agreement, providing that religious law will govern the dispute and that religious authorities will serve as the arbitrators applying that religious law. Accordingly, religious arbitration agreements include provisions that require the arbitrators to apply religious law, such

40 For a thorough description of the beit din, see Ginnine Fried, "The Collision of Church and State: A Primer to Beth Din Arbitration and the New York Secular Courts," *Fordham Urban Law Journal*, 31, no. 2 (January 2004): 633–55.

41 *See, e.g.*, *Isaacs v. Beth Hamedash Society*, 1 Hilt. 469 (N.Y.C.P. 1857).

42 *See, e.g.*, Beth Din of America, accessed January 8, 2018, http://www.bethdin.org; "CRC Beth Din," Chicago Rabbinical Council, accessed January 8, 2018, http://www.crcweb.org/bethdin.php; "Beth Din," Rabbinical Council of California, accessed January 8, 2018,https://rccvaad.org/beth-din/.

43 Helfand, "Arbitration's Counter-Narrative," 3017 & n.91.

44 Ibid., 3017.

45 The arbitration agreements for Christian forms of arbitration have frequently found their way into U.S. courts and have been almost uniformly upheld. *See, e.g.*, *Prescott v. Northlake Christian Sch.*, 141 F. App'x 263 (5th Cir. 2005); *Fardig v. Hobby Lobby Stores, Inc.*, No. SACV 14–561, 2014 U.S. Dist. LEXIS 87284 (C.D. Cal. June 13, 2014); *Easterly v. Heritage Christian Schs., Inc.*, No. 1:08–cv–1714, 2009 U.S. Dist. LEXIS 76269 (S.D. Ind. Aug. 26, 2009); *Encore Prods., Inc. v. Promise Keepers*, 53 F. Supp. 2d 1101 (D. Colo 1999).

46 *See* R. Seth Shippee, ""Blessed Are the Peacemakers": Faith-Based Approaches to Dispute Resolution," *ILSA Journal of International & Comparative Law*, 9, no. 1 (Fall 2002): 237, 241; Grossman, "Is This Arbitration?" 177–78.

47 Shippee, "Blessed," 242–45 (describing some of the Christian ADR alternatives available). Notable Christian arbitration service providers include the Institute for Christian Conciliation. *See* "Open a Case," Institute for Christian Conciliation, accessed January 8, 2018, https://www.instituteforchristianconciliation.com/open-a-case/.

as "Ecclesiastical Islamic Law"[48] and "Jewish Law,"[49] or to apply "the Holy Scriptures (the Bible)" as the "supreme authority governing every aspect of the conciliation process."[50] And these choice-of-law provisions are then combined with arbitration provisions that identify a religious arbitration service provider and thereby ensure that religious authorities will apply the relevant body of religious rules to the dispute.[51]

While private dispute resolution, and particularly arbitration, generally affords participants a range of benefits, including lower costs, greater efficiency and speed,[52] parties pursuing religious dispute resolution seem to put a particular premium on the pursuit of shared religious values when entering this form adjudication. As I have described elsewhere, one way to identify the importance of religious values to the participants to religious dispute resolution is to compare the use of pre- and post-dispute arbitration provisions in both standard and religious arbitration. In the context of standard business arbitration, studies have demonstrated that the overwhelming majority of submitted disputes are conducted pursuant to pre-dispute arbitration agreements.[53] These numbers indicate that parties to either business to business or employment arbitrations are very reluctant to arbitrate after a dispute arises, which from the perspective of strategic decision-making is far from surprising. Once the parties know both the facts and relevant legal principles relevant to the dispute, it is unlikely that they both will simultaneously conclude that arbitration will best serve their interests; invariably, arbitration will be seen as preferable to one party or the other—but

48 *See, e.g.*, *Mansour v. Islamic Educ. Ctr. of Tampa, Inc.*, No. 08-CA-3497 (Fla Cir. Ct. Mar. 22, 2011), http://jameswebdesign.com/~theproce/images/1377729140.pdf.

49 "Standard Binding Arbitration Agreement," Beth Din of America Documents, accessed February 7, 2020, https://bethdin.org/forms/.

50 "Rules of Procedure for Christian Conciliation," Inst. for Christian Conciliation, accessed February 7, 2020, https://peacemaker.training/wp-content/uploads/2019/03/ICC_Rules_v2019_January.pdf.

51 *See, e.g.*, "Standard Binding Arbitration Agreement," Beth Din of America Documents, accessed February 7, 2020, https://bethdin.org/forms/ (boilerplate rabbinical arbitration agreement that submits dispute to the Beth Din of America); *Jabri v. Qaddura*, 108 S.W.3d 404 (Tx. App. Ct. 2003) (enforcing an arbitration agreement that submitted a dispute to the Texas Islamic Court).

52 *Stolt-Nielsen S.A. v. Animal Feeds Intl Corp.*, 559 U.S. 662, 685 (2010) (noting that parties selecting arbitration "forgo the procedural rigor and appellate review of the courts in order to realize the benefits of private dispute resolution: lower costs, greater efficiency and speed, and the ability to choose expert adjudicators to resolve specialized disputes").

53 *See, e.g.*, Lewis L. Maltby, "Out of the Frying Pan, into the Fire: The Feasibility of Post-Dispute Employment Arbitration Agreements," *William Mitchell Law Review*, 30, no. 1 (2003): 313–30; *see also* Linda J. Demaine and Deborah R. Hensler, "'Volunteering' to Arbitrate through Predispute Arbitration Clauses: The Average Consumer's Experience," *Law & Contemporary Problems*, 67, no. 1 & 2 (Winter/Spring 2004): 55–74; Christopher R. Drahozal and Samantha Zyontz, "Private Regulation of Consumer Arbitration," *Tennessee Law Review*, 79, no. 2 (Winter 2012): 289, 346–47; Theodore Eisenberg, Geoffrey P. Miller, and Emily Sherwin, "Arbitration's Summer Soldiers: An Empirical Study of Arbitration Clauses in Consumer and Nonconsumer Contracts," *University of Michigan Journal of Law Reform*, 41, no. 4 (Summer 2008): 871–96.

not both. And therefore securing both parties' assent to arbitration post-dispute is an unlikely outcome.

However, according to records of over five years of arbitration proceedings before the Beth Din of America—one of the largest religious arbitration service providers in the United States—nearly 97% of its arbitration proceedings between January 2008 and August 2014 were conducted pursuant to a post-dispute arbitration agreement.[54] This inversion of the general trend is also evident from websites of religious arbitration providers, which frequently offer boilerplate post-dispute arbitration agreements, but do not include model pre-dispute arbitration provisions.[55]

These indications offer a very different picture of the motivations driving the parties to religious arbitration; while strategic decision-making when it comes to standard commercial arbitration almost eliminates arbitrations conducted pursuant to post-dispute agreements, the same is not true with respect to religious arbitration. Thus, while parties to religious arbitration presumably engage in strategic decision-making, the broad use of post-dispute religious arbitration agreements indicates that other considerations not present in the context of standard arbitration—what I have suggested elsewhere are considerations of religious aspirations and values—drive the parties to mutually agree on arbitration.

The relative advantages of private law over public law for religious dispute resolution

So are there implications of pursuing religious dispute resolution under the private law framework as opposed to the public law framework? The short answer is yes. The private law framework, like its public law counterpart, affords parties the opportunity to pursue religious values—a fact manifested in both the provisions of a religious arbitration agreement and the timing of its execution. However, the fundamental difference between public law's and private law's treatment of religious dispute resolution comes in the award enforcement stage.

As a general rule, arbitration proceedings end with the arbitrators issuing an award resolving the submitted dispute. And the arbitration award, if issued pursuant to duly executed arbitration agreements, can then be enforced by either party in court.[56] To be sure, a party can challenge the award—and thereby seek vacatur of the award—on statutorily defined grounds,[57] which primarily consist

54 Shlomo Weissmann, Director of Beth Din of America, email message to author, December 2, 2014.

55 *See, e.g.*, "Din Torah-Halachic Arbitration," Chicago Rabbinical Council, accessed January 12, 2018, http://www.crcweb.org/dintorah.php (providing a post-dispute arbitration agreement, but no pre-dispute boilerplate provision); "Financial Arbitration & Din Torah," Rabbinical Council of California, accessed January 12, 2018, http://rccvaad.org/financial-arbitration-din-torah/.

56 9 U.S.C. §9 (2018).

57 *See Hall St. Assocs., LLC. v. Mattel, Inc.*, 552 U.S. 576 (2008).

of forms of procedural misconduct.[58] But so long as the award clears these two hurdles—the parties duly executing an arbitration agreement and the absence of any forms of arbitral misconduct—a court must enforce the award.[59]

In this way, the private law framework differs markedly from public law's hands-off approach. Instead of simply avoiding judicial involvement on constitutional grounds, private law's arbitration framework requires a court to enforce the decision on its terms. From the perspective of parties seeking the application of religious rules and values to the resolution of their dispute, enforcement—as opposed to abstention—has some decided advantages.[60] As noted above, a hands-off approach—which is an approach predicated on constitutionally mandated abstention—fails to ensure that the faith community's rules or values are actually applied to the resolution of the dispute. This gap between principle and practice is ultimately a function of public law's hands-off approach where a court simply remains on the sidelines as opposed to enforcing a decision that flows from the religious rules and values of the relevant faith community. To return to the example above of the terminated pastor, a court approaching the outcome from public law's vantage point might not enforce a determination as to whether the pastor's termination was legally justified. Instead, a court might conclude that its constitutional limitations required it to leave the parties where they stood, regardless of whether the right outcome was actually reflected in the legally enforced remedies.

By contrast, by integrating religious dispute resolution into private law's system of arbitration, an arbitrator can allocate liability—and even divide up liability—in whatever way he sees fit based upon the very religious principles that animate the parties' shared religious worldview. Using the aforementioned example of the terminated pastor, if an arbitrator determined that the pastor's termination was justified under the agreed upon religious rules, then he could not only excuse the church from liability, but also require the pastor to return the paycheck that was accidently deposited in his bank account. In turn, because courts enforce the arbitrator's decision, private law's framework for religious dispute resolution ensures that the ultimate liabilities imposed on the parties draw directly from the religious principles and values they had hoped would inform the ultimate outcome.

The benefits of private law's framework for religious dispute resolution extend beyond the benefits of enforcement over deference. They also extend to the

58 9 U.S.C. §10 (2018).

59 9 U.S.C. §9 (2018).

60 To be sure, the state's enforcement of arbitration awards, while it may provide advantages, still subordinates non-state law—and arbitral awards issued pursuant to agreements that incorporate such law—to the authority of the state. In the words of Ralf Michaels, "In all these situations, non-state communities produce their own rules and the state acknowledges them as law but only as law that is subordinate to state law." Michaels, "The Re-State-Ment," 1235. For more discussion of religious arbitration and its position in a "weak legal pluralism" regime, see Helfand, "Future."

ability of the judicial system to police certain forms of procedural misconduct. As noted above, when religious dispute resolution proceeds under the private law framework, the decisions of the religious tribunals—because they are fashioned as arbitration tribunals—are subjected to the same categories of judicial oversight as all other arbitration awards. Thus, the various grounds for vacating an arbitration award apply, in large measure, equally to religious forms of arbitration.[61] These categories include instances of "corruption, fraud, or undue means,"[62] "evident partiality or corruption in the arbitrators,"[63] various forms of procedural "misconduct,"[64] and cases "where the arbitrators exceeded their powers."[65] And while it is certainly the case that motions to vacate are typically unsuccessful,[66] the statutory grounds for vacatur provide procedural side constraints to ensure that the most blatant forms of bias and misconduct render awards unenforceable. As a result, when religious dispute resolution adopts the private law frame, participants retain some degree of protection from arbitral malfeasance, thereby ensuring that the ultimate decision more likely reflects the parties' selected religious principles and values—as opposed to corruption, partiality and fraud.

There was a time when courts, adopting the public law frame, also imposed similar side constraints. Under the framework adopted in its early cases exploring the institutional autonomy afforded religious institutions, the Supreme Court held that the decisions of religious institutions "are accepted in litigation before the secular courts as conclusive," but only after a "marginal civil court review"[67] ensuring the "the absence of fraud, collusion, or arbitrariness."[68] Indeed, as I have traced elsewhere, these constraints were embraced by lower courts as well.[69]

61 It is worth noting, however, that there are some potential grounds for vacating an arbitration award that cannot be easily applied to religious arbitration—most notably, when the grounds for challenging a religious arbitration award require investigating compliance with religious rules. In those circumstances, the strictures of the Establishment Clause's religious question doctrine prohibit courts from assessing claims that require judicial inquiry into matters of religious doctrine and theology. I have explored such circumstances, and my related criticism of applying the religious question doctrine, in Helfand, "Between Law and Religion," 141, as well as in Part III.A of Helfand, "Future."

62 9 U.S.C. §10(a)(1) (2018).

63 9 U.S.C. §10(a)(2) (2018).

64 9 U.S.C. §10(a)(3) (2018).

65 9 U.S.C. §10(a)(4) (2018).

66 Christopher R. Drahozal and Peter B. Rutledge, "Contract and Procedure," *Marquette Law Review*, 94, no. 4 (Summer 2011): 1103, 1151 (noting, in passing, that "only rarely do courts vacate arbitration awards"); Paul F. Kirgis, "Judicial Review and the Limits of Arbitral Authority: Lessons from the Law of Contract," *St. John's Law Review*, 81, no. 1 (Winter 2007) 99, 104 ("The bottom line is that awards are rarely vacated by courts on any grounds").

67 *Presbyterian Church in U.S. v. Mary Elizabeth Blue Hull Mem'l Presbyterian Church*, 393 U.S. 440, 447 (1969).

68 Gonzalez v. Roman Catholic Archbishop, 280 U.S. 1, 16 (1929); *see also Bouldin v. Alexander*, 82 U.S. (15 Wall.) 131, 140 (1872) ("In a congregational church, the majority, *if they adhere to the organization and to the doctrines*, represent the church" (emphasis added)).

69 Helfand, "Religion's Footnote Four,"1942–51).

However, as the Court increasingly incorporated the religious question doctrine into the constitutional framework governing religious institutions, this standard of judicial review was deemed unconstitutional. Thus, with respect to assessing the decisions of religious institutions for arbitrariness, the Court held:

> For civil courts to analyze whether the ecclesiastical actions of a church judicatory are in that sense 'arbitrary' must inherently entail inquiry into the procedures that canon or ecclesiastical law supposedly requires the church judicatory to follow, or else into the substantive criteria by which they are supposedly to decide the ecclesiastical question ... [which] is exactly the inquiry that the First Amendment prohibits ....[70]

And as other lower courts have noted, this logic—although not explicitly applied to judicial review for fraud and collusion—all but assuredly makes all such forms of oversight on the decisions of religious institutions a constitutional impossibility.[71]

As a result, public law's deference framework—which has defined the contemporary Court's treatment of religious institutional autonomy—undermines the ability of lower courts to police religious dispute resolution.[72] In this way, the relationship between courts and religious dispute resolution varies quite significantly, depending on whether it proceeds under the public law versus the private law umbrella. Under the former, courts lack the doctrinal resources to provide any meaningful review of decisions rendered via the dispute resolution process conducted by religious institutions. Under the latter, courts can leverage the statutory grounds for vacating arbitration awards to ensure minimum standards of procedural fairness. And these protections represent an advantage for participants who ultimately seek adjudication based upon substantive religious rules, principles and values—and not self-dealing, fraud and bias.

To be sure, from the perspective of religious communities, private law may present a significant disadvantage. Ultimately, under private law, the authority of religious institutions to resolve disputes is contingent on the agreement of the parties. And to the extent religious communities hope to organize life around religious rules and principles, private law's threshold requirement—that the individual parties agree to submit a given dispute to religious arbitrators—injects significant uncertainty into the viability of communal enforcement of religious

70 *Serbian E. Orthodox Diocese v. Milivojevich*, 426 U.S. 696, 713 (1976).

71 *See, e.g.*, *Young v. N. Ill. Conference of United Methodist Church*, 21 F.3d 184, 187 (7th Cir. 1994) (recognizing that the Supreme Court left open the possibility of review for fraud or collusion, but noting the "unlikely significance this "open issue" might have in some hypothetical case"); *Church of Scientology Flag Serv. Org., Inc. v. City of Clearwater*, 2 F.3d 1514, 1541 (11th Cir. 1993) (casting doubt on the constitutional viability of judicial review of religious decisions for fraud or collusion).

72 I have elsewhere criticized this shift in constitutional doctrine for this very reason. *See generally* Helfand, "Religion's Footnote Four," 1891.

norms. In any given instance, particular members may choose to reject community norms in favor of judicial resolution of a dispute.

Of course, this possibility will not be troubling to all advocates of religious dispute resolution. Indeed, for those normatively committed to the principle of voluntarism, the need for individual and individualized consent to religious dispute resolution holds the benefit that the application of religious rules and norms to any given dispute will flow from the voluntary choices of the participants. But irrespective of one's normative commitment, there is no doubt that a shift from public law to private law also represents a shift in authority from religious institutions to religious individuals. And to the extent that members within a particular community begin executing religious arbitration agreements—as opposed to relying on the authority of religious institutions to conduct internal forms of religious dispute resolution—that shift will cabin the ability of religious institutions to serve as a central adjudicatory force.

That being said, religious communities that rely on private religious dispute resolution still have methods to maintain adjudicatory standards among their membership. For example, religious institutions can integrate arbitration provisions into house-of-worship by-laws, requiring all members of the community to resolve all of their disputes with the institution via private religious dispute resolution.[73] Thus, instead of the institution itself conducting internal dispute resolution, it can select a neutral third party—such as a religious dispute resolution service provider—to resolve all disputes between the institution and any of its members. And communities that worry about individual members refusing to submit disputes for religious dispute resolution can adopt various forms of social sanctions in order to police compliance with religious standards, thereby imposing a cost on all those who do not agree to submit their disputes for religious adjudication.[74] In fact, courts have been willing to enforce religious arbitration agreements executed under the threat of social sanctions, notwithstanding claims that such threats rendered the agreements unenforceable on account of duress. No doubt, extreme forms of social sanctions undermine the voluntaristic impulse that animates private law's framework for religious dispute resolution, raising serious questions about whether judicial reluctance to invalidate agreements signed under the threat of social sanctions is advisable.[75] But from the perspective of communities worried that private law's framework undermines the ability of institutions to enforce religious standards for dispute resolution, creative drafting combined with limited social sanctions can help close the gap between private and public law.

73 *See, e.g.*, *Meshel v. Ohev Sholom Talmud Torah*, 869 A.2d 343, 362 (D.C. App. 2005).

74 I have argued that both under public and private law, religious institutions and religious arbitration should be governed by rules drawing from principles of voluntarism. *See supra* note 34.

75 I have argued that courts should be far more willing to invalidate such agreements. *See* Helfand, "Arbitration's Counter-Narrative," 3042–51.

Conclusion

Religious dispute resolution provides institutions and individuals with the opportunity to ensure that conflicts are resolved in accordance with religious rules and principles. So doing allows shared religious values to govern not only the daily lives of the religiously committed, but also the tense moments within religious communities when disputes disrupt communal calm.

But the decision to pursue religious, as opposed to judicial, dispute resolution is itself somewhat multifaceted. Both public law and private law provide divergent frameworks to institutionalize religious dispute resolution. Many religious communities have relied upon the constitutional protections afforded religious institutions in choosing to insulate religious dispute resolution. However, that choice comes with some significant consequences; most notably, public law adopts a judicial hands-off approach to religious dispute resolution, which prevents courts from both enforcing religious decisions on their terms and policing the process of dispute resolution for various forms of fraud and bias. In this way, public law's frame of abstention may not serve as the ideal method for religious dispute resolution.

Instead, as argued above, pursuing religious dispute resolution under a private law framework provides some significant advantages. As a form of arbitration, private religious dispute resolution allows participants to submit religious arbitration awards for judicial enforcement. Moreover, under the rubric of arbitration, courts also retain the ability to police private religious dispute resolution for adjudicatory malfeasance, including a range of misconduct that could otherwise undermine the religious principles and values that are meant to animate the arbitral outcome. While not without potential downsides for religious communities, creating space for religious dispute resolution through private law as opposed to public law—and shifting some degree of authority from communal institutions to individual participants—may create a mechanism for resolving conflict that adheres more closely to the ultimate objective of ensuring the disputes are resolved in accordance with shared religious rules and values.

Part IV

Torts

14 The moral of torts

Michael P. Moreland and Jeffrey A. Pojanowski

Introduction

Tort theory is an anxious field, either trying to explain the body of tort law through a unified account or surrendering to the view that torts is just an accumulation of ad hoc "policy" judgments without a consistent explanatory basis. In this chapter, we argue that the natural law theory in the Christian tradition breaks through this impasse in tort theory by showing how the basic outlines of tort law are properly derived from principles of morality, while the details within that framework are left open for choice among a wide range of reasonable arrangements. In our view, central aspects of natural law theory such as its account of the relation of law and morality and the manner in which positive law is derived from the natural law explain and justify tort doctrine.

In Part I, we set forth the vexing, ongoing debate in contemporary tort law between internalist and externalist accounts. We argue that both sides demand too much of the other and that the various external and internal accounts in the academic tort literature all suffer from serious shortcomings. It is hardly surprising that both the 1L student trying to make sense of torts and the longtime teacher of the subject find themselves torn between a view that torts is a tidy and unified system of rules and doctrines and a view that torts is just an accumulation of common law cases over the centuries with few, if any, unifying principles. The surveyor of contemporary tort law cannot help but sympathize with A.W.B. Simpson's view that "In such a system of law as the common law the explanation for the degree of consensus which exists at any one time will be very complex, and no *general* explanation will be possible."[1]

In Part II, we reset the discussion by starting with Aristotle's distinction between natural and legal justice, those principles of justice that are universal and those that are subject to convention and variation. This distinction in Aristotle is an important piece of the philosophical background to Thomas Aquinas's view about the relation of natural law (and the principles of morality attached to it) and positive law, all of which is set within a larger account of divine providential

1 A.W.B. Simpson, "The Common Law and Legal Theory," in *Oxford Essays in Jurisprudence (Second Series)*, ed. A.W.B. Simpson (Oxford: Clarendon Press, 1973), 96.

governance of the world and human knowledge of moral principles by rational participation. Aquinas's multivalent view of how natural law and positive law are related allows for both a strong relation of positive law to morality (including, as we will argue, the morality of non-maleficence at the core of tort law) and an open range of indifferent, though reasonable options. In this way, the natural law tradition in Christianity helps one see that the choice between either a unified "moralism" (in a broad sense of the term) or a wholesale skepticism about tort law is a false alternative. Through natural law—or, more precisely, a natural law account of the positive law—unsettled aspects of contemporary tort theory can be redefined and better understood.

In Part III, we use this Thomistic natural law framework to point out briefly areas of tort doctrine that have been difficult to understand in the usual debates in tort theory such as the central role of intentional torts, *respondeat superior*, and the pockets of strict liability in a tort regime dominated by negligence. In conclusion, we bring our discussion back to the theme of this book and show how a natural law account of torts is related to Christian critiques of private law.

The search for a grand unified theory of torts

Tort theory in American law in the past century offers a struggle between two types of accounts of the doctrine. First, there are external accounts that claim the surface of the doctrine obscures tort law's actual purposes and functions. Second, internal accounts contend that the best way to understand tort law is to take its stated rules, principles, and structure seriously.[2] Both kinds of accounts seek unifying theories of tort law, of a sort, though the external approach seeks explanation and justification outside the subject it seeks to theorize.

From early in the twentieth century until the 1970s, the dominant, unified theory was externalist, holding that tort law was primarily a continuous process of pragmatic, judicial policy adjustment. To that point its theory was, in an important sense, antitheoretical. Starting in the 1960s and 1970s, economic analysis of law began to offer more sophisticated and rigorous versions of this externalist account. From the latter quarter of the twentieth century to the present, however, tort law witnessed a ferment of theorizing that was critical of this externalist, instrumental view of tort law. Both corrective justice and civil recourse theories, whatever their differences, share the goal of demonstrating that tort law is more than ad hoc policy balancing and not simply public regulation by adjudicative means.

Yet despite the impressive and fruitful work of these more ambitious tort scholars in the past quarter century, nagging doubts about the interpretive and prescriptive completeness of those theories—or any such theories—remain. We find

2 On this distinction, *see* John C. P. Goldberg and Benjamin C. Zipursky, "Seeing Tort Law from the Internal Point of View: Holmes and Hart on Legal Duties," *Fordham Law Review*, 75, no. 3 (2006): 1563–1592.

Scott Hershovitz, a figure by no means hostile to tort theory, concluding that a "search for a Grand Unified Theory is misguided; we ought not expect simple explanations for complicated and contingent institutions, like tort."[3] Even less optimistically, we see legal philosophers Larry Alexander and Kimberly Kessler Ferzan contending that tort law remains best understood as "a motley collection of doctrines that are impossible to justify under any recognizable and attractive normative principles."[4]

We are not as pessimistic as Alexander and Ferzan, but we share Hershovitz's concern that the most ambitious, unifying theories of tort law either elide or fail to offer a satisfying account for the rough edges around the "motley" and "contingent" body of tort law. Taking an initial stab at the explanation will be the work of the second section of this chapter, but to set the stage for our positive argument we first offer a thumbnail sketch of the path that led tort theory to its current state of uncertainty.

Externalist tort theories

For much of the twentieth century, external, instrumentalist understandings reigned supreme in tort theory, if not always in practice. As with much of American jurisprudence, this strain of theorizing marched to the beat set by Oliver Wendell Holmes, who eschewed moralizing and was inclined to describe legal doctrine as the shifting superstructure atop so many judicial policy judgments. Beneath the surface of the tort lawyer's talk of duty, breach, and legal cause, lurk more ultimate questions like "how far it is desirable that the public should insure the safety of those whose work it uses."[5] According to Holmes, judgments on these questions of value, not the structure and elements of the doctrine, shape and explain the path of tort law.

As Legal Realism developed Holmes's framework, tort theory followed suit. Leon Green was exemplary in this respect. Tort law, Green contended, was simply public regulation by means of private adjudication, rather than a practice with its own goals or integrity internal to itself.[6] Reflecting the Legal Realist's skepticism of doctrinal rules, Green did not organize his casebook according to discrete torts and their elements, but rather grouped cases into situation types like "Railway and Automobile Traffic" and "Conduct of Children and Insane

3 Scott Hershovitz, "The Search for a Grand Unified Theory of Tort Law," *Harvard Law Review*, 130, no. 3 (2017): 943.

4 Larry Alexander and Kimberly Kessler Ferzan, "Confused Culpability, Contrived Causation, and the Collapse of Tort Theory," in *Philosophical Foundations of the Law of Torts*, ed. John Oberdiek (Oxford: Oxford University Press, 2014), 406.

5 Oliver Wendell Holmes, "The Path of the Law," *Harvard Law Review*, 10, no. 8 (1897): 467. For a general discussion on Holmes's regulatory conception of tort law, *see* John C.P. Goldberg and Benjamin C. Zipursky, "The Moral of *MacPherson*," *University of Pennsylvania Law Review*, 146, no. 6 (1998): 1753–1756.

6 *See, e.g.*, Leon Green, "Tort Law: Public Law in Disguise," *Texas Law Review*, 38, no. 1 (1959): 1–14.

Persons."[7] Doing so would allow students to get to the root of tort law, which was understanding judges' responses to the interests in play in different types of disputes.

Yet Green did go not far beyond the contention that tort law was seriatim judicial interest-balancing, a hesitance which gave the impression that torts was simply "the aggregate of cases administered" and that the subject as a whole was in "a disorganized or fluid state."[8] In this sense, Green is a paradigmatic Legal Realist social scientist, content to focus on tort law's concrete situation types.[9]

On the heels of Green, however, emerged a form of instrumentalism that sought to clarify the policy aims of tort law while also working within the received doctrinal framework. The central player here is William Prosser, the Reporter of the Restatement (Second) of Torts and doyen of mid-century tort scholarship. Unlike the arch-Realist Green's particularism, Prosser and deterrence-compensation theorists were willing to place an overarching grid on the entirety of tort law, viewing it as a (moderately) flexible framework for incentivizing against antisocial conduct, giving recompense to the victims of the undeterred, and spreading the risks of a modern industrialized society.[10]

The relationship between this theoretical framework and tort doctrine was complicated. No Restatement Reporter can be a doctrinal nihilist, and Prosser's rendition of torts left much of the traditional edifice intact. Yet traditional elements were re-theorized along the lines of the deterrence-compensation framework. For example, the duty element of negligence was reconceived as "a shorthand statement" that merely represented the "sum total of those considerations of policy which lead the law to say that a particular plaintiff was entitled to protection."[11] This stands in sharp contrast to the traditional, more relational understanding duty articulated by Justice Brett in *Heaven v. Pender* or Judge Cardozo in *Long Island Railroad v. Palsgraf.* Under Prosser's rendition, the topography of tort law has the same landmarks, though the justificatory ground beneath them shifted. The language of duty, breach, and legal causation point toward other public ends beyond the ambit of their private law argot and, compared to traditional tort law, their application changed accordingly.

The apotheosis of tort theory externalism, however, came with the law and economics movement, which sought to rigorize the back-of-the-envelope policy analysis that characterized mid-century deterrence and compensation theories. The regulatory vision of tort law remained: the purpose of tort litigation was to give actors the proper ex ante incentives to act with efficient precaution. This

7 Leon Green, *The Judicial Process in Tort Cases*, 2nd ed. (St. Paul, MN: West Publishing, 1939), xi–xii. On Green's casebook, *see* G. Edward White, *Tort Law in America: An Intellectual History*, 2nd ed. (Oxford: Oxford University Press, 2003), 85–87.

8 White, *supra* note 7, at 111.

9 *See* White, *supra* note 7, at 111–112.

10 For a more detailed explanation of deterrence compensation theory, see John C.P. Goldberg, "Twentieth-Century Tort Theory," *Georgetown Law Journal*, 91, no. 3 (2003): 521–537.

11 William L. Prosser, *Law of Torts*, 4th ed. (St. Paul, MN: West Publishing, 1971), 325–326.

may point toward a negligence regime, with Richard Posner grasping the Hand Formula to theorize the breach element in terms of cost-efficient precaution. Alternatively, as Guido Calabresi argued, economic analysis might point toward a regime of strict liability for reducing the cost of accidents. Either way, to the extent economic analysis was offered as an interpretation of existing tort law, it suggested that the surface discussion of doctrine concealed the practice's deeper regulatory purposes. When offered as a prescription for how tort law ought to work, economic analysis sought to remake the doctrine in its image. Hence, we see Posner reducing the rich contours of breach to cost-benefit analysis or theorists like Calabresi pressing for the expansion of strict liability.

Holmes, Green, Prosser, and Posner share the commitment that traditional tort doctrine is best understood as pointing at regulatory purposes beyond itself. The normative content of that vision was as vibrant as it was bloodless. Green's particularistic approach cohered with the agnostic strain of Legal Realism that simply sought to better understand the policy judgments courts made on the ground. Holmes's moral skepticism was notorious, but his approach to tort law had a prescriptive ethos, foreshadowing the cost-benefit analysis further elaborated by Prosser and the more nuanced economic analysis developed in the latter half of the century. Overall, the dominant strain of externalist thought views tort law as a rule-utilitarian operationalization of welfare economics with a side business in insurance.

Internalist tort theories

Starting in the latter quarter of the twentieth century, legal philosophers began challenging the dominant externalist paradigm. From these critiques emerged the competing theories of corrective justice and civil recourse, which focus on the structure and doctrine of tort law on its own terms, rather than understanding them as private law instruments serving external public goals.

Corrective justice approaches view tort law as an institution for requiring the beneficiary of a wrongful gain to return the loss he has imposed,[12] or, put slightly differently, for making those responsible for wrongful losses of others to fulfill their duty of repair.[13] The flowering of corrective justice theory coincided with, or grew out of, critiques of externalist approaches to tort law. Such instrumental approaches had trouble, for example, explaining: the requirement of causation (if we want to deter bad behavior, why punish only those who actually caused accidents?), the fact that injured plaintiffs have the *option* to sue (why not require them to sue to ensure effective precaution?), why breach instructions and lay juror intuitions do not follow the algebraic Hand Formula, or the persistence of the doctrine's moralizing language in general and the traditional duty

12 *See* Ernest Weinrib, *Corrective Justice* (Oxford: Oxford University Press, 2012), 17.

13 *See* Jules Coleman, "The Practice of Corrective Justice," *Arizona Law Review*, 37, no. 1 (1995): 15.

element in particular. Corrective justice, by contrast, better explains the bilateral structure of tort law, which predicates liability on a private suit by a party who can causally connect his loss to the wrongful act of the defendant.

Civil recourse theorists, while similarly committed to taking the doctrine and structure of tort law seriously, contend that corrective justice does not offer an adequate account of tort law.[14] Civil recourse theorists, of whom John Goldberg and Benjamin Zipursky are the most prominent, identify a number of explanatory gaps in corrective justice theory. First, tort judgments do not always obviously return the loss suffered. Few people, after all, would trade a generous lump sum cash payment for the loss of a leg or loved one. Similarly, corrective justice has a difficult time accounting for nominal and punitive damages, or for tort liability without fault. Furthermore, if tort law corrected an injustice that arose at the time of the wrong, one might expect pre-judgment interest awarded with tort damages, but that is not the case.

Thus, while civil recourse theorists think corrective justice gets a lot right about the structure of tort law, they contend that tort law is better understood as a publicly provided forum in which private parties can obtain redress for wrongs committed against them. As described by Goldberg and Zipursky, according to the principle of civil recourse "certain persons—including those whose legally recognized rights against injury have been violated by a breach of a corresponding legal duty of noninjury—are entitled to have the state provide them with civil recourse against wrongdoers."[15] There is a serious argument that civil recourse theory is in fact an improved version of corrective justice, one that understands corrective justice in a framework that is broader than the overly narrow Aristotelian picture of restoring equilibrium and more realistic about what legal institutions can do about injuries that cannot be undone.[16] Call it corrective justice in a vale of tears.

Compared to the externalist approaches, corrective justice and civil recourse theories offer a better account of much of the structure and content of tort law as we find it. Yet these approaches face their own challenges. As a normative matter, they can appear to be either too thick or too thin. On the thick end, for example, Arthur Ripstein offers a strongly Kantian theory that is hard to square with many central features of tort law.[17] Somewhere between the thick and thin lies Ernest Weinrib, whose approach to tort law is also thoroughly Kantian but rejects as crass instrumentalism the notion that tort law should serve higher moral purposes. Tort law, like love, exists for its own sake.[18] This notion is baffling for

14 *See, e.g.*, Benjamin D. Zipursky, "Civil Recourse, Not Corrective Justice," *Georgetown Law Journal*, 91, no. 3 (2003): 695–756.

15 John C. P. Goldberg and Benjamin C. Zipurksy, *Recognizing Wrongs* (Cambridge, MA: Harvard University Press, 2020), 112–13.

16 For this argument, *see* Scott Hershovitz, "Corrective Justice for Civil Recourse Theorists," *Florida State Law Review*, 39, no. 1 (2011): 107–128.

17 Arthur Ripstein, *Private Wrongs* (Cambridge, MA: Harvard University Press, 2016); Hershovitz, *supra* note 3.

18 Ernest Weinrib, *The Idea of Private Law* (Oxford: Oxford University Press, 1995), 6.

those who view human law as a project of practical reasoning about justice and the common good. Furthermore, the Aristotelian theory of corrective justice upon which Weinrib draws has little to say about what counts as a wrong and what counts as just compensation.[19]

On the thin end, Goldberg and Zipursky persuasively argue that tort is best understood as a system of recourse regarding private wrongs, but are hesitant to offer normative criteria for what ought to be regarded as a wrong.[20] In fact, they are careful to distinguish between tort wrongs and moral wrongs. This should not be surprising, as Goldberg and Zipursky understand their project in terms of H.L.A. Hart's descriptive jurisprudence,[21] and it is true that the overlap between moral wrongs and tort wrongs is not complete. But even on descriptive terms, a sharp distinction between tort wrongs and moral wrongs is troubling, given how much of the doctrine theorists seek to describe is morally laden. More critically, those unsatisfied with Hartian analysis will seek more. If tort law notions like "correction" and "restitution" are most plausibly understood as "parasitic on some prior determination" of what counts as a wrong,[22] it seems unavoidable for theorists and jurists to pursue such deeper questions for purposes of justifying the institution as a whole or reforming or extending particular doctrines in light of new circumstances.

The question remains whether it is possible to offer a normatively rich theory of tort law that accounts for the fact that tort law as we find it is untidy, a "complicated and contingent institution." Relatedly, one also seeks a theory that takes the doctrinal content and structure seriously on its own terms while also respecting the externalists' insight that tort law, like all legal institutions, serves purposes beyond itself.

Aquinas on natural and human law

What might the Christian legal and moral tradition contribute to this impasse or uncertainty in modern tort theory? At first glance, the question might seem an odd one, for all sides in the contemporary debate in tort theory have avoided strong claims about the "morality" of tort law altogether, with the partial exception of corrective justice theorists (sometimes drawing on Aristotle) and those such as Ripstein who have offered robustly Kantian accounts of tort law that place concepts such as autonomy and respect at the center of their theory. As noted, even the civil recourse view about the "wrongs" that tort law seeks to redress assiduously avoids discussion of "moral" wrongs. And it would also be flatfooted for those interested in Christian approaches to law to argue that tort law is a

19 John Finnis, "A Grand Tour of Legal Theory," in *Philosophy of Law: Collected Essays: Volume IV* (Oxford: Oxford University Press, 2009), 138.

20 John C. P. Goldberg and Benjamin D. Zipursky, "Torts as Wrongs," *Texas Law Review*, 88, no. 5 (2010): 917–986.

21 *See* Goldberg and Zipursky, *supra* note 2.

22 John M. Finnis, *Natural Law and Natural Rights* (Oxford: Oxford University Press, 1980), 178.

reflection, however pale, of Christian morality. The traditional sources of Christian moral teachings such as the Beatitudes and the Ten Commandments—with their exhortations to supererogation, love of God, and love of neighbor—surely go a great deal further than the seemingly minimal harm-policing of tort law, while, conversely, much of tort law is seemingly mundane and unattached from moral questions.

In at least one important respect, however, we believe that an element of the Christian moral and legal tradition provides a heuristic for addressing the debate in contemporary tort theory we laid out in Part I: natural law theory, as classically expressed in the thought of Thomas Aquinas (more precisely, the Thomistic account of the relation between natural and human law). In addition to any strengths natural law has as an account of morality in general (views about which have, of course, varied within the Christian tradition over history), in this particular way, we argue, natural law (precisely as a theory of law) is especially helpful in diagnosing and resolving the internalist and externalist divide in tort theory. But note also that, following Aquinas, we do not make any sharp distinction here between what today would be termed "morality" and natural law. As Jean Porter points out, for Aquinas "morality, understood in the distinctively modern fashion—that is to say, a coherent body of norms which can be discerned apart from revelation—is not included as a separate way of specifying the natural law."[23]

An important source for the Christian philosophical tradition on these matters is Aristotle, and so we begin by noting a distinction Aristotle draws in the *Nicomachean Ethics* between "natural" and "legal" justice:

> Of what is politically just, one part is natural, the other legal. The natural one is the one that has the same force everywhere and not because it does or does not seem to have it, whereas the legal is the one where at the start it makes no difference whether it enjoins one thing or another, but once people establish it, it does make a difference.[24]

Here Aristotle "is making a distinction within the category of justice as it applies to equal citizens," as Richard Kraut notes, "because legal justice rests on an arbitrary choice within a certain range, we will often find variations in what is legally just in different communities."[25]

Though there is a long tradition of commentary on this passage from Aristotle, for our purposes here we look to how this distinction in Aristotle was incorporated into Thomas Aquinas's discussion of the relation of natural law and human law. The so-called Treatise on Law in Thomas Aquinas's *Summa*

23 Jean Porter, *Ministers of the Law: A Natural Law Theory of Legal Authority* (Grand Rapids, MI: Eerdmans, 2010), 79.

24 Aristotle, *Nicomachean Ethics*, trans. C.D.C. Reeve (Indianapolis, IN: Hackett Publishing, 2014), 89 (v.7, 1135a).

25 Richard Kraut, *Aristotle: Political Philosophy* (Oxford: Oxford University Press, 2002), 128.

Theologiae comprises Questions 90–108 of the *Prima secundae*, and includes a discussion of the four types of law (eternal law, natural law, human law, and divine law) and Aquinas's famous definition of law as "an ordinance of reason for the common good, made by him who has care of the community, and promulgated."[26] The central text for Aquinas's account of the relation of natural law and human law is *ST* I-II.95.2, in which Aquinas poses the question of "whether every human law is derived from the natural law?"

The first objection cites to *Nicomachean Ethics* v.7 and states that the legally just is a matter of indifference but that "those things that arise from the natural law are not matters of indifference."[27] An implication of the objection is that for human law to be derived from natural law would entail that all of human law is derived from natural law in such a way as to share in the force of the natural law. Because that is clearly not true—human law deals with a variety of trivial and apparently indifferent matters at a far remove from natural law—it must be, so goes the objection, that human positive law does not derive from natural law.[28]

The second objection relies on the traditional distinction between natural and positive law in Isidore of Seville (560–636, a Father of the Church who wrote a treatise, *Etymologia*, that sought to synthesize classical sources) and—once again—*Nicomachean Ethics* v.7. But, as the objection states, conclusions drawn from natural law belong to the natural law (I-II.94.4), so positive law must be something else altogether from natural law or morality. Indeed, I-II.95.2 obj.2 anticipates later positivist views that a valid "law" need not depend logically on morality or other such extra-legal sources.

In the third objection, Aquinas notes the evident variation in positive law, which would seem to belie any origin in the natural law that is the same everywhere (once more citing v.7 in Aristotle's *Nicomachean Ethics* on natural justice). Finally, the fourth objection states that reasons can be given (are available) for that which is derived from the natural law, but that is not always true for the enactments of positive law. Aquinas quotes Justinian's *Digest* that "it is not possible to give the reason for all the legal enactments of the lawgivers."

In the response, Aquinas observes that "something may be derived from the natural law in two ways."[29] The first way is by way of deduction "from

26 Thomas Aquinas, *Summa Theologiae*, trans. Fathers of the English Dominican Province (New York: Benziger Brothers, Inc., 1947), I–II.90.4.

27 The separate questions or "articles" of Aquinas's *Summa Theologiae* proceed dialectically by articulating a series of objections, followed by Aquinas's "answer" to the question in the *respondeo*, and then the replies to the objections.

28 By way of clarification, Aquinas uses "positive law" to denote both human positive law and divine positive law (such as the Ten Commandments or the ceremonial precepts of the Old Testament). Throughout this discussion, when we refer to "positive" law we mean human positive law.

29 The full text of the response in the English Dominican translation is as follows:

> It must be noted that something may be derived from the natural law in two ways: first, as a conclusion from premises, secondly, by way of determination of certain generalities. The first way is like to that by which, in sciences, demonstrated conclusions are drawn from the principles: while the second mode is likened to that whereby, in the arts, general forms are

premises," and these conclusions are reached based on the "general principles" of the natural law. The second way is by "determination of certain generalities." The analogies Aquinas uses for each of these modes of derivation are, respectively, deduction from premises in the sciences and the "particulariz[ation] as to details" in the arts (Aquinas refers to architecture and states that the "craftsman needs to determine the general form of a house to some particular shape"). "Some laws are derived by a kind of deduction, as conclusions from principles—the substance of a just law of murder, treason, rape, fraud, or theft, for example; or the general provision for punishment of crime," John Finnis writes in summarizing Aquinas's view, "But many other laws, e.g., those stipulating penalties for specific classes of offence, are derived from morality not by deduction of conclusions, but by the process which Aquinas identifies and names *determinatio*."[30]

The replies to the objections all show that the objectors misunderstood or failed to apply this distinction between deduction and determination. In the reply to the first objection, for example, Aquinas writes that Aristotle "is speaking of those enactments which are by way of determination or specification of the precepts of the natural law." We can also begin to see Aquinas's distinctive understanding of the distinction and relationship between law and morality in practical reasoning. "True, according to Aquinas, both law and morality aim to make men good, but each ought to do this in a distinct, and mutually supportive, manner," writes James Bernard Murphy,

> Morality has a more comprehensive role in cultivating the full range of moral virtues and in directing the full range of human acts, reaching even to the harmony of our thoughts, words, and deeds; law, by contrast, has a much more limited role in cultivating mainly the virtue of justice (and, only secondarily, the other virtues supportive of the disposition to justice) and in regulating only deeds, not mere intentions and dispositions.[31]

Importantly, the English word "indifference" in the first objection of the article (echoing "no difference" in the Reeve translation of the *Nicomachean Ethics*)

> particularized as to details: thus the craftsman needs to determine the general form of a house to some particular shape. Some things are therefore derived from the general principles of the natural law, by way of conclusions; e.g. that "one must not kill" may be derived as a conclusion from the principle that "one should do harm to no man": while some are derived therefrom by way of determination; e.g. the law of nature has it that the evil-doer should be punished; but that he be punished in this or that way, is a determination of the law of nature.

Accordingly both modes of derivation are found in the human law. But those things, which are derived in the first way, are contained in human law not as emanating therefrom exclusively, but have some force from the natural law also. But those things, which are derived in the second way, have no other force than that of human law.

30 John Finnis, *Aquinas: Moral, Political, and Legal Theory* (Oxford: Oxford University Press, 1998), 266.

31 James Bernard Murphy, *The Philosophy of Positive Law: Foundations of Jurisprudence* (New Haven, CT: Yale University Press, 2005), 54–55.

is susceptible to a misleading interpretation. It is not as though choices made by determination of the positive law are unreasonable or completely arbitrary, only that there is a way in which those enactments of the positive law could be otherwise. As Finnis notes, "The more limited and accurate statement is that in such cases the lawmaker has a number of options none of which is 'in itself repugnant to natural justice'."[32]

Application

With this framework in place, we can begin to see how natural law theory helps us understand certain features of tort law. At its core, both historically and philosophically, torts is concerned with non-maleficence, the obligation not to harm others. Not coincidentally, then, intentional torts—purposeful harm to others such as battery—lie at the origin of tort law in English legal history.[33] To be sure, the early actions for "Trespass Vi et Armis" did not sharply distinguish between bodily harms that were inflicted purposefully and those that came about by carelessness, but a plea of accidental injuring was relegated to a defense. As John Baker writes, "Whatever the real facts, defendants in battery were almost always made to 'assault, beat, and wound' the plaintiff…." and "the kind of fault required to make the defendant liable would therefore only become relevant if he tried to make it so by excusing himself on grounds of accident."[34]

This prohibition on intentional harm is derived from basic principles of natural law about what we owe to other persons in justice with significant moral and pedagogical implications. Tort casebooks traditionally began with intentional torts generally and often battery specifically, motivated partly by the relatively straightforward elements of intentional torts compared to negligence. Some recent casebooks start with negligence, however, because of its prevalence in modern tort doctrine. But if our account here is correct, then there might be sound philosophical reasons for starting with intentional torts as they lie closer, by derivation, to the basic principles of morality and moving out to negligence and other under-determined aspects of tort doctrine.

It is also worth noting that purely instrumentalist accounts of tort law have a difficult time accounting for the "intent" part of intentional torts, i.e., why intent should matter at all for purposes of tort law. John Finnis has made this point by way of a criticism of an argument in an earlier edition of Richard Posner's *Economic Analysis of Law*, where Posner writes,

> Most accidental injuries are intentional in the sense that the injurer knew that he could have reduced the probability of the accident by taking additional precautions. The element of intention is unmistakable when the

32 Finnis, *Aquinas*, 268 n.82.

33 *See* S.F.C. Milsom, *Historical Foundations of the Common Law*, 2nd ed. (Oxford: Oxford University Press, 1981), 283–313.

34 John Baker, *An Introduction to English Legal History*, 5th ed. (Oxford: Oxford University Press, 2019), 429.

> tortfeasor is an enterprise that can predict from past experience that it will inflict a certain number of accidental injuries every year.[35]

Such a collapse of the intentional torts-negligence distinction is at odds with our view—sounding in the moral, natural law core of tort law—that there is something distinctive and important about intent. As Finnis retorts,

> Common, non-utilitarian morality's principle that one must never choose (intend) harm to the person of any human individual both expresses and preserves the understanding that each human individual is more than just a locus of utility or wealth...or a channel or conduit for maximizing that wealth or utility.[36]

Tort law is most closely deduced from the natural law in those aspects where it seeks to provide redress for willful injury of another, most clearly seen in the law of battery but with possible relevance also to other purposeful inflictions of wrong to create imminent apprehension of harm in assault, to cause severe emotional distress, or to invade another's property in trespass (as noted by commentators, however, trespass has aspects of both intent and strict liability).

In other areas of tort doctrine, though, the choices made by common law courts and legislatures are more open ended because they are not related to the natural law by way of deduction but only by determination. As Jules Coleman writes, "Much of the content of the first-order duties that are protected in tort law is created and formed piecemeal in the course of our manifold social and economic interactions."[37] In determining among reasonable alternatives, legislatures and courts can choose among various public policy aims and employ the benefits of cumulative judgments. For example, the various tools of economic analysis of law—whatever its shortcomings as a comprehensive account of tort law—could still be brought to bear in choosing among alternative rules in tort law. Thus, the insights of law and economics or other types of cost-benefit analysis are preserved in this account while also limited by certain first-order moral constraints. "Where a person or a society has created a personal or social hierarchy of practical norms and orientations, through reasonable choice of commitments, one can in many cases reasonably measure the benefits and disadvantages of alternatives," as John Finnis writes.[38]

These determinations have the force of law and thereby impose obligations on citizens, but the rules set by such determination are susceptible to variation,

35 Richard Posner, *Economic Analysis of Law*, 2nd ed. (Boston, MA: Little, Brown, 1977), 119.

36 John Finnis, "Intention in Tort Law," in *Intention and Identity: Collected Essays Volume II* (Oxford: Oxford University Press, 2011), 214.

37 Jules Coleman, *The Practice of Principle: In Defence of a Pragmatist Approach to Legal Theory* (Oxford: Oxford University Press, 2001), 34.

38 Finnis, *Natural Law and Natural Rights*, 111.

or "indifference" to use the terminology invoked earlier. To take a prominent example, the choice between strict liability and negligence in certain domains of tort law is one of the long-running disputes in tort theory.[39] In important areas such as products liability or ultra-hazardous activities, tort law has oscillated between strict liability and negligence. This grand alternative between strict liability and negligence and the associated difficulty with providing a theoretical basis for why tort law should adopt one or the other has bedeviled the academic tort literature. On our account, though, the choice between strict liability and negligence can reasonably depend on a range of considerations, some of which will perhaps be tethered to moral judgments (e.g., those who engage in ultra-hazardous activities should be made to pay damages resulting from such activities) while others will be subject to all things considered judgments about the better rule (e.g., the choice in design defect product liability cases between a rule approaching strict liability as in the Second Restatement and a rule that seems to incorporates aspects of negligence as in the Third Restatement).

Another example of an election in the common law of torts that does not seem a matter of deduction but instead determination from the natural law is the liability of employers for the negligent torts of their employees via the doctrine of *respondeat superior*. One can imagine a range of possible tort rules: employers not subject to liability at all for the negligently inflicted injuries of their employees, liability for negligence by employees acting within the scope of employment (narrowly defined), or broad liability by employers, even for intentional torts committed by employees. Our account captures both the insight that there is a moral dimension to the choice (because, say, considerations of justice or fairness lean toward a regime of *respondeat superior* for the employer who benefits financially from the work of its employees should be made to pay for the risks thereby created) and the way in which it does not seem that there is a determinate "right" answer to precisely what the rule of *respondeat superior* should look like.[40]

We mean here only to offer a selection of possible ways to map the deduction-determination distinction in Aquinas's natural law theory onto some doctrines in the law of torts in order to capture something of both (referring back to the discussion in the first section) the "thickness" of a moral account of tort law and the "thinness" of the under-determined choices made by judges and legislatures as to particular tort doctrines. Other examples might include the requirement (even in strict liability) to show causation,[41] an understanding of proximate

39 *See, e.g.*, Steven Shavell, "Strict Liability versus Negligence," *Journal of Legal Studies*, 9 (1980): 1–25 and Richard Epstein, "A Theory of Strict Liability," *Journal of Legal Studies*, 2 (1973): 151–204.

40 See the discussion of various approaches to the scope of *respondeat superior* liability in Taber v. Maine, 67 F.3d 1029 (2d Cir. 1995).

41 See the discussion of the complex relationship between causation and moral blameworthiness in Michael S. Moore, *Causation and Responsibility: An Essay in Law, Morals, and Metaphysics* (Oxford: Oxford University Press, 2009), 20–33.

causation based in judgments of practical reasonableness about foreseeability or the realization of a risk posed by the defendant's conduct (not in a freeform "policy" judgment made about whether imposing liability in a particular case would be fair or efficient),[42] the intersection of legislative judgments in negligence per se with common law standards of reasonable care, or the choice between contributory negligence and comparative fault. In each of these areas, a natural law account helps us see that there is an inescapably moral dimension to the choices being made (as a matter of justice, for example) while also acknowledging that, apart from intentional wrongdoing, a reasonable tort system might admit of vast differentiation as legal authorities set about the task of determination of human law from the natural law.

Conclusion: the moral of torts

The modes of derivation in human law from the natural law explain both the moral significance of tort law in its essentials and those contingent aspects that have only the force of human law—but are still law. The mistake in much of tort theory is to pose a stark alternative between skepticism and overly tidy moral (or non-moral) explanations or justifications for all of torts, between views that tort law is really about something else and that torts is an internally consistent body of private law rules. "The backbone of tort is a set of moral—natural law—principles identifying as wrongful all choices precisely to harm or to deceive," as John Finnis writes, "But the flesh-and-blood of tort is a set of standards embodying both 'natural law' elements and 'positive elements'."[43]

A final word about what all this has to do with a Christian critique of law. While natural law is often characterized as a "secular" or purely "philosophical" account, the view we adopt here is more nuanced than that. To be sure, the basic dimensions of morality reflected in the natural law are, in principle, known to all by virtue of practical reasonableness and do not require, as such, the aid of divine revelation. But while Aquinas and the other scholastics relied on Aristotle and other philosophical sources in their articulation of the natural law, they also drew upon a long scriptural and patristic tradition.[44] Indeed, one of the unfortunate effects of reading Aquinas's questions on law in the *Summa Theologiae* apart from other sections is an inaccurate divorce between natural law and theology. As James Bernard Murphy writes, "If God is the supreme legis-

42 H.L.A. Hart and Tony Honoré, Causation and the Law, 2nd ed. (Oxford: Oxford University Press, 1985), 254–90.

43 John Finnis, "Natural Law: The Classical Tradition," in *The Oxford Handbook of Jurisprudence and Philosophy of Law*, eds. Jules Coleman and Scott Shapiro (Oxford: Oxford University Press, 2002), 1, 45.

44 *See* Jean Porter, *Nature as Reason: A Thomistic Theory of the Natural Law* (Grand Rapids, MI: Eerdmans: 2004), 10: "[I]n its warrants and its overall contours, the scholastic concept of the natural law was profoundly shaped by their reading of Scripture as mediated through patristic commentary."

and theology. As James Bernard Murphy writes, "If God is the supreme legislator of natural order, then, as social and political animals, we participate in his divine providential government through deliberate moral choice and through deliberate legislation."[45] Deliberation on the moral requirements of the natural law and the derivation in human law of those requirements opens one to the whole range of questions about the human good. Even in as seemingly mundane a subject as torts, its core demand of non-maleficence and the commitment to human flourishing leads the reflective person to ponder the human good in all of its manifestations.

45 Murphy, *The Philosophy of Positive Law*, 50.

15 Tort law and its three Christian pillars

David F. Partlett

Introduction

The law of torts is a major segment of what we call private law. Private law is that set of principles and rules that regulates the way individuals interact with one another when engaged in activities hazarding harm. In contrast, public law determines the obligations and duties between the citizen and the state. The common law of torts evolved over the long history of civilization in England and thence to all those nations that accepted the common law framework. It is unsurprising that one finds a tight weave of the body of the law and Christian tenets that pervaded those societies. The threads of that weave have been explicated by scholars over the centuries but none more influentially than Harold Berman.[1] My task here is more modest. I suggest that there are three pillars that describe tort law that are deeply reflective of Christian thought.

I describe the pillars and then how we lost the Christian threads as twentieth-century tort scholarship became pragmatic and consequentialist in its analysis of the norms of the law. Lately however tort scholarship has turned to excavating the basic values that the rules exemplify. That generally is not explicitly oriented to Christian values and precepts. On deeper examination, we may see the Christian roots and this allows those interested in this corner of private law more accurately to interpret the law, its past, present, and future, and its metes and bounds.

Three pillars

Three core elements or themes run through the law of torts. These are not normative touchstones but rather are descriptive of the common law of torts. For laborers in the vineyard of torts they fit the interpretative endeavor of the common law that looks for principles in a disciplined practice of deliberate, practical reasoning: this is the artificial reason of the law. The term "artificial reason" is used here to contrast it with "natural reason." The rules and doctrines of the

1 Harold J. Berman, *Law and Revolution: The Transformation of the Western Legal Tradition* (Cambridge, MA: Harvard University Press, 1983).

common law have their standing and force through the process of its formation. It emerges from a system denoted by public-mindedness in solving problems with regard to justice, a reasoned discourse in shaping its rules and doctrines, a common endeavor by exercise of common practice, a forging of rules and principles in court, and a discourse disciplined by its focus on concrete cases tethered to past decisions and "structured by (a) analogical reasoning, (b) mindfulness of the temporal aspect of law, and (c) a keen sense of its practical task of ordering and coordinating social interaction in the community."[2] In short, we search for "a unified realm of legal meaning and purpose."[3] These pillars as I call the three have deep roots in Christian thought. That is, as Harold Berman's powerful thesis went, discerning connections between society and its needs and the currents of belief and practice in institutions that instantiated Christian principles.

The pillar of community

The first and earliest is the role of tort law—a coordinating mechanism that is the cement of societies. The early forms of action of trespass and trespass on the case were explicitly designed to bestow the King's Peace. This objective has roots in the Christian faith. The Hebrews, indeed, conceptualized law as constituting their community and their identity. The idea of covenant recognizes a rule of law. The density of rules in the Hebrew scriptures from diet to religious observance defines and separates the Jews and promises the fruits of order and law from obedience to a jealous God. A system of rules also defines the early Christian communities. St. Paul's letters, poetical as they are, contain detailed instructions on the internal coordinating norms of those communities. Paul defines what observance is; how they should comport themselves in leading Christian lives and preparing for the life beyond.[4] The transformative notion is the life, teachings, death, and resurrection of Jesus Christ. So much can be embraced in the image of his self-sacrifice. As David Ford says: "laying down one's life for a friend, redemption, reconciliation, exchanges, obedience, healing

2 "Editor's Introduction," in *Matthew Hale, On the Law of Nature, Reason, and Common Law: Selected Jurisprudential Writings*, ed. Gerald J. Postema (Oxford: Oxford University Press, 2017), xxvi, xlix (Hale, a famous jurist and thinker of the mid-seventeenth century, described the "special discipline of common law reasoning": "Common-law reasoning is reasoning in *media res*, tethered simultaneously to broad principles of justice, the common stock of experience and decision and the enacted rules which determine them, and systematic connections within the body of law.")

3 Jeremy Waldron, "Torture and Positive Law: Jurisprudence for the White House," *Columbia Law Review*, 105 (2005): 1722; *see also* Jeremy Waldron, "The Concept of the Rule of Law," *Georgia Law Review*, 43 (2008): 135.

4 The issues of the relationship of Christianity with Judaism was long lasting and deeply dividing. *See* Luke Timothy Johnson, "Law in Early Christianity," in *Christianity and Law: An Introduction*, eds. John Witte, Jr. and Frank S. Alexander (Cambridge: Cambridge University Press, 2008), 53.

alienation, and judgement."[5] Before the Lutheran idea of the righteous believer standing before Christ, the journey of intensification was the "satisfaction theory" of atonement produced by Anslem of Canterbury (1033–1109). Order out of chaos arose from a unity of the political, economic, and social, attaching to the individual's responsibility to honor and obey stemming from the freely obedient death of Jesus.

Early Christianity operated within the framework of small isolated communities that adopted norms in contrast to, and in tension with, the surrounding pagans. Right relationships between human and God have continued to be framed by sharing communities. Christian theological ethics contribute to the forming of hearts, minds, and wills of individuals and communities. The Trinitarian doctrine unites God, mankind, and the Holy Spirit. Thus, man lives in community and takes responsibility for judgments, decisions, and actions. Dietrich Bonhoeffer's ethic was "to live the responsible life before God."[6] In these ideas, we see the operation of free will and the requirements of responsibility to God and fellow humans. It was a life of responsibility that showed a new human possibility. In terms of charity and support of education of members it placed an example before the pagans.[7] Importantly, the relational life in community allowed contention about ultimate questions of life and existence. The private law turns on relationships and their regulation within groups. The irony, and epoch-making event, was that the Christian community, the Jesus movement, toppled the gods of the vast Roman Empire.

The early law of torts had a close affinity with the "law" as expressed in the Hebrew Scriptures, the law expressed in the Torah, the first five books of Moses. As in the common law the rationale was to limit conflict and apply a principle of "restitution."[8] Take Welker's words:

> The intention of the law is to remedy conflict thus defined [as endangering another party's security of expectation—the normal course of life] by restoring a pre-conflict state of affairs or when this is impossible, limiting the conflict through an encouragement of restitution, or, in the worst case, through an equal damage to the offending side.[9]

The lives of the Hebrews and the lives of medieval Englishmen turned on "security of expectation" in small communities riven by a lack of formal enforcement mechanisms. To live beyond a rude level, the law had to act as a pragmatic deterrent to aberrant behavior and inculcate a code of values. At the same time, the law of the Bible had to incorporate flex to render mercy or equity. As Welker

5 David Ford, *Theology: A Very Short Introduction* (Oxford: Oxford University Press, 2013), 112.
6 Eric Metaxas, *Bonhoeffer: Pastor, Martyr, Prophet, Spy* (Edinburgh: Thomas Nelson, 2011), 446.
7 N.T. Wright, *Paul: A Biography* (New York: Harper Collins, 2018).
8 Michael Welker, "The Power of Mercy in Biblical Law," *Journal of Law and Religion*, 29 (2014): 225.
9 Ibid.

points out "mercy and love" infuse Biblical law disclosing justice and worship.[10] Of course, the law of the Bible is transcendent and "opens our eyes" to the deeper secrets of love which is indeed the "sum" and the "fulfillment" of the law.[11] This could not be claimed in the secular world of the common law. Yet a reverence for Biblical law inculcates habits that undergird secular law encouraging room for the human spirit to find fulfillment. Life is real and Jesus in the Trinitarian concept lived life that we could have it more abundantly.[12] It is a righteous life full of His spirit.

I will demonstrate how the rules relating to the intentional torts and the reasonable person in negligence are shot full of community rules of coordination that turn on application of ideals of Christian ethics. The rules are instrumental in the sense that the thriving and functioning of communities are furthered through the rules. In the modern day, we are prone to call this a system of rules and practices that builds social capital. In constituting a community, tort rules give good but fallen people the chance to thrive and to live to the full. The community however is comprised of self-willed individuals who are free to make choices; they may benefit or suffer as a result of those choices. Paul stressed the essential relationship with God and between fellow citizens.[13] Each human, being created in the image of God, possesses inherent human dignity.

The second pillar is human dignity

There is here the deep Christian commitment to the worth of the person, to his or her essential dignity. Jesus taught this in the Gospels caring for the sick and the lame; He comforted the poor. He included women. The early Christian communities practiced it for example by tending to the sick and encouraging education. Women were accorded powerful positions. That equality would be reinforced in the protestant revolution in Luther's direct relationship no matter the person's station in life.[14]

To respect human dignity is to recognize that each person has autonomy to make life's choices. This has come to instantiate a normative theory of the law of torts. Tort theory has in the modern age stripped this element of its Christian roots and, to the extent morality operates, it is a secular ethic calling on ruling notions of Aristotelian corrective justice and Kantian ideas of right.[15] Tort theory often turns on a singular deontological concept of right, the breaching of which is a wrong. Redress theory in the world of Goldberg and Zipursky turns on tort liability as redress of the wrong and inculcation of responsibility. In

10 Ibid.
11 Matthew 22:40, Romans 13:8.
12 John 10:10.
13 Wright, *Paul: A Biography* (describing the Christian communities, and particularly Antioch where Paul, at [Barnabas' (?)] urging, repaired to inquire into and advise the community).
14 *See* Witte and Alexander, *supra* note 4.
15 Arthur Ripstein, *Private Wrongs* (Cambridge, MA: Harvard University Press, 2016).

corrective justice, it is the law placing the burden on the wrongdoer to correct the wrong in a bilateral relationship denoted by juridical equality.[16] None of this has to be accepted to acknowledge that the free and responsible human being is at the descriptive center of the law of torts. The jurisprudence of individual rights coheres when the source of the individual right is God given.[17]

The third pillar is protection of the vulnerable

Tort law doctrine reinforces the Christian value of charity, of love for the other. The foundation is in autonomy in the sense of respect for the dignity of the individual.[18] Dignity requires equal respect and the vulnerable are deserving of succor in an ethical and a legal order that is devoted, as tort is, to righting of wrongs and elevating of the reviled and weak in society. The rules of tort law are often a form of equity that metes out justice when strict rules of contract exact absolute accounting.[19] The neighbor principle in the law, rooted in Christ's story of the Good Samaritan, spreads a protection beyond that contracted for, to others who will be affected by wrongful acts. This was especially the case when the vast changes in society wrought by the Industrial Revolution resulted in disruptions of communities and an exponential increase in injuries. Wealth may increase but at a cost of greater inequality; communities' support systems were broken. While the private law could not stop the harm, it could through its principles ameliorate the consequences. In industrial England the full force of defenses of contributory negligence, voluntary assumption of risk, and common employment (the fellow servant rule) was gated to allow factory workers a better measure of recovery.[20] The law too threw a light on significant social needs prompting public legal responses such as Workers Compensation. Tort law was also a solvent to the evils of capital exploitation and fraud as uncovered in economic catastrophes that begin in the South Sea Bubble in 1720 and extend to the recent great recession.[21] As we will see the victims of bad luck cannot all be helped but they can be recognized and their plight given some suasion as to attract public succor.[22] In a later section I want to discuss the neighbor principle

16 Peter Cane, "Tort Law and Public Functions," in *Philosophical Foundations of the Law of Torts*, ed. John Oberdiek (2014), 149.

17 Michael Perry, "Christianity and Human Rights," in *Christianity and Law: An Introduction*, eds. John Witte, Jr. and Frank S. Alexander (2008), 237.

18 Ronald Dworkin, *Taking Rights Seriously* (1978).

19 The formal law of equity grew in taking off the sharp edges of the law. Joseph Story succinctly and influentially framed equity's jurisdiction. *See* Gerald T Dunne, "Story's First Writing on Equity," *American Journal of Legal History*, 14(1970): 79.

20 Gary T. Schwartz, "Tort Law and the Economy Nineteenth Century America: A Reinterpretation," *Yale Law Journal*, 90 (1980): 1717.

21 John Carswell, *The South Sea Bubble* (2011). For an analysis of the Great Recession, see Ben S. Bernanke, *The Courage to Act: A Memoir of a Crisis and Its Aftermath* (2015). For an overview see Niall Ferguson, *The Ascent of Money: A Financial History of the World* (2008).

22 At least in responsive democracies. And just as Christian Communities in the early Church established hospitals that tended to plague victims.

in negligence and its limits, the place of the vulnerable individual, and the educational role of tort law.

All these are common themes for those who pick grapes in the vineyard of torts. I hope to show that by giving each pillar, element, or theme its due place we may see the underlying Christian values even as our twenty-first century Western society becomes fractured and community-creating norms are lost in the clarion call of broad and national standards and a drumbeat of the market.[23] In our present society autonomy is described as being protected through overarching public law imperatives. Moreover, the values of equal human dignity and the protection of the vulnerable drop from view because of a faith in the magic of markets.

I will describe below the three pillars in more detail. They are best seen through the lens of the intentional torts and separately under negligence. I shall then show how the general tort law can be interpreted through the three elements or themes: community, individual autonomy, and vulnerability. Before setting forth my argument it is essential to note that American private law in general and torts in particular have not been fertile ground for the uncovering of Christian ideas throughout the twentieth century. It is the emergence of theories beyond the twentieth-century pragmatic boundaries that have enlivened the embers that were but faintly glowing in that century.

The realists and tort law: the pillars buried in instrumentalist sands

The ground for a rich theory of law that would take seriously its roots in shared tenets of Christianity appeared propitious as the nineteenth century began. Philip Petitt,[24] quoting Harold Berman, says the courts and the common law had developed in the Middle Ages and had assumed a decentralized, non-volunteeristic form and had given rise to:

> [F]irm assumptions about people's rights under the law—people's ancient rights, as they were so often described—even their rights against the powerful: they had provided people a sense that they lived under a constitution, an empire of law, of ancient and unquestioned standing.[25]

The founding fathers of the American Republic were steeped in the faith of the enlightenment and how law could regulate the abuses of power and form the conditions of the commonwealth. It is unsurprising, therefore, that

23 For an appraisal of capitalism as religion see Harari, *Sapiens: A Brief History of Humankind* (2015). *See also* Cristina Tilley, "Tort Law Inside Out," *Yale Law Journal*, 126 (2017):1320 (arguing that tort doctrine acknowledges two distinctive kinds of communities: the closed and open. For closed, moral notions of the law prevail; for open, efficiency norms predominate). In the definition of community see ibid., 1346.

24 Petitt, *Republicanism: A Theory of Freedom and Government* (Oxford: Oxford University Press, 1997).

25 Ibid., 21–22

the strong faith in the powers of American lawyers and legal writing shone through both public and private law. But other forces intellectual and social crimped an appreciation of the pillars of community, human dignity, and vulnerability.

The dominant figure in the formation of ideas about tort law in the twentieth century was Oliver Wendell Holmes. His famous book *The Common Law* was based on his lectures at Harvard Law School.[26] Holmes was concerned to give the law a more solid jurisprudential base. In tort law, his famous proposition was his "conservative principle" that fault was the trigger in shifting loss from the injured to the injurer. In this he accurately interpreted the law that had gone before and clothed the argument in society and its expectations. In fault there was a morality. But the law of negligence had clearly based liability on the objective reasonable person test. Thus, if a person were incapable of performance at an objective level he would nevertheless be liable. To justify such a departure from subjective standards of fault, Holmes adopted a pragmatic argument that a subjective test would be unworkable.[27] Standards of behavior would vary and render interaction between parties difficult to predict. Persons in society expect that others with whom they interact are reasonable persons. Of course, if we know of those others' idiosyncrasies steps can be taken in precaution especially if persons, through no fault of their own, would be rusticated from society.[28]

Holmes was to contribute greatly to a number of trends in academic analysis of tort and more generally private law. The age of the treatise in law and ascendency of the legal profession had passed, and an age of academic external explicit examination of the law had begun. University training moved to the center of legal education and scholarly work would turn to the task of explaining the nature of the law.[29] Law began to be viewed through the lens of other disciplines, most notably in the early twentieth century through the spectacles of sociology, and at the end of the century through economic analysis. The question asked was whether law successfully served certain identifiable ends. In private law the deeper—internal—history was forgotten. Perhaps because public law, mainly constitutional law, came to dominate, private law was reduced to a consequentialist theory devoid of reference to free standing rights.

26 *See* Oman and Solomon, "The Supreme Court's Theory of Private Law," *Duke Law Journal*, 62 (2013): 1114–1119.

27 Holmes' reasoning parallels that of Tindal C.J. in the 1837 case of *Vaughan v. Menlove*, 132 E.R. 490 (1837). *See* Goldberg and Zipursky, "Seeing Tort Law from the Internal Point of View: Holmes and Hart on Legal Duties," *Fordham Law Review*, 75 (2006): 1663 (stressing Holmes's influence on tort theory by arguing that Hart's views have replaced some of Holmes's thinner view of liability rules as sanctions; rather accepted social norms of socially accepted obligations explain tort liabilty).

28 *Roberts v. State of Louisiana*, 396 So.2d 566 (1981) (finding that persons had to take precautions against the presence of blind persons in the post office building).

29 Partlett, "Reflections: Personal and Institutional, on the Past and Future Southeastern Association of Law Schools," *UMKS Law Review*, 86 (2018): 559.

Take tort law. Its principles and rules were accepted, as instrumental in furthering certain social policies. The tenor of the age was that tort law was public law in disguise. It was a tool to be employed to reach desirable public ends. Thus, in the twentieth century influential voices pushed tort law to be refashioned to accommodate the need to compensate victims of accidents. Indeed, in New Zealand the law of torts for personal injuries was abolished and a compensation scheme was substituted. Short of this two lions of tort law, Prosser and Traynor, molded doctrine to introduce strict liability for defective products. This would push enterprises to make safer products, or, at the least, pay for the costs produced by their activities. Tort scholars were generally much in favor of snipping off parts of tort liability to "socialize the costs" as in non-fault liability for motor vehicle accidents. Jeremy Waldron, a New Zealander, saw the merit of compensation schemes as reducing the arbitrary role of luck in compensating the victims of accidents.[30] This appeared to be a rational and moral way of dealing with a social problem. And it was potent in political climates that favored government intervention for the common good.

Instrumentalists all

The successors to the sociologists were the economists who wielded the tools of micro-economics and welfare economics, to explicate the workings of liability rules. The two powerful scholars were Guido Calabresi and Richard Posner. Calabresi, adopting the lessons of economics, proposed a normative argument that liability rules ought to be fashioned to identify the least cost avoider.[31] Posner, in his 1972 article propounding an economic theory of negligence, found that the law could be described as a mechanism to find efficient solutions.[32] The rules operated as if guided by a hand toward an efficient solution. Their work was to take hold of the legal academy and up to the end of the twentieth century the streams of scholarship were either the "in vogue" law and economics or the much-derided, doctrinal analysis that undertook to explain emerging case law in the common law method. Some disciples of Prosser continued in a pragmatic analysis of suggesting normative reformulations of the law. Scholarship, mainly stemming from Oxford, was overtly philosophical in the vein of Hart and the positivists. This fitted nicely into a jurisprudential scene that itself was positivist and rejected morality as being the center of law. Ideas of the inner morality of the law promoted by Lon Fuller had little play.[33]

30 Jeremy Waldron, "Moments of Carelessness and Massive Loss," in *Philosophical Foundations of Tort Law*, ed. David G. Owen (Oxford: Oxford University Press, 1997), 387–408.

31 Calabresi, *The Costs of Accidents: A Legal and Economic Analysis* (New Haven, CT: Yale University Press, 1970).

32 Posner, "A Theory of Negligence," *Journal of Legal Studies*, 1 (1972): 29.

33 Lon Fuller, *The Morality of Law* (New Haven, CT: Yale University Press, 1969); *see* Segev, "Should Law Track Morality?" *Criminal Justice Ethics*, 36 (2017) (arguing that morality has no necessary place in the law; if the law reflects a moral value it is independent of the law).

In many ways torts followed contract in stripping away old religious theoretical vestiges replacing them with a "new rationalization and a new systemization."[34] The exception is that torts kept to the "communitarian postulates which informed both Catholic and Protestant legal traditions."[35] Perhaps it is that contract did stray more radically from those moral and communitarian roots. But if one took a snapshot at the end of the twentieth century, the roots Berman identifies lay well hidden beneath the terrain of the instrumentalists particularly the law and economists. The revival of tort theory that harkens back to the roots, moral and communitarian, can be attributable to a reaction to the pragmatism and the blunt instrumentalism of Posner and his followers. Of particular importance in the revival are a number of scholars: Ernest Weinrib, Arthur Ripstein, Ben Zipursky, John Goldberg, Stephen Perry, Robert Stevens, and Peter Cane.[36] Others like Jane Stapleton and Andrew Robertson eschew any monolithically theoretical basis for tort. In these pages, I have no intention to choose among the theorists or to advance a theory of tort law. My intention is simply to show links with the three pillars described that trace back to a concept of the law as instilling virtue in the form of prudence and benevolence and of autonomy and solidarity.[37] Law reflected a higher virtue. It was devised not simply to coerce but to educate and coordinate social relations.[38]

The higher virtue just identified has enjoyed a precarious place in concepts of tort law. Professor McBride relies on Alasdair MacIntyre's work in his book "After Virtue." MacIntyre suggests that moral philosophy has undergone a catastrophe over the last couple of centuries with the result that we do not understand what we are talking about when we discuss what is right and wrong. McBride thinks also that this is the case with the law of torts. With a non-American focus, that of the English, he sees decay. He puts it down to English left-wing politics. In America I described the same decay above, attributable, I contend, to the influence of the academy in taking on extra-legal frameworks for explicating the phenomenon of private law and for dismissing law as independent autonomous discourse. Compensation of the victims of accidents with the smell of socialism was never close to the American heart (or nostril).

McBride finds hope in modern scholarship. He sees torts in terms of "coercive rights we enjoy against each other, free of charge without having to contract for them, and in providing us with remedies where those rights are violated or threatened with violation."[39] But to take a rights-based approach as a singular

34 Berman, "The Christian Sources of General Contract Law," in *Christianity and Law: An Introduction*, eds. John Witte, Jr. and Frank. S. Alexander, 140.

35 Ibid., 140–141.

36 *See* Oberdiek, *Philosophical Foundations of The Law of Torts* (Oxford: Oxford University Press, 2014).

37 Raz, *The Morality of Freedom* (Oxford: Clarendon Press, 1988)

38 Isadore of Seville. *See* Partlett, *Remedies for Breach of Privacy: A Study of a Different Hedgehog*, ed. Jason Varuhas and Nicole Moreham (2018) (forthcoming).

39 McBride, "Rights and the Basis of Tort Law," in *Rights and Private Law*, eds. Nolan and Robertson (Oxford: Hart Publishing, 2012), 359.

theory is to not keep faith with the fabric of tort law. It then leads to questions whether the right must be joined with the remedy and whether it is part or not of responsibility for wrongful actions. A pluralist approach looks at the operation of tort principles in terms of justice and social welfare. Sometimes to view relational interests between the parties without a wider frame of community welfare would be to undermine the social role of tort law.[40] After all the rules do deter actions and encourage other actions. They operate in society, the health of which turns on the responsiveness of the law to render justice.[41] The law should foster right relationships between citizens. American law has neglected the realm of the private in a blinkered view of the operation of the law as mainly achieving public instrumental goals.

I turn to the three divisions in tort law to retrieve—to uncover—the three pillars.

The Intentional Torts

The intentional torts as they are known in modern tort law sprang from the Chancellor's writ of trespass. The writ was issued to extend the King's Peace to the realm and to ensure that the Normans were able to exert power through the King's Court bestowing judicial process that was superior to the old Hundred and District Courts that had limited tools in providing justice to aggrieved persons. The action covered harms directly caused to the person or property of the individual. In the absence of strong central law enforcement, the streams of criminal law and tort law ran together. There was little regard for the mindset of the actor. The major factor was the act and the resulting harm.

The importance of a wrongful act came later. This law was concerned about the solidarity of community and fits within the slavic tradition of Anslem of Canterbury that was to have great resilience bolstering medieval ordering of society, as noted above. The responsibility was to society and its peace. Gradually, the courts began to allow that a person may not be liable where his act could not be regarded as volitional. Responsibility as centered on the individual was emerging. A proper enquiry was to the actions of the individual. The forms of action were defined in trespass to the person and property. The elements were developed and the concept that the individual in society had certain protections in his person or property appeared. The complexity of changing society wrought by the Industrial Revolution forced a change from close communities to more national norms. A strict form of liability was incompatible with the rising numbers of accidents. At varying rates of doctrinal change, the trigger for liability became fault in the actor causing loss. From an injury-producing activity as lifting

40 Ibid., 457–8.

41 William Temple, former Archbishop of Canterbury, put it this way: "It is axiomatic that love should be the predominant Christian impulse and that justice is the primary form of love in social organization." Quoted by Lord Denning, *The Influence of Religion on Law* (Alberta: Canadian Institute for Law, Theology, and Public Policy, 1997).

a stick to break up a dog fight we observe the Massachusetts court concede that plaintiff whose eye had been injured by the lifted stick must prove fault in order to recover damages from the actor.[42] Fault depended on proof of intent or negligence. Thus, the law now examined the mind of the actor. His or her acting for the purpose of invading the protected interests of the plaintiff became the test. Persons were thus viewed as autonomous actors who owed duties and in breaching those duties acted wrongfully. If those wrongful acts caused harm liability would ensue.

> The rules of battery, assault and false imprisonment protected the integrity of the person. Trespass to land and chattels ensured property rights.

The rules coordinated the actions of persons in society. They provided for legal redress rather than the socially risky and potentially destructive mechanism of self-help. Individuals could consummate private arrangements against a default rule that respected certain elemental rights.

The defenses or privileges are particularly illustrative of the presumption of the individuals' decision-making autonomy and human dignity. The defense of consent is ubiquitous allowing for individuals to accept invasions of rights if they consent to them. But the law is jealous of rights where the rights to personal sovereignty are central. It follows that if a doctor should propose to operate on a person, she should obtain the consent that is absolutely free and fully informed. An implied or imputed consent is rare except in case of emergency. In other circumstances, the privacy accorded to women in giving birth dictates the highest respect and a utilitarian reason for introducing a person not trained in medicine could not suffice.[43] In the ordinary affairs of humankind, however, coordination rules dictate that imputed or implied or assumed consent is common. Thus, to brush against a person in exiting a room is not a battery.

Importantly in trespass to the person the dignity of the individual became paramount. For a claim to be valid, the right had to be invaded but the action did not depend on showing material harm. The plaintiff could bring an action for nominal damages thus vindicating his rights. Moreover, the invasion may touch a person's dignitary interests. In the well-known Fisher case[44], the Texas Supreme Court found that the plaintiff, an African-American in Houston, could bring an action in battery where a waiter shouted racial epithets at him when snatching a tray from him. The snatching of the tray was a sufficient touching to constitute battery and the surrounding conduct was sufficient to base substantial damages for his hurt dignity. The central lesson of the case is that as Texas society changed in the "New South" persons should be able to operate in society free of such abuse that would deprive them of full status as participating members of

42 *Brown v. Kendall*, 60 Mass. (6 Cush.) 292 (1850).
43 *DeMay v. Roberts*, 46 Mich. 160, 9 N.W. 146.
44 *Fisher v. Carrousel Motor Hotel*, 424 S.W.2d 627 (Tx. 1967).

society. These doctrines gird human dignity while recognizing responsibility to community and to other vulnerable persons.

Negligence liability

The story of modern tort law is the march of negligence to predominance. The roots again are ancient in the action on the case. The background is the assertion of the King's power and jurisdiction. It is based in society but also in the right of individuals to act in society free of hurtful acts by others. The fracturing of settled society by the Industrial Revolution and the increasing incidence of accidents with the rise of the city and the factory recall the "satanic mills" and prompted the development of liability rules that found liability where an actor by falling below the standard to care of a reasonable person caused harm to another. Note here that because this was an action on the case the gist of the action is damage.

The scope of liability was much disputed in the nineteenth century. The great debate about property, freedom of contract, and tort liability played out on the stage of a rapidly changing society. Negligence liability depended on relationships that engendered duties to others. These were usually found in accepted categories such as employer-employee, occupier of premises and entrant, dangerous products and injured consumers and other foreseeable bystanders, and professionals causing loss to clients and patients. Property and contract predominated in the mid-nineteenth century in the period of laissez-faire. This gave voice to autonomy of the individual but without the amelioration of social cohesion. It was built upon a hard-edged society that did not reflect Christian ethics. Persons were vulnerable and the certitudes of the market did not measure to the requirements of justice. To take the clash of property and liability rules is to see the debate in relief. In the nineteenth century a fundamental tenet of the law was the right of landowners to exercise full dominion over their real estate. It was the core of ownership. If a person should come onto another's property the owner or occupier had no duty of care to take reasonable measures for the physical safety of the trespasser. Property rights trumped personal rights. The submerging of responsibility for safety and welfare of others struck even an early nineteenth century as lacking justice. In *Bird v. Holbrook*[45] we witness the rebalancing of interests.

In this case a young boy Willie Bird, in pursuit of a stray fowl, entered the Holbrook's walled garden. Bird stepped on a wire that was attached to a gun. The gun was triggered by the footstep and Bird was shot in the leg maiming him. No notice was given of the presence of the spring gun. On the one hand, it was asserted that Holbrook, as owner, had every right to protect his property from intruders. He had a right to deter entry of trespassers in his absence. Best C.J. found that Bird's action in tort (on the case) was maintainable. Against the

45 4 Bing. 628; 130 ER 911 (C.P. 1825).

robust property right rested Bird's claim of "humanity" (Id., 916). The Chief Justice said:

> It has been argued that the law does not compel every line of conduct which humanity or religion may require; but there is no act which Christianity forbids, that the law does not reach; if it were otherwise, Christianity would not be, as it has always been held to be, part of the law of England... it is the object of English law to uphold humanity, and the sanctions of religion.

The strict property-based rule was ameliorated. During the late nineteenth and early twentieth centuries the court found a duty of care owed to child trespassers. This was built on solicitude for children injured on premises and later, as the House of Lords put it, on a duty to act with "humanity" toward those on premises illegally.[46] Even those adults coming onto the premises for unlawful purposes, such as burglary, are owed a duty to not be subjected to the arbitrary threat of lethal violence as with a spring gun.[47] Though if the landowner is threatened with bodily harm the landowner can protect himself with proportionate force.

In the constant to and fro between property rights and tort liability, we witness a softening of hard-edged rules granting full dominion to owners. Thus in the famous case of Vincent,[48] the wharf owner whose property was trespassed upon in order to secure defendant's boat against it in the teeth of a violent storm was found to have a conditional privilege to trespass upon the sensible notion that greater harm was thus avoided and that to compensate the wharf owner for damage would have been the bargain arrived at in the absence of the adventitious storm that unforeseeably had come down upon Duluth Minnesota that day.[49]

The great driving force was the generalization of the discrete categories of duty to a rule that accorded a duty to all those persons who would foreseeably injured by the negligent act of a person. This is the neighbor principle that drew explicitly on the parable of the Good Samaritan.

Two critical matters are in operation. The law is based on relationship. As Paul stressed the cornerstone of a faithful life in Christ was to be right relationship with Him and hence with your community of fellow human beings. The law of negligence expected persons' attention to those persons with whom they expect to relate. The second critical matter is the law's recognition that the vulnerable require succor. The courts beginning in the nineteenth century found that certain relationships imposed upon an actor a duty not to expose vulnerable persons to unreasonable risks of harm. The relationships such as employer-employee

46 *British Railways Board v. Herrington*, [1972] A.C. 877.

47 *Katko v. Briney*, 183 N.W.2d 657 (Iowa 1971).

48 *Vincent v. Lake Erie Transp. Co.*, 109 Minn. 456, 124 N.W. 221 (Minn. 1910).

49 *See* Ripstein, *Private Wrongs* (2016) for discussion.

were characterized by such inequalities in power. Certainly, the categories were closed and the law was confined,[50] but this was to explode with the great case of the early twentieth century: *Donoghue v. Stevenson*. With its overt reference to scripture and Christian ethics, it stands as a center piece in the law of torts and ethical precursors found in Christianity.[51]

The great case

The case that revolutionized the law of torts had very humble beginnings. On an August evening in 1928 May Donoghue, a shop assistant, in search of refreshment arrived at the Wellmeadow café in Paisley, Scotland. (The proprietor was an Italian part of a wave of Italian immigrants that started cafes and sold gelatos.) With her friend she ordered an ice-cream float. The café owner, Mr. Minghella, placed some ice cream into a glass and poured some ginger beer from a bottle onto it. Donoghue consumed some of the delicious concoction and then her friend poured the remainder of the bottle onto the ice. Out slide a decomposed snail. She suffered, she claimed, a nervous shock and gastro-enteritis resulting from her consumption of the ginger beer. She could not sue the owner in contract because her friend had bought the drink; instead she sued the manufacturer of the ginger beer in tort. She alleged that the defendant manufacturer had negligently allowed the snail to enter and remain in the bottle. The opaque bottle had prevented any consumer from reasonably uncovering the gastropod.

Modest mundane facts do not defeat the epoch making judge. "Cometh the hour, cometh the man" and to the case came Lord Atkin who saw in the case an opportunity to escape the crimped nineteenth-century law and establish the law of negligence on a broad ethically driven base. His judgment established that the maker of the ginger beer owed a duty of care to May Donoghue in the face of precedent that confined the duty to established relationships. She was foreseeable as a person who would suffer harm if the manufacturer were negligent in producing an unreasonably dangerous ginger beer.

Of Welsh heritage, although born in Brisbane Australia, Lord Atkin had thought about the application of the Parable of the Good Samaritan to his judgment quite carefully. It was not idle rhetoric that drew him to it.[52] He had aired this with his family at dinner after church as recalled by his grandson many years later.[53] He had in a speech, two years earlier, displayed his thesis of the

50 *Winterbottom v. Wright*, 10 M. & W. 109, 152 E.R. 402 (1842).

51 It is to be noted that there was much correspondence between the English and American judges at this time. *See* "The Holmes Pollock letters," *The Correspondence of Mr. Justice Holmes and Sir Frederick Pollock, 1874–1932*, ed. Mark DeWolfe, Vols. 1 and 2 (2nd ed., 1941). Lord Atkin explicitly recognizes Justice Cardozo's famous decision in *MacPherson v. Buick Motor Co.*, 217 N.Y. 382 (1916).

52 Smith and Burns, "The Good Neighbor on Trial: Good Neighbors Make Bad Law," *University of British Columbia Law Review*, 17 (1983): 93.

53 Lewis, *Lord Atkin* (1983), 57.

moral foundations of the law.[54] English law, he says, sets up "a high, but not too high, attainable standard of honesty and fair dealing..." In a later speech in 1931 he referred to tort law: "I doubt whether the whole law of tort could not be comprised in the golden maxim to do unto your neighbor as you would that he should do unto you" (Luke 10:25–29).

In the Parable of the Good Samaritan in the concept of neighborhood Lord Atkin found his compelling encapsulation of the animating principle of tort law. The Samaritans were a conservative community outside the mainstream of the Jewish community. Members of the group would not have been regarded as neighbors—in fact they were reviled in Judea in the time of Christ. Christ's Golden Rule is universal.

If the question had been "Is the Samaritan my neighbor, too?" the predominant answer in Jewish society of the time would have been a clear cut "no." But Jesus now turns the whole matter on its head:

> The Samaritan...makes himself the neighbor and shows me that I have to learn to be a neighbor deep within and that I already have the answer in myself. I have become like someone in love, someone whose heart is open to being shaken up by another's need. Then I find my neighbor, or—better—then I am found by him.[55]

Such an all-embracing creed breaks with narrow concepts of the law for one is not justified through the law, but through faith. No doubt the "lawyer' in the Parable was trying to trap Jesus thinking of him as a rustic ignorant of Leviticus 19:18 ("Do not seek revenge or bear a grudge against anyone among your people, but love your neighbor as yourself"), Jesus shows his understanding of Leviticus and how it should be applied practically. Moreover, the lesson is a deep one for those subscribing to narrow and constricted views of the "law." The priest and the Levite pass the injured stranger rather than infringe the rules of their religion. The Golden Rule trumps such laws. As one scholar says: "Compassion should overrule code."[56] Mercy prevails even as admitted by the interrogating lawyer. "Which of these three, do you think, was a neighbor to the man who fell into the hands of the robbers?" Jesus asks. The lawyer responds: "The one who showed him mercy." Jesus says, "Go and do likewise." The law should not be blind to such injunctions if it is to act as a carrier of values. For Lord Atkin the lesson of the law of torts to the date of *Donoghue v. Stevenson* was that the narrow law carried within it a deeper lesson. It all tended to uphold the broad neighbor principle, just as the Jewish law, narrow

54 Chapman, *The Snail and the Ginger Beer: The Singular Case of* Donoghue v. Stevenson (2010), 111.

55 Ratzinger, *Jesus of Nazareth: Pope Benedict XVI* (London: Bloomsbury Publishing, 2008), 195; Galatians 2:15–21.

56 Holloway, "Introduction to The Gospel According to Luke," in *The Four Gospels: The Pocket Canons Edition*, (Edinburgh: Canongate Books, 2001).

as it might appear, carried within it the broader more inclusive lesson of universal neighborhood.[57] The tension between the law and the good is seen too in Luke 14.1–24. The principle Paul would apply is that law itself is of limited value for a more original life or order lives beyond it. Persons may live beyond the realm of death, scarcity, and pain that is the life of the law in terms of gift (1 Corinthians 12). But the virtue of charity—loving one's neighbor—shapes the law. As neighbors, we are a gift in service to one another.[58] The House of Lords found, supposing the facts to be established and read in favor of the Ms. Donoghue, that she was owed a duty of care. She was a foreseeable victim of the defendant's negligence that would have allowed the offending snail to crawl into the ginger beer. The case was settled in favor of Mrs. Donohhue who never would have thought that her name would be uttered down the corridors of English Common Law.

Foreseeability and a thousand ships

The articulation of duty as owed to all those who will foreseeably be injured as a result of a person's negligent act took immediate root in the law of torts. With the statements of Cardozo in *MacPherson*,[59] and *Palsgraf*,[60] Lord Atkin's neighbor principle launched the thousand ships of modern negligence law.[61] True it is that modern negligence law has been dominated by instrumental theories of the law but one can't gainsay that the power of Donoghue is its articulation of the ethical base of the law. It was "an integral part of [Lord Atkins's] overall objectives for the common law of negligence."[62] The use of the Parable has also a striking resonance with the inherent dignity of the individual found in tort law. The courts coming after Donoghue and the iconic Cardozo cases anxiously attempted to figure out the boundaries of liability. The disciples of Prosser saw these as mechanisms to control the extent of liability to "avoid the opening of the flood gates." But the significant courts facing the task of describing the range of liability would use the touchstone of responsibility: liability ought to be commensurate to the culpability of the defendant's action.[63] The balance is

57 Braun, *Feasting and the Social Rhetoric in Luke 14* (Cambridge: Cambridge University Press, 1995).

58 Harrison, "Serving and Being Served as Image of God," *St Paul School of Theology*, (unpublished), 5 ("Like the ancient prophets, we may be called to speak the truth and advocate for justice on behalf of our neighbors, or on behalf of the earth and its ecosystems."). *See* James 2:1–10,14–17 (demanding equal respect for the poor as "fulfilling the royal law .... You shall love your neighbor as yourself").

59 *MacPherson*, 217 N.Y 382.

60 *Palsgraf v. Long Island Railroad Co.*, 248 N.Y. 339 (1928).

61 Cardi and Green, "Duty Wars," *California Law Review*, 81 (2008): 671.

62 Chamberlain, "Lord Atkin's Opinion in *Donoghue v. Stevenson*: Perspectives from Biblical Hermeneutic," *Law and Humanities*, 4 (2010): 94.

63 Wagon Mound No. 1, [1961] A.C. 388, Privy Council on appeal from Court of Appeal of New South Wales.

relational. The paradigm is right relationships and the law of torts addresses and corrects wrongful actions that disrupt those right relationships.

A redoubt against invasion of the private: the limits of the duty to rescue

The Restatement Third of Torts § 7 defines the compass of the duty of care in negligence. Liability turns on defendant's act causing physical harm. The intriguing question concerns liability for omissions. This is usually expressed in terms of a denial of a duty to rescue. How is it that the common law would deny a duty of care when in cases like *Donoghue v. Stevenson*, the court seeks a Christian ethical basis for liability. Surely a person who should foresee that a person will be harmed should go to that person's rescue. No doubt the ethical obligation is firmly established.[64] The instrumentalist answer to the no-duty anomaly is in the ethical duty. In the usual case a person through ordinary compunctions of morality will go to the rescue. That is sufficient stimulus to perform the act. In a civilized society, failure to rescue draws social approbation. Indeed, to impose a duty of care may undermine the moral impetus since fellow citizens will presume the rescue has been prompted by dint of a liability rule. A good society is one that uses legal compulsion parsimoniously. Autonomous individuals act generally through social norms. The law is necessary where the incentives to engage upon harm-producing activity overwhelm moral compunctions. For example, where a product manufacturer fails to take adequate precautions in putting dangerous goods into the market. But a parsimonious rule of no liability reinforces the private arena of freewill and inculcates a sense of personal responsibility that enhances the human dignity of the person rescued in an act of grace by the rescuer. If faith is to save us in the Lutheran sense, it is freely arrived at. The private sphere in which the law imposes no legal duties puts ultimate authority on the individual to make moral choices. In Mark 4:35–41, Jesus sleeps as a storm gathers. Afraid of perishing, the disciples wake him criticizing Him for his insouciance as to their plight. He calms the wind. But he takes them to task for their lack of faith. Humans have space to make their own decisions and must accept the consequences. God should not be responsible for everything.

As mentioned above the third pillar of tort law is vulnerability. Jane Stapleton has dubbed it the "golden thread" of tort liability.[65] It too stems from Lord

64 Lentz, "The Bystander in the Bible," *Utah Law Review* (2017): 616, reviewing and commenting on Guiora, *The Crime of Complicity: The Bystander and the Holocaust* (2017). *See also* Clive James, "Blaming the Germans," *The New Yorker*, April 22, 1996 (reviewing and criticizing Daniel Goldhagen, *Hitler's Willing Executioners: Ordinary Germans and the Holocaust* (1996)). The focus of liability is on the person or corporation or legal entity at fault. Group liability where actors are lumped by affiliation is unusual. This is for the good reason that condemnation of entire groups upon a wooden interpretation of text has led to some of mankind's worst crimes.

65 Stapleton, "The Golden Tread at the Heart of Tort Law: Protection of the Vulnerable," *Centenary Essays for the High Court of Australia*, eds. Stapleton and Cane (LexisNexis Butterworths, 2004).

Atkins's *Donoghue v. Stevenson* opinion. Who is your neighbor? The use of the Parable has also a striking resonance with the inherent dignity of the individual found in tort law. Throughout the Gospel, Jesus focuses on the person before Him, recognizing her humanity, her worth, her dignity.

Lord Atkin acknowledges that the law is not coterminous with morality While the Parable should teach us to look at neighbors broadly and act with charity, the common law does not itself impose on the Good Samaritan a duty to rescue. One may leave, the robbery victim as did the priest and Levite, on the side of the road and like them she would suffer ethical condemnation but not tortious liability. This is so even though those travelers would have been able to rescue the injured man with ease. It is clear law in the entire common law world that unless a person caused by his negligent act the injury he will not be legally responsible for it. As Justice Deane of the Australian High Court said in a torts case: "The common law has neither recognized fault in the conduct of the feasting Dives nor embraced the embarrassing moral perception that he who has failed to feed the dying man has truly killed him."[66] In the Parable of the Good Samaritan responsibility to all mankind is universal and allows no room for rejecting the outsider. Not well recognized is Lord Atkin's drawing of a limit to the duty of care. In law he gives the answer of those persons reasonably foreseeably injured by the negligent act. (As John Witte explains in Protestant theory, duties are reciprocal with rights. There is a duty to love one's neighbor but also the neighbor has right to claim "to induce one's neighbor to discharge his or her divinely ordained duty."[67] The rights and duties here are not legal but they inform the content of legal rules.)

Furthermore, the law of negligence will impose duties to take affirmative actions to protect another when defendant has a special relationship with the plaintiff or potential victim. Consistent with the freedom of choice the law stresses the role of voluntary assumptions of responsibility arising from the circumstances. Thus, a school owes a duty of care to protect a student from the criminal acts of a third party where the school has reasonable knowledge of the danger and control of the circumstances to diffuse the danger.[68] A university may have a duty to protect against a shooter where the requisite relationship can be demonstrated. Of particular concern will be the vulnerability of the victims because they invest reliance in the university or other institution for their protection. In one case the court was inclined to find a duty of care in the wife of a child molester who failed to inform the victim's parents of her suspicions about the husband's molestations.[69] A psychologist owes a duty of care in some states to warn the parents of murder victim where the murderer reveals his intentions during therapy.[70]

66 *Jaensch v. Coffey*, 155 CLR 549 (1984).

67 Witte, *God's Joust, God's Justice: Law and Religion in the Western Tradition* (Grand Rapids, MI: Eerdmans, 2006), 62.

68 *Commonwealth v. Peterson*, 749 S.E.2d 307 (2013) (Virginia Tech. Case).

69 *JS and MS v. RTH*, 714 A.2d 924 (1998).

70 *Tarasoff v. Regents of University of California*, 551 P.2d 334 (1976).

The duty to warn or take other reasonable precautions rests on the contract-like freely assumed relationship, the potential harm that is threatened to be perpetrated, the effectiveness of the warning, the ability of the defendant to diffuse the threat and the imminence and salience of the risk.[71]

Vulnerability is ubiquitous. The law's solicitude is so much the greater if the victims are children and others who are foreseeably affected. A blind person is owed a duty of care even though he or she could not reach the standard of the ordinary reasonable person. As stated normally the coordination rule requires that a person comport his behavior to expected interaction with normal persons. Yet to comport that behavior to the expected presence of blind persons is generally accepted because we respect that blind persons ought to be able to integrate and participate in society. The central driver is that each person deserves to have his or her humanity respected.[72] Moreover to extend the duty to incorporate those who are different is to serve as a lesson in what our moral attitudes ought to be.[73] There is no prodigal son, no excluded one; in the Spirit of the Son each of us is beloved.[74] Like God, to love one person does not, or should not, diminish love to all.[75] The abiding Christian ethic is to recognize God's call. It is not a legal duty but as Lord Atkin's hand fashioned it, the legal rule is inspired by it.

The common law, Lord Atkin, and wise courts coming afterward have had a sense of the limits of law. A virtuous society possesses the rule of law but runs effectively and mainly through social norms; it protects the private. Indeed, this is the very zone in which mediatory institutions like churches play a critical role in the formation of non-legal norms and the formation of social capital.[76] Indeed, Robert Cochran argues that tort law often protects "intermediate communities"—families, religious congregations, and other associations between the individual and the state.[77] He draws this from Calvinist and Catholic social thought but is more broadly rooted. The rules protect and impose responsibility on "intermediate communities…so important to human flourishing…"[78]

There is a close interaction between articulated legal norms and social norms. Courts as expositors of values instantiate those values in social interactions. Christian ethics do not generate legal rules but rather lay down principles, as do

71 *Kline v. 1500 Massachusetts Ave. Apt. Corp.*, 439 F.2d 477 (1970).

72 *Roberts v. State of Louisiana*, 396 So.2d 566 (1981).

73 The modern dilemma of regard for those who are different ought to be plain. Compassion for the outsider is at the core of the Gospels.

74 McIntosh, *Mysteries of Faith* (Lanham, MD: Rowman & Littlefield, 2000), 98.

75 Ibid., 99. The game theorist would say that this is a positive sum game. To extend love is to increase the sum of love.

76 Robert Putman, *Bowling Alone: The Collapse and Revival of American Community* (New York: Simon & Schuster, 2000).

77 Robert F. Cochran, "Tort Law and Intermediate Communities: Calvinist and Catholic Insights," in *Christian Perspectives on Legal Thought* (New Haven, CT: Yale University Press, 2001), 486.

78 Ibid., 492–493.

the parables, frameworks, for living life in society.[79] Note Aquinas's assertion about the purpose of law:

> It is evident that the proper effect of law is to lead its subjects to their proper virtue: and since virtue is that which makes its subject good, it follows that the proper effect of law is to make those to whom it is given, good, either simply or in some particular aspect.[80]

But Aquinas too is quick to point to the limits of law.[81] To overburden the person with law impinges on the cultivation of virtue. John Finnis also identifies the criticality for virtue of limited government.[82] Lastly, note Rowan Williams's thesis, in accord with Paul's intimation of the realm beyond law, signaling that space beyond law should be given for a more fundamental association based on gift, in which persons are to be valued for the exercise of their talents offered to a common life.[83] A Christian community is built through practices of forgiveness, penance, and charity and this is Christians' light to the world.[84]

The modern law of negligence would surprise Lord Atkin. But his principle has endured through many different social settings over the past 85 years. The law of torts has burgeoned as responsibilities to "neighbors" have expanded to cover an individual's manifold interests in a modern complex society. But it is at its best humble in the remedial restitutive capacity that it exercises in our human relationships. It will nevertheless continue to play an important role, to educate and coordinate relationships, that is expressive of what is good in society.[85]

Conclusion

Much has been omitted from this brief discussion. But the lesson is clear: three pillars are constantly at play in tort law that support the relationship of that law to Christian precepts. Community, autonomy, and vulnerability are often invoked in the post-realist age but like shags on a rock, without the explicit tie to Christianity that I contend for in this piece. With that tie, we may trace this centerpiece of private law back to the Western revolution that

79 Chamberlain, "Lord Atkin's Opinion" (explaining the uses of Parables and the force of the neighbor principle). Parables can be regarded as Lord Atkin's neighbor principle as object lessons, riddles, and subversive speech. Ibid., 99–104.

80 Aquinas, *Summa Theological of St. Thomas Aquinas* (1273), 1–11, q. 92, art. 1.

81 Ibid., 98–100.

82 Finnis, *Human Rights and the Common Good: Collected Essays*, vol. 3 (Oxford: Oxford University Press, 2011), 82.

83 Williams, *Secularism, Faith and Freedom. Faith in the Public Square* (London: Bloomsbury Publishing, 2012).

84 Matthew 5:14–16.

85 *Cf.* Cochran, op. cit. at 494–495 (extolling the expansion of liability to protect others through finding "special relationships").

Harold Berman powerfully showed was the source of this corner of the law as it was for much other.

In this version, the autonomous individual is not unmoored from social roots. Those are vital. We are to be in right relationship with God and our fellow human beings.[86] Tort law imposes obligations but they are limited. Private law gives individuals space to thrive and exercise our free will, always mindful of the duty expressed and practiced by Dietrich Bonhoeffer and William Wilberforce and their fellow-minded Christians. To act to protect through Christian love the weakest among us has the capacity to transform our relationships and transform society.[87] Tort law true to its pillars frames the private and social duty.

86 The notion of "right relationship" suffused Paul's writings. Take Romans 8:1–39:

> The good news is that God has enabled us to live in this right relationship with him. This righteousness comes from God. It is his gift to us. We cannot earn it. We receive it by faith. Nothing can separate us from God's love for us.

87 Eric Metaxas, *Amazing Grace: William Wilberforce and the Heroic Campaign to End Slavery* (New York, NY: HarperOne, 2007).

16 John Calvin's quarrel with civil recourse theory

Nathan B. Oman

Litigation is, traditionally, an un-Christian activity. While Christians have been taught to render unto Caesar that which is Caesar's and subject themselves to the "powers that be," their scriptures also insist that Christians ought not to take one another to court. Christianity thus bequeaths to its adherents an ambiguous stance toward the law, one that seems to place a great deal of emphasis on the venerable but today much maligned distinction between public and private law. Public law – the "powers that be" – is to be respected, but private law is deeply suspect. Suing can be a nasty business and the Christian critique of litigation has an intuitive logic to it, even to those who might ultimately reject its substance. Strikingly, however, it is difficult to even articulate the substance of that criticism within the categories of much of contemporary private law theory. The exception is civil recourse theory. Most of contemporary private law theory focuses on the idea of liability. For law and economics liability is a price placed on certain conduct in order to create optimal incentives. For moral theorists, such as partisans of corrective justice theory in tort law, liability is the manifestation of a duty of repair that the law imposes on wrong doers. Missing from these theories is the action of the plaintiff, yet this is precisely what Christianity has criticized through the centuries. In contrast to other contemporary approaches to private law, civil recourse theory emphasizes the way that private law empowers plaintiffs to act against those who have wronged them. This is the aspect of litigation against which the Christian critique turns.

This chapter traces in skeletal form a history of the Christian critique of litigation, with a focus on the well-articulated argument of the Reformation theologian John Calvin. Calvin is chosen for two reasons. First, he is undeniably an important Christian thinker. Second, he offers a detailed articulation of the Christian critique of litigation. In contrast to much of contemporary private law theory, Calvin's argument is indifferent to the scope of duties and liabilities. Rather, like civil recourse theorists, he focuses on the agency of plaintiffs. Calvin's argument, however, is critical of key assumptions of those theorists. First, it suggests that generally speaking instituting a suit is immoral. Second, Calvin's argument suggests that revenge and "the right to be punitive," which civil recourse theorists have offered as the basis for punitive damages, cannot be proper reasons for the law. Finally, and most controversially, Calvin seems to reject the "right to reparation" on which some civil recourse theorists have sought to normatively ground private law.

Anti-legalism in Christianity

Christianity contains a powerful strand of anti-legalism. In the Sermon on the Mount, Jesus offers a series of hypertheses in which he counsels his disciples to go beyond the letter of the Mosaic Law to find its spirit. "Think not that I have come to abolish the law and the prophets; I have come not to abolish them but to fulfill them."[1] He begins with the prohibition in the law against murder:

> You have heard that it was said to men of old, "You shall not kill; and whoever kills shall be liable to judgment." But I say to you that whoever one who is angry with his brother shall be liable to judgment; whoever insults his brother shall be liable to the council, and whoever says, "You fool!" shall be liable to the hell of fire.[2]

In this context of the damnable consequences of anger between brothers, Jesus condemns litigation.

> Make friends quickly with your accuser, while you are going with him to court lest your accuser hand you over to the judge and the judge to the guard, and you be put in prison; truly I say to you, you will never get out till you have paid the last penny.[3]

The context here is an action to collect a debt. The word translated as "accuser" above is αυτιδιχοσ(*antidikos*). It is the word used for an opponent in a lawsuit.[4] In the *Phaedrus*, for example, it is the term used by Socrates when discussing the eloquence in court of "parties to a lawsuit."[5] Likewise, the remedies against which Jesus warns – imprisonment for debt – are those of a creditor in a lawsuit. Read literally, Jesus seems to be giving a bit of homely advice about the benefits of paying one's debts rather than risking the hazards of litigation. However, in the broader context of the Sermon on the Mount, his criticism of litigation goes deeper than this. He presents litigation as a manifestation of anger. Like the man who calls his brother "Fool," Jesus implies that the litigant suffers from a defect of the soul that places him in danger of hell fire.

1 Matt 5:17.
2 Matt 5:21–22. The reference here is to the prohibition on murder in the Decalogue. *See* Exod 20:13 and Deut 5:17.
3 Matt 5:25–26.
4 See s.v. "αυτιδιχοσ" in Gerhard Kittel, ed., *Theological Dictionary of the New Testament*, 10th ed., 10 vols. (Wm. B. Eerdmans Publishing Co., 1984).
5 Plato, *Phaedrus* 261c. The term is also used in the Septuagint to refer to litigants in Proverbs 18:17.

The Gospel of Luke repeats the teachings from the Sermon on the Mount almost verbatim:

> And why do you not judge for yourselves what is right? As you go with your accuser before the magistrate, make an effort to settle with him on the way, lest he drag you to the judge, and the judge hand you over to the officer, and the officer put you in prison. I tell you, you will never get out till you have pad the very last copper.[6]

The rhetorical context, however, differs from the Sermon the Mount. Matthew presents this teaching in the context of Jesus's hyperthesis on murder and anger. Avoiding litigation is about fulfilling the higher inner spirit of the Mosaic Law against murder. In contrast, Luke presents the teaching in the context of Jesus castigating the multitude for their ignorance of what should be plain to them. "You hypocrites! You know how to interpret the appearance of the earth and the sky; but why do you not know how to interpret the present time."[7] Just as the hypocrisy of the multitude blinds them to the eschatological meaning of current events, litigation is a sign of their moral confusion. "Why do you not judge for yourselves what is right?"[8] Jesus asks. The resort to litigation thus represents an abdication of moral responsibility to the judge. Rather than outsourcing judgment, Jesus teaches, litigants should be reconciled among themselves.

Paul's First Letter to the Corinthians also offers a pointed criticism of private litigation. The epistle was likely written while Paul was at Rome in response to reports of dissentions and immoral practices among the Christian converts at Corinth. Among these reports was apparently one of members of the church taking one another to court before pagan magistrates. Paul wrote:

> When one of you has a grievance against a brother, does he dare go to law before the unrighteous instead of the saints? Do you not know that the saints will judge the world? And if the world is to be judged by you, are you incompetent to try trivial cases?[9]

Paul's criticism seems to echo that of Jesus in the Gospel of Luke. In the eschatological age to come, the members of the church are to sit as judges of the world. How are they to fulfill this cosmic function if they cannot judge their own disputes without the help of an "unrighteous" magistrate? Paul's response is to call on the local Christians to create their own tribunals to handle such disputes. "Can it be that there is no man among you wise enough to decide between members of the brotherhood," he writes. "But brother goes to law

6 Luke 12:57–59.
7 Luke 12:56.
8 Luke 12:57.
9 1 Cor. 6:1–2.

against brother, and that before unbelievers."[10] Indeed, in an earlier passage in the letter, Paul provides an example of such intra-Christian judgment, deciding a case at Corinth involving an incestuous relationship between a man and his stepmother.[11]

In part, Paul seems to have been motivated by fear of scandal. He twice expresses his horror that the "dirty laundry" of the church has been exposed publicly before pagan magistrates.[12] The creation of "private" fora to handle disputes between co-religionists or other kinds of smaller communities was common in the Greco-Roman world, in part to protect the reputation of minority groups in the larger society.[13] Paul, however, goes beyond such pragmatic considerations of local politics. Rather, as in the teachings of Jesus in Matthew, Paul associates litigation with the angry resistance of wrongs rather than meekly suffering them in love.

> To have lawsuits at all with one another is defeat for you. Why not rather suffer wrong? Why not rather be defrauded? But you yourselves wrong and defraud, and that even your own brethren.[14]

Paul's moral condemnation of fraud is unremarkable. More striking, however, is his condemnation of the victim of fraud. The suggestion here is that the resistance to wrongs can itself be an evil worthy of condemnation.

Medieval Christianity carried forward the anti-legalism of the New Testament. This attitude was captured in the maxim of "pactum legem vincit et amor iudicium"; "agreement prevails over law and love over judgment."[15] In its narrowest sense, this maxim meant that in private disputes, a "pactum" between the parties should control over contrary law. In other words, settlement agreements would be honored. However, it meant more than that. The idea that "amor" (love) could triumph over "iudicium" (judgment) became institutionalized in the so-called "dies amoris" (love day).[16] This seems to have been a formal procedure by which a litigant could demand that the court suspend its judgment to give the parties the opportunity to settle their dispute amicably. However, the form suggested more than simply a breathing space for negotiations. Rather, the goal was Christian harmony between disputing brothers. The judge would counsel the litigants to "be at one" until the next sitting of

10 1 Cor. 6:5–6.

11 1 Cor. 5:1–5.

12 *See* 1 Cor. 6:1 and 1 Cor. 6:6.

13 *See* Mathias Delcor, "The Courts of the Church of Corinth and the Courts of Qumran," in *Paul and Qumran*, ed. Jerome Murphy-O'Connor (London: Geoffrey Chapman, 1968), 69–84.

14 1 Cor. 6:7–8.

15 *See* Michael Clanchy, "Law and Love in the Middle Ages," in *Disputes and Settlements: Law and Human Relations in the West*, ed. John Bossy (New York: Cambridge University Press, 1983), 47–68.

16 *See* Clanchy, 58–60.

the court, at which they would be asked whether they "were at one."[17] Chaucer versified the procedure in way that suggests more than simply a formal settlement agreement, "Mo love-dayes and accordes/ Than on insturmentes be cordes."[18] Chaucer associates the dies amoris with "accordes." He contrasts these with formal "insturmentes," seeing in the "accorde" a superior source for the "cordes" of brotherly love. Indeed, in Middle English, "accordes" had a richer meaning than simply agreement.[19] It was used to refer to Christian unity, peace, and charity.[20] Less poetically, the "dies amoris" also appears in Bracton, the first treatise on English law, who insists that if a litigant protests his adversary's invocation of the love day, he can preserve his plea at the next sitting of the court "if love does not take him."[21]

In the centuries after Martin Luther nailed his 95 theses to the church door in Wittenberg, the radical strains of Christianity implemented the anti-legal tradition literally. For example, the Society of Friends, known more widely as Quakers, came out of the most radical Puritan circles during the English Civil War. They sought to apply Paul's edicts against litigation against co-religionists. As the 1697 rules for the New England Yearly Meeting put it, "when any friend or friends shall hear of any … difference betwixt any friends…they [shall] forthwith speak to and tenderly advise, the persons between whom the difference is, to make a speedy end thereof."[22] If tender advice did not work, Quakers were expected to submit their dispute to "impartial and judicious friends" rather than going to court.[23] Similarly, early Mormons, like the Quakers, placed a premium on church discipline, and created an elaborate three-tiered system of ecclesiastical courts. Among the activity that could land one before such a tribunal was the catch-all charge of "un-Christian like conduct," which generally meant a Latter-day Saint suing a fellow Mormon before a secular court.[24] In the case of such complaints, Mormon ecclesiastical

17 *See* Clanchy, 58–59.

18 Quoted in Clanchy, 61.

19 *See* "'Accord' Sv," Middle English Dictionary, accessed December 21, 2016, https://quod.lib.umich.edu/cgi/m/mec/med-idx?type=id&id=MED289.

20 The *Middle English Dictionary* gives these examples from contemporary sources dealing with Christian virtue, Saint Paul, the unity of the church, and the law:

> Pes and acord awey schol wende And alle charite schal cesse.
>
> But Seint Poul sett oon acorde in al cristendom & seiþ..Vnus dominus, vna fides, vnum baptisma.
>
> Goddis lawe wolde be betere knowun..for onehed of wit & more acord be bi-twixe reumes.
>
> See "'Accord' Sv."

21 Quoted in Clanchy, "Law and Love in the Middle Ages," 59.

22 Quoted in *Society of Friends New England Yearly Meeting, Rules of Discipline of the Yearly Meeting Held on Rhode Island for New England*, 1849, 3–4.

23 *Society of Friends New England Yearly Meeting, Rules of Discipline of the Yearly Meeting Held on Rhode Island for New England*, 3–4.

24 *See* Edwin Brown Firmage and Richard Collin Mangrum, *Zion in the Courts: A Legal History of the Church of Jesus Christ of Latter-Day Saints, 1830–1900* (Urbana, IL: University of Illinois

courts staffed by lay church leaders would hear and resolve the case, threatening those who refused to abide by its decisions with excommunication. From the 1830s until into the twentieth century, Mormon church courts exercised jurisdiction over civil disputes, resolving claims involving torts, contracts, property, bankruptcy, divorce, and the like.

John Calvin and contemporary private law theory

John Calvin provides one of the most thorough articulations of the Christian critique of litigation. He is a useful figure because not only was he an influential Christian theologian but he was also formally trained as a lawyer.[25] He explicitly treats the issue of civil litigation both in his *Institutes of the Christian Religion* and in his *Commentary on the Epistles of Paul to the Corinthians*.[26] In his commentary on 1 Corinthians 6, he acknowledges that in part Paul's criticism of civil litigation was that the Corinthian Christians "by this means made the gospel contemptible, and exposed it to derision."[27] This reasoning, however, was merely "particular," and Calvin insists that Paul had another "general" criticism.[28] The general criticism lies in litigation as a manifestation of moral failing. In the *Institutes*, he writes:

> For there are very many who boil with such a rage for litigation, that they never can be quiet within themselves unless they are fighting with others. Lawsuits they prosecute with the bitterness of deadly hatred, and with an insane eagerness to hurt and revenge, and they persist in them with implacable obstinacy, even to the ruin of their adversary.[29]

Elsewhere he argues that an "excessive fondness for litigation" takes "its rise from avarice."[30] Such people use the law as an excuse and a smoke screen for their moral failings. "Meanwhile, that they may be bout to do nothing but what is legal, they use this pretext of judicial proceedings as a defense of their perverse conduct."[31]

Press, 1988), 263–370 (discussing the resolution of civil litigation before Mormon ecclesiastical courts); Nathan B. Oman, "Preaching to the Court House and Judging in the Temple," *Brigham Young University Law Review*, 2009, no. 1 (2009): 157–224 (same).

25 *See* Joseph Allegretti, "'In All This Love Will Be the Best Guide': John Calvin and the Christian's Resort to the Secular Legal System," *Journal of Law and Religion*, 9, no. 1 (1991): 6.

26 *See* John Calvin, *Institutes of the Christian Religion*, ed. John T. McNeill, trans. Ford Lewis Battles (Philadelphia, PA: Westminster John Knox Press, 1960), IV.20.17–21; John Calvin, *Commentary on the Epistles of Paul the Apostle to the Corinthians*, trans. John Pringle, Kindle edition (Seattle, WA: Amazon Digital Services LLC, 2011), loc.4523–loc.4677.

27 Calvin, *Commentary on the Epistles of Paul the Apostle to the Corinthians*, loc.4524.

28 Calvin, loc.4524.

29 Calvin, *Institutes of the Christian Religion*, IV.20.17.

30 Calvin, *Commentary on the Epistles of Paul the Apostle to the Corinthians*, loc.4523.

31 Calvin, *Institutes of the Christian Religion*, IV.20.17.

Calvin sees litigation as a manifestation of two moral failings. First, he references "that command which forbids Christians to indulge revenge."[32] In bringing a lawsuit, the plaintiff seeks an eye for an eye, a tooth for a tooth. This the Christian may not do. However, Calvin links this to what he sees as a second, deeper moral failing. Jesus taught:

> Love your enemies, do good to those who hate you, bless those who curse you, pray for those who abuse you. To him who strikes you on the cheek, offer the other also; and form him who takes away your coat do not withhold even your shirt. Give to everyone who begs from you; and of him who takes away your goods do not ask them again.[33]

The demand of this teaching is not simply that the Christian refrain from retaliation but that he or she love his enemies. One should not simply give to the beggar but also to the thief. One is not to ask back even that which was taken. Calvin builds on this, writing:

> What Paul then condemns in the Corinthians is this – that they harassed one another with lawsuits. He states the reasons of it – that they were not prepared to bear injuries patiently. And, assuredly, as the LORD commands us not to be overcome by evils, but on the contrary to overcome injuries by acts of kindness, it is certain that those who cannot control themselves so as to suffer injuries patiently, commit sin by their impatience. If contention in lawsuits among believers is a token of that impatience, it follows that is faulty.[34]

In the *Institutes*, he goes farther, writing that Christians should be "so composed in the whole frame of their minds that, on receiving one offence, they were to prepare themselves for another, promising themselves nothing during the whole life by the endurance of a perpetual cross."[35]

Despite the scope of his criticisms of civil litigation, however, Calvin is at pains to carve out a space for legitimate private lawsuits. There are two reasons for this. First, he wishes to distance himself from radicals, such as the Anabaptists, who had advocated extreme antinomianism. His reasons, however, go beyond merely separating himself from a politically toxic sect. Calvin's second reason goes to his theological defense of secular authority. He takes Paul's admonition in the Epistles to the Romans of subordination to "the powers that be" seriously. For Calvin magistrates are instituted by God and "the vengeance of the magistrate

32 Calvin, IV.20.19.

33 Luke 6:27–30.

34 Calvin, *Commentary on the Epistles of Paul the Apostle to the Corinthians*, loc.4639 (internal scriptural citations omitted).

35 Calvin, *Institutes of the Christian Religion*, IV.20.20.

is the vengeance not of man, but of God, which as Paul says, he exercises by the ministry for our good."[36] Indeed, he argues that Christians are bound to obey even the unjust tyrant, who is used by God to goad the unrighteous to repentance and test the patience of the saints.[37] (Although Calvin does argue that one is not obligated to obey the tyrant when his commands conflict with those of God.)[38] If, however, Christians are categorically forbidden from resorting to secular magistrates it would seem to suggest that the function of those magistrates is illegitimate. Calvin's response is to delineate cases where a Christian might in good faith proceed against another in court.

First, he argues that no blame attaches to the Christian who appears in court as a defendant. "It is wrong...to institute of one's own accord a lawsuit against brethren before unbelieving judges. If on the other hand you are summoned to court, there is no harm in appearing and maintaining your cause."[39] Even in this case, however, the defendant should "without bitterness urge what he can in his defense, but only with the desire of justly maintaining his right."[40] More importantly, Calvin argues that it is permissible for a Christian to be a plaintiff in a lawsuit, provided that he can do so without bitterness or enmity toward the defendant.

> Let such persons then understand that judicial proceedings are lawful for him who makes right use of them; and the right use ... for the pursuer, when undeservedly attacked in his life or fortunes to throw himself upon the protection of the magistrate, state his complaint, and demand what is just and good; while, far from any wish to hurt or take vengeance – far from bitterness and hatred – far from the clamor of strife, he is rather disposed to yield and suffer somewhat that to cherish hostile feelings towards his opponent.[41]

Crucially, for Calvin, the permissibility of civil litigation does not turn on the justice of one's legal position.

> [W]hen minds are filled with malevolence, corrupted by envy, burning with anger, breathing revenge, or, in fine, so inflamed by the heat of the contest, that they, in some measure, lay aside the whole pleading, even the justest cause, cannot but be impious.[42]

36 Calvin, IV.20.19 (internal scriptural citations omitted); *see also* Allegretti, "'In All This Love Will Be the Best Guide': John Calvin and the Christian's Resort to the Secular Legal System" (discussing Calvin's political theology and is relationship to his teachings on civil litigation).
37 *See* Calvin, *Institutes of the Christian Religion*, IV.20.24 et seq.
38 *See* Calvin, IV.20.32.
39 Calvin, *Commentary on the Epistles of Paul the Apostle to the Corinthians*, loc.4539.
40 Calvin, *Institutes of the Christian Religion*, IV.20.18.
41 Calvin, IV.20.18.
42 Calvin, IV.20.18.

This, however, is a standard of charitable disinterestedness that Calvin concedes few litigants ever meet in fact. "I confess that in these times it is rare to meet with an example of an honest litigant; but the thing itself, untainted by accession of evil, ceases not to be good and pure."[43]

The most striking thing about Calvin's critique of litigation is that it is completely indifferent to the question of liability. In his telling, Christianity's quarrel with civil litigation does not revolve around the content of the legal duties that the private law prescribes or with the scope of liability that the law affixes to the breach of those duties. This is striking because the question of liability tends to dominate contemporary private law theory. Contract law scholarship, for example, has been centered on the question of damages and damage measures since Lon Fuller's seminal 1936 article "The Reliance Interest in Contract Damages."[44] Likewise, most of the major debates in tort theory have centered on issues such as the choice between negligence and strict liability or the scope of the duty of care. Nothing in Calvin's critique, however, turns on these or related questions. For him Christianity's uneasiness with private law has nothing to do with the scope of duties or liability. The problem is not that a Christian going to court is availing himself or herself of legal rules that create unjust or immoral duties or that there is some evil in the remedy available for their breach. Indeed, Calvin's criticisms of litigation assume that the substantive content of the law is just.

Rather the argument that he offers focuses exclusively on the activity of litigation. Indeed, Christian criticism of litigation from Jesus onward has focused mainly not on the content of the law, but on the agency of the parties that call on the law in their quarrels with others. This explains, for example, why Paul is vociferous in his denunciations of Christians invoking the private law but insistent on their obligation to comply with public law. Likewise, Calvin can argue in favor of the moral obligation to obey even the laws of a tyrant while affirming that only a moral hero can avail himself of the private law without sin. Private law involves the activity of litigation, while obeying the commands of the public law does not. However, the normative status of the activity of litigation is strangely absent from much of contemporary private law theory, making it difficult to situate the Christian critique within its debates.

The dominant approach to private law theory in the United States is law and economics. According to this approach, the normative goal of fields such as torts, contracts, and property should be to maximize social utility through the efficient allocation of resources. The law does this, so goes the theory, by creating incentives for parties to behave in efficient ways or alternatively by assigning legal entitlements efficiently when high transaction costs inhibit direct private ordering.[45] Law and economics has seen defenders and critics among Christian

43 Calvin, IV.20.18.

44 *See* L.L. Fuller and William R. Perdue, "The Reliance Interest in Contract Damages, Pt. 1," *Yale Law Journal*, 46 (1936): 52–96.

45 *See generally* R. H. Coase, "The Problem of Social Cost," *Journal of Law and Economics*, 3 (October 1, 1960): 1–44; Guido Calabresi and A. Douglas Melamed, "Property Rules, Liability

legal theorists. Some have argued that its assumptions simply reflect the reality of human behavior in a fallen world.[46] Others have claimed that its acceptance of human acquisitiveness and focus on material wealth reflects the vice of avarice and a rejection of the Spirit for Mammon.[47] None of these Christian interlocutors with law and economics, however, has considered their own tradition's long-standing critique of litigation.

From a law and economics perspective that critique is puzzling. While Jesus condemned taking a brother to law, he counseled that we render to Caesar that which is Caesar's. Yet for economic analysis the payment of damages is simply a Pigouvian tax. Damages – like a tax on pollution – internalize all of the costs of the agent's decision, which is now blessed by the alignment of private and social incentives. Damages are thus normatively indistinguishable – except in the details of institutional design – from a gasoline tax. Jesus, however, counseled against litigation while encouraging his disciples to pay their taxes. Why the difference in treatment? Law and economics gives us no apparent traction on this question. There is no place in the theory in which to situate the Christian critique.

The same is true of corrective justice theory, which in recent decades has emerged as one of the chief competitors with law and economics in private law theory. The key insight of these theorists is that private law relates a wrongdoer and her victim together in a way that is unique.[48] In a tort suit, for example, a victim and wrongdoer will be related to one another by the idea of civil liability. The remedy will flow from defendant to plaintiff. On this view, damages are not an externality-internalizing tax on behavior but compensation paid by the tortfeasor to the victim of his wrongdoing. In making this payment, tortfeasors discharge their moral duty of repair or corrective justice.

The basic structure of the argument goes back to Aristotle, who distinguished between distributive justice, which he labeled a geometric principle, and corrective or commutative justice, which he called an arithmetical principle. Distributive justice is a matter of seeing that deserts are allocated among individuals in ratio to the proper moral criteria, hence geometrically. Corrective justice, in contrast, is about rectifying wrongs by taking improperly realized gains and returning them to those from whom they are taken. Notice that once one fully specifies the structure of the duty of corrective justice, presumably by providing some account of wrongful action or a wrongful loss, the duty becomes much

---

Rules, and Inalienability: One View of the Cathedral," *Harvard Law Review*, 85 (1972 1971): 1089.

46 *See generally* Stephen M. Bainbridge, "Law and Economics: An Apologia," in *Christian Perspectives on Legal Thought*, ed. Michael W. McConnell, Robert F. Cochran, Jr., and Angela C. Carmella (New Haven, CT: Yale University Press, 2001), 208–23.

47 *See generally* George E. Garvey, "A Catholic Social Teaching Critique of Law and Economics," in *Christian Perspectives on Legal Thought*, ed. Michael W. McConnell, Robert F. Cochran, Jr., and Angela C. Carmella (New Haven, CT: Yale University Press, 2001), 224–40.

48 *See, e.g.*, Ernest Weinrib, *The Idea of Private Law* (Cambridge, MA: Harvard University Press, 1995); Jules Coleman, *Risks and Wrongs* (New York: Oxford University Press, 2002).

like any other duty that the law enforces. The duty not to commit murder is owed to particular individuals. One never commits murder in general. Rather, one always kills a particular individual. Likewise, the duty of corrective justice is owed between particular individuals. Both duties are enforced by the law. We are thus left with the problem we encountered earlier with law and economics: why should the Christian critique apply to litigation but not to the criminal law? Why does it single out private law?

There is one contemporary legal theory that places the agency of the plaintiff rather than the nature of liability at the center of its account of private law. Civil recourse theory begins with the recognition that private law does not simply specify duties and define the consequences of their breach. Rather, private law also empowers wronged plaintiffs to act against those that have wronged them. It is not simply a matter of efficiently pricing activity with consequences to others or enforcing corrective justice duties of repair. It is about victims holding wrongdoers to account. In Hartian terms, civil recourse theory is as concerned about the "power conferring" nature of private law rules as it is with their "duty imposing" character.

Civil recourse's key insight is that private law is fundamentally a system by which plaintiffs act to hold defendants accountable for their actions to plaintiffs. These theorists have provided a normative justification of the law's empowerment of plaintiffs based on a reading of John Locke's social contract theory.[49] In the *Second Treatise*, Locke writes that in the state of nature:

> Besides the Crime which consists in violating the Law and varying from the right Rule of Reason, whereby a Man so far becomes degenerate, and declares himself to quit the Principles of Human Nature, and to be a noxious Creature, there is commonly injury done to some Person or other, and so the Man receives damages by his Transgression, in which Case he who hath received any damage, has besides the right of punishment common to him with other Men, a particular Right to seek *Reparation* from him that has done it.[50]

According to civil recourse theorists, in the social contract we give up our natural right not only to enforce the law of nature but also to seek reparation through violent self-help. Civil magistrates acquire the rights originally held by all in the state of nature to enforce natural law. As part of this role, the magistrate suppresses private violence. However, the law, by providing individuals with a private cause of action against those who have wronged them, continues to recognize the right to "Reparation" held in the state of nature. The right, however,

49 *See* Benjamin Zipursky, "The Philosophy of Private Law," in *The Oxford Handbook of Jurisprudence & Philosophy of Law*, ed. Jules Coleman and Scott Shapiro (New York: Oxford University Press, 2002), 623–55.

50 John Locke, *Two Treaties of Government*, ed. Peter Laslett (New York: Cambridge University Press, 1989), 273.

is now civilized through the process of the civil law, shorn of private violence and limited in scope. Crucially, however, what is preserved is not a right to compensation per se, but rather the right to hold others accountable, a process that might involve compensatory damages but could take other forms, such as declaratory and equitable relief or punitive damages.

Christianity's quarrel with civil recourse theory

While the Christian critique agrees with civil recourse theory in seeing the agency of the plaintiff as a central feature of private law, this does not mean that Calvin's account of civil litigation and its moral implications accords with the civil recourse view of the private law. There are at least three places where Calvin's view of the moral status of the litigation diverges from the civil recourse theory. First, Calvin places enormous emphasis on the morality of the decision to sue, suggesting that generally speaking instituting a lawsuit is a moral wrong. Second, as they have been defended on non-economic grounds by civil recourse theorists, punitive damages seem to be flatly rejected by Calvin's view of the potential evils of litigation. Finally, and most radically, Calvin can be read as rejecting the legitimacy of "Reparations" in the Lockean sense understood by civil recourse theorists. Rather, Calvin seems to suggest that private litigation should be seen as an adjunct to the power of the magistrate in pursuing the broader public interest.

If private law empowers plaintiffs to sue, then one of the central moral questions raised by the law is how plaintiffs ought to use that power. This is a question on which civil recourse theorists have had very little to say. Methodologically this is unsurprising.[51] Ultimately, civil recourse theory is a theory of law. It is not a freestanding moral or political theory. Rather, it seeks to provide an interpretive reconstruction of the law that is more than a mere legal sociology but is nevertheless disciplined by the reality of the system of laws that we actually have. Without making overly ambitious claims of imminent rationality, it seeks to reveal the latent normative structures of legal doctrine and justify them in terms that seem most consonant with the law's own self-understanding. The question of whether to bring suit is not strictly speaking a legal question. It is not a decision that is guided by any legal doctrines, and one might thus say that it is outside of one's theory of the law, strictly construed.

However, for civil recourse theory the morality of bringing suit cannot be so easily elided. At the very least, the law must assume that there exists a very broad spectrum of cases in which bringing suit is at the very least morally unobjectionable and perhaps even morally laudable. One might agree that in some cases plaintiffs ought to forgive their wrongdoers or that in some instances bringing suit may be captious. However, the private law provides a very broad grant of

51 *See* Benjamin C. Zipursky, "Pragmatic Conceptualism," *Legal Theory*, 6, no. 4 (December 1, 2000): 457–85.

power to plaintiffs to bring suit. If the decision to bring suit were generally morally depraved then such a broad grant of power would be troubling. At the very least, it would be the sort of thing calling for an explanation. It may be entirely possible to construct such an argument; however, it seems that its complete absence rests on the assumption that it is not really necessary to provide it. That, in turn, rests on the assumption that generally speaking it is morally unobjectionable for the holder of a valid cause of action to bring suit.

It is this assumption, of course, that Calvin vehemently rejects. For him, righteous litigation is a possibility but it is extremely unlikely. He writes:

> For this must be a set of principles for all Christians: that a lawsuit, however just, can never be rightly prosecuted by any man, unless he treat his adversary with the same love and good will as if the business under controversy were already amicably settled and composed.[52]

This is a very demanding standard. The conflict of litigation can be risked only if it can be done in a spirit of love as though there were no conflict at all. As Calvin recognizes, this is a standard that is seldom met.

> Perhaps someone will interpose here the such moderation is so uniformly absent from any lawsuit that it would be a miracle if any such were found. Indeed, I admit that, as the customs of these times go, an example of an upright litigant are rare…[53]

Far from assuming that the exercise of the power to bring suit is sufficiently unremarkable that it doesn't require any particular explanation, Calvin argues that most litigation is immoral.

Few topics are as fraught in contemporary debates over the status of private law as punitive damages. The Supreme Court has declared that in some instances their award violates the Due Process Clause.[54] Some law and economic scholars have sought to defend them on efficiency grounds, but generally speaking punitive damages have been criticized as an ineffective mechanism for creating optimal incentives. For corrective justice theorists, the purpose of damages is to provide compensation to plaintiffs for their losses. Punitive damages, however, are by definition non-compensatory and thus constitute something of an embarrassment for those theories.

However, once one sees litigation as primarily about empowering victims to act against wrongdoers, then the explanation for punitive damages becomes more natural. Such damages are an extension of the plaintiff's justified resentment

52 Calvin, *Institutes of the Christian Religion*, IV.20.18.

53 Calvin, IV.20.18.

54 *See, e.g.*, BMW of North America, Inc. v. Gore, 517 U.S. 559 (1996) (holding that punitive damages awards that are excessive violate the due process clause); *see also* State Farm Mut. Auto. Ins. Co. v. Campbell, 538 U.S. 408 (2003) (same).

against the defendant based on the egregiousness of the defendant's actions.[55] Some scholars, for example, have argued that the origins of punitive damages lie in the quest for revenge resulting from humiliation and disrespect.[56] One writes:

> Under the model of punitive damages as revenge, the victim makes an argument for punishment based on reasons that she hopes the court will take as objectively valid. If they are, they she has secured her retribution over the defendant who, by his actions, "argued" exactly the opposite. The victory of her argument for punishment (and not the state's), when accepted by the court, is her redress.[57]

In a similar, if less provocative, vein, civil recourse theorists have argued that punitive damages should be awarded because in the face of egregious wrongdoing, plaintiffs have a right to be punitive. The plaintiffs' right to be punitive constitutes the core of a civil aspect of punitive damages, while the state's goal of inflicting punishment upon the defendant is the root of a criminal aspect.[58]

Calvin, however, rejected entirely the legitimacy of seeking revenge. Furthermore, he agreed with civil recourse theorists that it often formed part of the reason for private litigation, but insisted that such litigation could only be legitimate if purged of such impulses.

> For if it is a civil case, a man does not take the right path unless he commits his cause, with innocent simplicity, to the judge as public protectors; and he should think not at all of returning evil for evil, which is the passion of revenge.[59]

Elsewhere, he laments, "[t]here are very many who so boil with a rage for litigation" and "carry on their lawsuits with bitter and deadly hatred, and an insane passion for revenge and hurt."[60] For Calvin's argument there is thus no value in punitive damages as explained by civil recourse theory. It is not that he objects to the severe punishment of wrongdoing. Rather his theory suggests that to link that punishment with the plaintiff's desire for revenge is wrong.[61]

55 Peter F. Strawson, "Freedom and Resentment," *Proceedings of the British Academy*, 48 (1962): 1–25 (arguing that victims of wrongful conduct are morally entitled to feel resentful toward those that wrong them).

56 *See generally* Anthony J. Sebok, "Punitive Damages: From Myth to Theory," *Iowa Law Review*, 92 (2007): 957–1036; Anthony J. Sebok, "What Did Punitive Damages Do? Why Misunderstanding the History of Punitive Damages Matters Today," *Chicago-Kent Law Review*, 78 (2003): 163–206.

57 Sebok, "Punitive Damages: From Myth to Theory," 1029.

58 Benjamin C. Zipursky, "A Theory of Punitive Damages," *Texas Law Review*, 84 (2005): 107.

59 Calvin, *Institutes of the Christian Religion*, IV.20.19.

60 Calvin, IV.20.17.

61 John Finnis, "Natural Law: The Classical Tradition," in *The Oxford Handbook of Jurisprudence & Philosophy of Law*, ed. Jules Coleman and Scott Shapiro (New York: Oxford University Press,

Finally, Calvin can be read as rejecting the entire notion of a right to reparation as conceptualized in the Lockean-based argument for civil recourse. That argument differentiates between the state's right to punish wrongdoing and an individual's right to reparation, even though the two will often overlap in terms of the wrongs that they address. As one scholar has written:

> There is a natural right and power to seek compensation for an injury done to one. However, if each person acted on what he or she perceived to be an injury caused by another, and engaged in self-help remedies, this would lead to chaos. But the problem will be resolved if each entrusts to the state the power to ascertain whether such an infringement occurred, and the power to redress the injury by requiring the injurer to compensate the injured party. The state has the power to do this because individuals have entrusted it to the state; individuals are justifiably prohibited from doing this because the state will be doing it on their behalf.[62]

Hence, private law is not merely a matter of the state righting wrongs, punishing wrongdoers, or protecting the entitlements of citizens. It represents a distinct and primal kind of right. While Calvin, writing more than a century before Locke, does not use the language of social contract theory, he seems to reject the assumption that there is a right to reparation.

Calvin consistently conceptualizes a private lawsuit as primarily an appeal to the magistrate to enforce the law against a wrongdoer.[63] What makes civil litigation defensible, according to Calvin, is that in theory it can be divorced from the private grievance of the plaintiff, who merely becomes an agent in advancing the justice of the community. "The Christian endures insults," he writes, "but with amity and equity defends the public interest."[64] In another passage, he suggests that one of the risks of private litigation is that it will pollute the magistrate's care of the public interest with the private anger of litigants.

> Indeed, I admit that, as the customs of these times go, an example of upright litigant is rare; but the thing itself, when no corrupted by the addition of anything evil, does not cease to be good and pure. But when we hear that the help of the magistrate is a holy gift of God, we must more diligently guard against its becoming polluted by our fault.[65]

2002), 56–57 (condemning as illegitimate civil recourse's justification of private rights of action as providing a mechanism for plaintiffs to "get even" with defendants).

62 Zipursky, "The Philosophy of Private Law," 639.

63 *See, e.g.*, Calvin, *Institutes of the Christian Religion*, IV.20.18 ("the plaintiff, undeservedly oppressed either in his person or his property, puts himself in the care of the magistrate, makes his complaint, and seeks what is fair and good").

64 Calvin, IV.20.20.

65 Calvin, IV.20.18.

It is only through participation in the public spiritedness of the magistrate that the rare moral paragon can pursue private litigation, precisely because there is a sense in which such litigation ceases to be private. It is no longer a matter of pursuing a personal grievance. Instead, the litigant becomes a kind of petty magistrate, imbued with the God-given legitimacy of the magistrate. In Lockean terms, such a litigant is virtuous precisely because he is not seeking reparation but rather the enforcement of the natural law. In his emphasis on the legitimacy of the magistrate and denigration of the legitimacy of private litigation, Calvin leaves little if any room for a private right of reparation.

Conclusion

Christianity has a long tradition of hostility to private litigation. This tradition co-exists with an equally long tradition that generally accepts the legitimacy of the law, counseling believers to "render unto Caesar that which is Caesars" and be subject to "the powers that be." The reconciliation of these apparently conflicting strands of thought lies in the agency of plaintiffs in private litigation. In the well-articulated argument of John Calvin, the Christian critique of litigation is indifferent to the scope of duties and liabilities. What is morally objectionable is the activity of suing another. Mapping his argument on to contemporary private law theory it is rendered most coherent by civil recourse theory, which also emphasizes the agency of litigants. Calvin's argument is also critical of civil recourse theory on key points. Ultimately, civil recourse argues persuasively that providing victims with an avenue of self-assertion against wrongdoers is one of the primary goals of private law. Calvin, however, suggests that for the Christian such self-assertion is always morally dangerous. Rather than using the legal power conferred on them by the private law to haul wrong doers before the courts, Christians, he argues, ought to turn the other cheek and do good to those that despitefully use them. Wrongdoers should be left to the powers that be rather than the private law.

17 Tort law and intermediate communities

Catholic and Calvinist theories*

Robert F. Cochran, Jr.

Tort law is commonly thought to be individualist in character.[1] Some tort law theorists celebrate its individualistic character.[2] Others lament it.[3] But tort law theorists have failed to give attention to a countervailing strain in tort law. Many tort rules are not individualist in character; many were designed to protect and many others to make demands on intermediate communities—the families, religious congregations, and other associations that stand between the individual and the state.

These tort law rules can best be understood based on what I will call "intermediate communitarian" theory, a theory drawn from Calvinist and Catholic social thought, but which is likely to find support in other religious and nonreligious traditions. Intermediate communitarian theory recognizes that intermediate communities are crucial to the health of both the individual and the broader society. As to tort law, intermediate communitarian theory can play both a descriptive role, helping us to identify and understand the intermediate communitarian strain that has generally gone unnoticed in the tort literature, and a normative role, suggesting ways that tort law might both protect and make demands on intermediate communities in the future.

* Reprinted with permission from Robert F. Cochran, Jr., "Christian Traditions, Culture, and Law," in *Christian Perspectives on Legal Thought*, eds. Michael W. McConnell, Robert F. Cochran, Jr., and Angela C. Carmella (New Haven, CT: Yale University Press, 2001). Some citations have been updated with sources in brackets. *See also* Robert F. Cochran, Jr. and Robert M. Ackerman, *Law and Community: The Case of Torts* (Rowman & Littlefield, 2003). I am grateful to Zach Carstens and Aaron Foltz for their research assistance.

1 *See, e.g.*, Robert A. Baruch Bush, "Between Two Worlds: The Shift From Individual to Group Responsibility in the Law of Causation of Injury," *UCLA Law Review*, 33 (1986): 1473; Richard L. Abel, "A Critique of Torts," *UCLA Law Review*, 37 (1990): 831; Richard A. Epstein, "A Theory of Strict Liability," *Journal Legal Studies*, 2 (1973): 203–04; David Owen, "The Moral Foundations of Products Liability Law: Toward First Principles," *Notre Dame Law Review*, 68 (1993): 498–99.

2 *See* Owen, "Moral Foundations," 498–99, and Epstein, "A Theory of Strict Liability," 203–04.

3 *See* Robert M. Ackerman, "Tort Law and Communitarianism: Where Rights Meet Responsibilities," *Wake Forest Law Review*, 30 (1995): 651 and sources cited therein.

Intermediate communitarian theory

Calvinists and sphere sovereignty

Abraham Kuyper (1837–1920) was a philosopher, a theologian, founder of the Free University of Amsterdam, and prime minister of Holland. In his social philosophy, Kuyper responded to Rousseau's Enlightenment individualism and Hegel's collectivism with the notion of "sphere sovereignty." Kuyper shared the traditional Calvinist belief in the sovereignty of God. In his speech at the founding of the Free University, he said, "There is not a square inch in the whole domain of our human existence over which Christ, who is Sovereign over *all*, does not cry: 'Mine!'"[4] But he also believed that God "delegates his authority to human beings." God delegates authority to the state, but also delegates authority to other entities, each of which is sovereign within its sphere. Kuyper recognized the church, the state, families, universities, guilds, and other associations as having spheres within which they are sovereign. He recognized two special responsibilities for the state:

> [The State] must provide for sound mutual interaction among the various spheres, insofar as they are externally manifest, and keep them within just limits. Furthermore, since personal life can be suppressed by the group in which one lives, the state must protect the individual from the tyranny of his own circle.

Nevertheless, Kuyper warned, "Do not forget that every State power tends to look upon all liberty with a suspicious eye." The state should not become an octopus, stifling the whole of life.

Sphere sovereignty has its roots in Calvin's thought. Calvin saw the church and the state as separate entities, each with its own God-given authority. Neither is subordinate to the other. The Calvinist ideal is a free church in a free state. Just as under the government of the Protestant churches, all believers and congregations are of equal standing, so are all citizens and groups within a nation.[5]

Kuyper found the basis for sphere sovereignty "in the order of creation, in the structure of human life," but also in scripture. He cited the examples of Jews and Christians resisting the governing authorities, as well as the "LORD's maxim concerning what is God's and what is Caesar's."[6]

4 Abraham Kuyper, "Sphere Sovereignty (1880)" in *Abraham Kuyper: A Centennial Reader*, trans. George Kamp (1998), 488. Quotations that follow in the text are from 466, 468, and 472.

5 Abraham Kuyper, *Calvinism* (1943), 96, 106, 63.

6 Kuyper, "Sphere Sovereignty," 480.

Catholics and subsidiarity

The Catholic notion of subsidiarity received its first expression in Pope Leo XIII's encyclical *Of New Things (Rerum Novarum)* in 1891.[7] He presented subsidiarity as an alternative to the individualism of unrestrained capitalism and the collectivism of Marxism. Leo had strong language for each. Capitalists should pay their workers wages sufficient to provide for their families; socialists should respect the right of private property. Leo emphasized the importance of institutions between the individual and the state remaining independent, using language similar to that of Kuyper. According to Leo, state administration of property would "bring State action into a sphere not within its competence." In addition, "A family, no less than a State, is ... a true society, governed by a power within its sphere."

Nevertheless, there appears to be greater room for interaction between the family and the state under subsidiarity than under sphere sovereignty.

> If a family finds itself in exceeding distress, utterly deprived of the counsel of friends, and without any prospect of extricating itself, it is right that extreme necessity be met by public aid, since each family is a part of the commonwealth. In like manner, if within the precincts of the household there occur grave disturbance of mutual rights, public authority should intervene .... But the rulers of the State must go no further: here nature bids them stop.

In *Of New Things*, Leo also discussed the importance of other intermediate institutions. The church, private benevolent foundations, labor unions, and religious orders all serve the needs of human beings and all face the danger of interference from the state. Leo's special concern in *Of New Things* was the relationship between business and labor. Here, again, he preferred a limited role for the state. Wages and working conditions should be improved through organizations of employers and workmen and strong labor unions, "in order to supersede undue interference on the part of the State."

Subsidiarity has received further development in papal encyclicals since *Of New Things*, most recently in Pope John Paul's *Centesimus Annus, The Economics of Human Freedom*, an encyclical commemorating *Of New Things*' one hundredth anniversary. John Paul wrote,

> *The principle of subsidiarity* must be respected: a community of a higher order should not interfere in the internal life of a community of a lower order, depriving the latter of its functions, but rather should support it in case of need and help to coordinate its activity with the activities of the rest of

7 Pope Leo XIII, "Of New Things (1891)," reprinted in *The Papal Encyclicals in Their Historical Context*, ed. Anne Fremantle (1956), 166 [hereinafter *Papal Encyclicals*]. Quotations that follow in the text are from pages 168, 171, 172, and 187–89.

> society, always with a view to the common good. Needs are best understood and satisfied by people who are closest to them, and who act as neighbors to those in need.[8]

Under the Catholic notion of subsidiarity, "Communities must enable and encourage individuals to exercise their self-responsibility and larger communities must do the same for smaller ones."[9]

Like sphere sovereignty, subsidiarity is grounded in both human nature and Scripture.

John Paul said,

> In the Christian vision, the social nature of man is not completely fulfilled in the state but is realized in various intermediary groups, beginning with the family and including economic, social, political, and cultural groups that stem from human nature itself and have their own autonomy, always with a view to the common good.[10]

Leo quoted Ecclesiastes 4:9–10 to illustrate the very practical value of community.

> It is better that two should be together than one; for they have the advantage of their society. If one fall he shall be supported by the other. Woe to him that is alone, for when he falleth he hath none to lift him up.[11]

Although there are differences between the Calvinist doctrine of sphere sovereignty and the Catholic doctrine of subsidiarity, their similarities are greater than their differences. There is probably greater interaction among the Catholic subsidiary communities than among the Calvinist sovereign spheres. Nevertheless, both doctrines recognize the importance of intermediate communities, for the sake of individuals as well as of society, and both recognize the dangers that either individualism or totalitarianism creates for intermediate communities.

The value of intermediate communities

Intermediate communities are important for several reasons. First, they have inherent value. As Peter Berger and Richard John Neuhaus have noted, the megastructures of modern life (big government, big business, big unions) are

8 John Paul II, "Centesimus Annus, The Economics of Human Freedom (1991)," in *Doing Well and Doing Good*, Richard John Neuhaus (1992), 301; for a similar description of subsidiarity, *see* Pope Pius XI, "Quadragesimo Anno (1931)," in *Papal Encyclicals*, 230.

9 Jean Bethke Elshtain, "Catholic Social Thought, the City, and Liberal America," in *Catholicism, Liberalism, and Communitarianism*, ed. Kenneth L. Grasso et al. (1995), 105, citing Joseph A. Komonchak, "Subsidiarity in the Church: The State of the Question," *The Jurist* 48 (1988): 301–02.

10 *See* John Paul II, "Centesimus Annus," 289–90.

11 Pope Leo XIII, "Of New Things," 189 (emphasis in the original).

"typically alienating, that is, they are not helpful in providing meaning and identity for individual existence," but in the modern world's alternative, private life, "the individual is left very much to his own devices, and thus is uncertain and anxious."[12] In a sense, in modern America we are all homeless.[13] Intermediate communities provide opportunities for fellowship, friendship, and meaning.

Second, intermediate communities are the source of the psychological and moral formation of individuals. In the words of Michael Sandel, community is "constitutive" of the self. For most people, intermediate communities are a source of personal identity. As Alasdair MacIntyre has said, "[I] inherit from the past of my family, my city, my tribe, my nation, a variety of debts, inheritances, rightful expectations and obligations. These constitute the given of my life, my moral starting point."[14] The experience of living in community teaches people how to relate to and treat others. This is especially true of the family. As Mary Ann Glendon has said, "[In the family,] citizens acquire the capacity to care about the common good"; "people learn to view others with respect and concern, rather than to regard them as objects, means, or obstacles"; and "a boy or girl develops the healthy independence of mind and self-confidence that enables men and women to participate effectively in government and to exercise responsible leadership."[15] From love of the smaller community, love of the larger society can, we hope, grow. Tocqueville called communities "little schools for citizenship."[16]

Third, intermediate communities provide "social services," both to their own members and to other people. The family is the greatest "social service provider." Some suggest that the United States is now going through crises in education, child care, and health care. But the problems that we have are minuscule compared to what they would be if families did not voluntarily meet a substantial portion of all of these needs. The costs of reproducing these services through government or in market transactions would be overwhelming.

Most religious communities teach that members should care for one another, but they also teach that their members have a social responsibility beyond the religious congregation. "The most anomic individuals in our society, the denizens of skid row for example, are cared for almost exclusively by voluntary associations, usually religious in character."[17] Studies show that people from religious congregations are the most active in both charitable giving and public service volunteering.[18]

12 *See* Peter L. Berger and Richard John Neuhaus, *To Empower People*, vol. 2 (1977).
13 *Cf.* Elshtain, "Catholic Social Thought," 106.
14 *See* Alasdair MacIntyre, *After Virtue*, 2nd ed. (1984), 220.
15 *See* Mary Ann Glendon, *Rights Talk: The Impoverishment of Political Discourse* (1991), 129.
16 *See* Mary Ann Glendon, "Communitarian Wager," *Responsive Community* (Summer 1992): 56 (quoting Alexis de Tocqueville).
17 Berger and Neuhaus, *To Empower People*, 32.
18 *See, e.g.*, Robert Franklin, "Charitable Giving Up 7.3% in U.S.," *Minneapolis-St. Paul Star-Trib.*, May 29, 1997, 10A; "Religiously Affiliated Americans Remain Most Generous," *Dallas Morning News*, October 12, 1996, 3G (citing a 1996 Gallup Independent Sector survey);

Not only do intermediate communities provide many social services to many people, they probably do a better job of providing services than does the state. Care by communities is likely to be more individualized, more tailored to the specific problems faced by those in need, than the care given by the state. As Pope John Paul II has said, "Needs are best understood and satisfied by people who are closest to them, and who act as neighbors to those in need."[19]

Finally, intermediate communities can provide a source of moral insight to the state and the surrounding culture. Religious communities draw from a source of values beyond the state. This can give them strength to speak a moral voice to the broader community. In the United States, the American independence, antislavery, child labor reform, labor rights, prohibition, antiwar, civil rights, and pro-life movements all have had religious leaders among their leaders. In England the fight against the slave trade, in Eastern Europe the fight against Communism, and in South Africa the fight against apartheid all were led by religious communities.[20] The religious leaders in all of these movements operated in the tradition of the Hebrew prophets, who challenged the state and the culture on behalf of the poor and oppressed.

Tort law's individualist character

Tort theorists have tended to view life through individualist lenses. Robert A. Baruch Bush summarizes the "individual responsibility" principle underlying American tort law: "The individual is responsible for all he does, but for only what he does."[21] Robert Ackerman says, "Modern tort law repre-

---

Cindy Kranz, "So You Want to Volunteer," *Cincinnati Enquirer*, May 15, 1997, C3. [*See also* James A. Roberts and Meredith E. David, "Holier Than Thou: Investigating the Link Between Religiosity and Charitable Giving," *International Journal of Nonprofit and Voluntary Sector Marketing*, 24 (June 2018), https://onlinelibrary.wiley.com/doi/full/10.1002/nvsm.1619 (religiosity has a positive effect on charitable giving); Bradford Richardson, "Religious People More Likely to Give to Charity, Study Shows," *Washington Times*, October 30, 2017, https://www.washingtontimes.com/news/2017/oct/30/religious-people-more-likely-give-charity-study/ (62% of religious households give to charity, compared to only 46% of nonreligious households); Robert David Sullivan, "Charitable Giving Is Highest Among the Most Religious," *America Magazine*, January 7, 2016 https://www.americamagazine.org/content/unconventional-wisdom/blue-states-get-dinged-almanac-american-philanthropy (noting that "religious people are more likely to give to charities of all kinds."]

19 *See* John Paul II, "Centesimus Annus," 301.

20 *See, e.g.*, James W. Skillen, "Toward a Contemporary Christian Democratic Politics in the U.S.," in *Christianity and Democracy in Global Context*, ed. John Witte, Jr. (1993): 89; Aldon D. Morris, *The Origins of the Civil Rights Movement, Black Communities Organizing for Change* (1984): 4–8; Stephen V. Monsma, *Pursuing Justice in a Sinful World* (1984): 5; Mary L. Gautier, "Church Attendance and Religious Belief in Postcommunist Societies," *Journal for the Scientific Study of Religion*, 36 (1997):289–90 (Poland and Eastern Europe); Joseph Punjer, "Contribution of the Reformed Churches to the Fall of Communism in Hungary and Romania," in *Research on Democracy and Society: Democratization in Eastern and Western Thought*, eds. F.D. Wells, et al. (1993): 111–32.

21 Bush, "Between Two Worlds," 1474.

sents a perverse triumph of radical individualism."[22] Tort law's individualist character is epitomized for many by the tort rule that says one need not go to the aid of someone who is in danger: if you see a child drowning or a blind person stepping in front of a car, you have the right to remain silent and enjoy the show. Mary Ann Glendon says, "Buried deep in our rights dialect is an unexpressed premise that we roam at large in a land of strangers, where we presumptively have no obligations toward others except to avoid the active infliction of harm."[23]

Tort law's treatment of intermediate communities

I agree that tort law is primarily individualist in character. Nevertheless, little noted by tort law theorists in any systematic way have been a host of tort rules that are not individualist. These rules were designed to protect or impose responsibilities on the same intermediate communities that the doctrines of sphere sovereignty and subsidiarity identified as so important to human flourishing—the families, friendships, religious congregations, neighborhoods, charities, labor unions, and towns that lie between the individual and the state. I will consider first several rules designed to protect intermediate communities, then several rules that were designed to make demands on them. My point is not that all of these rules are good rules. In some cases, these rules may have even been counterproductive, causing damage to the intermediate communities that they were designed to protect.

I focus primarily on rules of law that affect families and religious congregations, two of the communities that have been of primary concern both within the Calvinist doctrine of sphere sovereignty and within the Catholic doctrine of subsidiarity. The family and the religious congregation have received substantial attention from tort law. This is not surprising, since they are the most common, the closest, the most intense, and the most active intermediate communities. They are the intermediate communities that have provided the most care and service to people. They are communities with power, power that can be used for good or ill.

Protecting intermediate communities

A significant number of traditional tort rules were designed to protect the family. Spousal immunity, parental immunity, and the parental discipline privilege protected defendants from suit by their spouses and children. These rules were designed to reinforce authority within the home and to insulate "families from the vagaries and rancorous effects of tort litigation."[24] In recent years, most ju-

22 *See* Ackerman, "Tort Law and Communitarianism," 651.
23 Glendon, *Rights Talk*, 77.
24 *Renko v. McLean*, 697 A.2d 468, 478 (Md. 1997) (retaining the doctrine of spousal immunity).

risdictions have overturned spousal and parental immunities, though they have retained the parental privilege for reasonable parental discipline.

Under the alienation-of-affections cause of action, a spouse could seek recovery against a third party who had maliciously or intentionally interfered with the marital relationship. However, many states have abrogated this cause of action. Among the justifications that courts have given for abrogation are "changed social concepts of family solidarity ... [and] increased freedom of association between each spouse and the outside world."[25]

Associational immunity protected unincorporated associations in many jurisdictions from liability to members and from liability for the torts of one member against another, and charitable immunity protected charities from liability for injuries to their beneficiaries.[26] Most jurisdictions have abandoned associational and charitable immunity in recent decades.[27]

In defamation and privacy causes of action, courts recognized a qualified immunity that enabled communities to protect themselves. A defendant who communicated to someone to protect a common interest was subject to liability only if the defendant communicated the information beyond the protected community, acted primarily from ill will, or negligently communicated a false statement.[28] This qualified immunity rule has been undercut in recent years. In 1989, the Oklahoma Supreme Court held a church and its leaders subject to liability for advising its members to withdraw fellowship from a member who continued to engage in an adulterous affair.[29] In an earlier day, it is likely that the church's advice would have been protected as a communication in the common interest of the community.

Imposing responsibilities on intermediate communities

A second group of tort rules impose special responsibilities on intermediate communities. There are even communitarian aspects of the rule that for many epitomizes the individualistic character of tort law, the no-duty-to-rescue rule. The law does not impose a duty to aid strangers, but it does impose a duty to aid those with whom the plaintiff has a special relationship. Special relationships giving rise to an affirmative duty of care include the common carrier-passenger, innkeeper-guest, landlord-tenant, employer-employee, jailer-prisoner,

25 *Lentz v. Baker*, 792 S.W.2d 71, 75 (Tenn. 1989).

26 On associational immunity, *see MacDonald v. Maxwell*, 655 N.E.2d 1249, 1250 n.1 (Ind. 1995); *Calvary Baptist Church v. Joseph*, 522 N.E.2d 371, 374 (Ind. 1988); *Cox v. Thee Evergreen Church*, 836 S.W.2d 167, 169–70 (Tex. 1992); *Zehner v. Wilkinson Mem'l United Methodist Church*, 581 A.2d 1388, 1389 (Pa. 1990); *Marshall v. Int'l Longshoremen's & Warehousemen's Union*, 371 P.2d 987, 990 (Cal. 1962).

27 *See* Daniel A. Barfield, Note, "Better to Give Than to Receive: Should Nonprofit Corporations and Charities Pay Punitive Damages?" *Valparaiso University Law Review*, 29(1995): 1194–95, 1197 n.15 and cases cited therein.

28 *See Prosser & Keeton on the Law of Torts*, 5th ed., eds. W. Page Keeton et al. (1984) § 115, 828–30, 832–35 and § 117, 868. *See also Restatement (Second) of Torts* §§ 652F & G.

29 Guinn v. Collinsville Church of Christ, 775 P.2d 766, 783 (Okla. 1989).

hospital-patient, school-pupil, and business owner-customer relationships.[30] Here the law attempts to expand the range of relationships within which citizens care for others. The law acts to create communities among those that might not generally see themselves as being in a community. As we have seen, tort law traditionally prohibited suits among people within the closest community—the family. It left it to the affection and goodwill of people within families to generate care for those who suffered injuries.

Tort law also imposes a duty to protect third parties from people with whom one has a special relationship.[31] Relationships giving rise to such a duty include parent-child, employer-employee, and psychotherapist-patient. For example, parents who know of the dangerous behavior of their children and fail to take reasonable steps to control them are subject to liability for the torts of the children. The legislatures in many jurisdictions have also adopted statutes that impose strict liability on parents for their children's torts.

In addition to parental responsibility for their children's torts to third parties, many jurisdictions hold parents subject to liability for torts that they commit against their children. Within some jurisdictions, the abrogation of parental immunity merely opened parents to the same responsibilities to their children that other citizens have. New York, for example, has limited the abrogation of parental immunity to those cases in which liability would have been imposed on the parent had he been an unrelated person.[32] Under this rule, a parent is subject to liability to a child for negligent driving (since reasonably safe driving is a duty that courts impose on every citizen), but not for negligent supervision (since supervision of children is not a duty that courts impose on every citizen). Other states, however, have imposed liability on parents for failure to reasonably comply with the special responsibilities of parenthood. The California Supreme Court adopted such a rule, stating:

> The standard to be applied is the traditional one of reasonableness, but viewed in light of the parental role. Thus, we think the proper test of a parent's conduct is this: what would an ordinarily reasonable and prudent *parent* have done in similar circumstances?[33]

This amounts to liability for parental malpractice.

Tort law may create similar risks for religious congregations. The abolition of associational and charitable immunity exposed religious congregations to liability on the same basis as other businesses. The religious congregation is subject to liability when a parishioner or visitor slips in the parking lot. Plaintiffs in a few cases have attempted to push the liability of religious congregations much

30 *See Prosser & Keeton on the Law of Torts*, § 56, 383; *see also* Funkhouser v. Wilson, 950 P.2d 501, 508–09 (Wash. Ct. App. 1998).

31 *See Prosser & Keeton on the Law of Torts*, § 56, 383–85 and cases cited therein.

32 *Holodook v. Spencer*, 324 N.E.2d 338, 346 (N.Y. 1974).

33 *Gibson v. Gibson*, 479 P.2d 648, 653 (Cal. 1971).

further.[34] They have alleged "clergy malpractice." In some of these cases, the plaintiff has claimed that the clergy failed to provide reasonable pastoral counseling. A few lower courts have allowed clergy malpractice claims, but so far they have been reversed on appeal.

Courts generally have held clergy liable for having sexual relations with counselees and children, but they generally have held that religious congregations are not subject to vicarious liability in such cases because the clergy have been acting outside of the scope of their employment.[35] In some cases, however, courts have found churches liable for the sexual activities of their clergy based on negligent supervision. Courts have held churches subject to liability where they know of a clergy member's proclivity toward sexual exploitation and fail to take reasonable steps to control him.[36] Under such a rule, the fact finder may need to evaluate the reasonableness of the religious congregation's disciplinary steps toward clergy. Other courts have rejected such claims as an improper interference within religious matters.[37]

Intermediate communitarian tort law theory: some preliminary considerations

This overview of torts, families, and religious congregations illustrates that tort law is far from purely individualistic in character. Many rules have given special consideration to intermediate communities, either providing special protection to communities and their leaders or imposing special responsibilities on them. The overview reveals two trends in the law:

1. The rejection of rules that provided special protections for intermediate communities; and
2. The imposition of responsibility on intermediate communities for failing to fulfill responsibilities according to the standards of the broader society (for example, the failure to act as "reasonable" parents or "reasonable" religious congregations).

These trends in tort law are squeezing intermediate communities from both ends of the ideological spectrum. From the individualist end, individuals—for example, children and members of religious congregations—are winning cases

34 *See, e.g.*, *Nally v. Grace Community Church*, 763 P.2d 948, 949–50 (Cal. 1988) *and F.G. v. MacDonell*, 696 A.2d 697, 700 (N.J. 1997). [*See also* https://abcnews.go.com/Primetime/story?id=132074&page=1.]

35 *See, e.g.*, *Swanson v. Roman Catholic Bishop of Portland*, 692 A.2d 441, 445 (Me. 1997); Destefano v. Grabrian, 763 P.2d 275, 284, 287 (Colo 1988).

36 *See, e.g.*, *Erickson v. Christenson*, 781 P.2d 383, 386–87 (Or. 1989); Smith v. O'Connell, 986 F.Supp. 73, 81 (D.R.I. 1997).

37 *See L.L.N. v. Clauder*, 563 N.W.2d 434, 441 (Wis. 1997); *Pritzlaff v. Archdiocese of Milwaukee*, 533 N.W.2d 780, 790 (1995); *Schmidt v. Bishop*, 779 F. Supp. 321, 332 (S.D.N.Y. 1991).

against intermediate communities with the argument that communities have no basis for making claims on them. From the collectivist end, the broader society is imposing standards on intermediate communities as to their internal operations. Intermediate communities are losing to an alliance of individuals and the state. In recent years, tort law has moved power to the individual and the state at the expense of intermediate communities.

My point is not that intermediate communities should always win in conflicts with individuals or the state. As the doctrines of both sphere sovereignty and subsidiarity recognize, the state has a role to play in regulating the interaction between intermediate communities and protecting individuals within intermediate communities. Tort law might be a means whereby the larger community can encourage smaller communities to exercise their self-responsibility and advance the common good. Nevertheless, as sphere sovereignty and subsidiarity also warn, the state poses dangers to intermediate communities. Tort law can destroy the very communities that it seeks to call to greater care.

The state should give communities some protection from tort liability based on Hippocrates' first law of moral duty: do no harm. Tort liability can harm communities in several ways. Obviously, tort liability can impose financial responsibilities on communities, in the form of damages or of insurance payments. These can be very destructive, especially for smaller and poorer communities. But in addition, the fear of tort liability may lead communities to alter their practices. Tort liability may cause some communities to become passive or dependent and lose their vibrancy as the state takes over the responsibility to set their standards. If communities are not allowed to resolve their internal affairs, there is little reason for their existence. Like individuals, as communities exercise responsibility, they are likely to grow in the ability to exercise responsibility.

Not only should courts hesitate to impose tort liability on communities because tort liability damages them, internal community practices are likely to accomplish many of the goals of tort law without state intervention. There is generally no need for the state to create incentives for members of communities to care for one another. Within most communities, there is an internal affection between members. Members of families, religious congregations, and other close communities generally care for and nurture one another naturally in ways that the law could not command (and our culture could not live without). Tort law generally can rely on this internal affection to govern relationships between community members. When there is injury within a community, people within the community may be better able to fashion an appropriate remedy than those from the outside. For example, if a member of a family or religious congregation is injured, the family and religious congregation may provide meals, comfort, and other forms of care that may better meet the injured party's needs than money damages.

There are reasons for protecting communities from tort liability, but there are also areas where state regulation of communities through tort law may be appropriate. The ultimate goal of the state, as well as communities, should be to protect individuals. Under the theories of both sphere sovereignty and subsidiarity, the state may intervene in intermediate communities in order to protect individuals. Communities have power; they should use that power to benefit people, not to harm people. In some situations, where communities have caused harm to people, the state should provide a remedy to the injured party.

In their study of intermediate communities, Peter Berger and Richard John Neuhaus make the following recommendation: "*Public policy should protect and foster mediating structures*, and *Wherever possible, public policy should utilize mediating structures for the realization of social purposes.*"[38] It may be that tort law can pursue both of the ends suggested by Berger and Neuhaus—both protecting intermediate communities and utilizing them for social purposes. To some extent, this is a matter of balancing two interests that are in conflict. Using intermediate communities for social purposes may undercut their authority and damage them. Nevertheless, there may be ways that courts and legislatures can hold such communities responsible, without undercutting their power and discretion. In the following sections, I shall consider some ways that tort law might treat intermediate communities within the familiar bases of tort liability: intent and recklessness, negligence, and strict liability.

Holding communities responsible for intentional and reckless injury to the person

Tort law should give communities substantial discretion, but in cases in which there is a high risk of serious injury and communities or their leaders act with intent or recklessness as to that risk, courts should hold those communities and those leaders responsible. In such cases, tort liability may serve as a needed supplement to the incentives of criminal law. Cases raising this issue include those where a member of the clergy engages in sexual relations with a child or counselee, a parent maliciously injures a child, or a parent or religious community denies a child urgently needed medical care.

Clergy who engage in sexual exploitation of children or adult counselees should be subject to liability for the damage that they cause. In these cases, liability helps to protect individuals and reinforces the norms of both the religious community and the broader community. In such cases, courts have rightly stated that clergy may be held individually liable on battery, intentional infliction of emotional distress, and breach of fiduciary relations theories.[39] The more complex question is whether the sins of the clergy should be visited on the religious congregation. I shall discuss in subsequent sections the possibility of imposing

38 Berger and Neuhaus, *To Empower People*, 6 (emphasis in the original).

39 *See, e.g.*, *Byrd v. Faber*, 565 N.E.2d 584, 587 (Ohio 1991) (battery); *Destefano v. Grabrian*, 763 P.2d 275, 286 (Colo 1988) (en banc) (intentional infliction of emotional distress); *Bear Valley Church of Christ v. DeBose*, 928 P.2d 1315, 1321 (Colo 1996) (en banc) (breach of fiduciary relations).

liability on religious congregations under negligence or strict liability theories when their clergy engage in sexual exploitation.

Some early decisions granted parental immunity, even in cases where parents caused malicious or reckless injury.[40] Courts today are agreed, however, that parents should be subject to liability.[41] Admittedly, a tort suit by a child against a parent may cause conflict within the home, but the incentives of tort liability may be needed to deter child abuse. Protection of children, the culpability of the parents, and fairness to the children justify this limited interference with family autonomy.

The third case is much more difficult than the other two. Where parents or religious leaders deny a child medical care for religious reasons, they not only are acting based on religious convictions but generally are doing what they believe to be in the child's best interests. Nevertheless, in these cases, the interests of children are sufficiently important and there is a sufficiently broad and a sufficiently strong consensus concerning proper medical care that the state should intervene and impose tort liability.[42] The danger to the child may be sufficiently great that the failure of the parents to act may properly be deemed reckless. The risk of tort liability may provide a needed incentive for the parent either to provide medical care or to notify state officials of the child's condition so that they can provide medical care.[43]

40 The first explicit recognition of parental immunity occurred in 1891 in *Hewlett v. George*, in which the Mississippi Supreme Court denied a daughter's claim for false imprisonment against her mother, who had committed her to an insane asylum. The Court based its decision on concern for "the peace of society, and of the families composing society." 9 So. 885, 887 (Miss. 1891).

41 *See, e.g., Attwood v. Attwood*, 633 S.W.2d 366, 370 (Ark. 1982); *Barnes v. Barnes*, 603 N.E.2d 1337, 1342 (Ind. 1992).

42 For example, in *Lundman v. McKown*, 530 N.W.2d 807 (Minn. Ct. App. 1995), a diabetic child died after three days of Christian Science care.

> Although juvenile-onset diabetes is usually responsive to insulin, even up to within two hours of death, the Christian Science individuals who cared for Ian during his last days failed to seek medical care for him—pursuant to a central tenet of the Christian Science religion.

Id. at 813–14. The Minnesota Court of Appeals allowed the natural father to recover from the mother, the stepfather, and a Christian Science nurse practitioner. The court held that the state's compelling interest in the child's life overcomes the free exercise-of-religion protection. *See id.* at 818; *see also Prince v. Massachusetts*, 321 U.S. 158, 170 (1944).

43 Michael McConnell has suggested to me that the best compromise is a statute that would require parents who wish to rely on spiritual healing to notify state protective officials of the child's symptoms. The state can then take temporary custody for purposes of authorizing medical care. Such notification does not violate Christian Scientist beliefs. The parents can continue to provide Christian Scientist healing, in addition to the medical care that the state provides. Such a statute would leave the possibility of a tort suit if the parents failed to notify the authorities of a child's illness.

Liability for "unreasonable" community care

When we move to cases against communities and their leaders based on allegations of mere negligence, the argument for respecting community autonomy becomes stronger. The argument for community autonomy is especially strong in cases in which the community is alleged to have failed to exercise reasonable care in performing community functions, such as raising children or pastoral counseling. As noted previously, some courts have adopted negligent-parenting and "clergy malpractice" theories. There is a great danger that through such rules, the state can control parental and religious practices.

As to the matter of child discipline, parents are in a particularly difficult position under current tort doctrine. They can be subject to liability for either too much discipline or too little discipline. In claims brought by a child alleging excessive parental discipline, a "parent is privileged to apply such reasonable force or to impose such reasonable confinement upon his child as he reasonably believes to be necessary for its proper control, training or education."[44] In claims brought by a third party against parents for an injury caused by their child, parents are subject to liability if they knew of the child's dangerous tendencies and failed to take reasonable remedial measures.[45] In both types of cases, the parent is held to a reasonableness standard, but the existence of both types of claims gives parents little or no discretion. If they err in either direction, they are subject to liability. The dilemma of parents is worse than a mere lack of discretion; they may be in trouble no matter what they do. Given the differences in views about child discipline in our culture, a spanking might lead some juries to impose liability on parents for battery to their child, and the failure to spank the child in the same circumstances might subject parents to liability to a third party for failure to exercise reasonable control over the child.

Some jurisdictions subject a parent to liability to a child not only for unreasonable discipline but for unreasonable supervision as well. As noted previously, California holds parents to a reasonable parent standard. In a pluralistic culture, where there is so much disagreement about the way to raise children, society should not dictate such matters. As Justice Rogosheske of the Minnesota court has said, allowing a negligent parenting cause of action "creates [a] potential for judgments discriminating against parents whose conduct does not conform to prevailing community standards."[46] Only in the most extreme cases, such as those involving maliciousness or reckless endangerment, should courts intervene to judge parental decisions.

Clergy malpractice claims create a similar danger of imposing society's values on and discriminating against minority communities. In *Nally v. Grace Community Church*, parents sued a church, alleging that it was responsible for their adult son's suicide. The parents' expert witnesses, members of the clergy from

44 *Restatement (Second) of Torts* § 147(1) (1965).
45 *Restatement (Second) of Torts* § 316.
46 Anderson v. Stream, 295 N.W.2d 595, 603 (Minn. 1980) (Rogosheske, J., dissenting).

other denominations, sought to establish "the standard of care to be followed by pastoral counselors" when confronted with a suicide risk.[47] But imposing liability on such a basis would dictate uniformity for religious congregations. The state has no business creating a common religious standard, in the absence of a compelling justification.

As suggested above, courts properly impose intentional tort liability on clergy who engage in sexual exploitation of children or counselees. Such claims do not require the state to create a common religious standard; clergy actions can be judged against the reasonable expectations of counselees. But cases against religious congregations alleging negligent supervision of such clergy can create problems that are similar to the problems of the clergy malpractice claim. Negligent supervision claims may require the state to evaluate the reasonableness of the religious congregation's practices.[48] As the Wisconsin Supreme Court has said, rejecting a negligent supervision claim, "Such claims would require a court to develop a 'reasonable cleric' standard of care, which would involve the interpretation of church canons and internal church policies."[49] In such cases, religious congregations have communitarian incentives to see that their clergy do not exploit children and counselees; they provide such services in order to care for members' needs. But religious congregations also have incentives to protect their clergy. As the noted Catholic natural law theologian Germain Grisez has acknowledged,

> I believe that the real problems presented and revealed by the conduct of priests [who take sexual advantage of young counselees] have hardly been acknowledged by bishops [and] that thus far they have developed no adequate policy or procedure for dealing with those problems.[50]

It may be that religious congregations need the additional incentive of tort law to encourage greater oversight. In the following section I shall suggest a method of encouraging oversight without imposing a uniform religious standard on congregations

47 The California Court of Appeals held that such evidence should be admitted into evidence, 240 Cal. Rptr. 215, 221 (1987), but it was reversed on appeal by the state supreme court, 763 P.2d 948, 953 (Cal. 1988). [*See also* https://abcnews.go.com/Primetime/story?id=132074&page=1.]

48 In general, attempts to impose *respondeat superior* liability on churches have failed. *See, e.g.*, *Moses v. Diocese of Colo*, 863 P.2d 310, 330 n.28. ("When a priest engages in oral sex with a mentally ill parishioner, the priest is not acting within the scope of employment.")

49 *See L.L.N. v. Clauder*, 563 N.W.2d 434, 441 (Wis. 1997).

50 Germain Grisez, *The Way of the Lord Jesus, Vol. 3: Difficult Moral Questions* (Chicago, IL: Franciscan Herald Press, 1997). [*See also* Ira C. Lupu, David Masci, Jesse R. Merriam, and Robert W. Tuttle, "Churches in Court: The Legal Status of Religious Organizations in Civil Lawsuits," *The Pew Forum on Religion & Public Life*, March 2011, https://www.pewresearch.org/wp-content/uploads/sites/7/2011/03/Pillar_Autonomy.pdf.]

Simultaneously broadening the accountability of and preserving the discretion of communities through limited strict liability

As noted previously, there are significant reasons for both giving discretion to communities and holding them responsible. It may be that the tensions between these two goals can be reconciled in some cases by imposing limited strict liability on intermediate communities. Under such a rule, intermediate communities would be accountable for results but have autonomy as to means.

Communities often claim that they know their members better than outsiders and that they are best able to train and discipline their members. A rule of strict liability would encourage communities to prevent injury but allow them to determine, in light of their wisdom and insights into their members, how best to do so. Although a system of strict liability creates the greatest possibility of liability, it is not as intrusive a standard as negligence. A strict liability rule does not apply an external standard, as does a negligence rule. It leaves communities to determine what action is least likely to cause loss. It internalizes the decision-making process. A strict-liability rule would tell communities that they can chart their own course but that they bear the responsibility for the results. The law would encourage care without interfering with the inner workings of communities. It may be that a limited strict-liability rule is the best approach to parental responsibility for their children's torts and to a religious congregations' responsibility for sexual exploitation by their clergy. Through a limited strict-liability rule, courts may be able to hold communities responsible without micro-managing them and undercutting their authority.

Many states have statutes that impose limited strict liability on parents for the torts of their children. Statutory limits vary greatly.[51] My preference is for a rule that imposes strict liability on parents for any type of tort committed by a child, with a fairly high limit. Parents should have a strong incentive to control their children, but this responsibility should not ruin a family.

Similarly, courts or legislatures might impose limited strict liability on religious congregations when their clergy engage in sexual exploitation. In my opinion, such liability should be imposed only when the religious congregation or clerical supervisors are on notice of the clergy member's propensity toward sexual exploitation. Only then does the congregation know of the need for special action. Strict liability would avoid the state having to evaluate the reasonableness of the religious congregation's response. Nevertheless, strict liability would create an incentive for the church to take effective steps to protect children and counselees.

In cases of clergy sexual exploitation there should be a significant limit on a religious congregation's damages. There is a great risk that juries will punish

51 *See* L. Wayne Scott, "Liability of Parents for Conduct of Their Child under Section 33.01 of the Texas Family Code: Defining the Requisite Standards of 'Culpability'," *St. Mary's Law Journal*, 20 (1988): 72–3 and Appendix A.

minority religious groups.[52] As Judge Noonan reminds us, "Respect for the religious beliefs of others is particularly difficult when one does not share [their] beliefs."[53] Legislatures might impose damage limits in such cases, and courts should freely exercise the option of *remittitur* in cases where there is the danger of religious prejudice.

Concerns with corrective justice, individual rights, practical court administration, and economic efficiency have all influenced the development of tort law. Protection of intermediate communities has also been, and should continue to be, an important factor in this development. As both the Calvinist doctrine of sphere sovereignty and the Catholic doctrine of subsidiarity have taught, the health of both individuals and the broader society depends on our having strong intermediate communities. I do not suggest that intermediate communities should always win in conflicts with individuals or the state, but a balance of power will benefit individuals, intermediate communities, and the state.

52 *See, e.g.*, the jury verdicts in the following cases: *Wollersheim v. Church of Scientology*, 260 Cal. Rptr. 331, 353 (Ct. App. 1989) (punitive damages of $25 million for shunning the plaintiff, encouraging church members to break existing contracts, and threatening plaintiff); George v. International Soc'y for Krishna Consciousness, 262 Cal. Rptr. 217, 221 (Ct. App. 1989) ($32 million in compensatory and punitive damages for "brainwashing" plaintiff); and *Lundman v. McKown*, 530 N.W.2d 807, 815 (Ct. App. Minn. 1995) ($5.2 million in compensatory damages against mother, stepfather, and Christian Science practitioner and $9 million in punitive damages against the church for death of diabetic child). Most of these verdicts were reduced by judicial grant of remittitur.

53 *EEOC v. Townley Eng'g & Mfg. Co.*, 859 F.2d 610, 624 (9th Cir. 1988) (Noonan, J., dissenting).

Index

Note: Page numbers followed by "n" denote footnotes.

For Product Safety Concerns and Information please contact our EU representative GPSR@taylorandfrancis.com Taylor & Francis Verlag GmbH, Kaufingerstraße 24, 80331 München, Germany